Marching with the First Nebraska

August Scherneckau. CN014521, Oregon Historical Society, Portland.

Marching with the First Nebraska

A Civil War Diary

By August Scherneckau

Edited by James E. Potter and Edith Robbins
Translated by Edith Robbins

University of Oklahoma Press : Norman

Also edited by James E. Potter

(with L. Robert Puschendorf) *Spans in Time: A History of Nebraska Bridges* (Lincoln, Nebr., 1999)

Courthouse Rock on the Oregon Trail, by Merrill J. Mattes (Lincoln, Nebr., 2001)

Lewis and Clark on the Middle Missouri, by Gary E. Moulton (Lincoln, Nebr., 2001)

Library of Congress Cataloging-in-Publication Data

Scherneckau, August.
Marching with the First Nebraska : a Civil War diary / by August Scherneckau ; edited by James E. Potter and Edith Robbins ; translated by Edith Robbins.
p. cm.
Includes bibliographical references and index.
ISBN: 978-0-8061-3808-4 (cloth)
ISBN: 978-0-8061-4120-6 (paper)
1. Scherneckau, August—Diaries. 2. United States. Army. Nebraska Volunteer Regiment, 1st. 3. Nebraska—History—Civil War, 1861–1865—Personal narratives. 4. United States—History—Civil War, 1861–1865—Personal narratives. 5. Nebraska—History—Civil War, 1861–1865—Regimental histories. 6. United States—History—Civil War, 1861–1865—Regimental histories. 7. United States—History—Civil War, 1861–1865—Participation, German American. 8. German American soldiers—Nebraska—Diaries. 9. Soldiers—Nebraska—Diaries. I. Potter, James E. (James Edward), 1945–. II. Robbins, Edith, 1937–. III. Title.
E518.51st S34 2007
973.7'482092—dc22
[B]

2006024524

The paper in this book meets the guidelines for permanence and durability of the Committee on Production Guidelines for Book Longevity of the Council on Library Resources, Inc. ∞

To all Nebraskans
who have served their country

Contents

Illustrations

Figures

Maps

Preface and Acknowledgments

NEBRASKA TERRITORY, CREATED IN 1854 BY THE KANSAS-Nebraska Act, furnished 3,157 soldiers to the Union army during the American Civil War by official count. While numerically few, these soldiers represented about one-third of Nebraska's military-age male population in 1860 and about one-ninth of the 28,841 citizens of the territory as enumerated by the federal census. Given the small number of Nebraska soldiers, firsthand accounts of the war from among their ranks are rare. Rarer still are documents such as August Scherneckau's lengthy diary, which is remarkable for its rich detail, keen insight, and vivid description of life in the First Nebraska Volunteer Infantry (later cavalry) from 1862 to 1865, as the regiment served in Missouri, Arkansas, and Nebraska's Platte Valley.

Most of Scherneckau's diary survived the war because he mailed it in installments to relatives and friends living in the German settlement at Grand Island, Hall County, Nebraska Territory, where he found it waiting upon his discharge from the army. The diary accompanied Scherneckau in 1870 when he left Nebraska and moved to Oregon. It was mostly intact when he began to revisit his Civil War experiences about 1899 and to transcribe his diary, an exercise he continued from time to time until 1918, supplementing the diary with several letters he had written during the war. In 1984 the typescript diary (in German) was deposited in the Oregon Historical Society, where Edith Robbins discovered it, along with an English translation, during her research on the Germans of Grand Island. She recognized the potential treasure Scherneckau's text represented and felt it deserved a new translation and publication. Because German is her native tongue, Robbins was well qualified to retranslate the diary.

When Robbins learned that James E. Potter, senior research historian at the Nebraska State Historical Society, had a longtime interest in Nebraska's Civil War history and had authored several articles on the subject for the Society's quarterly, *Nebraska History*, she sent him a few translated pages. When Potter enthusiastically agreed that the diary should be published and volunteered to help edit it, Robbins began the laborious task of preparing a new translation.

Friends and colleagues have assisted us by providing reference materials and illustrations, responding to questions, or reading parts of the diary and offering comments on the translation or annotation. They include Jerry Green, Clayton, Georgia; Paul L. Hedren, O'Neill, Nebraska; Susan Lintelmann, U.S. Military Academy Library, West Point, New York; Douglas C. McChristian, Tucson, Arizona; John D. McDermott, Rapid City, South Dakota; Freeman K. Mobley, Batesville, Arkansas; Dennis Northcott and Amanda Claunch, Missouri Historical Society, St. Louis; Eli Paul, Kansas City, Missouri; Liisa Penner, Clatsop County Historical Society, Astoria, Oregon; and Sheri Salber, Warrenton, Oregon. Richard Engeman, Shawna Gandy, and Lucy Berkley of the Oregon Historical Society in Portland were particularly helpful and supportive as the project unfolded.

The research opportunities provided by the Stuhr Museum of the Prairie Pioneer in Grand Island, Nebraska, and the Nebraska State Historical Society in Lincoln, along with the support of their respective staffs, were crucial to this project. John Carter, Patricia Gaster, and Steve Ryan of the Nebraska State Historical Society aided greatly with photographs, indexing, and maps. Renae Morehead of Lincoln, Nebraska, did a superb job of copyediting. Charles E. Rankin, Steven Baker, Emmy Ezzell, and Alice Stanton of the University of Oklahoma Press shepherded us through the publishing process. Finally, we are deeply grateful to the Oregon Historical Society for granting permission to publish August Scherneckau's diary.

Edith Robbins
James E. Potter

Introduction

James E. Potter

BEYOND ITS VALUE AS A UNIQUE DOCUMENT IN ITS own right, several attributes distinguish August Scherneckau's diary from other Civil War soldier accounts. First, Scherneckau provides a German immigrant's perspective on his experiences as a Union volunteer. While many Germans fought for the Union (estimates range as high as 450,000 first- and second-generation Germans among a total of some 2.1 million soldiers and sailors), firsthand accounts of their wartime service will always be fewer than those penned by their American comrades-in-arms.[1]

Second, Scherneckau served with that tiny band of Union soldiers from Nebraska Territory, only seven years removed from its political origins when the war broke out. Because Nebraska's contribution of troops was small, barely exceeding three thousand men, correspondingly few diaries and letters from its soldiers have survived.[2] Scherneckau's diary of his three years with the First

1. Estimates appear in Kaufmann, *Germans in the American Civil War*, 70, and Lonn, *Foreigners in the Union Army*, 576–78. James M. McPherson, in *Ordeal by Fire*, indicates that foreign-born soldiers constituted approximately 24 percent of Union forces (358).

2. In Dyer, *A Compendium of the War of the Rebellion*, Nebraska was credited officially with furnishing 3,157 soldiers to the Union army (11). However, Dyer did not include in his tabulation four companies of Nebraskans who served in the Curtis Horse (Fifth Iowa Cavalry). As Nebraska newspapers reported, other Nebraska men enlisted singly or in small groups in Kansas and Missouri units. On the other hand, one company of the First Nebraska contained mostly men from Page County, Iowa, while another mustered many Germans from St. Joseph, Missouri. During its service in Missouri and Arkansas, the regiment recruited heavily, and many of these men never set foot in Nebraska before, during, or after the war. In the broader sense, few of Nebraska's Civil War soldiers had put down roots

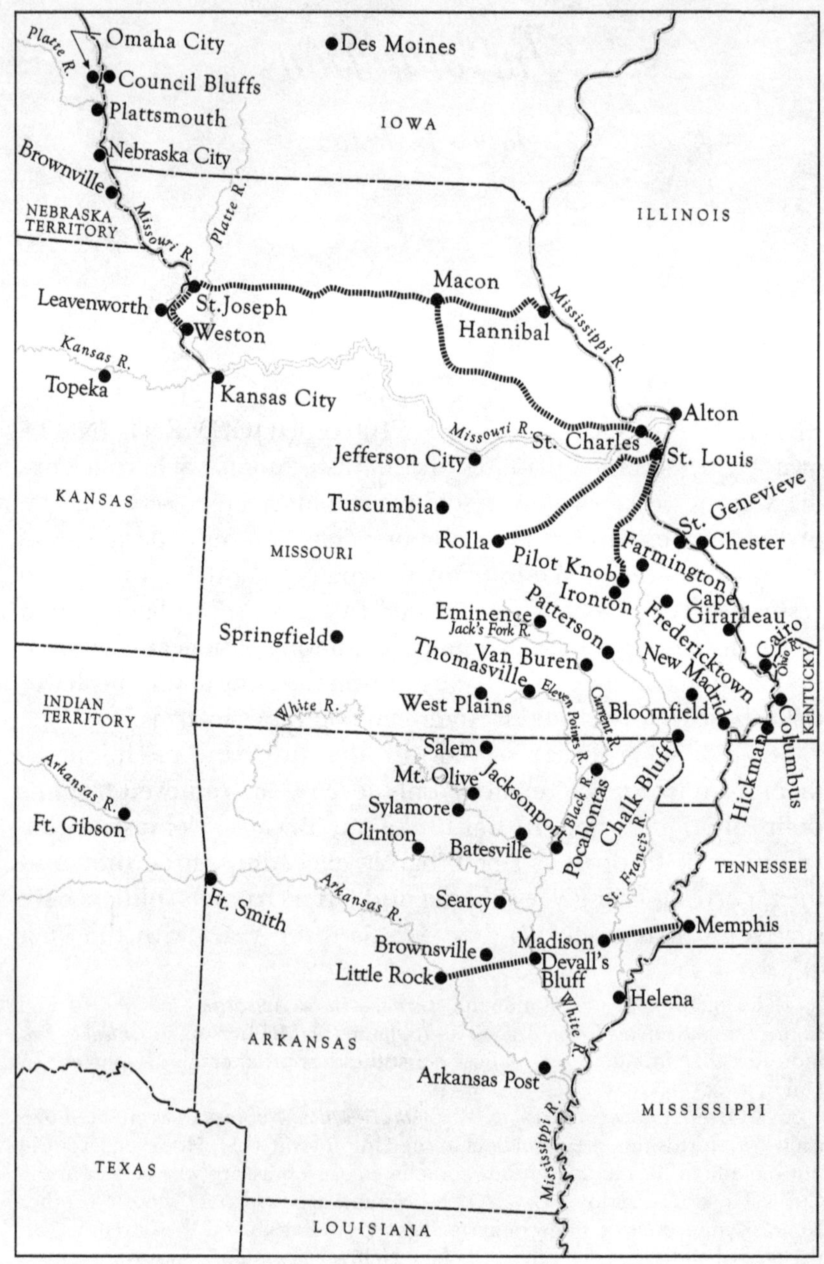

The First Nebraska's theater of operations, 1862–64. Map by Steve Ryan.

Nebraska Volunteer Infantry (later cavalry) in Missouri, Arkansas, and Nebraska Territory is the most extensive personal record of a Nebraska soldier's service that has yet come to light.

Finally, Scherneckau's account ranks with the best of Civil War diaries, regardless of origin. No mere recording of the weather or miles marched, the diary is filled with lengthy and detailed observations and insights rendered by a literate and perceptive soldier. Scherneckau's gaze took in far more than the First Nebraska Regiment's tents and campgrounds. His pen provided context and perspective on campaigns, military strategy, leadership, politics, ethnicity, emancipation, and many other topics.

Although Scherneckau saw men killed and wounded during the sporadic guerrilla and Indian warfare in which the First Nebraska engaged during most of its service, and was injured by friendly fire himself, he never experienced the carnage of a major battle. Most of the casualties he recorded came from disease or accidents. He fired his musket at an enemy once or twice but admitted he was dubious about whether his shots harmed anyone. Given the often mundane nature of Scherneckau's service, it is remarkable that he felt inspired to document his experiences, and those of his First Nebraska comrades, in such detail. But he was writing primarily for the benefit of his friends and relatives back home in Nebraska, so they could see the war through his eyes.

His meticulous record provides an insider's look at life in a Civil War volunteer regiment. Although Scherneckau's assessment of his fellow soldiers seems to have been colored by feelings of superiority stemming from his good education and his upbringing among his homeland's privileged class, his revelations that the regiment, "the noble Nebraska volunteers," as it was sometimes called, included its fair share of drunkards, deserters, and deadbeats will come as no surprise. While ennobling characteristics such as patriotism, courage, honor, and determination are rightly ascribed to Civil War soldiers, the men were not saints. In this, the First Nebraska probably differed little from most other volunteer regiments. And, writing not for publication but to inform friends

---

in the territory, which had been organized in 1854 and was by 1861 still very much a way station for Americans moving west.

and relatives, Scherneckau could be candid, an attribute encouraged by the absence of any censorship of soldiers' writings during the war. His diary, therefore, provides an astonishingly vivid portrait of one regiment of Union volunteers, spanning three years of service in the trans-Mississippi theater of the war.[3]

August Scherneckau (Sure-nuh-cow) was born on Christmas Day, 1837, in Rendsburg, Holstein. His parents were Friedrich Nickolas Rolf Scherneckau and Auguste Henriette Dorothea (Meyer) Scherneckau. His grandfather had been an architect, as was his father. In 1841 Friedrich Scherneckau became the first architect of the city of Kiel, a position he held until 1865. While little is known of young Scherneckau's upbringing, except that he was baptized in the Evangelical Lutheran Church of Rendsburg and that he spent his childhood in Kiel, his writing reflects an excellent education.[4]

Also prominent in the affairs of Scherneckau's native province was his uncle Friedrich (Fred) Hedde, who would be instrumental in Scherneckau's decision to come to the United States. A university-educated lawyer and journalist who also lived and worked in Kiel, Hedde energetically supported the 1848 movement for Schleswig-Holstein's independence from Denmark. Although he was not forced to flee his homeland for his support of the independence movement, as were many of his contemporaries, the movement's failure prompted Hedde to emigrate in 1854. He went to Davenport, Iowa, where many "Forty-Eighters" had settled, and there he joined a town company being organized to establish a new settlement in the Platte Valley of Nebraska Territory.[5]

The company-sponsored colonists, comprising some thirty Germans and a few Americans, arrived in Nebraska in the spring of 1857 and staked out a town site they named Grand Island City,

3. For the motives and mentality of Civil War soldiers, as well as a discussion of their literacy and the lack of censorship of their writings, see McPherson, *For Cause and Comrades.*

4. Baptismal record, copy in August Scherneckau Pension File, SC139–742, Civil War and Later Pensions, RG15, Records of the Veterans Administration, National Archives and Records Administration (hereafter cited as Pension File); Stoy, *Kiel auf dem Weg*, 86–87.

5. E. Robbins, "A Forty-Eighter," 67–69.

Fred Hedde. RG2411, Nebraska State Historical Society, Lincoln. Digitally enhanced and restored.

located in Hall County. Except for Forts Kearny and Laramie and a few road ranches scattered along the Platte Valley overland route, the Grand Island settlement, some 150 miles from the Missouri River, was the westernmost white enclave in Nebraska Territory. Despite the town company's failure during the Panic of 1857, most of the settlers stayed on, surviving by selling farm produce and supplies to the army at Fort Kearny and to travelers en route to Oregon, California, Utah, or the gold mining camps in present-day Colorado. By 1860 the fledgling settlement had 116 residents, of whom two-thirds were Germans.[6]

Exactly why August Scherneckau decided to come to the United States is unknown, but it was likely due to his uncle's influence, along with the opportunities that attracted so many other German immigrants during the nineteenth century. For whatever reasons, Scherneckau came, arriving in New York City in March 1857. He went immediately to Davenport, where Hedde had arranged for the young man to work on Nicholas J. Rusch's farm. Hedde thought this interlude would help Scherneckau become accustomed to life in America and learn something of farming and the climate before he moved to the Nebraska frontier. Scherneckau arrived at Grand Island with the second group of settlers in July 1858.[7]

The tiny settlement's appearance was not very impressive. Scherneckau found the Germans occupying four double log houses fortified for protection against Indians; only two log structures were standing in the "town" of Grand Island City. Most of the settlers had staked out "squatter's claims," pending completion of the government survey. Scherneckau first moved in with Hedde and by 1860 was living nearby in a twelve-by-sixteen-foot cabin on some land he was farming. In the spring of 1861 the Civil War broke out.[8]

When President Abraham Lincoln called for troops to put down the rebellion and the First Nebraska Volunteer Infantry was

6. E. Robbins, "A Forty-Eighter," 70–71. See also Stolley, "History of the First Settlement"; C. Robbins, *Physicist Looks,* table 3.

7. Scherneckau, "Her Quota Furnished," 77–78.

8. Scherneckau, "Her Quota Furnished," 78–79; 1860 Population Census of Hall County, N.T., National Archives Microfilm Publication M653, roll 665, RG29, Records of the Bureau of the Census.

formed, the demands of his farm kept Scherneckau from enlisting, despite his feelings as "an ardent abolitionist and [with] the desire to assist in the carrying out of these views as well as the sense of duty to my adopted country."[9] His opportunity to serve would come in the fall of 1862, when the acting governor of Nebraska issued a proclamation calling for recruits to fill up the depleted ranks of the First Nebraska.

The regiment in which Scherneckau would enlist had already made its mark. The First Nebraska Volunteer Infantry was mustered in at Omaha in June and July of 1861, drawing men primarily from counties and towns near the Missouri River, which held the bulk of Nebraska Territory's approximately thirty thousand inhabitants. Some of the men had been members of prewar territorial militia units, and others had barely set foot in Nebraska. Company B, "the German company," enlisted Nebraskans of German ancestry, as well as fellow countrymen from St. Joseph, Missouri. Company F was filled mostly with men from Page County, Iowa, and neighboring counties, whom Iowa authorities permitted to join the First Nebraska after the men voted to do so.[10]

The First Nebraska, commanded by Col. John M. Thayer, began departing Omaha for the South on July 30, 1861, to the dismay of many Nebraskans who believed the regiment had been raised to defend the territory against the threat of Indian attack now that the regular army garrisons of western forts were being withdrawn to the main theaters of war. During the fall and winter of 1861–62, the regiment was stationed at Pilot Knob in southeastern Missouri and later in west-central Missouri near Georgetown and Syracuse. During the first months of its service, the regiment performed mostly scouting and garrison duties.

9. Scherneckau, "Her Quota Furnished," 79.

10. The 1860 census recorded 1,742 Nebraskans of German nativity in a total population of 28,826. Hall County in 1860 had 73 persons of foreign birth (mostly Germans) in a total population of 116. Kennedy, *Population.* Data on the soldiers and companies from records compiled by the Nebraska adjutant general can be found in Dudley, *Roster of Nebraska Volunteers.* For Iowans in the First Nebraska, see *Page County Herald* (Clarinda, Iowa), June 21, 1861, and April 25, 1863. Andreas, *History of Nebraska,* contains an overview of Nebraska's Civil War military history.

In February 1862 the First Nebraska was sent to join Ulysses S. Grant's army in the campaign against Forts Henry and Donelson in northwestern Tennessee, where the Nebraska soldiers made a significant contribution to Union victory in the Battle of Fort Donelson, February 13–15.[11] Not quite two months later, the First Nebraska saw action on April 7 during the second day's fighting at Shiloh, helping drive the Confederate army from the field in that closely contested Union victory. The regiment participated in the subsequent Union advance upon Corinth, Mississippi, and spent much of the summer of 1862 at Memphis, Tennessee, and Helena, Arkansas, before returning to Pilot Knob.

While the First Nebraska had suffered few battle casualties, the rigors of army life, including disease, accidents, and desertion, had taken their toll. On September 16, 1862, acting Nebraska governor Algernon S. Paddock issued a proclamation calling for 315 recruits to fill up the regiment.[12] Each county in Nebraska Territory was assigned a quota based on its population in the 1860 census. Hall County was to furnish two men.[13] This call prompted Scherneckau to attend a "war meeting" at Schuller's Saloon in the Grand Island settlement, where he agreed to become one of Hall County's recruits. The second volunteer, whose name may have been Jackson according to Scherneckau's recollection, never entered the army.[14]

11. Cooling, "First Nebraska Infantry Regiment"; Cooling, *Forts Henry and Donelson.*

12. A letter from "G.H.T." to the *Nebraska Advertiser* (Brownville), dated September 27, 1862, and published in the October 18 edition, reported that the regiment then had no more than 200 effective men. When Scherneckau reached the regiment, he estimated on December 7, 1862, that about 250 men were fit for duty. On March 6, 1863, the *Nebraska Advertiser* noted that the regiment numbered about 600. A full strength infantry regiment would have about 1,000 officers and men.

13. General Orders No. 3, Executive Department, Omaha City, September 16, 1862, published in the *Nebraska City News,* September 30, 1862.

14. "Only Civil War Veteran Here," *Grand Island (Nebr.) Daily Independent,* June 5, 1920. No one by the name of Jackson appears in the 1860 Hall County census, nor is any such soldier from Hall County found in the records of the Nebraska regiment. Scherneckau may not have been Hall County's only Civil War soldier, however. Dudley, *Roster of Nebraska Volunteers,* 98–99, 189, lists Pvt. Benjamin F. Hurley of Hall County on the roster of Company H of the First Nebraska. Hurley had first joined the Second Nebraska Volunteer Cavalry January 5, 1863, and was

The recruits assembled at Nebraska City, and it was there on November 1, 1862, that Scherneckau began keeping his diary, a practice to which he remained remarkably faithful throughout his three-year enlistment. After three weeks at the Nebraska City recruiting depot, followed by a steamboat and railroad journey to Pilot Knob, Missouri, via Fort Leavenworth and St. Louis, Scherneckau was assigned to Company H of the First Nebraska on December 7. It was the eve of a campaign that would sorely test the new soldier's stamina and patriotism.

For much of the winter of 1862–63 Scherneckau and the First Nebraska tramped through the rugged Ozarks of southern Missouri and northern Arkansas with Brig. Gen. John W. Davidson's Army of Southeastern Missouri. The army sought to counter guerrilla activity in the region and mount a campaign, via Batesville, Arkansas, to threaten the state capital at Little Rock. After floundering through mud and snow and barely surviving on scanty rations for several weeks, the Army of Southeastern Missouri was back at Pilot Knob by late February 1863, having accomplished little. From there the Nebraskans marched to St. Genevieve, then steamed down the Mississippi to garrison Cape Girardeau, both towns located on the river's western shore south of St. Louis. Scherneckau's company, however, was soon detached to St. Louis for provost duty and missed the First Nebraska's participation in an April 26 battle at Cape Girardeau and the subsequent pursuit of the Confederate raiders back into Arkansas.

From mid-April to early June 1863, Scherneckau and his comrades from Company H remained in St. Louis, where they gained a different perspective on the war. Assigned to the provost marshal's office, the Nebraska soldiers experienced all the hustle and bustle connected with the city's wartime role as headquarters for the

---

discharged December 1, 1863, when that regiment was mustered out. He reenlisted in the First Nebraska on December 29, 1863, and is recorded as deserting at Gilman's Station in the Platte Valley on September 5, 1865. Hurley's Compiled Service Record records his residence as Wood River on his first enlistment. Compiled Service Records, First Nebraska Volunteer Infantry/Cavalry; Second Nebraska Volunteer Cavalry, National Archives Microfilm Publication M1787, roll 35, RG94, Records of the Office of the Adjutant General (hereafter cited as Compiled Service Records).

Union army's Department of the Missouri and as a major staging point for troops and supplies en route to the theaters of operation. Here were vast complexes of barracks and warehouses, military hospitals and prisons, the Mississippi River steamboat wharves, and the navy yard at Carondelet, where gunboats were being constructed. All these installations had to be guarded.

St. Louis, whose population exceeded 166,000 by the 1860s, also served the needs of soldiers in ways not authorized by army regulations. Brothels, saloons, theaters, and gambling dens flourished by the score, and one of the provost guards' principal tasks was scouring these establishments to round up the soldiers they were sure to find there. Deserters and soldiers committing crimes against their fellows or civilians had to be arrested and military justice applied.

As the principal city in an important border state, whose citizens' political orientation ran the gamut from rabid abolitionist to lukewarm unionist to confirmed secessionist, St. Louis was a hotbed of intrigue. Union authorities were always mindful of the need to suppress disloyalty, however they may have defined it at the moment, and the provost marshal's office was the instrument to help implement these policies. One such effort, aimed at St. Louisans the Union commander had deemed disloyal, gave Scherneckau and some of his fellow Nebraska soldiers an unexpected junket on board a Mississippi River steamboat. They formed part of the guard detail when several prominent St. Louis citizens, accused of giving aid and comfort to the enemy, were banished from the city in May 1863 and escorted south within the Confederate lines.

His St. Louis assignment also gave Scherneckau various opportunities to rub shoulders with his fellow countrymen, because German immigrants made up about a third of the city's inhabitants. They included prominent politicians, soldiers, and journalists, such as Theodor Olshausen, editor of the *Westliche Post* and a close friend of Fred Hedde.

In St. Louis and elsewhere during his service, Scherneckau also observed the plight of slaves, or those who had recently been slaves, and his empathy for them is apparent in his diary. Although support for abolition was one reason he gave for joining the army, it is doubtful whether Scherneckau had much, if any, firsthand knowledge of the so-called peculiar institution or of the unfortunate people upon whose labor it depended. Fred Hedde's strong antislavery views, which were held by many other German Americans, likely influenced Scherneckau, along with the German American press, such as the *Westliche Post*, which was solidly in the abolition camp. Scherneckau endorsed the Lincoln administration's emancipation policies, favored the enlistment of black soldiers in the Union army, and had harsh words for those of his comrades who seemed lukewarm or even hostile to these initiatives. On one occasion, he intervened directly to help secure the freedom of a former slave.

By the time Scherneckau rejoined the regiment in June 1863, it had returned to Pilot Knob, where the Nebraska soldiers helped build Fort Davidson, an earthwork that would play a pivotal role in the September 27, 1864, Battle of Pilot Knob. As the fort was nearing completion in August 1863, however, the entire First Nebraska was ordered to St. Louis, where Scherneckau's company was sent to guard the navy yard at Carondelet, while other companies were posted at prisons and barracks.

For six weeks Company H enjoyed light duty at Carondelet, where Scherneckau observed the construction of four Union ironclad monitors and again took in St. Louis attractions during his off-duty hours. In late October orders came that the First Nebraska Infantry was to be mounted and designated as the First Nebraska Cavalry. Much of the fall of 1863 was occupied trying to transform foot soldiers into capable horsemen.

On December 10, 1863, the First Nebraska Veteran Volunteer Cavalry (enough men had declared their intention to reenlist to earn the regiment veteran status) began a march from Rolla, Missouri, to Batesville, Arkansas, where regimental commander Col. Robert R. Livingston had been ordered to take command of the District of Northeastern Arkansas. The regiment arrived in Batesville on Christmas Day, 1863, and remained in the Batesville-Jacksonport–DeVall's Bluff area of the White River valley for nearly six months, scouting for and skirmishing with guerrillas and roving Confederate forces. Although the Union army controlled most major towns and waterways in northern Arkansas, including the capital of Little Rock, Confederate and irregular troops infested the countryside, launching hit-and-run raids against federal enclaves and supply lines.

Scherneckau had often lamented the assignments that kept him and his comrades from service in the field and the prospect of engaging the enemy. "I did not enlist to be so inactive," he wrote on June 15, 1863. The regiment's posting to Arkansas finally provided the excitement for which he had been yearning. The life of a cavalryman, however, proved even more strenuous than he had expected. Lacking time to write in his diary every day, he substituted lengthy letters to friends and relatives back home whenever duty allowed, summarizing the marches, expeditions, and skirmishes in which he had participated. After a nearly a year and a half in the army, and despite exposure to the hardships and dangers of the irregular warfare in Arkansas, Scherneckau seemed to be thriving as a soldier. The reality of war hit home for him, however, on March 31, 1864, when he was accidentally shot in the leg by one of his own comrades.

Scherneckau observed the rest of the First Nebraska's Arkansas sojourn from a hospital bed and resumed writing in his diary. With his wound not yet healed, he came home to Nebraska in June 1864 with the regiment's reenlisted soldiers when they were released on their veterans' furlough. As the Nebraskans traveled from Arkansas to Omaha, via St. Louis and St. Joseph, Scherneckau recorded the accolades the returning veterans enjoyed. From July 1864 until February 1865, he lived with Heinrich Egge, another of Grand Island's first settlers, while he recuperated from his injury.

This interlude was not uneventful, even though Scherneckau stopped keeping his diary for most of this period. He renewed friendships with many of the Grand Island settlers and helped them with their farm work. When the Lakotas and Cheyennes began raiding stage stations and road ranches along the Platte Valley overland route in August 1864, the Grand Island Germans fortified Henry A. Koenig and Fred A. Wiebe's O.K. Store and William Stolley's residence, the latter dubbed "Fort Independence." Although no Indians attacked Grand Island, Scherneckau joined other young men in patrolling the nearby countryside, admitting he was still "half an invalid" on account of his wound.[15]

By the time Scherneckau was well enough to return to the regiment in late February 1865, his comrades in the First Nebraska Veteran Volunteer Cavalry had been defending the home front since the previous August. Upon the outbreak of the Indian raids of late summer 1864, the First Nebraska veterans were quickly recalled to Omaha and dispersed to garrison forts and small outposts strung out along the Platte River, protecting the vital lines of communication and commerce to the west.[16] The men of the First Nebraska would serve in this role until they were mustered out in July 1866, never again reunited under the regimental banner.

When Scherneckau rejoined his Company H of the First Nebraska, he found it posted to Midway, a stagecoach and telegraph station some sixty-five miles west of Fort Kearny. Perhaps because his officers had previously observed him scribbling in his diary or writing letters home, he was assigned to be the company clerk. It took a literate soldier with good penmanship, talents Scherneckau possessed, to prepare the multitude of orders, morning reports, muster rolls, and descriptive books the military bureaucracy required. By now he had become adept at speaking and writing in English. Moreover, the lingering effects of his wound may have disqualified him from performing some of the more strenuous duties characteristic of a cavalryman's life.

Soldiering in the Platte Valley offered Scherneckau and his comrades many new experiences. Now the enemies were Cheyenne and Lakota warriors, and the Nebraskans campaigned with former Confederates—ex-prisoners of war who volunteered for service in the West and who became known as "Galvanized Yankees"—instead of fighting them. Although the Great Plains landscape was a marked contrast to the Missouri and Arkansas Ozarks, the First Nebraska's new foes proved no less elusive than the bushwhackers with whom the men had sparred during their service in the South.

15. Stolley, "Defense of Grand Island"; Stolley, "History of the First Settlement," 51–56; Scherneckau, "Her Quota Furnished," 79.

16. A more recent book on the 1864 phase of the Indian War is Becher, *Massacre along the Medicine Road*; a classic is Ware, *Indian War of 1864*.

From his vantage point at Midway and other nearby posts, Scherneckau observed a constant parade of stagecoaches, freighting contractors' "bull trains," and emigrant wagons passing up and down the Platte Valley. Protecting this vital supply and communications artery from Indians was the reason for the First Nebraska's assignment, and the seemingly endless procession provided fodder for Scherneckau's pen. He witnessed the buildup for Gen. Patrick E. Connor's 1865 Powder River campaign against the Indians, saw the comings and goings of volunteer regiments that had been sent to the Great Plains, and noted important passers-by, both military and civilian.

While duty in Nebraska was no picnic, Scherneckau escaped some of the hardships and danger his comrades experienced. He rejoined the regiment too late to take part in a 360-mile winter march to the Republican River in January 1865 that disabled some fifty soldiers and many horses by frostbite and injuries while failing to find any Indians. In May 1865, while escorting officers, he arrived at a Platte Valley road ranche only moments after Indians had killed one Nebraska cavalryman, wounded a soldier from his own company, and made good their escape with stolen horses.

Perhaps Scherneckau's greatest good fortune was simply being mustered out of the army on October 22, 1865, soon after his company had been ordered west to guard the trail between Fort Sedgwick at Julesburg and Mud Springs in the Nebraska Panhandle. The order came just as Company H had spent much of the summer building substantial quarters at Midway. Now the men faced spending the coming winter in rude huts and dugouts while patrolling a long and dangerous route lacking water and firewood. The new assignment infuriated Company H's officers and men, who believed they had been treated unfairly, and desertions increased dramatically, continuing until the First Nebraska Veteran Volunteer Cavalry was finally mustered out of service on July 1, 1866. Meanwhile, Scherneckau was happily receiving his honorable discharge at Fort Kearny and settling back into civilian life.

Scherneckau's diary is a significant contribution to the literature of the Civil War in the Trans-Mississippi theater and supplements or informs previously published works. For example, his day-by-day commentary on the Army of Southeastern Missouri's exhausting and fruitless winter campaign is a worthy companion to John F. Bradbury, Jr.'s, article "'This War Is Managed Mighty Strange': The Army of Southeastern Missouri, 1862–1863." Much of what Scherneckau recorded during the march also resonates with Bradbury's article "'Good Wood & Water, but the Country Is a Miserable Botch': Flatland Soldiers Confront the Ozarks."

While he was stationed in St. Louis on provost duty, and during several other visits, Scherneckau saw the city from street level, recording a soldier's insights on the German inhabitants, military prisons, gunboat construction at Carondelet, and federal policies on disloyalty and slavery, topics Louis S. Gerteis explores in depth in *Civil War St. Louis.* Scherneckau reinforces Gerteis's analysis of German support for emancipation and attests to Gen. John C. Fremont's popularity among many St. Louis Germans, an opinion Scherneckau shared.

The guerrilla conflict that characterized the Civil War in Missouri and Arkansas is a major theme in Scherneckau's diary. His comments on this "inside war," as Michael Fellman called it in his compelling 1989 book by that name, provide additional insight about the complexity and brutality of a mode of warfare that, in the end, proved mostly irrelevant to the Civil War's outcome.

Scherneckau and his First Nebraska comrades experienced the apex of their guerrilla war during the early months of 1864, while the regiment was based at Batesville, Arkansas, the seat of Independence County. Nola A. James sets the stage in her 1969 article "The Civil War Years in Independence County," and Scherneckau provides a look behind the scenes. Although Scherneckau's diary was not available for the preparation of Freeman K. Mobley's *Making Sense of the Civil War in Batesville-Jacksonport and Northeast Arkansas,* the diary confirms many of the episodes discussed therein.

Daniel E. Sutherland's "Guerrillas: The Real War in Arkansas" and Kenneth C. Barnes's "The Williams Clan: Mountain Farmers and Union Fighters in North Central Arkansas" provide context for Scherneckau's story of the violence and conflicted loyalties typical of the guerrilla war in Arkansas. During its time there, the First Nebraska served alongside an Arkansas Union regiment, nicknamed "mountain feds," enlisted from the Batesville vicinity. Arkansas unionist and scout William Monks served briefly with the

First Nebraska, and his memoir of wartime episodes on the Missouri-Arkansas border is the only published account by a Union guerrilla from that region.[17]

Scherneckau's diary also includes his account of the First Nebraska's service along the Platte Valley overland route in 1865. Truly, this was one of the war's backwaters in which worn-out, poorly supplied, and wretchedly mounted soldiers sought to prevent Indians from severing the vital lines of communication and supply between the Missouri River and the settlements, military posts, and mining camps to the west. In this part of his diary, Scherneckau offers a soldier's-eye view that supplements Eugene F. Ware's memoir, *The Indian War of 1864*, and John D. McDermott's study *Circle of Fire: The Indian War of 1865*. During his Nebraska service, however, Scherneckau saw more that was familiar and less that was exciting or unusual, and his commentary suffers by comparison with his account of soldiering in the South. His diary for this period has been summarized and excerpted in the epilogue to this work.

In his introduction to the 1993 edition of Wiley Britton's *Memoirs of the Rebellion on the Border, 1863*, Civil War historian Phillip Thomas Tucker notes, "No theater of operations in the most written about conflict in American history has been more overlooked than the Trans-Mississippi. . . . The soldiers of both sides who fought in this much-neglected arena wrote little of their struggle west of the Mississippi, and they have been largely forgotten as well." Britton's memoir "does much to illuminate this forgotten theater of war, making a substantial contribution to Civil War historiography." Surely the same can be said for August Scherneckau's insightful diary.[18]

Notes on the Diary and Translation

With few exceptions Scherneckau provided detailed accounts of his experiences nearly every day, in part because he wanted to record them for his friends and relatives. He evidently kept daily notes and completed the more extensive entries soon afterward. After a trip escorting deserters on a Mississippi River steamboat,

17. Monks, *History of Southern Missouri.*

18. Tucker, introduction to *Memoirs of the Rebellion*, 5–6.

he wrote, "I will now transfer these days from my pocket notebook in which I had continued my diary during this time." In an 1864 letter he mentioned that the busy life of a cavalryman prevented him from keeping a diary "recording daily happenings," as he had done while an infantryman. He lamented not having time "to make daily notes."

Whatever his method, the entries' immediacy indicates that he finished them within a few days of the events he describes in order to mail the installments to Grand Island, most being sent to Heinrich Egge or Fred Hedde. Moreover, Scherneckau frequently exchanged letters with Grand Island correspondents, as well as with his parents and friends in the Old Country and with former army comrades. Except for a few letters that Scherneckau inserted to fill gaps in his diary, the whereabouts of this extensive correspondence is unknown.

A few pages of Scherneckau's diary were lost before he could send them home, once when his knapsack disappeared. Nor was he able to write in the immediate aftermath of his being wounded on March 31, 1864, although he resumed the diary during his lengthy hospital stay. The largest gap dates from mid-June 1864 to late February 1865, while he was on medical furlough in Grand Island and living again among his friends and relatives.

The diary accompanied Scherneckau when he left Nebraska and moved to Oregon after the war. Except for an extended stay in Germany from 1912 to 1920 (he was living there when World War I broke out) and a brief period in California before his death, he spent the rest of his life in Oregon.

In 1984 Frank Hildebrand of Astoria, Oregon, donated a typescript of Scherneckau's diary to the Oregon Historical Society. Hildebrand was the son of August Hildebrand, who had been born in Emden, Germany, in 1869 and who came to Astoria, Oregon, in 1883. August was one of the founders of the Clatsop County Historical Society and held the title of historian in 1928. In that year he wrote an article about Astoria's Civil War veterans titled "Roll Call." This circumstantial evidence suggests that August Hildebrand and August Scherneckau, who had moved to Astoria in 1887, probably had become acquainted due to their common German ancestry and Hildebrand's interest in Astorians who had served in the Civil War. One can imagine Hildebrand's delight at meeting a countryman who not only had been a soldier but also kept an extensive record of his experiences. It is easy to speculate that Scherneckau (who had no children) entrusted his Civil War diary to Hildebrand and that it then passed through his son, Frank, to the Oregon Historical Society.[19]

The 144-page typescript diary is single-spaced on legal-size paper. The German text represents the language as spoken and written by well-educated Germans during the 1860s. Apparently Scherneckau must have begun reviewing the original diary and notes about 1899, based on his introductory statement that he began keeping the diary "seven and thirty years ago." The first entry is in the fall of 1862. The final line in the typescript, "copy completed today, May 15, 1918," was written while he was living in Germany. Evidently he took the original diary, paper, and a typewriter with him to Germany in 1912, where he completed the transcript while he was stranded there during World War I. According to Edith Robbins, the typewriter on which the transcript was made was an American machine, lacking the umlauts characteristic of a German typewriter. Nor is legal paper common in Germany. The fate of the original field diary and related notes is unknown.

As Scherneckau mentioned at the beginning, he did not intend to edit the diary significantly, and, except for a few asides inserted in his transcription, it appears that he made no major alterations. Perhaps it was while he was typing the diary that he inserted several of his Civil War letters to friends or family to help fill gaps. It is likely, though impossible to be sure, that his frequent use of English words in the transcript was also characteristic of his field diary. Soon after his enlistment he remarked that the association with his fellow recruits provided "a good chance to perfect my English." Later, while visiting with some fellow Germans in the First Nebraska, Scherneckau reported, "I got stuck, since I mixed in English words."

19. Biographical information on August and Frank Hildebrand and additional information on August Hildebrand's role in Clatsop County history is courtesy of Liisa Penner, archivist, Clatsop County Historical Society. Penner to James E. Potter, January 4, 2005. Letter in author's possession.

Working from Robbins's initial translation, both she and James E. Potter tried to provide a final translation in modern English that accurately reflects Scherneckau's text, the meaning he sought to convey, and that also conforms to the military terminology of the American Civil War. For example, when he refers to artillery firing "grenades" or "bombs," the words have been changed to "shells." The "cover" for a foraging party has become the "escort," and "putting rifles in pyramids" is now "stacking arms." Minor words that contributed to smoother sentence structure have been silently inserted. More significant editorial insertions, corrections, or speculations appear in brackets—for example, when Scherneckau occasionally recorded the wrong day of the week for a given date or vice versa. A few words that could not be deciphered are indicated with a blank (_____). Scherneckau's own asides, presumably inserted when he made the transcription, appear in parentheses.

Scherneckau's dense typescript has been divided into chapters, and further divided into paragraphs. His occasional misspelling of names of officers, localities, or military units has been silently corrected when the proper spelling was known. Individuals mentioned in the diary have been identified, when possible, in a note. If identification of the same individual seemed necessary at a subsequent mention, this identification is usually provided in brackets within the text. The editors have italicized the names of newspapers and steamboats. Scherneckau's treatment of numbers, military titles, and dates was inconsistent, and the editors have followed the *Chicago Manual of Style*, 15th edition, in such matters. Punctuation has been added for clarity throughout. Potter provided the bulk of the annotation, assisted by Robbins's notes accompanying her translation.

Marching with the First Nebraska

CHAPTER 1

A Recruit for the First Nebraska Volunteer Infantry, September 21–December 8, 1862

1862—Seven and thirty years have passed since I wrote down—often in haste—the following fragments of my diary. Some have been lost over the years; some notes never reached my friends and relatives to whom I sent them whenever I had a chance. After so many years I will try, as best I can, to complete these fragments, to make them comprehensible, and to remind myself of the exciting times I lived through.

September 21, 1862—On a Sunday I find myself in Grand Island, Hall County, Nebraska, in those days still a territory. A proclamation of the governor had reached us too, the most western of all [Nebraska] settlements. I was present at a meeting that afternoon, held at Schuller's Saloon, and I agreed to serve in the army as one of the two recruits the governor had requested. A second man who joined me at the time changed his mind before departure.[1]

Fourteen days later I was on my way to Omaha, then the capital of the territory. Just these first few pages of my notes are lost. After a very superficial examination by the recruiting officers stationed in Omaha, I was accepted.[2] A few days later, I was sent down the

1. D. Schuller had the first saloon in town, operated a store, and was postmaster of Grand Island in 1864. "The German Settlement of Grand Island," *Mississippi Blätter* (St. Louis, Mo.), January 8, 1864, appendix 1 in Manley, *Platte Valley Chronicles*, 243–44.

2. Aside from a brief physical inspection, the examining officer asked the new recruit a series of questions about his health, including, "Have you ever had fits?" "Are you in the habit of drinking?" "Have you ever had the 'horrors'?" See "Form for Examining a Recruit" in Compiled Service Records, roll 1.

☞ Come Up Boys! Capt. Gillette is waiting to swear you in for service in our brave First Regiment. If you are halting between two opinions, as to the relative merits of the regiment under Col. Livingston and the cavalry "for frontier protection," take our word for it you had better choose for the former. The service will be parlor lounging compared to the irksome monotony of the frontier forts or the hardships of galloping over an unsettled country, where no hen-roosts are, and your boiled beans will be as hard and indigestible as buckshot and slugs. Choose the First, and call on Capt. Gillette for confirmation of your decision.

At the time Scherneckau enlisted, recruiting was under way to fill up the First Nebraska, as well as to form the Second Nebraska Volunteer Cavalry, a nine-month regiment that would serve in Nebraska and Dakota territories. The editor of the *Nebraska City News* showed his sympathy with the First Nebraska's recruiting efforts in this editorial comment published November 1, 1862. Nebraska State Historical Society, Lincoln.

river by steamboat to Nebraska City with several other recruits. Here was the headquarter for the officers recruiting in the North. And starting here I find some of the notes from my diary on my experiences as a recruit. From now on I will let these notes tell the story, and I will add to them only if it seems necessary.

Saturday, November 1—I want to express my enthusiasm about the patriotism that has inspired my comrades, patriotism I had not expected to this degree among Americans. But perhaps they, I mean my comrades here, are the better kind representing the nation. The lukewarm, indifferent ones, those opposed to rules and regulations, stay back and have not rushed to take up arms as we have.

Sunday, November 2—Many went to the different churches today. I am lucky to have fatigue duty.[3] The day went by as usual, only singing was more common than on other days, not uplifting songs, but songs of the most indecent kind. A rather old man has arrived here as a recruit, who is somewhat tinged with Puritanism. He reads his Bible regularly and, what's worse in our minds, continually tries to convert us. After coming back from the church service today, he preached to us boys that we should not desecrate the Sabbath by singing worldly songs. More than likely all of us would soon be exposed to danger; enemy bullets could surely find us all, and we should not be unprepared to face them. But he has encountered the wrong men. Even liberal-minded Germans could not have been more blunt with him.[4] Naturally, we tried to annoy him even more. Since then, we call the old man "Preacher." The religious debates here are not nearly as serious as those of a political nature. Puritanism is not much represented here.

Monday, November 3—Was on guard duty as usual. A new corporal has been appointed. This afternoon three men departed for a place fifty miles from here to arrest a deserter. I have eaten very green apples here, greener than I ever had before in America. They cost one to two dollars a bushel. Usually one of us treats everyone to a bushel, or we pool our money to buy one.

Jayhawking, as the expression goes, is practiced too. I believe the local neighborhood will be happy when these bandits march on.[5] But then we all wish to march on soon.

3. He is probably being sarcastic.

4. Scherneckau's roots were anticlerical and liberal, which explains his reaction to the "puritan." E. Robbins, "A Forty-Eighter," 75.

5. "Jayhawking" was the term originally applied to the activities of bands of men with free-soil sympathies who roamed the countryside opposing "border ruffians," who had proslavery sentiments. The term probably originated during the 1850s in "Bleeding Kansas," where armed bands raided back and forth across the Kansas-Missouri border. As time passed, however, jayhawking came to mean theft, horse stealing, or terrorism against civilians by any armed paramilitary or predatory band during the Civil War. Few such groups, if any, had official government sanction. The Nebraska territorial legislature considered and tabled an anti-jayhawking bill in 1861. On January 2, 1862, Governor Alvin Saunders issued a

Tuesday, November 4—As usual, on duty and drilling. The old puritan is being teased a lot. Therefore, the "stove pipe" expedition.[6] He complains to the noncommissioned officers, but even if they wanted to protect him they could not. I wrote to friend Egge but did not finish.[7]

Wednesday, November 5—On guard duty. The complaints about jayhawking are increasing daily. Recently we had a full beehive with the best honey. I don't know where it came from. Today a complaint was made that the inhabitants of the barracks had stolen a bunch of woolen blankets. I have no doubt the culprit is among us. Where the stolen goods are hidden I do not know, but I know that last night one of these blankets kept me warm. My bunkmate seems to be one of the leaders of this operation. This morning the blanket had vanished. One of the recruits was arrested for drunkenness. My above-mentioned bunkee was taken before the captain, being suspected of thievery. Naturally, there was no evidence.[8]

---

proclamation calling for such groups to disband. Lewis, *Messages and Proclamations,* 1:219.

Though jayhawking or bushwhacking was never a serious problem in Nebraska Territory, Missouri and Arkansas during the war experienced these activities to a degree without precedent in American history. See Fellman, *Inside War,* and Sutherland, "Guerrillas." In an April 17, 1864, letter to a friend in Germany (see chapter 14), Scherneckau characterized jayhawkers or bushwhackers as nothing more or less than highwaymen.

In the context that Scherneckau mentions jayhawking here, however, it seems likely that the complaints had to do with the foraging of food and other commodities by the recruits and that the local residents considered the recruits to be jayhawkers.

6. Scherneckau's meaning is unclear. Berrey and Van Den Bark, in *The American Thesaurus of Slang,* list "stovepipe session," which is defined as a discussion around the fire, telling stories or perhaps making fun of one another. Clearly the recruits had played some sort of practical joke on their overly religious comrade.

7. Heinrich Egge was one of the first settlers in the Grand Island area in 1857. Stolley, "History of the First Settlement," 3. Egge was the recipient of many of Scherneckau's diary installments and letters, and one of his closest friends.

8. The location of the recruits' barracks is not known. They were probably quartered in a private building the government had leased. There was no permanent military post at Nebraska City.

In the afternoon a six-mule wagon and an escort of three men arrived from Fort Kearny to pick up our deserters.[9]

Thursday, November 6—It is said that our equipment can be expected with the next boat. It is now severely cold at night, and the blankets we can get here are quite expensive and are worse than the ones the government hands out.[10] The guards had to be reinforced this night, since two more men have been arrested on charges of drunkenness, so now five prisoners have to be guarded. We posted three guards. The deserters for Kearny are guarded especially strictly. Tonight I was part of the guard.

Friday, November 7—I was on guard duty. This morning chains were riveted to the legs of our two regulars at the blacksmith shop. Hopefully they will be handed over soon, so we will be released from this strenuous guard duty. No drill. The two deserters are guarded especially closely.

Saturday, November 8—This morning, while I was still on guard duty, we turned over our prisoners to the detail that had come from Kearny, and now we are free of the exhausting night duty. The guards were immediately reduced to mere sentry duty. Therefore, I was off duty. No drill the whole day. The men of the expedition to capture the deserter returned without him. He had disappeared before our men arrived.

This afternoon I took a long walk across the creek [Table Creek] to that part of town that is called Kearny.[11] Nebraska City

9. These were deserters from the small, regular army garrison at Fort Kearny, comprising soldiers of the Tenth U.S. Infantry. The *Nebraska City People's Semi-Weekly Press,* October 30, 1862, noted that Captain Gillette had arrested two deserters. Capt. Lee P. Gillette, Company D, First Nebraska Volunteer Infantry, was the officer assigned to recruit south of the Platte River. *Nebraska City People's Semi-Weekly Press,* September 4, 1862.

10. At this time, the recruits had not yet been issued uniforms or other military equipment.

11. Kearny (or Kearney) was an addition to Nebraska City named for Stephen Watts Kearny, the officer who located the first Fort Kearny on Table Creek in 1846. Sweet, "Old Fort Kearny," 233–37. Kearny was adjacent to the old fort site.

viewed from different places always presents a new sight. It is a nicely situated town, only [the buildings are] too scattered. A war meeting at Union Hall this afternoon was poorly attended. One of the officers spoke to solicit for the recently authorized cavalry regiment, and the main point was to gather recruits, find horses, and raise money for this new regiment.[12]

A few of our men went on leave, but they have to expect to be called back any minute, since the captain has the notion that we will soon be sent to our regiment. Thank goodness! Tonight another batch of honey was brought to our barracks, God only knows from where. We have a few boys with excellent talents in this line of business.

Sunday, November 9—Very boring as usual. Two meals, no duty except roll calls, men on guard duty. Since a poster marked with our daily schedule is nearby, I will copy it here: reveille, 6 A.M.; guard mount, 8 A.M.; drill from 10 A.M. until dinner at 12n; drill, 4 P.M.; retreat and inspection of arms at 5 P.M.; supper at 6 P.M.; tattoo at 9 P.M.; taps, nine o'clock, thirty minutes.

This afternoon at two o'clock our Sergeant Harding read the so-called Articles of War to us.[13] They are quite long and contain more than twenty paragraphs. They are so tiresome that it will be difficult for our soldiers to remember them, even more so since they have to be read to us only once every six months.[14]

12. This unit was soon to be enlisted as the Second Nebraska Volunteer Cavalry. Gen. John Pope, commander of the Department of the Northwest, authorized recruitment of the regiment following the Minnesota Sioux uprising in the summer of 1862. Pope's September 29, 1862, order appears in the *Nebraska Advertiser* (Brownville), October 4, 1862.

13. Sergeant Harding has not been identified. There was no such noncommissioned officer in the First Nebraska. One of Scherneckau's fellow recruits was Pvt. Amos Harding of Nebraska City, whose father was prominent businessman N. H. Harding. Perhaps Private Harding had been given temporary sergeant's authority over the other recruits. The elder Harding provided space for Gillette's recruiting office. The Hardings appear in Dale, "Otoe County Pioneers," 4:1099–1100, 1103–6. The *Nebraska City People's Semi-Weekly Press*, November 24, 1862, mentions that Sergeants Richey and Rhoades were recruiting in Gillette's absence. These men were likely Joseph E. Richey of Company F and Albert K. Rhoades of Company D. Dudley, *Roster of Nebraska Volunteers*, 44–45, 66–67.

14. The Articles of War is the army's list of regulations governing soldiers'

In the evening at the barracks we again had a beehive filled with honey. Here these days I have eaten the best honey I have ever tasted, straight from the hive. There is a lot of singing here, finer and more beautiful melodies than I expected from the Americans. I am the only German among the recruits, and because the pronunciation of my name is so difficult, everybody calls me "Little Dutchman."[15]

Monday, November 10—This morning and afternoon, we drilled as ordered; also inspection of arms, but very informal since we have these weapons only temporarily. Nobody wants to clean them if they have to be returned soon. In two or three days our uniforms should arrive; it is also said that we will leave soon to join our regiment.

Tuesday, November 11—On police, or fatigue, duty, which means to fetch water and wood for the barracks and to sweep the floor as often as necessary. One of the men was arrested today because the sergeant found him sleeping on guard duty last night. Heavy rain last night, and this morning an equally strong snowstorm, accompanied by a cold wind from the north.

Yesterday evening the order came to put nametags on our bunks, as well as to have our weapons and other baggage in good order on top of the bunks or hanging somewhere. Toward evening the weather improved slightly. We did not have a drill and had only two meals. In the evening a foraging party arrived with a stolen beehive that contained at least fifty pounds of honey. What a feast! Almost every evening the woodpiles in the neighborhood are heavily plundered, since it is much easier to steal firewood than to chop it.

Wednesday, November 12—I had a cold night; our blankets are not adequate to keep us warm. On guard duty today. The weather is better but cold; some places are still covered with snow. No drill. A

---

conduct and punishments for specific transgressions. McDermott, "Crime and Punishment," 246.

15. Scherneckau was five feet four inches tall, with blue eyes and brown hair, according to his file in Compiled Service Records, roll 20. Germans were commonly called "Dutch," a corruption of "Deutsch."

soldier on leave returned today in order to move south with us. Foraged as usual in the evening!

Thursday, November 13—A cold night, fair but cold weather. Today two of the boys received leave for seven days. It does not look like we will be ordered away soon. I wrote Caroline H. today, and to Martin, and took the letters to the post office around noon.[16] In the morning and afternoon we had bayonet drill. In the evening we received rations. A beehive with the best honey was brought in this evening. A great banquet upstairs in the barracks; one of the recruits who lives here [in Nebraska City] delivered pies for his comrades; with that we had bread and the best honey fresh from the hive. This afternoon I had to repair my pants thoroughly, since they are falling apart. Uncle Sam has not yet issued any clothing.

Friday, November 14—A beautiful day, no drill. I was not well all day, had some toothache. This afternoon we set up our kitchen on the [ground?] floor of this building. A cook stove was requisitioned, with all the utensils. It was like magic: goods were being used here that the owner still considers hidden. Everything is taken if we can use it. No wonder the recruits are not much loved in this area.[17]

Among us [recruits] is an old, trained hotel and steamship cook. Released of his duties, he has taken over the kitchen.[18] Last

16. Caroline was Fred Hedde's wife and Schernekau's aunt. For a biography of Hedde, see E. Robbins, "A Forty-Eighter." It is possible that Scherneckau's other correspondent was George Martin, an English emigrant who had a ranch south of the Platte River in Hall County. Martin's two sons, Robert and Nat, were involved in a famous incident during the 1864 Indian raids in the Platte Valley. When Indians surprised the father and sons in a field near their home, the boys sought escape by riding double on the same horse. They became targets for numerous arrows, one of which passed through Nat's body and lodged in Robert's back, pinning them together. Both survived after the attackers left them for dead. Stolley, "History of the First Settlement," 48–49.

17. Obviously, the stove had been stolen.

18. Perhaps Thomas Bagley, thirty-two years old, a native of New York City, whose occupation was listed as "baker" and who enlisted September 25, 1862. Company K Descriptive Book, Orders, Morning Reports, and Descriptive Books, First Nebraska Volunteer Infantry/Cavalry, RG18, roll 3, Records of the Nebraska Military Department, microfilm, Nebraska State Historical Society (NSHS), Lincoln (hereafter cited as NSHS RG18, roll 3).

evening and this morning we noticed the improvement this change has brought in our meals. Until now, the wife of one of the married soldiers had cooked for us, and we ate there. She was reimbursed with our rations and leftovers we did not need, often quite a lot. Now, since we have taken over this business, we can trade the remaining rations for things we would like to have but that are not issued to us. Besides, the meals are better prepared, and the table can now be supplied with additional delicacies, obtained through nightly foraging, which of course we could not take into another's [the previous cook's] house. But here among us the booty is safe; no stranger is allowed to enter the barracks unless he has a pass from one of the officers or is introduced by one of the soldiers. Nightly foraging really means evening, since no one can leave the barracks after nine thirty, although the guards are not that strict if it is to everyone's benefit.

Saturday, November 15—On guard duty today. Our meals are improving amazingly. We have a talented cook, indeed, to lead our kitchen department. We pick up our bread from a [local] German baker, one hundred pounds of flour exchanged for one hundred pounds of bread. This baker knows Rawohld very well. Rawohld, by the way, has entered a Missouri regiment. Rawohld never owned a thing.[19] This evening there was a grand foraging expedition: cabbage and other produce, not to mention the chickens and a large turkey. No drill today.

Sunday, November 16—Parade and weapons inspection at eight o'clock in the morning. Only two meals today, but we can get something in between if we are hungry. Big dinner this afternoon. Our sergeants, who are married and don't live here [in the barracks] but with their families, had been ceremoniously invited. The doctor, who visits us daily, came just at dinnertime and so took part. Solemnly, like a good member of the church, he blessed the feast, which consisted mainly of stolen goods: roasted and stuffed

19. Perhaps Otto Rawohl, who is mentioned as accompanying William Stolley on a Nebraska buffalo hunt in the fall of 1860. Stolley identifies him only as "a certain Otto Rawohl." Stolley, "History of the First Settlement," 35.

turkey, chicken stew, slaw, bread, cakes, pies, and black coffee with lots of sugar. The cook received great, well-earned praise.

Yesterday it started to rain, and it is still raining today. This evening I went with some of my comrades over to the Methodist Church. The service was well attended, and it was very warm there. The preacher was a good speaker. The congregation often interrupted the prayers with emotional outcries. Right after the service a general raid was undertaken to bring in the necessary firewood for the night. How fitting!

Monday, November 17—On guard duty today. I had stomach trouble this morning. The day went by as usual. Cloudy weather; a little drilling in the afternoon. In the evening a piglet was killed with a revolver shot in the basement of this building, butchered, and taken into our kitchen, skinned, and the head, skin, and intestines disposed of. Everyone in the barracks knows about these things, and everyone helps, more or less. No one is troubled about it since the pigs roam around freely by the hundreds. The owners probably don't know how many they have.

Tuesday, November 18—On guard duty. In my free time I chopped wood for a man in the neighborhood, for which I received about twenty cents an hour. Cloudy and rainy weather. No drill. In the evening two new recruits arrived here from Plattsmouth. All recruits on leave, and the ones who have been at other recruiting places have been ordered to come back. We are supposed to be sent off definitely with the next boat.

Wednesday, November 19—Beautiful weather. A steamboat came by here today on its way to Omaha. At one o'clock it was announced that we should be ready to march tomorrow afternoon at four. Next, the captain came to the barracks on account of the stolen honey. General delight that finally we are going to march on.

Thursday, November 20—This morning I received one letter from Hedde and one from Martin, wrote back to both immediately. Preparations for departure are being made; provisions for ten days are issued. The letter from Martin was touching; I was as happy as if

I had received a letter from my dear parents. All the recruits are now arriving here little by little, but the boat has not yet come. It is said that it will not arrive before tomorrow afternoon.[20]

Friday, November 21—On fatigue duty today. Everything is packed and ready. In the evening all our belongings were taken to a warehouse by the landing, where we also had supper. But we still slept this night in our old quarters. It was a very cold night.

Saturday, November 22—After breakfast, which we ate at the landing, the boat came into view and soon docked. The recruiting officer, Captain Curran of Omaha, with one of the sergeants, was on board, as well as some recruits.[21] We took our baggage on board and soon were steaming down the Big Muddy. Captain Gillette went on board with us; the two sergeants of the recruiting party stayed behind. We went down to the lower deck with our belongings. A guard was posted to watch the baggage and the gangplank at the landings. I was assigned to guard duty for the last mentioned.

We went down the river fast and soon were across from Missouri, the first slave state I have seen, although I have not set foot there. Lindsay was the first small landing place there. In the afternoon we reached Peru, Nebraska, the home of our delegate Daily.[22] He and his son came on board. Brownville was the next stop. It is a pretty big town, nicely situated. St. DeRoin in Nebraska, fifteen miles from the Kansas border, consisting of only a few houses, was where we stayed overnight. I slept quite warm; all the others had good lodgings too.

Sunday, November 23—At daybreak we went on down the river. The scenery was fantastic, steep bluffs alternating with bottomland

20. These must be the recruits who had been granted leave.

21. The *Nebraska Advertiser* (Brownville), November 22, 1862, reported that the steamboat was the *Emilie.* Capt. Sterrit M. Curran, Company E, First Nebraska Volunteer Infantry, was the recruiting officer assigned north of the Platte River. *Nebraska City People's Semi-Weekly Press,* September 4, 1862.

22. Samuel G. Daily of Peru, Nemaha County, was delegate to Congress from Nebraska Territory. His biography appears in Morton, *Illustrated History of Nebraska,* 1:405–6.

covered with cottonwood, and wide, spread out sandbars reminding me of the Platte at home. Here and there were clearings and cornfields between tree stumps and trees still standing, also saw- and flour mills. Here and there were little towns, which appear to be on the decline, crippled from the start. Empty houses, unfinished buildings started in a grandiose manner, others in decay, all give clear evidence of these fast-paced times.

Shortly we were between Kansas and Missouri. In White Cloud, a little place in Kansas, a substantial quantity of grain was loaded, and also quite a number of raw buffalo hides. The boat by now is really loaded. In the afternoon a large quantity of firewood was taken on board where, at that point, the steamboat ran aground and was stranded. The booms at the front of the boat were moved into position to free the boat with a pulley and get us afloat. We passed by several little towns. St. Joseph, Missouri, located on the bluffs, came into sight just at sunset. But about a mile upstream from St. Joseph the boat ran aground again, and it took until midnight to get us loose, after which anchor was cast close to the Kansas shore.

Monday, November 24—At daybreak the boat was moving again, and we steamed past the city toward the landing, right by the station of the St. Joe and Hannibal Railroad. We have permission to go ashore until four o'clock this afternoon, when we will probably be transported farther by rail. Daily went ashore here. I did not speak to him since, indeed, my clothing was in no condition to appear decently in his cabin. It is time that Uncle Sam is providing us with clothing.

Now since I have walked through the town, I have a little more material for my diary today. St. Joseph is really an important town. But what was so noticeable in the little towns along the Missouri exists here too, only on a much larger scale. Buildings are in ruins; complete rows of houses are empty.[23] But it is quite lively in the business district, a lot of splendid stores. There are nice looking homes

23. St. Joseph was in Buchanan County, whose population was 10 percent slave. The city had been wracked by strife in 1861 as Union and Secession factions struggled for control. Secessionist militiamen and Union troops took turns occupying the town, looting, and destroying property. Filbert, *The Half Not Told*, especially chapters 2, 3, and 5.

in this town that, by the way, is laid out quite similarly to Davenport, Iowa—a bottom at the river and steep bluffs through which, with hard work, streets have been cut.[24] Some of the houses are twenty to thirty feet above the streets; others are almost buried. Besides, all the main streets are macadamized, and there are good side streets.

I went with one of my comrades to a wool-spinning mill operated by steam engines.[25] Raw wool was brought into the lower floor and appeared as finished fabric at the upper floor (third floor). The spinning process was most fascinating. After the wool had been shaped by three machines into a loose strand, the thickness of a finger, the last of these machines carried it onto large spools. Twelve of these spools were now brought together at a spinning machine to be spun in no time at all into a fine thread, the strength of average knitting wool. Since every spool contains 18 threads, the machine is therefore spinning 216 threads at the same time, which are rolled up on smaller spools. These will be put on the weaving frames [looms], shooting forth and back. On the last floor eight of these weaving frames now process these wool threads. A girl is working on each weaving frame. This would be something to see for friend Sass; I mean the machines, not the girls.[26] This mill is small compared to the huge plants in the eastern United States. But since this was the first such mill I had seen, it was quite remarkable.

Here in town almost everyone is in uniform. Everyone who does not belong to the militia belongs to the Thirty-seventh Missouri Volunteer Regiment, which is just forming here. On the western end of the town on top of the bluffs are fortifications, which control St. Joseph as well as the river. However, they are not armed anymore and are already in ruins.[27]

24. Scherneckau had emigrated from Germany to Davenport in 1857, where many "Forty-Eighters," including Fred Hedde, settled after leaving Schleswig-Holstein. E. Robbins, "A Forty-Eighter," 68–70.

25. This likely was the Buell woolen mill, started in 1860 by Norman and George Buell. *Daily News' History*, 286.

26. Detlef Sass was one of the first settlers in the Grand Island area. Stolley, "History of the First Settlement," 4.

27. This was Fort Smith, built in September 1861 by Illinois troops and named for Col. Robert Smith, Sixteenth Illinois Volunteer Infantry. Filbert, *The Half Not Told*, 50–51.

Across from St. Joe in Kansas is a little town called Elwood. St. Joseph takes up quite a terrain. Between the different parts of town are cornfields; the bluffs are only sparsely wooded. Around four o'clock we brought our baggage to the depot. We had our supper here, and we are now waiting for our train, which should take us farther downstream. The steamboat that brought us here has taken on freight the whole day, for the most part government supplies consisting of all kinds of things—clothing from head to toe, and other equipment for man and horse, to provide for the Nebraska regiment in Omaha [the Second Nebraska Volunteer Cavalry]. At eleven o'clock in the evening we left the depot of St. Joseph in passenger cars. At _____ o'clock we went on board a steamboat near the Iatan railroad depot.

Tuesday, November 25—We had a cold night on the lower deck of this filthy steamer, *Majors of Omaha.*[28] Early, at daybreak, the steamer started to move down the river, and about seven thirty we docked at the landing at Fort Leavenworth.[29] Beautiful limestone quarries form the landing here. Several imposing warehouses, made from the same material obtained at the quarries, are built down by the landing. The fort with its numerous buildings is positioned on top of the bluffs. Many buildings are made of limestone; others are built with bricks; only a few are wooden. The fortifications are hardly worth mentioning and, as it seems, have been erected since the beginning of the war. A weak battery armed only with a thirty-six-pounder [thirty-two-pounder?] controls the river. From the riverside, for protection of the land north and west, a few guns have been set up on some low ramparts. Furthermore, some stockades with loopholes for the infantry have

28. This vessel was the *A. Majors,* named for freighting and Pony Express magnate Alexander Majors. Way, *Way's Packet Directory,* 3. Most of the civilian steamboats that Scherneckau mentions in his diary are listed in *Way's.*

29. Fort Leavenworth, on the Kansas side of the Missouri River, was established by the Sixth U.S. Infantry in 1827 after Fort Atkinson on the Council Bluff was abandoned. Fort Leavenworth was a major depot for posts farther west and during the Civil War was the headquarters of various military jurisdictions west of the Missouri River. Hart, *Old Forts of the Southwest,* 110–12.

been erected. However, the stables, the large supply of hay, and other buildings are all outside of this weak defense system.

Ten horse stables, each one quite a bit larger than the government stables at Fort Kearny in Nebraska, lie to the north of the fort.[30] Large stone warehouses, three or four stories high, contain the supplies for quartermasters, also blacksmith shops and other kinds of workshops. The center of the fort [parade ground] is exactly like the one at Fort Kearny, only on a grand scale, and like at Fort Kearny, barracks surround it on two sides; on the third and part of the fourth side [it is surrounded] by elegant houses for officers and offices. At the southwest corner, almost on the highest point of the terrain, lies the massive guardhouse.

Outside of this square, quite a few nice residences are scattered, all occupied by officers and government officials, I believe. This enclosed place, gently inclining toward the middle, is overgrown with large trees. In the middle is a round, massive brick building, the powder magazine as I understand, very much out of place, I think. Seven huge hay barns, as I believe, containing no less than three thousand tons of hay, are next to eight silos filled with corn, and several other buildings, all surrounded by stockades. Besides these, several large buildings are still under construction. So there is a lot of activity. Stonemasons and carpenters are busy in the large yards to prepare the material.

The garrison consists of four hundred men of different Kansas volunteer regiments, also cavalry and six brass field guns. As soon as we arrived, the steamer *West Wind* came down the river from St. Joseph, and a large amount of government supplies of all kinds was unloaded and immediately hauled by six-mule-team wagons to the fort. We also brought our baggage on shore, and after we had our lunch at the landing, the wagons finally arrived and the order came to move to quarters in the fort.

Here we have a large room on the ground floor in one of the barracks on the east side. It is built from limestone. One door on

30. Fort Kearny on the Platte River was established in 1848, replacing the earlier fort by that name located near present Nebraska City, Nebraska. Scherneckau would have been familiar with the second Fort Kearny because it was the major military outpost in the Platte Valley and was not far from the Grand Island settlement. Mantor, "Fort Kearny and the Westward Movement."

the east, or back side of the building, leads from our room into a courtyard, and the windows on this side open a view to a part of the river and a thick grove on the other bank. The door on the west side leads to a veranda and from there to the macadamized road that runs around the entire square. A fireplace, in which cordwood in its entire length makes a wonderful fire, heats the room and gives us an opportunity to cook.[31] The best oak and hickory wood—all nicely dried—is delivered daily to the different buildings by teams. Also every day, water in barrels is transported from the river to the fort in special water wagons, each hitched with eight mules. We had the opportunity to observe all this while waiting at the landing for our transportation. It was quite cold, and some snow was falling. Therefore, the fire in the fireplace was very much appreciated. I had a bad toothache for the rest of the day.

At the moment our officers pay little attention to us. We are told that we will receive our uniforms tomorrow. All kinds of supplies in large quantities are stored here. These buildings far surpass my expectations after I had seen Fort Kearny. The city of Leavenworth is supposed to be much larger than St. Joseph; it is located one mile away from the fort down the river, and I have not had the opportunity to see it.

The space taken up by the government buildings here surpasses, I am convinced, the layout of the same kind in Rendsburg [Holstein] as far as I remember. But here they are not well maintained. Fenzen [fences] lying on the ground, plaster missing on the rooms' ceiling and walls, and broken windows and doors give the buildings, viewed closely, a bad appearance, but from a distance, the place looks nice.

The whole area resembles a hilly park, decorated with groups of beautiful oak, hickory, walnut, and other nice trees. A train of about fifty wagons, each one hitched up with eight mules, loaded with all kinds of supplies, left this afternoon for Fort Scott [Kansas] and, indeed, without any military escort. In my estimation this is a mistake in a state where bands of guerrillas recently

31. A cord of wood is defined as a stack eight feet long, four feet high, and four feet wide. He evidently meant that the fireplace would accommodate four-foot logs.

roamed, and secessionists are certainly still sheltered. Even in peacetime it seems appropriate to provide such transport with a guard. American indifference or, even worse, treason?

Wednesday, November 26—A cold night, lying on the floor, covered only with a light woolen blanket. Today nice weather, but brisk air. On guard duty. Today we received our complete uniform, except for the weapons. Listed here are the different items I received and the prices the government has established: a light blue overcoat, $7.25; a dark blue jacket, like the ones we have frequently obtained from soldiers in Grand Island, $2.63; a light blue pair of pants, $3.03; a hat with a black feather, the left side of the brim turned up, and attached to it a brass ornament with the inscription "E pluribus unum." The feather is placed on the right side, a bugle adorns the front with the number of the regiment and the letter of the company. The price is $1.85. We could take as much underwear as we wanted. I took one pair of underwear, $.50, one woolen top shirt, $.88.[32]

In Omaha such top shirts would cost somewhere between one and a half to one and three-quarter dollars. We did not receive our caps, since they were not yet available.[33] Besides that, we received the following accoutrements: a knapsack made from strong canvas, oiled and varnished, black with leather reinforcements, by the way, a horrible looking thing if it is not packed carefully to make it a compact square. The outfit is sensible and, as far as I can judge, practical. A so-called haversack, made out of the same black canvas, is to be carried over one's shoulder like the well-known travel bags.[34] I think I remember that the Schleswig-Holstein army used similar bags, made out of white canvas. And finally, a metal canteen covered with gray canvas, to be carried with shoulder straps.

32. The cost of these items was deducted from the soldier's clothing allowance of forty-two dollars a year. Shannon, *Organization and Administration*, 1:98–99.

33. This was the so-called forage cap or kepi. Army headgear, uniforms, and weapons are described in Pritchard, *Civil War Weapons*.

34. The haversack was canvas, painted black. Pritchard, *Civil War Weapons*, 60.

Part of the bounty due to us will probably be paid tomorrow.[35] This afternoon I took another walk around this area and found more sights, beautiful homes hidden in the woods with vistas hacked out overlooking the river. Tonight was the first in my uniform; if not on guard, one had to sleep on the hard floor in this room.

Thursday, November 27—Cold and windy. Today is Thanksgiving Day, and everything, as usual on an English Sunday, is dead and quiet.[36] In the morning I wrote to Egge and Martin. Afterward I took a walk in the neighborhood and discovered a large number of government buildings, obviously built not long ago as hospitals, laboratories, and for other purposes. Most of these buildings are covered with slate and are the first I remember seeing here with this kind of roof. They are constructed very solidly and in a grand style and far surpass the older installations of the fort.

When I spoke before of fortifications, one should not assume a fortified place. It is, in fact, not much more fortified than Fort Kearny.[37] At a closer look, I find that only the less important part of

35. Bounties were offered as an inducement to enlistment or reenlistment. The *Nebraska City People's Semi-Weekly Press*, September 4, 1862, carried an advertisement titled "200 Recruits Wanted," which offered a $100 government bounty to each enlistee. Sometimes bounty money was supplemented by private subscription. The *Tri-Weekly Nebraska Republican* (Omaha), November 7, 1862, carried a recruiting advertisement offering a $25 advance bounty payment to each three-year enlistee, with the balance of the $100 from the government payable upon the soldier's muster out of service. Each recruit would also receive a $3 premium for enlisting. One theory behind bounties was that men were often reluctant to enlist because army pay was insufficient to support their families and that they could earn higher wages outside the army. The bounty would help offset these drawbacks to military service.

In June 1863 the government offered a $402 bounty for five-year volunteers and for those soldiers already in the army who were willing to reenlist for a three-year term. October 1863 regulations provided that any new three-year volunteer for an existing, or "old," regiment would receive $300. "Bounty jumpers" frequently abused the system. Shannon, *Organization and Administration*, 2:62–63; McPherson, *Ordeal by Fire*, 356.

36. He means that Thanksgiving, as a religious holiday, resembled a Sunday.

37. Forts in the West were rarely fortified with walls or stockades. There were no fortifications at Fort Kearny until a temporary stockade was erected on the east edge of the building complex at the time of the 1864 Indian raids in the Platte and Little Blue river valleys. Mantor, "Fort Kearny," 203.

the building area is surrounded with earthen fortifications, and this part is controlled by the neighboring heights so that there can be no thought of resistance once cannons are brought into action.[38]

The hills that surround the buildings, partly covered with nice trees, are all being landscaped. Old trees are uprooted, the standing ones trimmed, and always arranged in picturesque displays. Vistas are hacked through where necessary, and what surprised me most, even the stumps are taken out. Much is also being done on the roads; good bridges lead across sloughs, steep hills are dug down, and low spots filled in and covered with gravel. A nice stockade fence runs around a large section, which includes the arsenal, the hospitals, and many residences, where the cows of the officers and officials are out to pasture. Down toward the river, in the direction of the town, extend the large yards for cattle, mules, and horses. Leavenworth City is about two and a half miles from here. For twenty-five cents a person, wagons will make the connection.

This afternoon I walked into town with two friends. But we did not have a lot of time to look around. It was a bustling place where we were; only a few buildings were closed because of Thanksgiving. It appears to me that the town is at least as large as St. Joseph. There were a noticeable number of saloons in the north end, close to the fort, obviously brought about by many requests for "substance" by the garrison.

Friday, November 28—This morning, as I was strolling around the fort with a few comrades, "march" suddenly sounded. When we came to our quarters all baggage had been loaded on government wagons, and the men were in rank and file. We rushed to take our places, and after we marched out of the fort, we assembled in an open area, and an officer of the company swore us in, or as the expression is, "mustered us in." We went directly down to the river on the bottom of the Kansas side, which has a grove of trees. After we had marched about two miles, we came to a ferry, took our baggage on board, steamed up the river, and then across to the fairly large town of Weston, at the southern end of the railroad along

38. He means that once an enemy force controlled the heights, it could bombard the fort with impunity.

the river.[39] The riverbanks on the Missouri side are quite steep, consisting of nice limestone. In some places the railroad was laboriously cut right through.

At one thirty in the afternoon we left by train and arrived here in St. Joseph at sunset. We are quartered in the waiting room, so early, at three o'clock tomorrow morning, we can go on by train to Hannibal.[40] This evening I sent my suitcase to Pundt and Koenig in Omaha, wrote to them, also to Hedde.[41] Today we had the nicest weather of our journey, and everyone is in the best of spirits.

Saturday, November 29—After we had slept some hours in the waiting room, we left from St. Joseph by train at three thirty this morning. Lovely country on both sides of the track, trees alternating with stretches of prairie, as flat in many areas as our Platte bottom. The bluffs and steep hills really belong to the railroad leading along the Missouri River, which we had used on our journey to and from Leavenworth. We passed the now-famous Platte Bridge in the dark.[42] At daylight we could see that troops were posted at nearly all bridges, and nice log cabins were constructed,

39. The Platte County Railroad, which connected Weston and St. Joseph, was completed in April 1861. Glaab, *Kansas City and the Railroads*, 95.

40. The Hannibal and St. Joseph Railroad across northern Missouri was a common route to move troops to St. Louis. From Hannibal, steamboats took soldiers and supplies south on the Mississippi River to the town. As Scherneckau later reports, however, the Nebraska recruits changed to the North Missouri Railroad at Macon, where it intersected with the Hannibal and St. Joseph. For a map of railroads in Missouri during the war, see Fellman, *Inside War*, 9.

41. Henry Pundt and William Koenig operated a general merchandise store in Omaha. William's brother, Henry Koenig, clerked in the Omaha store before enlisting in Company B of the First Nebraska Volunteer Infantry. Henry Koenig had been discharged for disability before Scherneckau enlisted. A December 26, 1861, letter from Henry Koenig to his mother, written from Georgetown, Missouri, is found in the Pundt and Koenig Papers, RG0790, NSHS. Henry Koenig later opened a store in Grand Island.

42. He had heard of the sabotage of the railroad bridge over the Little Platte River, which collapsed under the weight of a train on the night of September 3, 1861. The wreck killed between seventeen and twenty persons, Union soldiers and civilians. Many others were injured. The saboteurs were presumed to have been anti-Union guerrillas. Filbert, *The Half Not Told*, 37–46. Correspondence about guerrilla activity in northern Missouri, including the firing into troop trains and efforts to suppress these attacks, is found in *The War of the Rebellion*, ser. 1, vol. 3, for example, pp. 135, 173, 423–24 (hereafter cited as *OR*, with the series,

surrounded by stockades. The troops were mostly cavalry from various Missouri regiments.

At about eight thirty we stopped at a station, Brookfield, to eat breakfast, which came to twenty-five cents per man. This was advanced by the captain and later will be withheld from our pay. After we moved on again and had gone about twelve miles, the train suddenly stopped, the engine whistled several times, finally unhooked, and drove forward. In half an hour it came back again and picked us up. We soon learned what happened.

Two trains, one packed with cattle coming from St. Joseph, the other a so-called construction train transporting dirt, with several cars attached where workers and their families lived [had collided]. One locomotive was completely thrown off the track and headlong down the embankment, which here is at least ten to twelve feet high, running through low bottomland. Two or three of the following cars were completely splintered and the pieces strewn about. The cars behind were shoved on top of each other, the last ones thrown off the track. Rails were broken as though they were kindling, a frightful sight.

Most ghastly, however, was the sight of a person, the fireman of one of the locomotives, who was sitting on the engine, pressed against the boiler by pieces of the other, and his head literally crushed. He was penned in by so many splinters and broken pieces that he could not yet be taken out, since the collision had taken place only about an hour before our arrival. Three other people were injured, one seriously. We had to unload passengers and baggage from our train and wait until a train came from the other side, which took us.

At about one thirty we left the scene of this tragic accident, this time pushed by the engine. After some twenty miles we came to Macon City, from which the North Missouri Railroad branches off. We changed to the cars of the North Missouri and St. Louis Railroad, and off we went again. From here I mailed a letter to Hedde. After it was dark, we stopped for supper in Warrenton, where we

volume, part, and page). The *Nebraska Republican* (Omaha), September 19, 1861, noted that rebels were at Platte City, Missouri, and had been engaged in the recent bridge burnings on the Hannibal and St. Joseph Railroad.

had a good meal [such as] in the morning. Forty miles farther on, we came to St. Charles on the Missouri, which we crossed by steam ferry. On this side, we got into railroad cars again and were taken quickly to St. Louis, where we arrived about eleven thirty at night. The station is located on the levee. For the night we were lodged very comfortably in the ladies waiting room. For once, we slept very well on a soft carpet, close to a well-heated stove and in a room with gaslight until sunrise of

Monday [Sunday], November 30—At that time we were expelled from this paradise, simply put out on the street with our things, where we had to wait until about twelve o'clock noon. A wagon then took us with our baggage to "Schofield's Barracks," where we are now quartered.[43] These are extensive buildings. The sleeping rooms are equipped with three rows of beds, one on top of another.[44] The single soldier or entire troops like us passing through St. Louis are quartered here until transportation is available. We probably won't stay here long. It is not very pleasant in these rooms. Moreover, I was ordered for guard duty this evening. We have to set up three posts to prevent anyone from entering or leaving. Only those who have written permission may pass, but it is not supposed to be easy to get such permission. The windows facing the street are equipped with strong bars; the doors lead only to the interior of the building; the yard is surrounded with twelve-foot-high planks; and the exits, as mentioned, are guarded. Indeed, the place looks more like a prison than a barracks for free men. Apparently this is necessary in this big city.

Until now the recruits have been given too much freedom, which they have often abused. Two or three of our men have already been

43. This was a "transportation barracks," where troops were housed in transit to or from their units. It was located near the St. Louis railroad stations and the Mississippi River, convenient to the places where soldiers arrived or departed. The barracks was named for Gen. John M. Schofield, who was posted in St. Louis before being given command of the District of Southwestern Missouri, Department of the Missouri, from September 24 to November 10, 1862, and again from March 30 to May 24, 1863. On the latter date, he assumed command of the Department of the Missouri, a position he held until January 30, 1864. Sifakis, *Who Was Who in the Union*, 355.

44. He evidently means that they were bunk beds stacked three high. Later in this same entry, he refers to "these triple beds."

left behind when we departed from Nebraska City. Another one in St. Joseph was evidently drunk and then arrested there, so that he could not come with us because we left at night. Still another got lost here yesterday morning, before we reached these quarters.[45] I cannot tell you very much about St. Louis, since I have not had the opportunity to see the city. Nevertheless, it is a very large city, and among its inhabitants are quite a number of Germans.[46]

Now just a few words about the gunboats under construction. They are lying on the levee a little above the North Missouri Railroad yard, and construction on both has advanced up to the covering with iron plates.[47] And despite it being a Sunday, at least one hundred workers were hard at work. On one of them [they] had already started with the iron sheathing, complete both underneath and above the water line. The flat, rather long, and, toward the top, quite round and closed-in things look very strange. What's more, they seem to be very strongly built; I should think the not-so-powerful shots would bounce right off. Over the very strong oak ribs, arranged tightly together, is first placed a layer of three-inch-thick planks and, over this, another layer of the same planks crosswise. These are caulked and painted. On top of these, large, two-inch-thick iron plates are placed, which are nailed down tightly with foot-long, one-inch iron bolts. Each plate, about two to three feet wide by six to eight feet long, is attached with ten to twelve such colossal bolts. In my estimation each single plate must weigh at least five hundred pounds. Hatches for cannons, as well as slits for rifles, have been provided in various parts of the boat. Real monsters of cannons were lying at the landing. These were designated for the boats.[48]

45. He probably wrote this part of the entry the next day, that is, December 1.

46. By 1860 Germans made up about a third of St. Louis's population of 166,773. Gerteis, *Civil War St. Louis*, 43; Winter, *The Civil War in St. Louis*, 3.

47. He evidently observed the gunboats while the recruits were waiting on the street in the vicinity of the North Missouri Railroad station, which was near the Mississippi River levee, although the principal shipyard for the construction of these vessels was farther south, at Carondelet.

48. Several ironclad gunboats were under construction at St. Louis or Carondelet at this time. Scherneckau's description is not precise enough to be certain which two he observed, but the likely candidates are *Lafayette* and *Choctaw*, river steamers being converted to ironclads, and nearing completion. Commodore William D. Porter had designed the two gunboats. Progress reports on several gunboats, along with the histories and specifications of *Lafayette* and *Choctaw*,

USS *Choctaw*, one of the Union gunboats Scherneckau observed at the levee in St. Louis in December 1862. NH55218, Naval Historical Center, Washington, D.C.

There are a lot of military [personnel] here, especially in this area (Chouteau Avenue), where several barracks and guard stations are located. General [John C.] Fremont's headquarter is on the corner just across from us in a palace-like building.[49] In general this seems to be a fashionable part of town, since all buildings more or less resemble palaces. McDowell's college is only about eighty rods from here, and is occupied by our secesh friends.[50]

Our barracks here, Schofield's Barracks, had been built by the general for whom they were named. They consist of "fachwerk" construction, the outside covered with fir wood, the roof covered with a double layer of boards. Inside, the walls are whitewashed. Three stoves heat each of the long buildings. However, at present only one is about half-occupied. In each building 112 men can sleep in these triple beds, built one above the other. The yard, formed by the two dormitories, is almost completely taken up by a double building, which is used as a kitchen and dining room. The

---

appear in *Official Records of the Union and Confederate Navies*, ser. 1, 23:418, 23:453, 23:636, and ser. 2, 1:57, 1:124. Drawings and specifications of Union and Confederate warships are found in Gibbons, *Warships and Naval Battles*, with *Lafayette* and *Choctaw* at 46–48. James B. Eads and his company, which built many of the gunboats, are discussed in Coombe, *Thunder along the Mississippi*, 18–20, and Gerteis, *Civil War St. Louis*, 236–41, 249–52.

One wonders how Scherneckau learned so many details from his look at the gunboats. Perhaps he spoke with one of the workmen, or some other St. Louis resident, after the boats had piqued his interest.

49. John C. Fremont, noted for his western explorations, was the first Republican candidate for president in 1856. His fame and political connections led to his appointment as commander of the Western Department in July 1861. Fremont proved inept as a military commander and insensitive to the administration's need for delicate maneuvering in the treacherous political waters of wartime Missouri. President Abraham Lincoln removed him November 2, 1861, after the general had issued an independent emancipation proclamation without approval from Washington and taken other actions that dissatisfied the president. Sifakis, *Who Was Who in the Union*, 143–44; Faust, *Encyclopedia of the Civil War*, 291. While commander in St. Louis, Fremont occupied the three-story Brant mansion on Chouteau Avenue between Eighth and St. Paul streets. Gerteis, *Civil War St. Louis*, 142; Winter, *The Civil War in St. Louis*, 71–73.

50. McDowell Medical College, on the corner of Eighth and Gratiot streets, was used as a military prison during the war. St. Louis military prisons are discussed in Gerteis, *Civil War St. Louis*, chapter 6, and Winter, *The Civil War in St. Louis*, 79–80.

space on the street between the two dormitories is taken up by a two-story building containing the office and guard station. But I am getting too long-winded and will end this day, adding only that it was cold and boring on my guard duty.

Tuesday [Monday], December 1—Cold and unpleasant in this big city. Still no chance of getting permission to go outside. I wrote in my diary, also to Hedde and Martin. I have a good opportunity here to observe the different groups as they come and go. I am lucky to have such good comrades. Of all the different troops who come and go, I have not yet found any, relatively speaking, that include such good elements as our group. As comrades, as well as educated men, they are more outstanding than any group of the same size that I have ever met in this small and eventful world.

The Germans I have met so far are all South Germans. These South Germans are the ones who start all these rackets and fights; they have convinced me even more that I should not enlist in a company formed entirely of Germans.[51] Certainly the inferior, poor German they speak would keep me from joining such rough fellows. In fact, many do not even realize that I can understand their German.

Without bragging too much, I can say that I have improved considerably in the English language since there are, of course, so many well-read and educated men among us [recruits]. I have had the opportunity to be corrected by them in the pronunciation of words, as well as in the choice of accurate expressions and the composition of sentences. For this reason, if possible, I will probably stay with this company. I like the men, and I have a good chance to perfect my English. Most of them intend to enter Company A, and, therefore, I will apply for the same. The captain is our present commander, Captain Gillette. I have already established my address, my letters [should be] directed to St. Louis, from where they will find their way to the regiment.

51. Company B of the First Nebraska was composed almost entirely of Germans, many of whom enlisted from St. Joseph, Missouri. Dudley, *Roster of Nebraska Volunteers*, 22–29.

Today I had an opportunity to see how fast, how marvelously fast, news travels across this huge country. The evening *Republican* already contained the proceedings of the Congress that had opened this morning in Washington and [the paper] was offered for sale here at the barracks around four o'clock in the afternoon. We backwoodsmen [in Grand Island, Nebraska Territory] are very much behind the times![52]

Wednesday [Tuesday], December 2—It freezes quite severely here, yet it is warm in our barracks. This morning at roll call we were not detailed for duty with the others, a sign that we will be leaving soon. One of our comrades was sent to the hospital. He was suffering from a severe case of "mum" [mumps?]. But this evening he came back again. He found it so unpleasant there that he would rather stay with us than be treated in the hospital.

Since there is still no prospect of getting permission to leave the barracks, I decided to climb over [the wall] somewhere in order to see something of St. Louis at least, and to speak once with Mr. Olshausen.[53] I found an unguarded corner, climbed over the high wooden fence and the roof of the barracks, and landed safely in an alley. So as not to be picked up on the street without a pass, I borrowed civilian clothes and certainly looked somewhat shabby when I got to Olshausen's, but he recognized me at once as being somebody from Davenport and was very friendly. I conveyed regards from Hedde and told him about Nebraska and our settlement.

52. An evening edition of the *Missouri Republican*, published in St. Louis. The Grand Island settlement had no newspaper at this time, and Omaha or Nebraska City newspapers that reached the settlers would not always have included the latest news from the East.

53. Theodor Olshausen was a prominent journalist and political leader who emigrated from Schleswig-Holstein to the United States in 1851. He lived in Davenport, Iowa, from 1856 to 1860, when he moved to St. Louis and assumed the editorship of the *Westliche Post*, which became one of the most important German-language newspapers in the country. A strong supporter of the Republican Party and of the abolition of slavery, Olshausen was unhappy with Lincoln's removal of Fremont as commander of the Western Department. Scherneckau undoubtedly had met Olshausen during his Davenport stay, and Olshausen was a friend of Scherneckau's uncle, Fred Hedde. For a biography of Olshausen, see Bärner, "A Forty-Eighter Who Returned."

Theodor Olshausen, editor of the *Westliche Post.* Foto Kieler Stadtarchiv. Digitally enhanced.

Since there had been a message in the *Westliche Post* with this content: "A letter for Lieutenant Ernst Arp is in our office and anyone who knows his whereabouts should notify us," I immediately inquired about him. Mr. O. told me that Ernst, now a lieutenant in the Twelfth Missouri Volunteer Regiment, had left St. Louis to meet his regiment, which was somewhere in Arkansas or Tennessee. But he never arrived, and no one has heard from him again. The letter was from his Uncle Schricker. I did not get all the details of when this happened, nor to which company of the regiment he belonged.

I did not want to trouble Olshausen any longer than absolutely necessary, but to my great surprise, I heard further that Mr. Rusch was here and in the army. He belongs to the regular troops and has the rank of quartermaster. I obtained his address; he is living close to the office of the *Westliche Post* and, as far as I know, does not have his family here. I was there three times, yet did not find him. I left my card but still have not heard from him.[54]

Around noon I was back here. It is not difficult to get in, only to get out. Today at noon we received three dollars a man for pocket money, which each recruit who has volunteered is entitled to. The twenty-five-dollar bounty is still not available. I was lucky to receive permission to go outside this afternoon. I wandered around the city with several comrades. Some of them got ambrotyped—four pictures, a good image, and quite large, for a dollar. I bought a pair of suspenders since the trousers provided are so large and heavy that I cannot keep them up with only the belt. In addition, I also got paper and envelopes, as well as a couple of handkerchiefs, etc. By the time it got dark I was here again. In the meantime our route of climbing over the fence had been discovered and a guard posted there.

54. Nicholas J. Rusch (or Rausch) employed Scherneckau on his farm near Davenport, Iowa, in 1857. Fred Hedde had made the arrangements. Scherneckau, "Her Quota Furnished," 77. Rusch had been elected lieutenant governor of Iowa in 1859. Bärner, "A Forty-Eighter Who Returned," 96. Rusch was appointed captain and assistant quartermaster of volunteers September 27, 1862. He died September 22, 1864. Heitman, *Historical Register*, 1:852.

Thursday [Wednesday], December 3—Cold and freezing during the night, rather pleasant during the day. This morning a couple of Nebraska boys were discovered as they tried to make their way over the roof into the street. They were taken to the guardhouse but soon were released. In this establishment we have the advantage of not having to do guard duty or other fatigue duty, yet it is difficult to be kept like a prisoner. This morning, however, I was lucky to be able to sneak out again.

Immediately I went to look up Mr. Rusch. I met him at the restaurant where I had been told to go. He was still the same old fellow, except for the insignia of his captain's rank on his shoulders. He received me very warmly. We remained together until noon. During this time several glasses of Rhine wine were consumed, while we chatted about old times. He has been here about three weeks and was appointed three months ago. He has the freedom to choose a division to which he would like to be assigned as quartermaster. He likely will join one of the expeditions that will be sent soon to attack the South. I hope he will come to the same division to which I am assigned. He is just building his department. I was introduced to a German who had applied for a clerk's position in Mr. Rusch's office. I learned that he [Rusch] possibly would employ twenty clerks and, except for his chief clerk, intended not to take any Americans. He talked a lot back and forth and suggested that I also apply for a position under him. I declined to do so, but he promised me that he would always support me, as far as it would be in his power, if we meet again. He too knew nothing more about Ernst Arp; he had known him quite well, since he had lodged with him in the same house where Ernst had disappeared, leaving his things behind. Once more I went to Mr. Olshausen, and he too knew nothing more about Arp but told me in confidence that it would probably be better if Ernst did not surface again. Ugly rumors were circulating about missing funds, etc. With what I know about E.A.'s past, I assume that there is some truth to it, and therefore I have dropped the matter.[55] The name

55. In his diary entry dated November 21, 1863, Scherneckau reports hearing that Arp had stolen money entrusted to him by men in his unit.

of the German mentioned above is Hammerstein, an elderly gentleman, formerly from Davenport, and as it became apparent, a creditor of our friend W. Stolley. But he said he had given up his claims for 10 percent.[56]

Around noon I left Mr. Rusch and went directly back to our quarters. However, in the afternoon I had a chance to go outside again and take another look at this very busy city. Almost half the men are in uniform, or at least partially militarily dressed. The McDowell college is located only one block from our barracks and surrounded with numerous [guard] posts. My bunkmate had a brother who was a prisoner there and paid him a visit; he found him to be a fanatical secessionist.[57]

Tomorrow morning at six o'clock we will leave on the Iron Mountain Railroad to join our regiment. Parts of St. Louis are almost entirely German. Nothing but German is spoken there, and one can see German announcements, faces, and traditional costumes.

Thursday, December 4—Pilot Knob. Somewhat closer to the front lines! This morning, about six o'clock, we left St. Louis on the Iron Mountain Railroad and arrived here at twelve o'clock noon. As the name says, the railroad goes through a mountainous, iron-containing area. On the last stretch it really earns its name, mountains of iron! Everything is red and rusty; the trees on this poor soil are, therefore, just gnarled, but stones and boulders are plentiful, in fact, "more than I ever saw." In places, the railroad practically had to be forced through boulders. Now and then pine trees come into view, but not large and stately ones, also cedar trees.

We are now resting at the station without tents. We hope to be able to march farther on tomorrow morning. The First Missouri Regiment has also set up their tents here. Some earthworks have

56. William Stolley was a partner in an outfitting store in Davenport, Iowa, which went broke during the Panic of 1857, and was also one of the leaders of the original German colony at Grand Island.

57. Because many persons came to Nebraska Territory from border states, or elsewhere in the South, it is not surprising that some of them, or members of their families, favored secession. Territorial newspapers during this period occasionally mention former Nebraskans who had enlisted in the Confederate service.

been erected around the station but without cannons. My friend Foster and I went on an expedition to the top of the iron mountain, Pilot Knob.[58] One has quite an extensive and rewarding view from the jagged peak. The little towns Pilot Knob, Ironton, and Arcadia lie at one's feet. Quite a few pits have been dug into the mountain, yet the supply [of ore] still seems inexhaustible. At the moment the smelting furnaces are not active, yet large supplies of iron ingots are lying at the railroad at the foot of the mountain. The ore appears to be very rich, since it is unusually heavy. It is a peaceful, nice day, yet quite fresh since the sun is slowly setting. Since I am writing outside on the back of an ambulance, it is getting too cold for me, and therefore I am closing for today. Many Germans live here, and furthermore, there are many countrymen among the troops located here.

Friday, December 5—Last night we slept quite well in a shed near the railroad, where hay was stored for the government. I was on guard duty today—even for commissary stores. Around noon we loaded our knapsacks and rations on a wagon ordered for that purpose and marched off, heading in the direction of Patterson. Two wagons, besides the one we loaded, made up our train. Close to Pilot Knob we met a wagon train from our regiment, which was supposed to load supplies. About five miles from P. Knob, six companies of the Twenty-fifth Missouri Regiment were camped, who had repaired the road, which needed it very much indeed. Everything here was wood and stone; now and then we saw single pine trees. We went about seven miles from the town into camp. Without tents it was an unpleasant, cold affair, and I slept little.

At daybreak [Saturday, December 6] everything was ready for departure, and we went forward again, over hill and dale. Today we came to more and more impressive-looking pine trees growing on top of the mountains on very rocky soil. By sunset we reached the Big River. Four companies of the Twenty-fifth Missouri Infantry Reg-

58. Richard B. Foster enlisted at Nebraska City on September 17, 1862. Dudley, *Roster of Nebraska Volunteers*, 118–19, 122–23. Since Scherneckau mentions Foster by name, perhaps the two were bunkmates before they were assigned to different companies.

iment were camped here, and they had almost completed a bridge across the river. We camped right next to them, and I slept in the tent of the cook of a German company. The German comrades were definitively sick of the soldier's life and moaned and complained, and would certainly have deserted if only they had been paid. Again, it was a really cold night with heavy frost.

Sunday, December 6 [7]—Early this morning we went on. We forded the river. The area was frightfully wild, the road we followed, rocky. The big, heavily loaded government wagons sometimes banged so hard against stones and stumps that I believed they surely would break, yet everything went well. Two miles this side of Patterson we passed the outposts of the unit to which our regiment belonged and afterward came to the division headquarters. Here was the camp of the First Wisconsin Cavalry Regiment, a little farther on, a six-pounder Missouri battery was encamped. Soon afterward we came to an almost level area, a cultivated field, on which the First Nebraska, the Twenty-fourth Missouri, and the Twenty-third Iowa regiments camped. Each company has its own row of tents, and at the front of these rows, the tents of the officers are pitched.[59]

After our wagons had arrived, we assembled, and our names were called by Adjutant Cramer.[60] Then we were handed over to the commander of the company to which we had been assigned. We did not have a choice to join the company we had chosen, for the weakest companies had to be filled up. I was assigned to Company H with two others; twelve of the recruits went to Company I and twelve others to Company K.[61] The regiment has been

59. The First Nebraska, along with six companies of the Twenty-fourth Missouri, constituted the Second Brigade, Second Division, Army of Southeastern Missouri. The Twenty-third Iowa and the Twenty-fifth Missouri made up the First Brigade. The First Wisconsin Cavalry was in the cavalry brigade. *OR*, ser. 1, vol. 22, part 1, p. 890.

60. Francis I. Cramer enlisted from Page County, Iowa. In October 1863 he was discharged to become a major in the First Alabama Cavalry Volunteers. Dudley, *Roster of Nebraska Volunteers*, 4–5.

61. Based on rosters and dates of enlistment given in Dudley, *Roster of Nebraska Volunteers*, the men were likely as follows: Scherneckau, George Shannon, and William West, Company H; Isaac Flinn, Amos Harding, Samuel Lockwood, John Predmore, Leonidas Quim, Lewis Laflin, William Rancier, Francis

reduced severely. At the moment not more than 250 men are presumed fit for service. My company now numbers only some 30 men.[62] In the afternoon we received our weapons: Springfield rifle-muskets, ammunition for them, pointed balls [minié "balls"], the cartridge pouch for them, and the same for the copper guards [percussion caps].[63] At four o'clock we had a dress parade. We marched up in lines, did several exercises, and then received a general order, read by our adjutant, according to which we had to march on Tuesday, the Twenty-fourth Missouri Regiment as advance guard, the battery in the middle, and our regiment as the rear guard.[64] Each man should take rations for two days in his haversack, and five days' rations were to be brought along on the company wagon. After we had completed all the formalities, we wheeled off into our tent alley.

Reed, William Roberts, Merritt Slocum, and Stephen Stoddard, Company I; and Abel Hill, John Adams, Chauncey Allen, Thomas Bagley, Charles Bates, Richard Foster, Joseph Beardsley, James Clark, George Cardwell, Henry Black, Hamilton Bridwell, James Clayton, and John McCarthy, Company K.

62. The Company H morning report for mid-December 1862 shows three officers and forty-five enlisted men present for duty, out of an aggregate strength of three officers and sixty-two enlisted men. NSHS RG18, roll 3.

63. This was likely a Springfield Model 1842 .69-caliber rifle-musket, although the regiment was not uniformly armed with this weapon until June 1863. Col. Robert R. Livingston, in a report dated December 25, 1863, said the regiment had first been supplied with arms of various kinds, including foreign muskets. In an ordnance report dated July 17, 1863, Livingston reported turning in 275 "Springfield muskets," .69 caliber, and nine thousand rounds of "buck and ball" cartridges, as well as some Prussian muskets in .69 and .71 caliber. Because "buck and ball" was smoothbore ammunition, this document reveals that the First Nebraska had been armed partly with smoothbore muskets before June 1863. Coming in as a new recruit in the fall of 1862, Scherneckau was fortunate enough to be issued a rifle-musket, confirmed by his reference to the "pointed ball," or minié bullet, that was used in such weapons. MS129, Robert R. Livingston Papers, NSHS (hereafter cited as Livingston Papers).

Because "musket" had historically been the term designating a smoothbore military long arm, Civil War soldiers often referred to their weapons as muskets even after the rifled version had replaced the smoothbores as the primary infantry arm.

64. The artillery consisted of Battery B of the First Missouri Light Artillery and Battery M of the Second Missouri Light Artillery. *OR*, ser. 1, vol. 22, part 1, p. 890.

I slept well this night and for once warm in our tent, about twelve to fifteen men in each. These are the so-called Sibley tents. They are round and have a post in the center, which rests on an iron tripod. We lie with our feet toward the center. In every tent there is a small iron stove like a sugarloaf, which warms it quite comfortably if it is not too cold.

Monday, December 8—Today we had plenty to do just to polish our rusty muskets and accoutrements a little. I am feeling weak and sick. I caught a bad cold on the trip here from Pilot Knob, and my chest hurts from a lot of coughing. We drilled a little this morning. In the evening, parade again. Once more orders were read, whereupon strict discipline is to be observed on the upcoming marches, and the officers were made responsible for the conduct of their men. Each man is to place forty cartridges into his cartridge pouch and to carry the knapsack. The wagons will bring the blankets and remaining baggage.

CHAPTER 2

With the Army of Southeastern Missouri, December 9, 1862–February 21, 1863

Tuesday, December 9—Early, at four o'clock, the signal sounded, and soon drums and fifes struck up reveille. We were quickly wide awake, and after eating breakfast, we packed our things and waited for the signal to break camp. As soon as the bugle sounded, one tent after another came down. Each company has a wagon to transport its things. These wagons were then loaded tightly and compactly up to the bows. As soon as everything was packed, the drums sounded to start. We lined up in our tent streets, from which we wheeled and joined the remaining companies of our regiment. We marched with the rest of the sections of our brigade in close rank, and at that time were inspected by Brigadier General Davidson. He is the supreme commander of this expedition.[1]

Soon afterward everything was set in motion, and we marched at the end of the column, followed by our wagon. We marched in a southwestern direction on little-used roads, stopping only now and then as the wagon train ahead of us was occasionally held up. A pioneer corps was ahead of us, improving the road where necessary, as well as occasionally replacing broken wheels or axles of the wagons. The road was rough and rocky, like from Ironton to here,

1. John W. Davidson commanded the Army of Southeastern Missouri, Department of the Missouri, from October 1862 until February 23, 1863. In August and September 1863, he led Union troops from Missouri as part of a successful campaign to capture Little Rock, Arkansas. After the war he commanded cavalry in the West, including the Second U.S. Cavalry, and was lieutenant colonel of the Tenth U.S. Cavalry (buffalo soldiers). Sifakis, *Who Was Who in the Union*, 105; DeBlack, "1863," 90–94; Davidson, *Black Jack Davidson*. The winter campaign of 1862–63 is reviewed in Bradbury, "This War Is Managed."

Brig. Gen. John W. Davidson. Arthur Marchand Collection, U.S. Army Military History Institute, Carlisle Barracks, Pennsylvania.

but the pine trees were more numerous and taller. We rarely saw a house. The few that we did see were often deserted, and the fields were not cultivated. If there were still inhabitants there, they were mostly women and children.

Besides the forty cartridges we had to carry, already a very considerable weight, we had the bayonet and musket and the haversack with the rations. Besides, we were marching rather fast. Finally, about four o'clock in the afternoon, after General Davidson returned with his bodyguard, we stopped and set up our tents in an old clearing that, however, was now overgrown again with hazel brush. The battery and the wagons took up the middle, and the other regiment the left wing. Extremely tired, I sank down, chest and shoulders aching terribly. I felt I would not be able to march again the next day with a full pack. Some of the others were in the same state, although we had marched only twelve miles. Since our wagon, to make good use of the space, could still take our knapsacks, we received permission to load them on, as did most of the other companies.

Wednesday, December 10—Early, as usual, the military music woke us up. The wagons were quickly loaded, and we moved on, our regiment at the head this time, only a detachment of skirmishers and the pioneer corps in front. I felt three times lighter than yesterday; my feet were in good shape and not, as with so many others, swollen or full of blisters. I have to thank a pair of comfortable boots (which Court made for me); they have strong soles and light uppers.[2] Besides, I did not have wet feet as did many in small shoes, who had to wade through the small streams that the road crossed every minute, or followed their beds—the simplest way to have a road. The sharp stones were a tough test for the durability of the soles, and if the soles were thin the feet felt it too. Today we marched even faster than yesterday with fewer stops.

2. Court is undoubtedly Frederick Court, an Omaha boot- and shoemaker who emigrated with his family from Prussia, according to the 1860 Census of Nebraska Territory, Omaha, second ward, 28. His advertisement appears in the October 23, 1860, issue of the *Daily Omaha Nebraskian* and in surrounding issues. Later Scherneckau mentions sending some of his pay to Court for safekeeping.

At twelve o'clock noon we reached the Black River. We marched up in line; our camp was being marked off and was soon set up again. The battery is positioned so that it controls the ford in the river. The enemy advance post had been three miles on this side of the river today; we found their fires still burning. But since we did not have cavalry with us, naturally we could not think of pursuing these mounted bush-nags [bushwhackers] to bring them in. Likewise, they could not capture such a large column as we were. The Black River is a nice clear river, with dark green water; there is no bridge crossing it in this area. Farther below, where the main road crosses the river, a bridge has been built by the troops stationed there. Our advance posts were set up this afternoon and moved forward across the river.

Thursday, December 11—Nice weather, like all these days. And what is so pleasant about it is there is no wind, as we are used to in Nebraska. I have not noticed wind since we left St. Joseph. It is already warmer here; at least it did not freeze as hard as the nights in Patterson. We are about twenty-five miles south of there. It looks as though we will stay here somewhat longer; in the morning we drilled some and in the afternoon had to modify the camp somewhat, and for that reason we had to take down all the tents and set them up again.

Friday, December 12—We drilled some in the morning, and in the afternoon, as we marched out for the same purpose, it started to rain, and we were ordered back. Since then it has rained constantly. Otherwise everything is going along as usual. The pioneers are cutting down the trees in front of the battery in order to open up a wider field of fire across the river for the cannons. Thirty to forty wagons cross the river every day and get corn; they often also bring back hogs and cattle. Each day the foraging train leaves with a large detachment as escort. A lot of corn is still in the field, and it is carelessly picked and thrown into the wagons. Secessionists, who have left their possessions behind, lose everything. Union people, or those who pretend to be, receive a receipt for which they can request payment.

Saturday, December 13—After it rained the whole night, nevertheless, there is a good shower every ten minutes today. Therefore, we are sitting in the tents and feeling sorry for the men who must be outside. However, the weather is still warm, and I am sitting in the tent in shirtsleeves and writing this without fire in the stove. I wrote to Egge and Martin today; ceaseless rain, everything wet and cold.

Sunday, December 14—Still raining, nevertheless, I was sent out with the foraging expedition today. We crossed the river, using the ford, but the water came into the wagon bed. We then drove five to six miles farther in a southwesterly direction on terrible roads and in pouring rain. The farmer we visited had all his corn in two cribs, and it was enough to load all the wagons, some twenty in number. We were four or five men with each wagon, so somewhat over one hundred men in all. We saw or heard nothing of the enemy. When we came back to the river, it had risen further. We made it through all right with our wagon, but the one following had an accident with its harness. The four front mules got tangled in the harness chains and were saved only when we cut them free and sacrificed the leathers. All of this took place in pouring rain.

We then unloaded and could go home. It was evening, and still it rained on without a break. I was soaked through to the skin; my coat weighed a ton. Weapons and other equipment were all wet, and the shiny rifle nicely moist, ready to rust.[3] There was little prospect of getting my things dry. They had to stay on my body and get dry as well as possible, yet it was, with all the wetness, not very cold. Wrapped in the damp woolen blankets, I finally fell asleep after the toothache had diminished somewhat.

Monday, December 15—Continuous rain. Today I was sent out again with a fatigue detachment, which was to raise a sunken ferryboat. It had been sunk by the rebels about five miles downstream. The

3. Scherneckau used three different German words to refer to the arms he and his comrades were issued: *Muskete* (musket), *Büchse* (rifle), and *Gewehr* (gun). The varied terminology is a reflection of the confusing variety of smoothbore and rifled arms used during the Civil War.

river had risen so much that it filled all the sloughs and bottomlands. We had to travel on the high bluffs to reach our destination.

When we finally got into the area, we found wide and deep streams that separated us from the boat, which were impossible for us to cross. We, some one hundred men strong, were therefore sent back, and now discovered that the rising river had almost cut us off from the camp. A little after noon we reached our quarters, which we had to take down immediately and load on the wagons, since the still-rising river threatened to flood the whole area. We went back a little on the bluffs into the woods, where we set up camp again. All this took place in steady rain; only toward evening did it let up and begin to clear.

Today I had to face the rain without my overcoat, since it was too heavy and wet to be used. Naturally, I became as wet as I could get, yet I will be content if only it will clear up. This evening the river covered all the area where our tents had been this morning. Even after tattoo, a detachment had to go down to rescue the mules from drowning. The sutler of our regiment lost three of his four mules this way. Still later at night, some of us had to get out to move the quartermaster's supplies to safety. The whole area looks like a large lake, in which wagons or other objects left behind are stuck here and there. Our advance guard, on the other side of the Black River, has not been relieved this morning, since it is impossible to get across; a nice opportunity for the secesh to capture some forty men if there really are gangs here strong enough to attack them.

Tuesday, December 16—Finally, nice clear weather today. It was quite cold at night. I was detailed for foraging again, but when we reported at headquarters, we received a counter order and could go back to our tents. Now we had to clean the camp; each company had to clear away all the underbrush in its alley. I was detailed with a fatigue party of about fifty men from our regiment and the same number from the Twenty-fourth Missouri Regiment to husk the corn in the cribs. After an early noon meal, we were kept busy there the rest of the day.

Wednesday, December 17—It was very cold last night, good clear weather today. A train was sent out again today to bring in corn.

The pioneers are repairing the bad spots in the roads. Other detachments are busy with husking corn. A flatboat is being built to reestablish the connection with the other bank, where the advance guard still remains—unrelieved.

At this time our life here in camp is about as follows: at daybreak the bugle of the regiment's bugler sounds, and as soon as the drummers have gathered, they join with drums and fifes, drumming for about a quarter hour, during which time the men fall into ranks in their tent alleys. As soon as the drums are quiet, the first sergeant begins the roll call of his men. Half an hour later the bugle sounds again, this time for breakfast call. After this is over, sick call comes for the sick, who now have to report. At roll call in the morning, the sergeant announces the names of those who have duty for that day and what time they have to be ready. At seven thirty the bugle sounds for those assigned to fatigue duty, as well as for the escorts of the forage trains. At eight o'clock there is a bugle call that marks the relief of the guard detachment chosen yesterday; this, of course, again takes place with full drumming and piping. Guard duty here requires quite a few men at the moment, since we have to post an extensive advance guard line, and besides that a strong camp guard and provost guard.

Usually no signal is given again until sunset; however, officer and orderly calls often happen in the meantime—the first for the officers to gather, the latter to call the orderly sergeants into the headquarters to receive orders or the like. At sunset retreat sounds, at which the men gather for roll call. At nine o'clock there is tattoo that, like reveille in the morning, is carried out with full music. Half an hour later a bugle call, taps, is blown, with which the military life closes for the day.

Now that I am in a little better spirits, I can better describe the life and activity here. Since I am lucky enough today to be spared from duty entirely, I have the opportunity to write. There is plenty to eat and drink, coffee with lots of sugar or at times tea; with that, these large crackers, called pilot bread, which are quite good.[4] Furthermore, smoked or salted bacon, cooked or fried, fresh meat

4. He is referring to hardtack.

usually every other day. Of course, there are plenty of beans, likewise hominy, the latter cooked either with the meat or just in water and then sweetened with sugar. The last one I like very much. The toothache is again bothering me a great deal this evening.

Thursday, December 18—This morning it was very cold again. It had frozen so hard last night that wagons and animals went across the frost without breaking through. I was with the forage detachment, this time [going] back in the direction from which we had come; about thirty wagons with a one-hundred-man escort came with us. We had to pick the corn in the field, and we threw it with the husks into the wagons, which were quickly filled. Corn does very well here in some places, especially on the strips of bottomland, which are less stony than all the other land. This field contains at least sixty acres; the owner was not there. Most cobs are thicker in diameter than the corn we raise in Nebraska but no longer. The individual kernels are longer and therefore cause the circumference to be much larger.

Today I used my bayonet for the first time, stabbing a hog, which had been shot, with it, until another man came and cut its throat so that the penetrating squealing would end. This easily could have alarmed the officers, who, of course, are supposed to see to it that such things do not happen. But I was surprised how easily the bayonet, which did not seem to be very sharp, went straight through the animal. The booty was thrown on the wagon, and at three thirty we were at camp. The drums are rolling for retreat, so I must close for tonight. Things change quickly in the life of the soldier; until now I still wrote at the Black River.

Friday, December 19—I was ordered to relieve the advance guard and was just preparing myself with rations for twenty-four hours when an orderly call sounded. Orders reached us to recall the advance guard and to have everything ready to march at nine o'clock in the morning. Of course, I did not get to the post, but ten minutes later, I was busy packing up everything. At eight o'clock strike tents was blown, and at nine o'clock the entire force stationed here marched. Our regiment formed the rear guard today. We marched back the way we had come, and in the evening we set up our tents again on the same place we had occupied for one night when we came [from Patterson]. Soon we were comfortably set up after the rapid march we had completed. As so often, I suffered from a severe toothache this evening.

Saturday, December 20—At four o'clock this morning reveille was sounded, and before daybreak we were on the march. Today we had the lead, and at the quickstep we went uphill, downhill, toward Patterson. We often had to wade through brooks now risen much higher, and since I got my feet quite wet, one boot began to rub, and marching became more difficult for me. We also had to carry our knapsacks today, according to orders. For the most part, however, they were almost empty, since we had packed all the heavy items in our wool blankets and loaded them on the wagons. Somewhat after ten o'clock this morning, we marched into Patterson again, where two regiments, the Twenty-fifth Missouri and Twenty-third Iowa, were just marching off.[5] We set up our tents close to the deserted campground. The Twenty-third Iowa Regiment is at least three times as large as our regiment now is and, as it marched by, gave the appearance of the way one imagines a regiment to be.

The weather now is really pleasant. It did not freeze at all last night, while the night before it was cold enough to freeze the ground solid, so wagons went over the frozen ground without breaking through. But marching today in the mud was not pleasant at all.

Sunday, December 21—By daybreak we had already marched a mile. No one knew where we were going. We soon left the road to Pilot Knob. On little-used roads we went through thick woods, over steep hills, covered for the most part with majestic stands of pine trees, stopping only rarely. At about four o'clock in the afternoon we overtook the troops who had marched away from Patterson yesterday. They encamped on the banks of the Black River, where we

5. These regiments made up the First Brigade, Second Division, Army of Southeastern Missouri. *OR*, ser. 1, vol. 22, part 1, p. 890.

also stacked our muskets in order to set up our camp as soon as the wagons with the tents would arrive. But there it went wrong; they did not come, as much as we longed for them. The road had been too poor, and we had marched too far, about twenty miles.

Night came, fires were started, and the few provisions we had were soon consumed. Coffee and tea were rare items. Most of us, like myself, had not planned on the absence of the wagons and therefore had not burdened ourselves too much with rations. I was lucky enough to snatch half a tin cup of warm coffee, also crackers enough to still the greatest hunger. But now there was another problem. Nightfall came; it was not very cold but still unpleasant enough to lie under the open sky without blankets or overcoat. As did many others, I had sent all needless things with the wagons, making it easier to march. Now I was without blankets and did not even have my overcoat with me! I found it not very pleasant lying next to the fire. The ground was too damp and cold to keep warm. The tent of the camp guard, which had arrived with the quartermaster wagon, is the only tent we have, besides that of the regimental staff and the Quartermaster Department. I found a little space in the guard tent, but without blankets I could not fall asleep, although I was very tired from the rapid, long march we had made.

At ten o'clock in the evening wagons and men were sent out to our train to bring it into camp, and about two o'clock the first of these arrived. Our company wagon had overturned, as had many others, in the abominable holes of the road. Others were broken and could not go on. Since reveille was to be sounded at four o'clock, the tents were not set up, just blankets taken out to try to catch a couple of hours' sleep. In the meantime, I helped the cook prepare breakfast, since our black man was missing. Fresh meat was fried with bacon, and coffee was boiled in huge pots. Reveille sounded before we had breakfast completely ready. The groups lying about the various fires began to stir, and as usual one company after the other turned up in formation for roll call. Next we had a quick breakfast, which for many was the supper of yesterday. The wagons were loaded again, although the wagons of three or four companies were still not here, and again the drums were rolling to fall in.

Monday, December 22—At daybreak we came to the banks of the Black River, which we had left only two days ago. But now we were about thirty or forty miles farther upstream, close to its source. Incidentally, it was still quite considerable and very rapid. The pioneers of the troops preceding us had put over a footbridge of logs, or more precisely in it, since in many places the water gushed through. It was a very makeshift arrangement, yet it did take us across successfully.

The Twenty-fourth Missouri Regiment marched in front today, then came the battery, and then us. After that followed the wagons belonging to both these regiments, then came the Twenty-fifth Missouri and Twenty-third Iowa regiments, as well as a battery of twelve-pounders. The supply train of the division followed slowly, protected by some cavalry. A cavalry company formed the advance unit of the entire column.

We again marched rather quickly, yet the frequent crossings of so many small streams caused quite a bit of delay. The arrangements for the crossings were very inadequate. Trees were felled across them, and everyone had to try to balance his way across as best he could. Many fell in, to the great amusement of the rest. Often a tree, blown down by the wind, or a tree trunk washed ashore were the only bridges, similar to when at the settlement we went over to the big island across the branch of the Platte and did not use Hans Wrage's bridge.[6] But these streams were considerably more rapid and most of the time much wider than that branch of the Platte. We must have crossed one single brook, whose valley we followed for a long time, at least twelve to fifteen times. Otherwise, the road was better for the teams today, mostly stony but also sandy.

The land is not worth much around here, except for some small places. Everything is dense woods, often very nice, much of it pine.[7] On this uneven and rocky road, my feet began to hurt very

6. Hans Wrage was one of the Germans who settled in Hall County in 1857, and he lived near the Platte River. Stolley, "History of the First Settlement," 3. Evidently Wrage had constructed a bridge of some sort.

7. For a review of how Union soldiers from the Midwest reacted to the landscape of the Ozark highlands, see Bradbury, "Good Water and Wood."

much, and I was close to collapse when we finally reached the end of our day's march, a small town by the name of Barnesville, containing three or four houses. It lies on a small plain, surrounded by hills with pine, and looks quite charming. We camped among the houses on a large open area. Besides us, only the Twenty-fourth Missouri Regiment and the battery had arrived. Our wagons came in the course of the evening, with the exception of some, which belonged to the other companies. We put up our tent, and tired as I was, I slept extremely well, sincerely pitying the comrades who camped outside without any protection.

Tuesday, December 23—We slept until daybreak this morning and had high hopes we might be given a rest day. But it turned out otherwise; we were still at breakfast when the signal was sounded to strike the tents. I was assigned to the camp guard, which I took up before the troops started to march. From Barnesville we went in a westerly direction. The current regimental guard marches behind the regiment, the prisoners in the middle. Furthermore, it picks up and drives on the looters and, in general, maintains order. Our prisoners today were the one deserter we have escorted here from Nebraska, and for whom still no decision has been made, and several from our corps who were caught by the colonel on the pig hunt.

Today the road, in general, was somewhat better; we did not have as many streams to cross as yesterday. There were more hills and stone roads, which we passed. It rained pretty hard for a while, but my coat kept me dry. Since we were at the head today we marched quite rapidly, and when we stopped at about two o'clock in the afternoon, we had made twelve miles.

We now set up our camp in a valley about eighty rods wide. The hills on both sides were covered with oak and pine, and on the plain, like in a park, were groups of leaf and pine trees. The Twenty-fourth Missouri Regiment, as well as the Missouri battery, camped here too. This night I slept in the guard tent and altogether had to be on the post only four hours out of the twenty-four, since we have to have only one post in front of the guard tent. Honor posts, in front of officers' and generals' quarters, I have not yet seen in this army.

Wednesday, December 24—Christmas Eve! At three o'clock this morning the sergeant of the guard was to wake one of the drummers to sound reveille. At three thirty everyone in the camp was busy eating breakfast, either around the fires or in the tents with lamps. Crackers were in very short supply this morning; meat and coffee were nearly the only things one could get. The companies whose wagons had not yet arrived had to borrow from the others whose rations had arrived. Besides, we had to give several days' rations to the Twenty-fourth Missouri Regiment, since their wagons, sent for supplies, had still not returned. This put us on short rations too. Before we marched off, the guards were released, and I came back to my company.

Today we formed the rear guard and started about eight o'clock. Our way went through a lot of pine forest, and we passed several quite extensive farms. Otherwise we saw only few people and works of man. About ten o'clock we came to the foot of a steep hill, and the artillery slowly moved up into the heights, following the road. We followed, climbing, and finally found ourselves on a ridge from which we saw other hills around, covered with pines, nothing but rocks, hills, and pine forest. The tops of the giant pines in the canyons reached almost to our feet. Everything around was wild and deserted. The artillery now followed the road to our left, while we on the ridge kept more to the right. This way we had to climb several steep hills without a path or a road, just following a leader.

Finally, after several hours' strenuous march, we saw a river at our feet, the Current River. Along the bank on this side we saw widespread rows of tents, as well as a few houses on the far bank, forming the town of Van Buren. This was the destination of our march, although there had been many different opinions about this. In fact, where we were being led and what was intended remained a mystery for everyone. This last part of our march, through such a roadless area, even gave us the idea that we would be in action at once, and a battle was before us. However, it appears to have been only one of the usual mistakes of our gentlemen officers that chased us over boulders and mountains. I can justly call these mountains; we are in the Ozark Mountains.

The artillery, the baggage, as well as the remaining regiments of the division arrived soon after we did and had far better roads than those we had to take. We set up our tents behind those of the troops who had arrived earlier, so we are quite a ways from the river.

Christmas Eve, surrounded by the loveliest evergreen trees, provided many opportunities to obtain a Christmas tree, but for whom? And with whom? I felt lonesome in the middle of thousands of comrades, almost had some sort of homesickness. It was, of course, the first Christmas Eve I had to spend without having some friends or relatives around who like myself—and we North Germans in general—were accustomed to observing this evening. The pine branches that we brought into camp tonight reminded me very vividly of our homeland, as likely was the case for the other Germans among us. But we used them only as a mattress for our beds, since one sleeps softly on them, and at the same time they keep the moisture away.

Thursday, December 25—Christmas Day. The most miserable I have ever spent. The weather is so mild and warm that we don't have a fire in the tent. Besides, our officers kept us at work to keep us warm. We had to clean the whole camp, each company its tent alley and also around the tents of its officers. All bushes had to be cut down, the leaves swept away and burned. The rocks, with which the ground is covered, had to be thrown onto piles, etc. I was busy with this work when I was ordered to report to the quartermaster. There I received the assignment, with about twenty more men, to chop wood for burning charcoal. One from our company was an expert, a charcoal burner. He set up the charcoal kiln, while the rest of us brought in the wood. This pleasant work kept us going until evening, when we could go back to our quarters.[8] Thus passed my twenty-fifth birthday!!

Friday, December 26—This morning there was regimental inspection. Rifles and equipment had to be polished and clean! This was a harsh demand after we had made such an exhausting march and, what's more, in mostly wet weather. We had been on fatigue

8. He is being sarcastic.

duty the whole day yesterday, and today we are required to have clean and polished equipment, without being given any longer time than from breakfast until ten o'clock this morning! Before long we marched up and survived the inspection without much criticism, since the officers likely understood that they could not expect much fancy work under these circumstances. Major [Lieutenant Colonel] Baumer inspected us personally.[9] In the afternoon we had several hours of company drill; in the evening, as usual, was dress parade.

The weather is mild and nicer than we from the North are used to seeing at this time of year. But the roads are bottomless in the vicinity of this camp; the countless wagons, the artillery, and the cavalry make the roads poor beyond all comprehension. The division's train is now arriving here little by little. It consists of one hundred wagons, each pulled by six mules. The heavy wagons sink down to the axles, and the poor mules are horribly mistreated.

Saturday, December 27—Today I was assigned to escort a forage train. We went with about thirty wagons and an escort of eighty men across the river on a pontoon bridge thrown across by the pioneers and then went in a southwestern direction, through pine forest and over steep hills. We passed several farms with enough corn and forage, but we went onward until we reached an entirely deserted area, where there were neither farms nor forage. Finally we had to turn around and go back the same way and then load up where we first had driven past.

Just as the train turned around, several riders showed up on a hill to our left. Apparently guerrillas, since heavy smoke rising in the same direction made one suspect a camp of the enemy. The riders soon disappeared from view, and we arrived back across the

9. William Baumer, a native of Munster in Prussia, came to the United States in 1851 and lived in Dubuque, Iowa, and St. Joseph, Missouri, before coming to Omaha in 1861. He helped raise Company B, the "German" company of the First Nebraska, and became its captain. He was promoted the regiment's lieutenant colonel on October 4, 1862. Dudley, *Roster of Nebraska Volunteers,* 4–5. For a biographical sketch of Baumer, see his obituary in the *Omaha Weekly Herald,* October 27, 1869, and Watkins, *History of Nebraska,* 528.

river and into our camp without being attacked. Today, for the first time, I had loaded my musket with a good pointed ball but had to remove it since I had no opportunity to take a shot.[10]

Sunday, December 28—This morning, inspection again. Our regiment marched up in full glory, but it turned out as usual. I wrote in my diary and started a letter to Egge. I was ordered away from this to go to the river with a wagon and get two loads of gravel and spread it out in the quartermaster's tent. This pleasant Sunday afternoon fun kept me busy until almost evening; however, I had time to complete my letter. Yet at sunset we had dress parade, at which a great number of orders were read. Among other things, one of them decreed how the detachments going out for forage are to be armed and what marching order is to be observed. Also an order from General Davidson, which dictated that not less than fifty wagons with appropriate cavalry and infantry escort should go from here to Patterson, etc. Every place around us appears to be full of guerrillas, and we will have to guard our trains well.

Monday, December 29—Today I had to go across the river with an escort again. We had about thirty wagons; sixty men marched at the head of the train; the same number formed the rear guard. I was in this one. In addition, eighty men were distributed among the wagons. Today we went downstream and then followed the course of a brook, which emptied into [the river]. Of course, we had to cross it frequently.

After we had gone some three miles, we came to the place where the skirmish had been yesterday. It was a large farm; the train had been in the cornfield and was being loaded by the men. There had been forty men from the Twenty-fourth Missouri Regiment with these wagons as escort. All were taken captive, except the ones who had been badly wounded and left behind. Our ambulances and doctors met us, transporting these poor, shot-up cripples to the camp. The rebels had been four to five hundred

10. He means a conical bullet, generally called a "minié ball," used in rifle-muskets.

men strong, and all well mounted; a number of dead horses were still lying around, and many bloody spots revealed where men had been killed.[11]

In the quite sizable farmhouse the body of a secesh was still lying. He was the son of the owner of this farm. Since July he has been in the Southern army, contrary to the will of his father. Yesterday he had led the rebel band to this place but did not get to the house of his parents alive. Tragic but true, a picture of the misery that prevails in this part of Missouri. The old man was arrested and taken with us to camp to investigate whether, perhaps, he had acted in collaboration with his son and betrayed our men. Yet, here, he is generally believed to be a Union man.

We had taken preventive measures well today to fend off any possible attack. A chain of flankers was drawn about the entire place. The escort stood under arms, while the corn pickers carried their rifles slung over their shoulders, but nothing showed up. Oats and hay were also taken. At sundown we arrived back at camp, quite exhausted. A mile from camp we passed a sawmill, driven by water. It was in good order and had already been activated by our men. The owner had abandoned everything, and of his possessions only the sawmill remained intact; the house and stable had been burned down.

Tuesday, December 30—At six thirty this morning, I had to report for the relief of the advance guard with rations for twenty-four hours in the haversack. A strong chain of outposts was set up on this side of the river. About 150 men strong, we marched to a point on the road to Centerville, where the pickets and reserves were stationed. Thirty men remained behind there, while the rest relieved the outposts to our right and left.

I remained behind with the reserves, and after darkness had fallen advanced forward about half a mile along the road with two

11. Thomas E. Keen, also of Company H, mentioned this skirmish in a January 7, 1863, letter to his parents: "Since we have been here one of our forage trains was attacked by the guerrillas. They captured 7 wagons and 34 men, they wounded 5 of our men and we killed two and wounded 6 of them. There was about 500 of them. They got off with their booty." Potter, "I Thought It My Duty," 148.

other posts. It was a very cold night, and since we were not allowed to have a fire, we had to endure considerable cold. And even after we had been relieved, we still could not sleep lying there on the hard, cold ground. With only one woolen blanket over us it was not possible for me to get any sleep, as tired as I was. Yet the night passed, and at daybreak we returned to our reserves.

Wednesday, December 31—Our relief came around eight o'clock, and toward eleven o'clock we were at camp again. We had to report immediately, since our regiment was to be mustered for pay. After an inspection the colonel read all the names on the muster roll, and the respective company commanders had to report on those who were absent. After all this was over we had our noon meal. In the afternoon I had to gather rations, wrote in my diary and to Hedde. But I didn't get very far, the bugle sounded once again to report, this time for dress parade, which was held late this evening. At midnight the brigade band played to celebrate the New Year, 1863.

Thursday, January 1 [1863]—The New Year dawned for me in the tent; it was really cold again this morning, but I had slept nice and warm in my bed. At eight o'clock this morning the signal to strike the tents suddenly sounded, and soon everything was loaded on the wagons. We had to wait quite a while since the other regiments had to cross the river ahead of us. Our turn to cross finally came, and we set up camp on the hill behind Van Buren. Our position here controls the river; a battery that came up behind us rakes the bridge, as it fires away overhead.[12]

This afternoon, after we had just settled down a little, I was ordered to a detachment for fatigue duty. We were to build a cattle yard in Van Buren and to get some fifty head of slaughter animals from the other side and drive them into the newly built yard. General Davidson also moved his headquarters here today. A train of seventy-five wagons came from Patterson under heavy escort. As

12. He must mean that the artillery was firing some practice rounds, for there was no report of any engagement with the enemy. He reports artillery practice again on January 3.

far as I, a common soldier, can ascertain, we now have one brigade of this division on each side of the Current River. Furthermore, there is quite a bit of cavalry along the road between here and Patterson for the protection of the telegraph line.[13]

Friday, January 2—It rained almost constantly last night and this morning. I had to take up camp guard. This is pretty good duty, since, when not at the post, a good tent with a stove protects us against the weather. There is a lot of activity around here: troops come and go; loaded wagon trains arrive and empty ones depart to get more supplies. Everything must be obtained from Pilot Knob or Patterson. It really is not an easy job when supplies of all kinds must brought in from so far away over bad roads, even when only four to five thousand men have to be provided for.[14] The duty is quite a strain now, since so much manpower is needed to do the necessary and often also the unnecessary work.

Saturday, January 3—Relieved from guard duty this morning, I had some time to clean my rifle, and I wrote to Martin. In the afternoon we had to clean out bushes and trees around our camp. This work is producing many an acre of cleared land in Missouri, since we must move our camp so often and must do the same work over and over again. In the evening it began to rain severely and kept it up almost the whole night. This day our artillery had shooting practice, as it fired round shot and also shells.

Sunday, January 4—This morning the weather is clear and nice. It was never cold during the wet weather. This morning, company inspection. Shortly afterward I was ordered to report at the adjutant's office with an axe; from there I was taken with an entire detachment of axe men to our headquarters. Here we joined a detachment of the Twenty-fourth Missouri Regiment and reported

13. For tables of organization of the Army of Southeastern Missouri, see *OR*, ser. 1, vol. 22, part 1, p. 890, and ser. 1, vol. 22, part 2, p. 90.

14. The Army of Southeastern Missouri totaled approximately eighty-six hundred officers and men present for duty as of January 31, 1863. *OR*, ser. 1, vol. 22, part 2, p. 90.

to the division headquarters, where we were instructed to cut down the timber on our front to maintain a free range for our artillery. The dense forest soon fell crashing under the axe blows of one hundred men, and by noon a sizable gap had been made.

I then returned to camp and had my noon meal. I wrote in my diary, as well as to Hedde. While writing, I was ordered to be ready for guard duty in the afternoon at three o'clock. At the appropriate time we reported to division headquarters. From there, the various details were sent off to the places to be guarded. At sunset we came to the place assigned to us. We were ten men under the command of a sergeant and several corporals. We had to guard the office and the supplies of the quartermaster of the brigade. At about eight o'clock I, together with two others and a corporal, was ordered to cross the river, where we were to guard a train that had just arrived. It was loaded with supplies for the quartermaster. Lying around a new, good fire, we had quite a good night.

Monday, January 5—At daybreak we crossed the river with the wagons, and since there was nothing more for us to do, we returned to our tents. In the afternoon, however, we had to report for duty in order to be relieved by the newly reporting guard. At about four o'clock the relief came, and we were dismissed.

This afternoon I had the chance to see quite a few superior officers who were members of the court-martial that was in session in the same building. They were General Benton, Colonel Boyd, and the majors of Indiana regiments Eight and Eighteen.[15] The night was cold and stormy, and I almost froze in the tent; it also rained somewhat.

Tuesday, January 6—Clear and cold. I did not have duty today; wrote in my diary and washed some of my clothing.

15. William Plummer Benton commanded the First Division, Army of Southeastern Missouri, from October 1862 to March 1863. Sifakis, *Who Was Who in the Union*, 30. Sempronius H. Boyd was colonel of the Twenty-fourth Missouri Volunteer Infantry, commanding the Second Division, Army of Southeastern Missouri. *OR*, ser. 1, vol. 22, part 1, p. 890. The majors were likely Thomas J. Brady (Eighth Indiana) and John C. Jones (Eighteenth Indiana). *Report of the Adjutant General*, 48, 158.

Wednesday, January 7—This morning I had to take off with a foraging train. We had to take rations with us for twenty-four hours. We went back the same way we had come from Patterson. After we had gone about seven miles and had just found several wagon loads, an order reached us to return to camp immediately.

At sunset we were in Van Buren again. I found the tents of the camp taken down, except one for each company. The order had gone out to be ready to march the next morning at eight o'clock and to leave all tents behind, except one for each company. Each man was to take along two days' rations in his haversack, and rations for eight days would follow on the wagons, and only one wagon is permitted for every two companies. I slept in our tent tonight.

Thursday, January 8—Reveille woke us early indeed. Soon we heard that the order to march had been recalled; however, we were to line up at nine o'clock for a review. Since we did not know whether we had to march immediately after the review, the knapsacks were packed with great care. We marched about half a mile, where there was a sizable clearing that had been partly planted with corn. There we not only had to pass in review but also had to endure a full scale field maneuver in which the entire brigade participated, including the artillery. We maneuvered in columns, and our regiment finished the matter, in that it had to proceed in an extended line and go through all the skirmisher exercises. At twelve thirty we returned to camp, naturally very tired since we had been packed so heavily.

Countless were the curses that rained down on the head of General Davidson, who, with his staff, looked on smugly as we, heavily loaded, charged with the sweat running down our faces. In the evening we had dress parade at which the order was read to march the next morning at eight o'clock. No one knows where to.

Friday, January 9—In compliance with the order read yesterday evening, we marched this morning. A lot of property was thrown away or burned beforehand, since no one wanted to load himself down too much. The one wagon for two companies could not hold any of our things. I had to leave a nice, large, new U.S. blanket behind. My knapsack could hold only one light woolen blanket, one pair of underpants, a few pair of stockings, one woolen shirt, a pair of shoes, one towel, some writing paper, and handkerchiefs. Furthermore, I had to take along my overcoat. The knapsack seemed light, but toward noon it became quite heavy, since the other equipment of a soldier is of considerable weight.

We went over the pontoon bridge and followed an eastward course. The Twenty-third Iowa Regiment marched ahead, then came ten cannons—eight six-pounders and two twenty-four-pounders—then us, and finally the Twenty-fourth Missouri Regiment. The bad roads slowed us down greatly, since the artillery cut in very much, and often they had to double the teams.

At four o'clock in the afternoon we made camp, after we had gone about thirteen miles. We slept tonight camped around countless fires. In the beautiful moonlight this seemed truly romantic. The green pine needles make a nice mattress; therefore, it is usually the first business on each campground to fell trees and to pick off the needles for bedding. One blanket kept me just barely warm; however, for several hours following this strenuous march, I had a really healthy sleep.

Saturday, January 10—At three thirty we had to line up for roll call. The breakfast was very meager; many had nothing at all left of their rations. I barely could still my hunger. I had just a tin cup of tea, but the outlook for the rest of the day was very depressing. The large majority of us would have nothing for dinner, and, especially if we march farther on, our wagons with the supplies will certainly not reach us, since yesterday they had gone less than half the distance that we had covered. However, other orders seemed to have come during the night. At five o'clock in the morning we lined up and turned our faces toward the west, marching back the same way we had come yesterday. Five cannons were ahead today, then we came, and the rest of the cannons and regiments. Halfway, we overtook our wagons that likewise were going toward the river.

At eleven thirty we once more crossed the Current River and passed by our old campground, going about two miles farther upstream, where we set up our camp on a steep hill, very tired and hungry indeed!! After we had stacked our muskets and stretched out to rest, we had to line up again and change our position. We had to repeat the same maneuver three times. Why, God only knows. Of course, the tired men were very angry to be fooled like that.

What this retreat signifies, no one knows, at least in our group. Some say the rebels are threatening Springfield, and they had cut off the supplies of the army under General Blunt in Arkansas, so we would have to march to Springfield. Then, again, it is said our troops have suffered a defeat at Vicksburg and we would need to march to Rolla, in order to go via the Pacific Railroad to St. Louis and farther down the Mississippi to strengthen the troops there. It is possible that both rumors are wrong.[16] After several hours our wagons arrived here too, and with them, food. Coffee was soon made, bacon fried, and a splendid supper brought the day to a close.

The march today was very strenuous, not even two-thirds of the men were in ranks as we finally stacked our rifles. It was all I could take. Lieutenant Colonel Baumer himself was, as it appeared, very bitter to have to march around like this, and I heard him say he wished the boys had their four months' back pay and then [they] would break up this whole farce. Indeed, hungry and discontented men are much inclined to mutiny!!! As we lined up this morning in order to march, many gave vent to their anger by whistling, curses, and shouts such as "breakfast," "rations," and "transportation," namely, for our knapsacks. It was still completely dark, and the individual shouters could not easily be discovered. Colonel Livingston, very angry, rode to the front and gave sort of a speech, which ended about in this way: "You will catch hell if you

16. On December 7, 1862, Brig. Gen. James G. Blunt's Union forces defeated Confederates under Maj. Gen. Thomas C. Hindman at the Battle of Prairie Grove in northwest Arkansas. The battle secured northwest Arkansas and southwest Missouri for the Union. Shea, "1862," 51–58; Faust, *Encyclopedia of the Civil War*, 599. Also in the fall and early winter of 1862, Maj. Gen. Ulysses S. Grant began his first campaign against Vicksburg. On December 11 and 20, Confederate cavalry raided Grant's supply lines and depots, thus bringing an end to his first attempt on Vicksburg. Faust, *Encyclopedia of the Civil War*, 781. The probable cause of the movement, however, was a December 1862 and January 1863 raid aimed at Springfield, Missouri, by Confederate general John S. Marmaduke. See *OR*, ser. 1, vol. 22, part 1, pp. 194–98.

don't follow my advice," followed by general laughter.[17] Then we marched. This night, as the previous night, we slept around a fire, but I still had a good, sound sleep.

Sunday, January 11—At six o'clock reveille woke us. To celebrate the day, company inspection; after that the campground had to be cleared and cleaned up, since our tents were to be delivered to us. A little before noon they arrived, and soon the ten rows, each comprising a company, were standing in the official order. I wrote to Egge and in my diary, since I had free time the whole day, although rather large detachments were assigned for foraging and guard duty. It was a very warm day.

Monday, January 12—Again very nice, warm weather. At eight thirty we had to fall in for battalion drill. We marched down from our mountain to a clearing, where we joined the Twenty-fourth Missouri Regiment and had to drill until twelve thirty. Hungry and tired, we were then released to our quarters. Nonetheless, even before I had finished my noon meal, I had to report for fatigue duty—this time to repair roads between here and the river. The pioneers and detachments from the combined regiments camped here were busy improving all the bad spots in the low-lying bottom. General Davidson came toward evening, personally inspecting the work. He made the comment that we had to make the road so durable that a train of three to four hundred wagons could pass over it. When I came back to camp there was dress parade, but I did not attend, since I had just come from duty.

Tuesday, January 13—Due to orders read yesterday, we had bayonet drill right after breakfast. That lasted one hour. After that, com-

17. Col. Robert R. Livingston of Plattsmouth commanded the regiment at this time, as well as the Second Brigade, Second Division, Army of Southeastern Missouri. *OR*, ser., vol. 22, part 1, p. 890. He was a native of Canada, trained as a medical doctor, who came to Nebraska Territory in 1859. In 1861 he enlisted the men of Company A, First Nebraska, and was appointed their captain. He rose to the rank of brevet brigadier general by war's end. He returned to his medical practice at Plattsmouth and served two years as surveyor general of Iowa and Nebraska before his death in 1888. Sheldon, *Nebraska*, 2:144–45.

Col. Robert R. Livingston. RG3323:1-1, Nebraska State Historical Society, Lincoln. Digitally enhanced and restored.

pany drill from nine to eleven o'clock. At about twelve o'clock it began to rain, so the battalion exercise was cancelled. In the evening orders came to march off the next morning. At ten o'clock in the evening we drew rations for three days. It rained steadily all night.

Wednesday, January 14—At four o'clock the drums woke us up, even though it was raining dreadfully. Around eight o'clock in the morning the wet tents were finally loaded, three for each company and one officer's tent. We marched in a southwesterly direction; the roads were bottomless. Mud ran in and out of my shoes. The whole division was moving; the artillery up ahead of us went through up to the axles and caused considerable delay. After we had made about eight miles, we lined up to camp.

We had barely stopped when advance guards were posted, and I was chosen for this duty. We were to advance on the road leading to the southwest. I remained behind with the reserve outpost. We finally had a good fire going, after we had changed our location several times. The thirty of us had only three posts to guard, so there was only one hour of standing guard for each man. The rain let up, and it became colder. I had to guard my post from nine until ten o'clock. There were two of us on the road, and we had orders not to let anyone pass who did not have the password. Cavalry and officers moved in and out. We had fun to order them down from their horses in the deep mud to come over to us and give the password.

After I was relieved, it soon began to snow. I tried to sleep a little, wrapped in a blanket, but it was just too cold. The snow fell steadily, and when morning finally came, several inches of snow were lying on the ground, and still more continued to come down.

Thursday, January 15—At daybreak I went into camp with several comrades to get food. Since our wagons had not yet arrived yesterday when we were sent to this outpost, we had not taken along any rations. But we found out that even now our wagons had not yet arrived. Our company, like several others, sat around the fire in deep snow, without tents and food, and longingly awaited the teams. These had been prevented from coming by the bottomless roads. So we had to return to our post empty-handed.

I now decided to do something to secure a breakfast, even if it were only meat. Taking my rifle I went out to shoot down some stray pig. A tent mate was with me, an Irishman, a jolly eccentric who, when he is in the mood, gets our whole tent laughing. He is remarkably witty and has seen a lot, since he was a soldier all over the world and has served many masters. The snow was still falling, and it was not easy to stir up a young pig. I scared up a rabbit, which sat down just a few steps away from me. I shot, but my ball went several inches over Lampe's head. Since these rifles are regulated only for greater distances, they shoot very high.[18] I loaded again and let my comrade shoot, but he also missed, although he is a good shot. Some time ago he had shot two geese with one shot of his musket at eighty paces—one through the head, the other through the neck.

Just as I was shoving a third ball into the barrel, since the rabbit had not moved, a three-man patrol came and arrested us, since we had shot inside the guard area, which is strictly forbidden. However, this is usually not taken so seriously. The comrades who are on guard duty often look the other way, if at all possible, and pretend not to notice. Shots fell all around just as we were arrested. The patrol that took us captive was made up of men from the Twenty-fourth Missouri Regiment, who paid no attention to comradeship. They took us along to their outpost. There the sergeant in charge sent us under guard to our fire, where a lieutenant from our regiment had the command. He, however, let the matter rest, and before long the relief came and we marched back into camp. The tents had now arrived, and soon we had coffee, fried bacon, and crackers. Only toward evening did it stop snowing, and it turned bitter cold.

Here a page of my original diary has been lost; however, I find the next fragment from

18. According to Edith Robbins, Lampe is the name of the rabbit in a popular German fable. Civil War rifle-muskets were designed for accurate shooting at a much longer range than "a few steps," so it is no surprise he overshot the target. It is doubtful, however, that he or many other new recruits in the First Nebraska had ever fired their weapons. In an earlier entry Scherneckau mentioned having loaded his musket for the first time. Civil War soldiers were seldom provided with marksmanship training.

[Monday] January 19—I was again on advance guard duty; the weather cold! Wrapped in a woolen blanket, despite the cold I still had several hours of sleep after being relieved from my post. This outpost was assembled of details from the Twenty-fourth Missouri, the Twenty-third Iowa, and our men. I had a delightful debate with a staunch, stupid puritan about religious matters, especially with regard to the war. The guard line here is quite strong, and no less than six hundred men were on the outpost. At ten o'clock in the morning we were relieved. I slept nearly all the rest of the day.

[Tuesday] January 20 and [Wednesday] January 21—Had no duty, cloudy weather, not much to eat. Today we received flour, and bread baking began on a massive scale. Our mess built an oven in the following manner: a flour barrel, placed on its side, was covered all around with prepared clay. Likewise the part now forming the bottom was coated with clay. Next a fire was ignited in the barrel and the wood burned away. This caused the clay to harden from the heat and to change into a compact mass in the shape of the barrel inside, remaining as an oven. The bread baked this way turned out quite well. Sad that such scanty rations are given to us!—about two-thirds of the amount that we are entitled to.

[Thursday] January 22—This morning I was sent out with a train for foraging. We were some sixty men with twenty-five wagons, and an equally strong train soon followed us, but they took a somewhat different route. I saw only a few houses. We loaded the wagons in the cornfield, as we picked corn with the husks and threw it into the wagons. We placed some straw on top and turned back toward the camp. The soil here is quite stony, and the corn, therefore, was very mediocre—small, poorly filled-out ears. About two o'clock I was back and had peace for the rest of the day.

[Friday] January 23—This morning at nine o'clock the first brigade with all the cavalry left its camp next to ours; I cannot say where to. We had brigade drill in a nearby field. General Davidson was present in an ambulance. After the meal I had to go on advance guard duty. Lieutenant Colonel Baumer was officer of the day and

posted the guards on the line, which was now pulled back considerably, since the camp had become so much smaller.

Toward evening intense rifle fire, numerous volleys and single shots, disturbed us a great deal, and it seemed that our advance guard was being attacked on the other side of the camp. Since no alarm was sounded, we calmed down and discovered that the men released from picket were firing off their rifles at the same time as the men of the escort from the returning foraging train. Before entering the camp they fired their rifles in order to clean them for the inspection the next morning. Usually we have to pull our loads, since shooting is not allowed in camp and also is not permitted near the advance posts.[19] The night was dark but not very warm. It passed quickly, since everyone had to be on his post for only two hours and could rest by the fire for six hours.

[Sunday] January 25—At two o'clock this afternoon we were relieved by the new advance guard detail. Around noon it began to rain and lasted through the day. I was resting in the tent the remainder of the day. We did not have roll call this evening, since it was raining so hard.

Monday, January 26—It rained hard all night and still does now. Wrote in my diary and to Egge and Martin. At noon I was ordered to picket duty again. However, I was sent back without doing duty, since the officer of the guard had enough men. It was still raining steadily, and I was not exactly angry to be able to return to the tent.

Tuesday, January 27—During the night it stopped raining and a very sharp frost arrived. This morning marching orders came for us. We were supposed to be ready to march the next day at daybreak. At noon I was ordered to division guard. Prisoners and quartermaster supplies were to be guarded. Forty captured guerrillas, most likely residents of this area, were housed in a building, and our assignment was to guard them there. I had to stand guard

19. Because the troops were armed with muzzle-loading arms, the load would have to be extracted manually if the gun had not been fired.

for four hours during the night; it was very cold and at the same time, a sharp wind.

Wednesday, January 28—At daybreak our regiment, as well as the Twenty-fourth Missouri Infantry and the artillery, was marching. This was the entire rest of our division, which had remained in camp here. I was not yet relieved when the troops started to march, and I had to catch up to my regiment. It was in the advance guard position and appeared to march extremely fast. We crossed a rather large brook, Warm Creek, and proceeded mostly in a southwest direction, through hilly, very rocky parts, in the average on a very good road.

The area was not densely settled; the few residents are all taken along as prisoners. "I am a good Union man," I heard a farmer say this morning, as the officer of the guard commanded him to join us. "I will make a better one of you," was the lieutenant's answer. Funny scenes often take place when we must deal with these butternuts.[20] Around four o'clock, very tired, we came to our campground. Our wagons soon reached us as well. We had passed the other brigade of our division in their camp about two miles before. It was a very cold, yet bright day; we had made fifteen miles.

Thursday, January 29—At five o'clock in the morning we had reveille. Yet we did not march before ten o'clock, since the other brigade had to pass by first, also the artillery, and we were forming the rear. But then we went rapidly ahead. Like yesterday the area was barely populated and had only a few trees but often small stretches of prairie. Yet the ground was very stony, and the already worn out soles of our footwear were finished off here. Since our train had not come to Alton, we could not get shoes. Many boys walked in their stockings directly on the ground. My shoes, received at the Current River, were almost worn out at the soles.[21] The road was quite good, and the artillery did not delay us often.

20. A reference to the homespun cloth worn by many Southerners, colored with dyes made from walnut shells.

21. The quality of the footwear was so poor that even General Davidson took notice. On January 31, 1863, he wrote, "I have sent up for shoes. The paper soles

Toward evening we passed the first brigade and went into camp about three miles farther near a large farm. For the last miles the area was more developed; large farms with very respectable houses cover the area. Firewood was here for once, but only meager, crippled oak provided us with minimal burning material. At sunset the wagons reached us, and soon the tents were set up. Three pigs, which we had killed along the way, produced a good evening meal for us, even though the salt was missing and the crackers were in short supply. An icy, cold wind blew through this open area. Today I was a camp guard, and I had to be on post for two hours in the guard tent. The rest of the night I slept in my own quarters. We had made at least sixteen miles today; therefore, I was very tired when it was finally my turn to sleep.

Friday, January 30—At eight o'clock this morning we again assembled in rank and file and started out at the head of the brigade. Before we marched off, Colonel Baumer told us that we had to march only about six to seven miles and therefore he wanted us to hold out. In response to this announcement the men cheered him on. How different this is from our Colonel Livingston, who with his orders does not accomplish anything, while today scarcely a man remained behind!

The area was well settled, and we saw the best farms we had yet encountered in this part of Missouri. Just before the town of West Plains we met part of the Third Iowa Cavalry Regiment. The rest of them were standing in ranks in the town itself and we marched past them with sounding music and waving flags, moving to camp on the south side of town. Soon afterward, the Twenty-first and Twenty-second Iowa regiments arrived here as well. They belong to Gen. Fitz-Henry Warren's brigade.[22] In the afternoon the first wagons of the large train from Pilot Knob also reached us here.

---

the contractors now furnish render their frequent renewal a matter of vexation." Davidson to Maj. H. Z. Curtis, assistant adjutant general, *OR*, ser. 1, vol. 22, part 2, p. 87. Shannon, *Organization and Administration*, 1:94–98, discusses the poor quality of army clothing and footwear, including the notorious material known as "shoddy."

22. Fitz-Henry Warren, colonel of the First Iowa Infantry, had been promoted brigadier general of volunteers on July 16, 1862. Heitman, *Historical Register*,

The town consists of thirty to forty very prettily painted frame buildings; however, only a few are occupied at the moment. In some of them we had to guard a number of war prisoners, perhaps over one hundred men in all. They were mostly inhabitants of the area. Besides the above-mentioned troops, cavalry regiments from various states are also camped in a semicircle around the town. There are now quite possibly not less than eight to ten thousand men [camped here]. Four to five hundred wagons jam the town; there is a lot of activity. Because the town lies on top of a hill, the white covers of the wagons can be seen from far away.

Saturday, January 31—We are still camped here. Food is in short supply—plenty of meat, but no salt. This morning I had no more crackers, and no more are to be issued until tomorrow! It rained some last night.

Sunday, February 1—At seven thirty this morning I had to go out with a train for foraging. From the Twenty-fifth Missouri Regiment and from ours, together we had close to fifty men with twelve wagons. We went about nine miles in a northwesterly direction from the town, and by sunset we were in camp again with our load.

Monday, February 2—It froze hard last night. At eight thirty we were standing in ranks, our tents loaded, and then we marched off in a southerly direction. The road was good, although stony, destroying our shoes. Only our brigade, the Twenty-fourth and Twenty-fifth Missouri and our regiment, as well as the artillery attached to us, marched. Even swampy, low spots were quite easy to cross today due to the hard frost. The area was similar to the one we passed yesterday, only the woods were somewhat denser and the trees larger. Today we were in the rear guard, yet since the roads were good, we moved ahead quickly.

The Third Iowa and Fourth Missouri cavalry regiments overtook us in the afternoon and went all the way to Salem [Arkansas]

1:1003. In the winter of 1862–63, he commanded troops in the District of Rolla. *OR*, ser. 1, vol. 22, part 1, p. 895.

that same evening. At four o'clock we set up camp, the wagons arrived at the same time. A fence, which, of course, disappeared in a minute, provided us with firewood, and, very tired, I soon fell asleep. Several sheaves of wheat, which I had dragged here myself from about three miles away, served as an exceptionally soft mattress. Once again it was a very cold night. We had made eighteen miles today.

Tuesday, February 3—At four thirty, reveille woke us up. At sunrise everything was packed, and we marched on. Today in the lead, we marched ahead quickly in the sharp winter air over solidly frozen roads. At eight o'clock we crossed the border and marched into Arkansas. At first a stream delayed us in our march, and we would have to cross it five times before we reached Salem, our next destination. We were led around great detours, where we saw neither people nor houses, so that our route became twice as long. We made at least twenty miles by the time we finally reached the little town and camped in a field close by, an old campground.

I immediately had to go on picket duty and was stationed with twenty more men on the road leading to Batesville. It was an extremely cold night, bright moonlight, and windy. Like most of the others I could not sleep and was sincerely happy when daylight finally came.

Wednesday, February 4—Several inches of snow fell, and it began to snow seriously when we were finally relieved at two o'clock in the afternoon. Tired as I was, I slept quite warm in our tent. It snowed the whole night.

Thursday, February 5—Ten inches of snow. I was ordered to go out with a detachment to cut down the timber in front of our position. A pleasant assignment in deep snow and in shoes such as I, and most others, had. By noon our work was done, since our detachment contained about thirty men. We returned to our quarters, where I wrote in my diary and to Hedde.

Friday, February 6—I was instructed to be ready to go out with an expedition for foraging when the signal to strike the tents suddenly sounded. No one knew where [we were going] to march, but it soon became apparent that we had to go back. The air was very sharp and [conditions were] bad for marching, even though a regiment and the artillery preceding us made something of a path for us. It was about nine o'clock when we left our camp.

The sun had already set when, after marching about eighteen miles, we finally formed the line for a camp. It was completely dark when we had set up our tents, and after a meager supper, we prepared our places to sleep in the deep snow as well as we could. However, the night was not quite as cold as the previous one.

Saturday, February 7—Early this morning we were moving on after a really cold night spent on the snow. We had to march, but where to was a mystery again. Most of us believed we were going back across the border into Missouri. The cavalry is now in the rear, since it had preceded us on the march toward Batesville. It is said they had a skirmish with the enemy there.[23] Yet we went farther north toward West Plains, back over the same road over which we had come, but today as rear guard of the column.

Around three o'clock we once more marched into town, through it, and set up our tents again near our old campground. The troops that we had left behind here were still camped about the town. It is said that they are partly paid off, and we too are supposed to receive our pay. The troops camped here, as we were told, received full rations, while we, marching through snow and cold, had less than half rations. Of course, our men had helped themselves wherever they could get anything edible. Houses were plundered and pigs were taken at liberty. Our company had three of the latter, so this evening we had a really good supper. Some cornmeal, cooked as mush, helped out somewhat, replacing the missing hardtack.

Another big defect is the lack of shoes. The rocky roads wear them out inconceivably fast. The soles of a new pair of these shoes

23. Davidson's cavalry, the Third Iowa and Fourth Missouri regiments, briefly drove Confederate forces out of Batesville, but the effort was only a reconnaissance, and the cavalry rejoined Davidson's column. "February 4, 1863, Skirmish at Batesville, Ark.," *OR*, ser. 1, vol. 22, part 1, p. 227.

are worn through in a few days, while the rest is, so to speak, still new. One cannot get them repaired, so they are thrown away. Such a rapid consumption of footwear had not been expected, and the result is that many are now marching in the snow in their bare feet.[24] A large amount of mail was here for us yesterday evening but no letter for me! It was considerably warmer today, and as a result the snow melted, changing the roads into a dirty mud puddle!

Sunday, February 8—The weather was warm. Today we slept until daybreak for once and got a good rest after this strenuous two-day march. At eleven o'clock the signal to strike tents sounded for us, after most of the troops had marched off earlier. We then went north on terribly poor, muddy roads, made virtually bottomless by the many wagons and the artillery. We still made eleven miles today, whereupon we made camp in an open area with few trees, just our brigade, since the other troops had taken other roads.

Monday, February 9—At daybreak we were on the march again. Around noon we again reached the pine region, and the area became more mountainous and rugged. The road itself, however, was considerably better than on the preceding days. Our food supply had been exhausted when we left West Plains. The adjutant then promised us that by this evening we would be provided with crackers as well as with shoes, which we needed so very much.

Toward evening, in the vicinity of the quite beautifully situated town of Thomasville, we overtook the other brigade consisting of the Twenty-first, Twenty-second, and Twenty-third Iowa regiments.[25] They camped in the town, which had been burned down except for a few houses. In the immediate vicinity are really nice farms, with imposing frame houses. Pine trees are everywhere. We marched four more miles until we reached a mountain ridge,

24. Fellow Company H soldier Thomas E. Keen reported that leather had been confiscated from a tannery near Salem, Arkansas, and issued to the men, who used it to repair their shoes. Potter, "I Thought It My Duty," 150.

25. The Twenty-first and Twenty-second Iowa were from Gen. Fitz-Henry Warren's command, not initially part of the Army of Southeastern Missouri. *OR*, ser. 1, vol. 22, part 1, p. 895.

Union troops foraging in Missouri. *Frank Leslie's Pictorial History of the American Civil War*, vol. 2, part 10, p. 147. Digitally enhanced.

where we set up our tents under tall pine trees. However, it was nine o'clock in the evening before our exhausted [teams?] brought them to us; we had made some twenty miles.

Coffee, mush, and fresh beef were now our only food. And, except for the meat ration, it was also so little that I could not even once adequately eat my fill. There was something available only early in the morning and then again late in the evening, since we had to march strenuously during the whole day. A pig killed now and then gave us a little variety and made the rations somewhat larger. Since the officers could not keep their word to provide the soldiers with food, nothing was said when the hungry men took whatever was edible in the houses along the road. And it did not end there; the residents were completely plundered; often their belongings, which could not be used, were destroyed by the marauders. Unfortunately, there are too many such men!

Tuesday, February 10—We left our campground at seven o'clock and marched quickly ahead, for the most part on good roads. The area was just barely settled. Many pine trees, yet also clearings, almost little prairies, could be found. On one such bird's prairie we set up our camp after an exhausting march. We had made twenty-one miles. This night I had to be on picket guard. We had a good fire going, and the night passed quickly; it rained somewhat toward daybreak. This evening we signed the muster roll.

Wednesday, February 11—At seven thirty we again formed ranks to march. Lieutenant Colonel Baumer rode to the front and cautioned the men to stay in ranks on the march today. We had only ten miles to go, and some whiskey would be distributed among us this evening after our arrival in camp. This last announcement caused general cheering. At that point we marched off, but the "ten" miles did not want to end. Good Baumer had been deceived in order to make us march farther, since many, as a result of insufficient nourishment, were too weak to march far. I, myself, felt very exhausted.

Today we came to an imposing farm, which had been totally plundered shortly before. Two shots were fired from the house on our cavalry that had gone ahead as our advance guard. After we had marched some fifteen miles we came to the Jack Fork of the Current River. We were taken across in ambulances and with our company wagons. We set up our camp on the other side in a large field. Since we camped in such a low place, we got six inches of water in our tent, for it rained hard last night.

Thursday, February 12—After a meager breakfast the wet and heavy tents and things were loaded again, and we marched on with the definite assurance that we would meet the train this evening, which had food for us. I was almost sick today, and therefore could not keep up with the regiment and stayed back with the wagon train. It was a bad road, steep hills and muddy bottomland. Several times we had to double up the teams and finally came again to the Current River, across from the town of Eminence. This is our destination for the time being.

This town, located on a hill, consists of only two houses. We had made twelve miles today. No foodstuff was here; the train is still supposed to be eight miles away. After supper I had to go as escort with several empty wagons to meet the train. We crossed the river twice, whereby two mules drowned. We then camped on the riverbank, lying around a big fire, without a single blanket, yet I slept quite well.

Friday, February 13—At daybreak, the remaining wagons were brought over as well, and we went farther on toward the train, which we met a mile from the river. Hungry as we all were without breakfast, we attacked the cracker boxes and thoroughly supplied ourselves and our pockets. These last eight days we had experienced reminded me vividly of the first Nebraska winter.[26] How often had I envied a luckier or more frugal comrade for his bite of cornbread or cracker! To suffer hunger and still have to march with a pack is truly no fun!

As soon as we loaded our teams, we drove back again, always eating. We reached camp around ten o'clock in the morning, where I made my tent mates happy with crackers I had brought along. Soon rations were provided for the companies, and a generous noon meal was prepared. All troops had crossed over the river in the meantime and camped near the so-called town. I wrote in my diary and to Egge.

Saturday, February 14—We had some rain last night. Today I rested. The regiment was paid off, our company immediately after noon. I received about thirty-one dollars—from October 18 to December 31 of last year.[27] I then bought some things from our sutler that I needed.[28] I wrote to Court and Martin.

26. Scherneckau arrived at the Grand Island settlement in July 1858. The first two winters were very hard for the settlers, in part due to the 1857 financial panic. The Bank of Davenport, Iowa, which had promised to supply the colony, went broke, and the supplies could not be shipped. Stolley, "History of the First Settlement," chapters 3 and 4.

27. Privates were paid thirteen dollars per month, plus Scherneckau likely received about five dollars additional pay for his partial month's service in October 1862. Shannon, *Organization and Administration*, 1:72.

28. There is a token marked "P. Hoddy, sutler, First Nebraska," in the Nebraska State Historical Society collections, though it is unknown when he served as the regimental sutler.

There is a lot of activity in camp today; money deals of all kinds are being made. The chaplain of the regiment is going to Nebraska and is taking with him all the money for safekeeping. He enjoys everyone's trust.[29]

Prisoners from the Southern army are now being brought in from time to time. The Third Iowa and the Fourth Missouri cavalry regiments, which had been as far as Batesville in Arkansas, came back here today bringing in fifty prisoners. Like us, these riders had to manage without food. Food is already beginning to be in short supply again. Furthermore, forage for our teams is not to be had.

Sunday, February 15—I had camp guard duty today. Company inspection. For wintertime the weather is quite mild. I visited the various sutler stores; all make profitable deals. The greenbacks are really easy money for them. In the afternoon I went up to the town, which is the county seat of this county. It [the county] holds the name Shannon.[30] The town consists of only two log houses opposite each other. One is the jail, and the other, also two stories, is the courthouse, now a hospital. I turned over fifteen dollars to Chaplain Tipton in care of Court in Omaha, and wrote to Hedde, as well as in my diary.

After roll call at retreat, an order from Colonel Livingston was read, which contained many strange things. He spoke disapprovingly about the behavior of the men on the last march. Driven by bitter hunger, they only tried to grab provisions necessary to sup-

29. Thomas W. Tipton of Brownville, Nebraska Territory, a lawyer and Congregational minister, was chaplain of the First Nebraska from 1861 until July 1865. After the war, Tipton was elected one of Nebraska's first two U.S. senators. Thomas E. Keen described Tipton as "one of the best army chaplains I have ever seen. He is a kind, good man and a perfect gentleman." Potter, "I Thought It My Duty," 159. On February 16, 1863, Tipton applied for a twenty-day leave to carry back to Nebraska about ten thousand dollars that the men of the regiment had entrusted to him. Compiled Service Records, roll 23.

30. The county was named for Pvt. George Shannon, a member of Lewis and Clark's Corps of Discovery, according to a Missouri historical marker at the courthouse in Eminence. Shannon had been appointed U.S. district attorney for Missouri in 1829. Morris, *Fate of the Corps*, 164–67.

port their lives. Without a doubt some men went too far, for they stole and destroyed things that were of no value to them. But instead of preventing this and punishing the individual evildoers, the order says, furthermore, that the extra guard duty that was imposed upon us a few days ago would be ordered anew for this reason and would continue until the troops returned to good discipline and demonstrated better behavior.[31]

Of course, this order is condemned by one and all in the entire regiment, just like a similar order at the time in Van Buren. There it was said that the commander noticed with regret that the officers under his command were placing themselves too much on the same level with the "common men." They even forgot themselves to the extent that they ate together, played cards, and drank whiskey. He ordered then that such behavior had to stop and that common soldiers and noncommissioned officers no longer associate so intimately with the commissioned officers. This order was actually read by the regimental adjutant at a public parade, in the land of freedom and equality, in the year of grace 1863!!! (Of course, I think somewhat differently about this now and would in no way maintain my point of view of that time.)

On the other hand it was much better that rations were issued. They were distributed for five days but had to last eight days, so we were told. Still only half rations! Hopefully, by the time these are used up we will be in Pilot Knob, where we are now returning. This night an extra guard was posted at the tent of our chaplain to prevent the theft of the money entrusted to him.

Monday, February 16—Was released from guard duty this morning. Our tent raised $2.50 to buy a box of crackers to make our rations last a little longer. These crackers were bought from the quartermaster in the name of a commissioned officer. It was quiet in the tent today, and I repaired my shoes for the impending march. In the afternoon it rained a little.

31. Thomas E. Keen attributes this order to General Davidson, and Keen, like Scherneckau, was outraged by it. Potter, "I Thought It My Duty," 151. For other soldiers' opinions of Davidson's leadership and the frustrating campaign, see Bradbury, "This War Is Managed," 42, 46.

Several officers, among them our captain, made a journey into the underworld, in one of the extensive caves with which these mountains are filled.[32] They found nothing unusual but signs of bears present. They returned from the underworld, dirty and tired, after they had gone at least two and a half miles below. Yesterday, I had been in one [cave] of smaller magnitude, which displayed beautiful stalactite formations. Unfortunately, I knew nothing of this [today's] expedition until it was too late. In the end I would probably not have been permitted to join them, since commissioned officers carried this out.

Tuesday, February 17—At daybreak we stood in rank and file, ready to march. The adjutant read General Order No. 4, whereby it was impressed on us not to break ranks during the march and to plunder, as happened previously, since now we would come to an area inhabited by people friendly to us. Then we marched on.

Today we were the first regiment of our brigade; the other brigade took another road. The route we followed had obviously been used only little, proceeding first over steep, rocky hills and then following the valley of a creek. Seventeen times we had to cross this rather large creek in the course of the day, and the pioneer corps had plenty to do to construct bridges for us, often very temporary ones. Very tired, we finally reached our campground near a burned-down sawmill. Our wagons arrived very late, some not at all. I was detailed for camp guard duty, which had been ordered as punishment for our brigade. I stood my four hours in front of the headquarters tents. The rest of the time I was lying at one of the many fires and got some sleep, since it was a warm night.

Today I saw a Dithmarscher, a member of the Missouri battery.[33] To speak Low German was difficult for me after I had been speaking English almost exclusively for the last three months. We had made nineteen miles today.

32. Capt. William W. Ivory enlisted from Nebraska City in 1861, and was promoted captain September 7, 1862. Dudley, *Roster of Nebraska Volunteers,* 90–91. Thomas E. Keen had little good to say of him. Potter, "I Thought It My Duty," 159.

33. According to Edith Robbins, Dithmarsch is an area in Schleswig-Holstein from which many of the early Grand Island settlers had come.

Wednesday, February 18—At daybreak we were released and had our breakfast, little bread but a lot of fresh pork; an illustration [of the futility] of the order read yesterday. Since not all the teams had arrived yet, we did not march until nine o'clock. We crossed the creek several times and then came to a better road, not criss-crossed by so many creeks. Still, the pioneers had to improve some bad spots to make it possible for the artillery to get through. We marched forward with only minor delays. A pain in my right leg, just above the foot, made it extremely difficult for me to keep up, but I made it through. After we had crossed the west fork of the Black River, only a modest stream here, we again set up our tents before darkness had fallen. Marched sixteen miles today.

Thursday, February 19—This morning, still dark; we lay quietly. A number of our wagons were sent back to lighten the wagons remaining behind in order to make it possible for them to catch up. I began a letter to Egge; however, I had to stop, since we started to march at twelve o'clock. We made our way over steep hills, while the wagons took a better road, which, nonetheless, was also longer. We were the last regiment of our brigade, and, after we had marched twelve miles, we arrived at our campground, an open cornfield, at sunset.

Our wagons reached us shortly before midnight. Most of the men had left the open field and made large fires in the sheltered ravines, around which they slept without having had much supper. I too lay down by a fire and slept a deep sleep, wrapped only in my overcoat, until the drums and pipes woke me up in the morning.

Friday, February 20—No breakfast this morning. The rations issued to us consisted only of flour, with which we could not do a thing, partly because we lacked time, and besides we did not have even a little bit of fat to be able to bake even slapjacks.[34] A cup of coffee was, therefore, all we had before we began our day's march at eight o'clock.

34. Slapjacks were made by mixing flour and water and frying the dough in grease. Shannon, *Organization and Administration*, 1:212.

Today we were the last regiment of our brigade. We crossed various creeks, as well as one of the sources of the Black River. Close to noon we left the side roads, which we had followed for so long, and reached the main road, where we met one of the other brigades of our division. We had to let them march past. They were the Thirty-third and Ninety-ninth Illinois regiments of infantry, the Eighteenth and Eighth regiments of Indiana infantry, as well as the First Battery of Indiana artillery. This brigade had always marched on our right, while to the left of us another column was moving toward Pilot Knob. We followed these troops, which had passed us, for several miles, then again shifted to a side road, where we soon set up camp. It was still early afternoon.

This evening I had to go to the advance post after I had eaten nothing all day and had marched about fourteen miles. At dusk I was released and went to a sizable farm nearby, where I was lucky enough to get five to six small biscuits and a live duck for twenty-five cents. In addition, during the day I had bought a canteen of syrup. As soon as we came to camp a decent, adequate supper was put together from these supplies. Rice and coffee were made, and plenty of biscuits were baked. During the free hours of our watch we slept quite warm at the fire.

Saturday, February 21—Only after complete daylight had arrived were our posts pulled back, and then, as we came into camp, we found everything packed and the regiment in rank and file, ready to march. We barely had time for some coffee with meat and bread, saved for us, before we had to get in line to march off.

Like yesterday we found the area today more settled, especially by larger farms and those well tended, while earlier the cleared land had been overgrown with weeds and usually the houses and fences had been neglected. We also passed a steam sawmill, however, that was not running. After we had gone six to seven miles it began to rain, which gradually turned into quite a severe snowstorm, when we finally reached Arcadia, a little town two miles from Pilot Knob. Here in an open field we stacked arms. We sought protection against the worst of the storm as well as we could beside the neighboring buildings. We could not go far, since guards, who turned everyone back, surrounded our entire camp.

Yet probably half of our men were already scattered around Ironton and Pilot Knob and, before long, totally drunk.

We arrived here at ten o'clock in the morning, and our wagons came around noon. We set up our tents during a real snowstorm. A rail fence provided firewood, along with neighboring sheds and small frame buildings. All boards and even the shingles of the roof were taken and placed on the ground in order to make it somewhat dry and tolerable for us. Today was the worst weather I had been exposed to since I became a soldier. The snowstorm stopped during the night, and a hard frost set in. We made ten miles today.

CHAPTER 3

In Camp at Pilot Knob, February 22–March 7, 1863

Sunday, February 22—This morning it was bitter cold but somewhat less muddy, since the ground is now frozen and little of the snow is left. I reported in sick today, since my right shin was swollen and hurting. Today we had many drunkards in the camp, and brandy was abundant. I wrote to Egge. In the evening we had a good whiskey punch.

Monday, February 23—The weather cleared up today; the little snow that was left melted, for the most part, and bottomless mud was the result. The doctor today reported me fit for service, although my leg is still swollen and also hurts.

At noon I was ordered to guard duty at a large hotel, located not far from our camp. We, two men and a corporal, did not have to occupy a post but were there only to protect the property in case our help was needed. A large room with sofas and rocking chairs was vacated for us, where we are sitting comfortably at the fireplace. This is the soldier's life: we have just escaped starvation during forced marches; now we find ourselves in a warm house, at a well supplied table, since the host must feed his guards.

Furthermore, we drew rations today—fresh bread, peas, bacon and ham, and so on. Again we lived in abundance without every little morsel being meagerly measured out, as has happened so often lately. In addition, clothing was issued today. I took a pair of pants, a pair of underpants, two pairs of socks, and a pair of shoes.

This is the first time that I have written at a table in a house since I joined the regiment. From my guard post I made a little trip to Ironton. Much dirt, lots of soldiers and military wagons; mainly,

Pilot Knob, Missouri. Guernsey and Alden, *Harper's Pictorial History of the Great Rebellion*, 1:171.

the drunken men made themselves noticed. I wrote in my diary. In the evening I had a pretty good meal in a private home nearby. The meals here in the hotel have stopped suddenly because food is so limited that they have trouble getting the bare necessities together for their boarders. We bought a number of apple pies, and with a good fire in the fireplace, we spent the night quite comfortably.

Tuesday, February 24—A nice day to sit comfortably by the fire. I wrote to C. Hedde and Martin. It is no wonder that the slaveholders like their black property so well. It is all too pleasant to have any and all work done and to be waited upon. There are at least twelve to fifteen blacks of both sexes in this hotel, and they do all the work. The proprietor is a colonel in our army and is absent. His wife is running the business; she has healthy lungs, and with a voice that would do honor to a drill sergeant, one hears her throughout the house giving orders to the blacks. At noon I went to eat, and then we were released, since the post was withdrawn. A splendid supper took place in our tent.

A ridiculous amount of money is now being squandered. After all the hardships that the men have experienced, they want to pamper themselves but often only ruin their stomachs with all the unhealthy sweets. And there is gambling for large amounts; fifty to one hundred dollars are won or lost in a few seconds. In the evening we had a good whiskey punch.

Wednesday, February 25—It rained and made our campground almost impassable, at least in shoes. At eight o'clock in the morning the regiment had to fall in under arms. Then strong detachments from all regiments of the brigade who, like us, were under arms, were sent against a battery camping next to us to arrest the men, since, as it was said, they had refused to obey orders. I was in the section, some eighty-men strong, leading the way. The whole brigade formed a wide semicircle and surrounded the camp of the alleged mutineers. We marched up in front of the tents of the artillery, where we found the men quietly eating their breakfast. There was no visible evidence that they would offer resistance; nevertheless, we were ordered to load. Then the officers went to the men and tried to convince them to conform. However, only about one third obeyed; the rest surrendered all their weapons, and we escorted them to the nearby fort.[1] They are mostly Frenchmen, but also quite a few Germans are among them. I could not find out what the real cause of the mutiny was. As we led them into the fort, they told us they only wanted their rights and nothing more. I believe this battery was recruited especially for the defense of St. Louis. The men did not believe they were obligated to march around so far out in the countryside as they had done. There was also the possibility that they would be required to do such duty in the future.[2] It rained almost the whole day, as well as the greatest part of the night. In the evening we had whiskey punch.

Thursday, February 26—Better weather today, and the morass around us dried up somewhat. Company drill took place in the morning, at which, however, the companies were very poorly represented. In the afternoon the entire regiment had battalion drill. In the evening there was parade as usual. On this occasion the whole regiment totaled not more than what two complete companies should be; the rest was on guard duty or scattered around, mostly drunk.[3]

Company G, mostly Irishmen, reported nineteen men absent without leave; in our company, only one, since the only man who had been regarded as a deserter had come back. The man from Company F who had been brought along by us recruits from Nebraska as a deserter was set free several days ago after a court-martial that had begun to investigate his case was interrupted as we left Van Buren. In the regiment, he is generally regarded as a deserter who only wished to have his parole. However, there are plenty of this sort. Many desertions are expected should we go to Vicksburg.

Friday, February 27—At eight o'clock this morning the bugle blew to strike tents, and everyone was happy to leave this wet and muddy

1. Fort Curtis, an earthwork located between Ironton and Arcadia.

2. This was likely Battery M, Second Missouri Light Artillery, which had participated in the expedition just ended. *OR*, ser. 1, vol. 22, part 1, p. 890.

3. In other words, only about two hundred men participated in the parade.

campground. I was ordered to strike the doctor's (first assistant surgeon's) tent and help load baggage, then go with the wagon and help set it up again; there are always three men ordered for this.[4] The whole brigade marched; our regiment was the last. The mutinous battery was filled up sufficiently with men from the Nebraska regiment that they had enough drivers to bring along the cannons and powder cars [limbers and caissons]. The march went through Ironton and Pilot Knob, along the railroad to Iron Mountain, six miles from Pilot Knob. The wagons followed on an appallingly poor road, which mostly ran parallel with the railroad.

Pilot Knob was full of soldiers, many of them drunk, even though all drinking places apparently were closed. In these times innkeepers and merchants of all kinds do a good business. Greenbacks are abundant here, and the money is of little value in the hands of most of the soldiers. After having endured so many hardships, they believe they have a right to indulge themselves. Pies, sausage, cheese, all kinds of cake, as well as candy and many other treats, are therefore bought in large amounts to compensate for the long time they had little food. I too had an upset stomach for a couple of days and did not get better until I changed back to Uncle Sam's simple but healthy food.

Most of the business houses here are owned by Germans, who chuckle and pocket the money the soldiers literally throw away. Gambling and drink, of course, generate fights as a third evil. If I am informed correctly, various murders have occurred since we have been camped here.

Early in the afternoon we arrived in Iron Mountain, a small place with a railroad depot and a smelter furnace in working order. The surrounding hills consist of almost pure iron ore. A one-time plank road, now macadamized, leads from here to St. Genevieve on the Mississippi, which we probably will use in case we receive orders to go down to the river.

After I helped set up the doctor's tent, I returned to my company. Our camp is in a thick underbrush, all young hickory and

4. Napoleon B. Larsh of Nebraska City, who enlisted October 25, 1862, and resigned November 28, 1864. Dudley, *Roster of Nebraska Volunteers*, 4–5.

oak, which we had to clean out before we could set up tents. At retreat this evening, the captain informed us that from now on, all absence from camp without permission would be severely punished; up to now allowance was made to compensate us for the hardships endured. The infamous camp guard fortunately was omitted today, since it is exactly the reason that drives the men away, to avoid doing this guard duty. It is so completely unnecessary. It rained nearly all night. I received a letter from each Egge and Martin.

Saturday, February 28—Some rain in the morning. The Twenty-fourth Missouri Regiment, belonging to our brigade for so long, left us today to go to Rolla, the terminus of the Pacific Railroad. The entire remaining army corps, as it appears, is now concentrated here, and an active military life prevails.[5] This afternoon inspection for two months wages took place, yet it went on very peacefully. I wrote to Egge and in my diary.

Sunday, March 1—Nice warm weather; wrote to Martin. Lighter guard duty now, neither pickets to set out nor camp and brigade guard. Today I was on cooks police duty, since our Negro cook, "Tom," had taken his leave and has gone to St. Louis. We now must assign three men daily to bring in water and wood, and also one man who is regularly employed as cook. Today we drew *full rations* for six days, except coffee. Also wrote to Caroline Hedde.

Monday, March 2—Good weather; we had just a short drill in the morning. In the afternoon battalion drill in a nice dry field sown with clover, right next to the railroad, a quarter mile from camp. Yesterday and also today we had to clean up and put our campground in order and thereby cleared another small farm. The young growth of hickory and oaks was so dense here that when we arrived we could hardly see one tent next to the other.

5. Scherneckau often uses the word "corps" but not always as the official military organization that, in the Union army, generally comprised three divisions. His reference here and elsewhere seems to refer to a group of soldiers having something in common, or associated under the same jurisdiction.

Since this whole warfare is a monstrous humbug and in most branches of the army officers and officials get away with what they can, the entire drill is mere pretense, to the extent that more orders and daily commands are issued than are really necessary. First, rarely are more than one-third of the men present, since there is so much opportunity to be absent. The maneuvers that are carried out seem, for the most part, to be understood neither by the subordinate officers nor by the common soldiers and, therefore, often turn out very wretchedly. When one speaks here of well-trained troops, one must not compare them to the skilled European soldiers. At least of the regiments that I have had an opportunity to see so far, one cannot speak of drilling in comparison with German soldiers. And yet our regiment is regarded as the best-drilled regiment of the army corps! In the evening it got colder and windy; at night some snow fell.

Tuesday, March 3—It is cooler today. We had battalion drill in the morning, as well as company drill in the afternoon, dress parade in the evening. The day's orders from Colonel Harding, brigade commander, were read in which he praised the troops for their good conduct during the hardships and privations of the last campaign.[6] In addition, various commendations and demotions of noncommissioned officers of our regiment were publicized.

Wednesday, March 4—Heavy frost; the sun was shining nicely, yet it was cold. Drilled in the morning and also in the afternoon; dress parade in the evening. Orders were read calling for a big review for tomorrow to be held before General Carr.[7] It was a cold night again.

6. Col. Chester Harding, Jr., of the Twenty-fifth Missouri Volunteer Infantry had commanded the First Brigade, Second Division, Army of Southeastern Missouri, and later the division. *OR*, ser. 1, vol. 22, part 1, p. 890; *OR*, ser. 1, vol. 22, part 2, p. 90.

7. Brig. Gen. Eugene A. Carr commanded the St. Louis District in the Department of the Missouri from November 13, 1862, to February 23, 1863, following the reassignment of General Davidson to field command. *OR*, ser. 1, vol. 22, part 1, p. 894. In February and March 1863 he commanded the Second Division, Army of Southeastern Missouri. Sifakis, *Who Was Who in the Union*, 67.

Thursday, March 5—Today I had camp guard duty. We had poor weather, and, as a result, the review was canceled. In the afternoon there was drill again; I was on guard over forage and our wagons. During the night it became somewhat warmer and rained severely. Drunken men filled the guard tent, since beer and whiskey are plentiful here. Sausages, cakes, and other sweets also sell like hot cakes from the sutler, since money is still abundant.

Since we have been in camp here, Lieutenant Colonel Baumer has been in command of the regiment, for Colonel Livingston has gone to St. Louis, and we can thank him [Baumer] for the light duty. The d——d Dutchman is more than ever in favor among the soldiers. Even to a German ear, his quite funny-sounding speeches in broken English always cause great amusement, but the men understand him and know he means them well.

Friday, March 6—Cloudy skies with rain. The Twenty-fifth Missouri Regiment left us today going to St. Joseph, it is said. Our regiment with the artillery is now the only one of the original brigade left here. Many rumors about our next destination are spreading through the camp. Now, it is said, instead of going downstream, we will go up the Missouri; where to is not yet decided—perhaps to Nebraska in order to recruit! Toward evening it began to rain hard and continued so during the night.

Today, I saw in the *Missouri Democrat*—we receive the St. Louis papers here on the same day that they come out—that the infamous "Dr. Henry" from Nebraska has been confirmed as the quartermaster of the army.[8] Of course, many in the regiment here know him, yet the men's opinions in general are not very much in his favor. The least that is said about him is, he is too d——d smart, while others openly call him a scoundrel.

Here in the army the *Democrat* is now almost exclusively purchased. Nevertheless, even ever so conservative men among the soldiers condemn the tendency of these halfway secessionist

8. Dr. Charles A. Henry, who later became chief quartermaster of the Seventh Army Corps under Gen. Frederick Steele. He had shot a man in Bellevue, Nebraska Territory, in 1854 but was never indicted, claiming self-defense. Henry's biography is in Morton, *Illustrated History of Nebraska*, 1:191–93.

papers.[9] Whatever the men's opinion may have been at the beginning of the war, now all who can form their own judgment agree to some extent on this, "to use all and every means to put down the rebellion." Even arming the Negroes and setting them free are now agreed upon by the old Democrats as being necessary, and Lincoln is praised for his measures aimed at accomplishing this.

Saturday, March 7—Review was to take place today, but a counter order came. We had miserable weather; the rain had turned to snow. Since we now can rest and receive the papers regularly, there are many political debates. The conscription law finds general approval among the soldiers here. Almost all agree that it is just to force the lukewarm and half-hearted Union men to do something for their country.[10]

Yesterday we received rations for ten days. As for meat, nothing but ham and shoulders; besides this, desiccated potatoes, coffee, sugar, tea, syrup, rice, grit (the latter is coarse ground corn), salt, soap, candles, and crackers.[11] Of the latter we will have at least eight boxes (about four hundred pounds) left over. I wrote to Kiel [Germany] and in my diary.[12] Always cloudy weather; some snow is falling. In the evening the march order came.

9. It is not known what may have prompted Scherneckau's remark. The *Missouri Democrat* was considered an unconditional unionist newspaper, and favored emancipation. Gerteis, *Civil War St. Louis*, 84, 265.

10. The Enrollment Act of March 3, 1863, made every able-bodied male citizen aged twenty to forty-five eligible for the draft. James M. McPherson notes that the act's real purpose was to stimulate volunteering, based on quotas assigned by the War Department to each congressional district. McPherson, *Ordeal by Fire*, 356.

11. Desiccated vegetables were dehydrated and formed into blocks. They could be reconstituted by boiling or adding them to soups and stews. Evidently they were not very palatable; some soldiers called them "desecrated" vegetables. McDermott, "No Small Potatoes," 167, 170n51.

12. His parents lived in Kiel.

CHAPTER 4

Posted to Cape Girardeau, March 8–18, 1863

Sunday, March 8—At three thirty the drums woke us up. We had our breakfast early, and by daybreak the tents fell. After it was complete daylight we formed ranks, and, contrary to all expectations and rumors that were in circulation in the camp these last days, we marched east. We used the plank road leading to St. Genevieve. Our teams were loaded with anything that could be tied to the wagons, since we had the chance to have a good road today.

This is the first time we have marched on a modernized road, which, of course, still left much to be desired, but all streams were well bridged. The larger bridges were built in the style of those on the military road in Nebraska.[1] At places where the planks were already rotten the road was poorly macadamized. The material for it is amply available along the road, since the area is very rocky and the ground consists mostly of gravel.[2] Another curiosity are the turnpikes, of which we passed two today, the first ones I have seen in America.[3]

A battalion of the First Wisconsin Cavalry Regiment preceded us, whereupon we followed. The remaining regiments and the artillery, which formerly had composed the Army of Southeastern

1. A route north of the Platte River from Omaha to opposite Fort Kearny, surveyed and constructed by the army, 1855–61. Most of the fifty-thousand-dollar appropriation was spent for bridges. Puschendorf and Potter, *Spans in Time*, 4.

2. Named for Scotsman James MacAdam, who invented the process, a macadam road was surfaced with crushed stone aggregate.

3. The original meaning, as used here, meant a barrier across a road, derived from the Middle English "turnpyke." Later the word came to denote a tollgate and, in modern usage, a toll highway.

Missouri, remained safely in camp near Iron Mountain. Many good farms, carefully cultivated, showed fewer signs of war than we had been used to seeing so far. Orchards with old trees indicated that this was an old settlement. In the southern part of the state we would see women and children alone at home. Here we also saw men of all ages.

Around midday we reached Farmington, a pretty little town with nice large brick buildings and obviously only a little or not at all touched by the war's unrest, yet all stores and businesses were closed because it was Sunday. Many Negroes of both sexes and all ages were seen in town. Around one o'clock we went to the east side of the town to camp in a large field. Nearby haystacks made good beds for us in our tents. Our present commander, Colonel Baumer, returned to Iron Mountain in the afternoon, since an order had arrived here that called him to St. Louis. Baumer is the darling of the regiment. Tonight a strong guard complement was in town, partly in advance posts, partly as provost guard.[4] We had made fifteen miles.

Monday, March 9—At daybreak we were on the march again. Captain Ribble, as the oldest officer present, was in command today.[5] Our Captain Ivory remained in Iron Mountain, since he has a seat on the court-martial, which is judging the mutinous artillerymen, I mentioned at the time [February 25]. Also, two men from our regiment stayed there in the guardhouse because they had been charged with murder. One was first sergeant of Company I.[6] Both are known as great loafers. In addition a bunch of drunks is still back there. Most likely, they will be brought along in several days. Indeed, a nice collection of drunkards found each other in this regiment. Otherwise the boys behave themselves very well on this

4. The provost guard were the military police of the day.

5. Capt. Henry H. Ribble of Company I was about twenty-six years old. Dudley, *Roster of Nebraska Volunteers*, 104–5. Perhaps Scherneckau means he was the senior officer present.

6. James Bangs's service record confirms that he was appointed first sergeant of Company I on May 1, 1862. Evidently nothing came of the murder charge, for Bangs was discharged for disability on November 6, 1865. Compiled Service Records, roll 1; Dudley, *Roster of Nebraska Volunteers*, 104–5.

march. This only happens out of love for Baumer, for whom they will do anything, while strict orders by Colonel Livingston accomplish nothing.

Today the road was not quite as good as yesterday, since in many places the planks were removed but not replaced with gravel. We soon passed a creek on which a small settlement is located, called Valley Ford. Here there was also a good sawmill, as well as a gristmill, both driven by steam, also a foundry and furnace with a number of houses. On both sides of the road were farms with nice buildings and green wheat fields. We made some seventeen miles and then made camp, right along the road in an open, wooded area.

Today we came through a settlement made up entirely of Germans. Besides, from here on up to the Mississippi the inhabitants are, for the most part, Germans or their descendants. A mile beyond where we made camp was a farm whose owner sold the nicest clear Catawba wine, while a mile back the way we came, a brewery was located. High spirits ruled the camp for that reason, of course. Our company had two kegs of beer, containing about twenty gallons, and five gallons of wine. I went to purchase wine and found out that the vintner was born in Baden. He had lived on this place for seventeen years, and he had a farm of two hundred acres. Winter wheat, wine, and fruit are the main products of the area; corn does not do well on this soil. The settlement, or rather the post office, is called Neu-Offenburg, since many of the settlers are from that area. Only really late in the evening did we finally quiet down in our tent.

Tuesday, March 10—At dawn I left the camp, going ahead of the regiment, which was not to march before eight o'clock. It was a glorious morning and a lovely area. The extensive farms, with well-kept fences, spoke very well of my fellow countrymen. Attractive houses, with even better barns, were visible everywhere, and blue smoke rising straight from the chimneys announced that the residents were up early. Well-situated hills supported vineyards, primarily with the magnificent Catawba grape. At the end of the fields, rows of mostly fruit trees were planted, carefully pruned. Everything was so alive, and at the same time so peaceful and safe, that nothing reminded one of the war raging so very nearby. I came past a large store, which at the same time accommodated the post office. Just now bells were ringing, and a large church of sandstone appeared and next to it a friendly looking vicarage. These buildings, as well as many of the farmhouses, are built of sandstone.

Several miles from town a farm wagon caught up with me, and with it I soon reached St. Genevieve on the Mississippi. I reached the river at nine thirty just as the steamer *Choctaw* was leaving. It had part of the First Wisconsin Cavalry Regiment on board.[7] St. Genevieve is a friendly town, with nice buildings, mostly of brick or sandstone, built to last. The inhabitants are mainly French Creoles and Germans. Naturally, I was one of the first of our regiment to enter the town.[8] It arrived about three hours later, and I joined the ranks, marching through town to the landing about two miles above. There we made camp close to the Mississippi.

Several boats came and went today, both upstream as well as downstream. We are once again on the banks of the Father of Rivers, the majestic Mississippi. The islands there with their stand of cottonwood and sycamores do not let one see much of the opposite shore of the state of Illinois. In a short time the camp was crawling with men, women, and children from the area, who offered all kinds of food and drink for sale. The prices went up amazingly as soon as soldiers came into the area. For example, I had bought eggs for ten cents a dozen before the regiment marched in. In a few hours one could no longer get them for less than twenty-five cents. Whiskey in large quantities was also smuggled in. Women had bottles of brandy under their skirts and, of course, sold them quickly. The result, for sure, was many drunks again. Heavy patrols were sent into town to keep order and restore peace by arresting the drunken brawlers. Otherwise we had no duty.

Wednesday, March 11—Very nice weather. Five men from each company received passes to go to town. Even more went without a pass,

7. This would have been about the time the *Choctaw* would have been proceeding downriver, following its conversion into an ironclad at St. Louis. It may have been ordered to transport some troops. The next day, as Scherneckau notes, a company of the First Wisconsin Cavalry accompanied the First Nebraska to Cape Girardeau aboard another steamboat.

8. Scherneckau does not explain the circumstances under which he was allowed to precede the regiment to St. Genevieve. Perhaps he simply left early.

risking the danger of arrest. Soon after noon the steamer *H. [Henry] Chouteau* came into sight upstream, and with that, the signal to strike the tents sounded. The things were brought on board, then the wagons were taken apart and stowed away. The mules also were brought on board. By sundown most of the men were quartered on the boat as well, our company on the hurricane deck [upper deck]. Finally, the guard delivered a number of drunken men from town.

Our boys had a fight there with men from the division—the one that had followed us from Iron Mountain and had moved into camp nearby. In this fight an artilleryman was mortally wounded by a bayonet thrust. It was a cool night; we were lying on deck, wrapped in our blankets; I got only a little sleep. Besides us and our baggage, a company of the First Wisconsin Cavalry Regiment was also on board.

Thursday, March 12—The boat left about one o'clock at night. As I got out of my blankets this morning just after sunrise, the city [Cape] Girardeau was before us, built on a steep hill. After much chaos, lots of running back and forth, complaining, shouting, and labor, the unloading and reloading were finally done.

At eleven o'clock the signal to assemble was given, and with flags flying and with drums and fifes playing, we marched through town and about two miles farther outside and made camp on an open, high field. A battalion of the Thirty-second Iowa Regiment is camped in town; part of the First Wisconsin Cavalry is camped near town too. A small fortification, armed with several cannons, controls the river and is furnished with the essential artillerymen from the Missouri regiment. These men belong to the same regiment as the men of a battery that rebelled in Arcadia. They had made the march into Arkansas with us. Those stationed here broke out in a mutiny as well.[9]

The city is built mostly of bricks and has many fine buildings, hotels, churches, etc. As far as I can judge now, it is larger than Nebraska City. The streets are well macadamized; also the highway

9. This was Battery D, Second Missouri Light Artillery, which was from the same regiment that furnished a battery for the winter Missouri-Arkansas campaign. *OR*, ser. 1, vol. 22, part 2, p. 345.

on which we marched here is just the same and kept in good condition. The bluffs are so steep that the streets are dug through in only a few places and therefore accessible for wagons.[10]

We left a sizable provost guard in town, together with the guards from the Iowa regiment and the cavalry to keep peace and order. The bad elements of our corps, however, seemed to be so firmly present that soon the jail could no longer hold all those arrested, and the order was sent into camp to strengthen the guard in town and to escort the prisoners to camp. Therefore, I had to march to town with forty others, just as the drums were signaling tattoo. Most of the drunken men there were turned over to us. We escorted them into camp, where they were then sent to their respective quarters. The night was mild, even though dark, so the tramp was not so unpleasant.

Friday, March 13—Like yesterday, today was also very nice. Very early the camp was overrun with women and children who offered all kinds of cake, eggs, butter, milk, etc., for sale. For the most part, they are Germans! This morning I washed a pair of underpants, socks, and a shirt, everything I have, and so must get along without these items of clothing until they are dry. In the evening, our colonel, as well as the chaplain, returned to the regiment.

Saturday, March 14—At eight o'clock I had to go on guard duty, to go to town with a strong detail and relieve the Iowa regiment, which is leaving. A formal guard parade with drums and fifes was held on the main street. I was sent to the steamboat landing with the detail to guard commissary supplies stored there. Another strong detail was assigned as provost guard. Boats came and went and brought much activity to the levee. The same boat that brought us here brought the Missouri battery (Welfley's) today, which had marched with us through this state.[11] The steamer also

10. "Nebraska," in a March 20, 1863, letter published in the *Tri-Weekly Nebraska Republican* (Omaha), March 30, 1863, estimated that Cape Girardeau had about four thousand residents.

11. Battery B, First Missouri Light Artillery, under Capt. Martin Welfley. *OR*, ser. 1, vol. 22, part 1, p. 890; Dyer, *Compendium*, 1313.

Cape Girardeau, Missouri. *Frank Leslie's Pictorial History of the American Civil War*, vol. 2, part 10, p. 147. Digitally enhanced.

had the Twenty-third Iowa Regiment on board and took it farther downstream, as it is said, to New Madrid. The artillery, as well as the Thirty-second Iowa Regiment (four companies of it), went on the road toward Bloomfield, while our regiment moved close to town, actually really into it, and set up a camp in nice open place.

In the afternoon a boat brought a large amount of supplies for the government in St. Louis, as well as one hundred cavalry and artillery horses. The following articles, all necessary for the feeding of the soldiers, were on the river bank under our guard: boxes with hard bread, flour in barrels, grit, coarsely ground corn, smoked bacon packed in large barrels, also ham packed the same way, sugar cured ham sewn into sacks, pork in barrels, barrels with salt and some with syrup, rice in barrels, coffee in sacks, boxes with tea, desiccated potatoes, these are dried and mashed, many barrels with sugar, then barrels with vinegar, boxes filled with candles and soap, and still some others. The night was warm and quiet. I slept quite well beside the guard fire, wrapped only in my overcoat.

Sunday, March 15—At about eight o'clock we were relieved and could rest. It was very warm. In the afternoon our chaplain preached in one of the churches, but I did not go. I hear, however, that his talk was praised very much. He is an extremely broad-minded man, who does justice to all kinds of views and therefore is loved by everyone. In the evening, dress parade.

Monday, March 16—It was nice weather like the last days; the roads are dry and dusty. At eight thirty we went out to drill, company by company. However, I was soon ordered to go into town with several others and two wagons to get clothing for our regiment. We had to wait a long time on the levee, where the office of the post quartermaster is. Finally we had the different articles, which we had loaded at just as many different places, and were in camp again about two o'clock. The government is using almost all the larger buildings on Front Street. A large hotel is utilized as a hospital; two large steam flour mills, built of bricks, five and six stories high respectively, are being used as warehouses, and the lower floors as horse stables.

A large number of Negroes work here for the government as teamsters and to feed the animals. Our patrols yesterday and the preceding days rounded up all Negroes who are not occupied that way and don't have a master. Today they were sent under guard to Whitewater, a river fifteen miles from here on the Bloomfield road, where they are to help building a bridge. Company G along with a detail from our regiment [company?] left with them.

I was hardly back in camp and busy eating my lunch when a new detail was ordered to go as guard into town. Since most of the members of my company were absent, I offered my help, even though it was not my turn. We reported, twelve men, two corporals, and a sergeant, at the headquarters in town, across from the St. Charles Hotel. Our colonel resides in this hotel.[12] From there we were sent to the quartermaster, who directed us to a wagon train that we were to guard during the night, since it was to leave the next morning for Bloomfield. Only one post was set. There were ten wagons, and as there were twelve of us, each one had to be on his post for only one hour during the night, which moreover, was nice and quiet. I had the first watch until eight o'clock. Thereafter I slept quite well during the night in a saloon cleared for us, near a blazing fire in the fireplace, until the morning gun at sunrise woke me up.

At night there had been a fire in town, which had been prevented from spreading further only by the efficient help of our guards. Something else happened during the night, which was more of our concern as the guardsmen of the train. A box of chewing tobacco had been stolen from one of the wagons. The loss was discovered before the guard left and also reported to the quartermaster, yet nothing was done, and we were ordered back to camp and released.

Tuesday, March 17—We barely had eaten our breakfast when we had to fall in again. We had to march back to headquarters. There our Colonel Livingston spoke to us and expressed the wish to find the thief who, despite the guard, had robbed the wagon. This speech brought no result, and we were taken to the office of the quartermaster, where we were interrogated once more. The result of this [interrogation] was that the said tobacco had been in the

12. At this time Colonel Livingston was the commander of the post of Cape Girardeau. *OR*, ser. 1, vol. 22, part 2, p. 187.

wagon until two o'clock. The sentries up until then, therefore, had done their duty. Luckily I was among these. Of course, the rest also knew nothing of the tobacco and swore nobody had come near the wagons during their time. This ended the matter for the present, and after the adjutant of the regiment had taken down our names and the company to which we belonged, we were released. I do not know who the thief is, yet he is, without doubt, one of the "noble" guards. I only wish he would be discovered to clear the rest of us of suspicion.

It is nice, but almost too warm. The people are preparing their gardens and fields. The river is alive with steamers going up and down. Those going downstream are now loaded mostly with troops, who earlier had formed the Army of Southeastern Missouri with us. They now are destined mostly for Memphis. The brewer whose property was saved by the efforts of our men from total destruction by fire last night sent us four barrels of beer today, which, when shared, made a tin cup full for each of us.

We are now living quite well; in place of the crackers we receive good fresh bread each day and sugar cured ham, sewn in cloth. I could rest today. In the evening, dress parade as usual. An order was read in which a sergeant of our regiment was demoted for a scandal performed while drunk, in which he seriously wounded a child.[13] Another soldier is under arrest, since he wounded a little girl in her arm and leg when he carelessly fired his rifle.

Wednesday, March 18—Dreary sky and some rain. I wrote to Egge. Toward evening, however, the weather cleared somewhat. I was lying in the tent, resting, when the call to arms sounded. The bugle blew assembly, and soon our whole regiment, that is, the remainder still present in camp, stood under arms. After the bad, or missing shells [musket cartridges], were replaced with fresh ones, we marched on the road leading to Bloomfield, out of town, where we were reinforced by an artillery detachment armed with muskets. They were the rest of the mutinous Missouri battery who still serve.

13. Probably Wilson Majors of Company C. Dudley, *Roster of Nebraska Volunteers*, 30–31, reports Sergeant Majors was "reduced to the ranks" on March 17, 1863. However, he survived this episode, was appointed second lieutenant on September 6, 1865, and was mustered out with the regiment in July 1866.

Now we learned that the Fourth Missouri Cavalry Regiment, which yesterday had come down the river, had rebelled and refused to march on, as they had been ordered. Half a mile brought us to their camp. There was no visible sign of resistance. The men were lying and sitting in and outside their tents. However, I noticed that whiskey and beer had been enjoyed too greatly, and even now, full canteens were circulating among them. The cause of the mutiny was general dissatisfaction. They had not received pay for seven months. Their commander had deluded them that they would be paid in Cape Girardeau. Instead there was the order to march up here. In their anger, my good fellow countrymen—the regiment consists for the most part of Germans—had drunk too much and had come to the too hasty conclusion to disobey the order.

As much as I am opposed to such insubordination by soldiers and always will lend my arm to suppress them, I believe, however, that under the same circumstances our regiment would not have reacted differently. I know what attitude has prevailed among us under lesser provocations.

We formed a line of battle against them and loaded our rifles. At that point their bugler blew to saddle up, and all obeyed, with the exception of three of the ringleaders, who were arrested at once. Soon thereafter, they [the rest of the Fourth Missouri soldiers] mounted their horses and galloped away, on mostly excellent horses. We then marched back to town and were released, after a guard had brought the three riders to the jail, which is now being used as a military prison. Forty captured rebels were brought in today from Bloomfield, where they had been taken by McNeil's cavalry.[14] These were also lodged in that jail.

14. John McNeil was colonel of the Second Missouri State Militia Cavalry as of June 30, 1862, and was appointed brigadier general of volunteers on November 29, 1862. Heitman, *Historical Register*, 1:679. He was in command of Union forces at Bloomfield, Missouri, when Confederate cavalry under Gen. John S. Marmaduke raided into Missouri and attacked Cape Girardeau on April 26, 1863. McNeil's reports for this period are in *OR*, ser. 1, vol. 22, part 1, pp. 255–60. His military career is outlined in Sifakis, *Who Was Who in the Union*, 259–60, and Winter, *The Civil War in St. Louis*, 114.

CHAPTER 5

Escorting Prisoners to St. Louis, March 19–24, 1863

Thursday, March 19—This morning, right after reveille, a detail was made up to go along as guards with the prisoners of war to St. Louis. Eighteen privates, three corporals, one sergeant, and one lieutenant were to be selected. Our company was to furnish two privates and one of the corporals. Only reliable, clear-headed men would be chosen, and I was very happy that the choice fell upon me, since I had not counted on being able to go along. After all, I am in good graces with my orderly sergeant and have often been granted small favors without having asked for them.[1]

We marched to town, got our prisoners out of jail, and went on board the *John Warner* with them, which had just come upstream from Vicksburg.[2] The boat had some two hundred prisoners on board, escorted by a detachment of the Fourth Iowa Infantry Regiment. Among them were the prisoners who had been captured below Vicksburg, on board *Era No. 5*.[3] The privates of this group belonged to Louisiana and Mississippi regiments. Our prisoners, on the contrary, were nothing more or less than guerrillas, a ragged

1. The soldiers from Company H were Corp. John H. Boon, Pvt. Frederick Elwood, and Scherneckau. Company H Morning Report, March 1863, NSHS RG18, roll 3. A letter signed "Nebraska," March 20, 1863, reported that the detail escorting the prisoners to St. Louis was commanded by Lieutenant "Paddock" (actually William A. Polock) of Company C. *Tri-Weekly Nebraska Republican* (Omaha), March 30, 1863; Dudley, *Roster of Nebraska Volunteers*, 30–31.

2. He means the Vicksburg vicinity, where Union forces were maneuvering against the Confederate stronghold, which would not fall until July 4, 1863.

3. *Era No. 5* was a stern-wheel steamboat captured from the Confederates on February 14, 1863. Gibbons, *Warships and Naval Battles*, 171.

and bodacious-looking gang. We brought them all to the lower deck, in the stern of the boat, where two sentries had them under guard. We made our quarters in the gallery around the cabins.

The weather was excellent. We went upstream quickly, only lightly loaded. We met several boats, mostly in the service of the government. One of them had the Eighteenth Indiana Infantry Regiment and the First Indiana Battery on board. In the afternoon we reached a sandbar in the river on which the *City of Alton* was stuck. It also had Indiana troops on board. After great efforts, our steamer got her going again, whereupon both went on their way, upstream and downstream respectively. One more post was set up in the evening. The night was lovely, and I slept really well until the morning bright. We had rations for three days in the haversack, soft bread, ham, coffee, and sugar—enough for soldiers accustomed to so little, as we had now become, to make an excellent meal.

At daybreak [Friday, March 20] we were only twenty-two miles from St. Louis. Soon we came to the suburb Carondelet. There in the shipyards several gunboats in the process of construction were moored that already had received their iron armor. It seemed that our prisoners, who had by now been brought onto the hurricane deck, did not like at all the black things with the bombproof deck visible above water. A few more miles and we squeezed between the long rows of boats on the levee. Not far from us was the large steamer *Ruth*, confiscated by the government a few days ago when caught in a smuggling operation with the enemy. Now she was taking government freight and troops on board for Memphis. There was tremendous activity at the landing, and a good part of this originated from the boats loading and discharging for the government.

In the afternoon, our prisoners were picked up by the provost guard, a Missouri regiment. We wandered about the city a bit and then toward evening headed for the Schofield Barracks, already well known to me. The Thirty-seventh Iowa Regiment had the guard there, nothing but old men, therefore nicknamed the Graybeards. Many of them were entirely white-haired, and as they mentioned, none of them under fifty years.[4]

4. The "Graybeard Regiment" comprised men forty-five years of age and older. One soldier was reported to be eighty years old. The regiment was organ-

The barracks were extremely crowded, at least three hundred men were there from all possible regiments of the western armies, waiting for transportation to various points. There were soldiers here from Michigan to Nebraska and from Tennessee and Arkansas regiments. Naturally, foolish activity reigned, and only late did one get to sleep in the over-filled rooms.

Since my last stay, this prison-like building has been made even more secure. More iron bars have been put in front of the windows, the surrounding board walls have been raised several feet, and worst of all, guards were stationed around the whole building, cutting off all possibility of climbing over. The Graybeards had to take up no less than eleven posts around the institution.

Saturday, March 20 [21]—In the morning I wrote to Hedde. Right after the noon meal we were dismissed, since our lieutenant had made the necessary arrangements, and I was sincerely glad to have the annoying gates behind me. Since we were not supposed to leave before Monday, it was a requirement that we had to return in the evenings. I looked for Mr. Olshausen in the office of the *Westliche Post,* where I learned that he had gone to Washington. In the evening I was looking around for a hotel or lodging house, and through a comrade who had lodged there earlier I found the "Pension, tenue par Fr. Simmon [boarding house, managed by Fr. Simmon]" where everything was French; good food and bed, as well as a friendly host, soon made me feel at home.[5]

Sunday, March 21 [22]—It rained. At the boarding house I wrote in my diary as well as to Egge. After supper I returned to the barracks, since I did not know for sure whether we would be leaving on Monday morning. Only with effort was I able to get a spot to lie down inside the building.

---

ized to relieve able-bodied troops from routine guard and other garrison duties. Faust, *Encyclopedia of the Civil War,* 321–22.

5. It seems obvious that Scherneckau ignored the requirement that he was to return to the barracks for the night.

Monday, March 23—There was no boat ready for our departure, and after we were let out of our prison, we explored St. Louis. I visited the U.S. steam cracker factory, where our hard bread is manufactured in large quantities. As the name says, the machinery is powered by steam, and the baking is done in many large ovens. Fresh and warm, the crackers are not so bad. In the evening I was back in our quarters.

Tuesday, March 24—Wrote in my diary, which later would be lost.[6] We mostly remained in the barracks today, since we had to board the boat in the afternoon. But this turned out to be a mistake; we had to spend another night in the building. However, it was quite interesting to observe the life and activities here. Late in the evening there was an uproar in our wing of the building. The sutler store, which is not absent here either, was broken into and all the merchandise hauled away. The sergeant of the guard arrived with his men, put guards at all the doors leading into the courtyard and all of us, as well as beds and knapsacks, were subjected to a thorough and tiresome search. Two or three of the men had some of the stolen goods in their possession, and they were led away to prison. Some of the stolen goods included tobacco, cigars, oysters in tin cans, playing cards, candles, knives, smoked herring, and many others.

6. The lost diary must have been a book in which he jotted notes for the more extensive installments he mailed to Hedde and others in Grand Island.

CHAPTER 6

Back to Cape Girardeau, March 25–April 10, 1863

Wednesday, March 25—After we had slept a few hours, we were back on our feet. Following breakfast our lieutenant came, and we marched to the levee. Almost everyone from the transportation barracks left with us at the same time. Two boats took the men. We were ordered to board the smaller one, called *[J. D.] Hinde.* The day was pleasant; our little boat, a stern-wheel steamer, although at other times quite slow, went downstream rather quickly, since it was not heavily loaded.

By sunset we reached the little town St. Genevieve. We did not stop for long but went about two miles farther downstream, where we moored both boats for the night. It was a nice moonlit night, and quite a number of us went ashore and to the city, less than two miles away. The Twenty-second Iowa Regiment was encamped there. Since all taverns were closed, we almost missed our beer, which we had counted on; nevertheless, I secretly secured a glass. Before midnight I was back on board and slept in the cabin, where it was very warm.

Thursday, March 26—At daybreak we went farther downstream, and around eleven o'clock, after we bade farewell to all the new friends, we were set ashore at our post, Cape Girardeau. Among these [friends] were a few from the Eleventh Indiana Regiment, Zouaves, who for a long time were with our regiment in the same brigade under the command of Gen. L. Wallace.[1] Both regiments

1. General Orders No. 6, February 21, 1862, assigned troops in the District of West Tennessee to brigades and divisions. Although this order placed the

respect each other greatly, and wherever men from these corps meet, they get acquainted with one another immediately. We had the same experience with these brave men. Their regiment is still located in Helena, and through one of them, Walsh by name, I have sent greetings to Mr. Rusch. So I was therefore home again, gladly welcomed with many handshakes, and after that we discussed news and our experiences.

In the afternoon I had to go out for battalion drill; in the evening there was dress parade. Many men here have families cook the rations they receive and, for this, pay one dollar a month. I, with six of my tent mates, do the same. An old woman and her daughter cook for us. Her husband is with the Thirteenth Illinois Cavalry Regiment, now in Tennessee. It [the cook's house] is not far from camp, and we receive good food. Our Captain Ivory is again with the company.

Friday, March 27—Today I had to go on guard duty. Since quite a few men are required every day, the duty is really strenuous. The provost guard in town is quartered in a comfortable furnished house. With drums and fifes [playing], the guard is inspected before it relieves the old guard. Furthermore [there are] a great number of military ceremonies, which are, to use the army slang, "putting on style." Shined shoes and ditto leather things, as well as highly polished rifles and brightly polished brass decorations on the cartridge pouch and belts, are now required to pass the inspection for guard duty. I was assigned to a detachment at the disposal of the post quartermaster. Toward evening it started to rain quite heavily, but our post was dry, and we slept really warm in a hayshed. A large train, which had taken provisions to Bloomfield, came back in the evening.

Saturday, March 28—Relieved at the usual time at eight o'clock in the morning, we were released to our quarters, and for the rest of the day I was not assigned further. I cleaned and polished my rifle

---

Eleventh Indiana in Gen. Lew Wallace's division, the Indiana regiment was assigned to the first brigade, while the First Nebraska was in the second brigade. *OR*, ser. 1, vol. 7, pp. 649–50.

Chaplain Thomas Tipton of the First Nebraska. RG2411-5631, Nebraska State Historical Society, Lincoln. Digitally enhanced and restored.

and other equipment. Yesterday evening, to my great joy, I once again received letters, one from Egge, the other from Martin. In the evening there was dress parade.

Sunday, March 29—The weather today was very cold and stormy; just as in Nebraska sometimes at this time of year, cold weather suddenly follows a warm, nice day. This morning at seven thirty there was regimental inspection by Lieutenant Colonel Baumer, but, considering the cold weather, it proceeded rapidly, and we were spared the long standing and freezing. The inspecting officer made only a few comments about pants not being brushed.

I received two letters again today, one from Hedde, the other from Martin. At ten o'clock our regiment's clergyman gave a sermon in the church of the Presbyterians. We had been officially informed about this. I went today, and there were quite a few soldiers present and also residents with their ladies. Our beloved preacher does not have a good voice, but he is a liberal-minded man, and he gave a truly good sermon. One forgot that one was in a church, since he spoke so naturally and simply; besides, he wore no official garb, so that everyone enjoyed listening, whatever denomination he might belong to. Reverend Tipton, indeed, is a man that a regiment like ours (and probably most of those in Uncle Sam's services) needs. He does not force himself on anyone, favors no religious group, and, furthermore, makes himself useful as postmaster of the regiment, distributing the letters and sending off those that have been written.

Monday, March 30—Went on guard duty at the same place again, but this time had a cold night. The wind was sharp and freezing cold like often in Nebraska. Such weather turns up here frequently in the spring, even during the month of April, as several residents have assured me. I wrote to Hedde, Egge, and Martin. Received a letter from Germany from Father and Faber. Some eighty prisoners were brought in from Bloomfield.[2]

2. Bloomfield, southwest of Cape Girardeau, was garrisoned by Union troops under the command of Gen. John McNeil. *OR*, ser. 1, vol. 22, part 2, p. 187.

Tuesday, March 31—This morning we were relieved; the weather turned somewhat nicer. The prisoners brought in yesterday were sent to St. Louis with an escort from our regiment on the ferry *Davenport,* which had come upstream. I had a bad cold and did not feel well. In the afternoon we had some drill, and in the evening, the unavoidable dress parade.

Wednesday, April 1—This morning I went to the doctor, who listed me as "sick in quarters" on the sick report. I received several powders and during the day had quite a fever.

Thursday, April 2—This morning I feel much better; have to take several pills. I wrote to Hedde and in my diary. The weather is still unpleasant—cold winds, as if we were in Nebraska. Regardless, peach and apple trees are in magnificent bloom.

Friday, April 3—The weather is still the same. Today I wrote to my parents. I feel quite well, except I have a bad cough. I have used only half of the medicine given to me. The salt, which I was supposed to take today, I did not use at all. Besides, I was still reported as sick in quarters today. The supply train from Bloomfield returned this evening.

Saturday, April 4—The weather today was warmer and nicer. Was still reported for quarters today.

Sunday, April 5—Was taken off the sick list today; the weather was warm and nice. Soon after breakfast I was sent to town with a fatigue party, reporting there at the headquarters. We found out that we were not needed, and therefore we were sent home. The men who had been to St. Louis as escort returned today at noon. With them came a dozen recruits and the recruiting officers and sergeants who had been in Nebraska. Our pastor will preach again this afternoon. I wrote to Mr. Olshausen in St. Louis and to Faber in Germany. In the evening we had dress parade. At sunset I had to go to town with a detail to put the commissary stores under cover, since it looked very much like rain. We worked until about eleven o'clock at night and then returned to our quarters. Whiskey was distributed among us.

Monday, April 6—Had to go on guard duty today. I was sent to Fort C, located right here by the camp. In each of the four forts only one post is set up with orders to let no one in. Here we had a tent with a stove. Also a stove in the sentry house at the rampart, which is especially pleasant for the man on duty on cold nights.[3] A member of the medical committee was here inspecting quarters, hospitals, and the like.

Tuesday, April 7—After I was relieved from guard duty, I was immediately sent to town with a detail to load merchandise that had been unloaded from a steamboat. We waited at the landing all day in vain, because no wagons came that we could load. So toward evening we went back to camp without having accomplished a thing.

Our regiment, together with the Missouri artillery stationed here, paraded through town today. Also a salute was fired from the fort to celebrate the anniversary of the Battle of Shiloh. Yesterday evening thirteen shots were fired, since it was said that Charleston, South Carolina, had been taken.[4] Colonel Baumer treated each company with half a barrel of beer, which naturally caused quite a bit of gaiety in the camp and, as a result, a few fights. Nice weather.

Wednesday, April 8—Today the Fourth Regiment, Missouri Cavalry, went on board a ship to go downstream. The First Wisconsin Cavalry Regiment camps next to us and, as they say, is going down the river as well. An Iowa regiment on a boat passed us yesterday going downstream. Numerous rumors are circulating right now that we might have to go to Nebraska in the event of a war with the Mormons.[5] I was on fatigue duty. Our wagons were fetching firewood, four cartloads for each company, which kept us busy all day.

3. Four earthen fortifications defended Cape Girardeau. "Nebraska" letter, May 4, 1863, in *Nebraska Advertiser* (Brownville), May 14, 1863.

4. Adm. Samuel F. DuPont had led a Union navy attack on Fort Sumter in Charleston Harbor, but the attack failed. *American Heritage Civil War Chronology.*

5. The stationing of U.S. troops under Gen. Patrick E. Connor at Salt Lake City in the fall of 1862 increased tension between the Mormon leadership and U.S. officials in Utah. Many gentiles thought the Mormons, particularly church leaders, were disloyal. By March 1863 it seemed possible that hostilities might break out between the Mormon militia and government troops. See Varley, *Brigham and the Brigadier*, chapter 6.

Thursday, April 9—Had to go on guard duty. Was assigned to picket and sent to the Benton Road, three men and a corporal. All persons passing our line must have a pass signed by the provost marshal and a permit for all merchandise that is being transported to the outside as well. War contraband, when found, is confiscated. In the evening the officer du jour came to give us a new password. He also informed us that patrols of our cavalry would be riding toward the advance post line, since they wish to catch an enemy spy. We, therefore, had to keep a sharp eye out on the road, yet the night passed quietly, and Mr. Spy was not caught.

Friday, April 10—This morning we were relieved. Returning to camp, we found the regiment assembled for inspection. According to an order by the secretary of war, an examination of the entire army is being held to judge the actual status of all troops [regiments] and how many conscripts are necessary to bring them up to normal strength.[6] The arriving guards escaped this inspection. Under orders by the officer of the camp guard, we emptied our muskets at a target. In the afternoon, as usual, some company drill and dress parade.

The president's proclamation, it seems, has already been effective for our regiment as well. A number of deserters, some absent from the regiment five to six months, have now come back, for they could return without punishment if they appeared by the first of this month.[7] I believe today's inspection is carried out to discover which men are still absent. I hope that they will be firmly punished when found. It is very windy today; large dust clouds enclose our camp, penetrate the tents, and make everything dirty and sandy.

6. General Orders No. 82, War Department, April 1, 1863, provided that there would be a general muster of all troops on April 10 for the use of the provost marshal-general in making drafts to fill up regiments and batteries under the Enrollment Act of March 3, 1863. *OR*, ser. 3, vol. 3, p. 109.

7. On March 10, 1863, President Abraham Lincoln issued a proclamation, as provided by an act of Congress, which granted amnesty to deserters who returned to their regiments by April 1. Deserters so reporting would not be penalized, except for forfeiture of pay and allowances during the period of their absence. *OR*, ser. 3, vol. 3, pp. 60–61. One of the deserters who came back to Company H was Pvt. Isaac Sager, who had deserted June 18, 1862. Company H Morning Report, April 1863, NSHS RG18, roll 3.

CHAPTER 7

Provost Duty in St. Louis and a Trip to Memphis, April 11–May 12, 1863

Saturday, April 11—The rain today was most welcome, since it settled the dust somewhat. One detachment of our regiment went to St. Louis yesterday evening with fifteen secesh prisoners. After I had written this, an order suddenly came for our company to get ready to march, in order to go to St. Louis with the next boat. All men detached from the company as drivers, clerks, or the like, had to return. For the same reason our second lieutenant, the regiment's quartermaster, also returned to the company.[1] With all these men, [the company] was now over fifty men strong. Only two remained in Girardeau, one who is the regiment's bugler, and the other was detached to Company G, which is building a bridge on the Bloomfield road.

With great ceremony, our drums and fifes at the head, we marched through town to the headquarters. There we stacked arms and received our wages, paid up to the first of March of this year. The paymaster was in a pool hall right under the headquarters. On the pool table the greenbacks were thrown toward us with unbelievable speed. Officers and privates, around sixty men, were paid off in four and a half minutes. After we received our money, we marched to the landing, where after some drill, we again stacked arms and waited for the boat. Naturally, of course, there were drunken men immediately, since there was money again, as well as beer and brandy.

1. Lt. Stephen W. Moore, who had served as regimental commissary sergeant. Dudley, *Roster of Nebraska Volunteers*, 90–91.

At about four o'clock a steamboat finally came upstream, the *Meteor* of Vicksburg, loaded with condemned horses. We marched on board and soon left the landing. Colonel Livingston shipped out with us, also ordered to St. Louis. In the evening we had our regular roll call just as in camp; the captain in person gave orders, for once. He seems to be quite dissatisfied with the condition of the company. We received the order to line up for inspection tomorrow morning at eight o'clock with the best pieces of our uniform, in order to find out what was needed for being suitably outfitted. It seems that Captain Ivory wants to put on a show with us. Apparently, the presence of our colonel on board has much to do with this. We know that he likes it if the men are well dressed, putting on style, as it is called. He wants our company to present itself as fancy soldiers in St. Louis. I slept quite well on the floor of the cabin.

Sunday, April 12—The boat was traveling all night. During the trip wood was taken on from a flatboat, which was tied down alongside, while we happily went upstream. Much brushing, polishing, and shining went on early this morning. The barber could barely keep up with the demand, although he had started before dawn. At daybreak, landed again to take on wood.

At eight o'clock the formal inspection took place in the cabin. The men had cleaned themselves thoroughly, were well scrubbed, and even the old muskets were passably shiny. We drilled for half an hour in the salon of the boat, while our colonel, sitting next to the stove and smoking his cigar, watched comfortably. At one thirty we reached the landing at St. Louis. After our captain returned from headquarters, where he had reported, we marched to the Schofield Barracks, too well known to me. We took up quarters in the rooms, only moderately occupied.

It is now said that we are assigned to do guard duty here in St. Louis. Our first lieutenant will take command of this transportation barracks; the second will go back to the regiment to complete his business as quartermaster and to turn over the books.[2] Our

2. William T. Clarke was the first lieutenant. Dudley, *Roster of Nebraska Volunteers,* 90–91. Schofield Barracks was an assembly point for troops returning to their regiments from furlough, hospitalization, or detached duty assignments.

Captain Ivory has been appointed to be a member of the court-martial here, while our colonel, as I see from today's *Democrat*, in accordance with Order No. 80, is appointed commander of the Invalid Detachment for the hospitals in St. Louis.[3] As always, we are kept here in strict custody, yet I hope this is just temporary and will come to an end when our lieutenant takes command here.

Monday, April 13—The situation is still the same as yesterday, only this much seems sure, for now we will remain stationed here in St. Louis. The barracks are now guarded by artillerymen armed like infantry; the men belong to the Second Missouri Artillery Regiment. One company of the same regiment is also stationed at Cape Girardeau. It is said that we are destined to take over their post.

Today our first lieutenant took over the command, and we now received permission to go into the city. I went to the office of the *Westliche Post.* Mr. Olshausen was not yet back from his trip to Washington. I paid for mailing the weekly edition to Father. Took a uniform coat, which I had bought as used from a comrade, to a cleaner of clothing. So far, I have gotten by without a so-called dress coat. The usual shirt worked well in the field but is no longer adequate here, where we will have to do garrison duty.

Toward evening, I returned to the barracks. However, soon afterward I made an excursion with our orderly sergeant, who is a good friend of mine.[4] I also am on good terms with the other officers. We strolled around in the city until a little after nightfall. When we came back I had to patrol the city with a private and a corporal, since quite a number of our men had not yet returned. Of course, we avoided meeting our comrades as much as we could and arrested only one, after we had given him every possible opportunity to escape. He had to spend the night in the guardhouse. After we had made this pleasant walk through the city, we returned to

3. The Invalid Corps, created in April 1863, consisted of disabled officers and men no longer fit for combat. There were two categories: those who could bear arms and perform garrison duty, and those who were fit only for hospital service. Faust, *Encyclopedia of the Civil War,* 383. The order is referenced in Livingston's file, Compiled Service Records, roll 14.

4. Probably Sgt. James I. Shaw, who served until the regiment was mustered out in July 1866. Dudley, *Roster of Nebraska Volunteers,* 90–91.

our barracks. Later at night most of the men we had not located came in, except three or four who arrived here after roll call on

Tuesday, April 14—Today we are busy setting up housekeeping, since it is said we will stay here for quite some time. Duty has not yet been required of us. It rained nearly all day. I wrote and passed the time as well as I could. Besides, it is now not at all difficult to get permission to leave. We have our regular roll calls as in camp, with the difference here, only one drummer and one piper plays, while if the regiment is together, six or eight drummers and just as many pipers call to fall in.

Wednesday, April 15—Like yesterday. I was in the city the better part of the day. Sent off a small box to Hedde. Today two men and a corporal left for Memphis with some prisoners. Another detail accompanied a transport of deserters and various soldiers who are returning to their respective regiments to the boat that would take them. Except for a few besides our company, the barracks are completely unoccupied. I wrote to Mr. Pundt and to Hedde.

Thursday, April 16—Nice weather; still no duty. Today the barracks were thoroughly cleaned and fixed up where necessary. This work is done by the soldiers who are waiting here, as well as by the military prisoners. We do not have to bother with this and play the gentlemen. However, we had to drill a little.

Friday, April 17—A glorious, warm day. One of our men was sent with a prisoner to Rolla today. Yesterday evening I attended the parade of the frequently mentioned Graybeards, the Thirty-seventh Iowa Regiment. The old boys took a lot of time in their drill. Hence the whole affair was a miserable sight, even for men who understand nothing about drilling. The commander of this department, Major General Curtis, was also present.[5] After the

5. Maj. Gen. Samuel R. Curtis, commander of the Department of the Missouri, September 24, 1862, to May 24, 1863. Previously he had commanded victorious Union troops at the Battle of Pea Ridge, Arkansas, March 7–8, 1862. Sifakis, *Who Was Who in the Union*, 99.

parade he spoke at length with the officers and privates of the regiment, since he is obviously well known as a former member of Congress from the state of Iowa.

Last night there was a fairly large fire about a mile from here. A soap factory burned down; five to six hose carts went past here, hurrying to the fire. This evening I took a walk through the neighborhood of the barracks. The residences of the business people and the wealthy of the city are, in general, very nice buildings, similar to the immediate vicinity of Hamburg, which also has such nice houses. Only here, the space is more limited. The lovely parks, which surround the houses of the money barons around Hamburg, here dwindle to miniature gardens, which nevertheless are painstakingly tended and cared for to bring small plants to grow.

Saturday, April 18—Very nice weather again. I took an extended walk upstream into the northern part of town, but I did not reach the city limits by a long shot, even though I had been walking for four hours. Factories and mills of all kinds, besides numerous churches, are included in this part of town. I got back to our quarters, exhausted, a little before noon. A large troop had arrived here, released from hospitals, paroled prisoners returning from furlough, and God only knows from where else the men had come, to wait for transportation to their variously assigned places. We now have two posts to man in the courtyard to maintain order and cleanliness.

A long time has passed since I wrote the previous notes. I was in Memphis, and I am now back here in St. Louis. I will now transfer these days from my pocket notebook, in which I had continued my diary during this time.

At two o'clock we left the barracks, three men—including myself—and a corporal, to escort seven prisoners to Columbus [Kentucky] and Memphis, respectively, who belong to various regiments and who were arrested as deserters. We marched with them on board the steamer *Nebraska*, which left at about four o'clock with a full load of army provisions. We set up our quarters in the back of the boat on a kind of middle deck. The boat moored thirty miles below St. Louis in order to take on wood. It was on the Illinois bank, and we stayed there for the night. Of course, we had to guard our prisoners during the night. The cavalrymen from the Fourth Missouri Regiment lost one of the prisoners under their guard; he had gone on shore in shirtsleeves with the deck hands and had then disappeared in the dark.

Sunday, April 19—At dawn the boat started to move again. Nice weather in which the boat, although fully loaded, went downstream quite rapidly. The *Nebraska* is a large, old boat, and very much in need of repairs. The cargo consists largely of flour in barrels and sacks, besides coffee, beans, peas, sugar, etc. Also some fifty head of fat oxen are on board. We were supplied with rations for ten days before we took off, consisting of bread, ham, tea, sugar, and soap.

It is a delightful journey in such excellent weather. The trees are radiant in their first green of spring; others still without leaves are covered with blossoms. Around one o'clock we reached Cape Girardeau landing but stopped just for a moment to let some passengers disembark. Next we went on farther around the peninsula; on its tip—reaching farthest into the river—rests the Catholic seminary, or cloister, high up and beautiful, an attractive building. On the other side of this peninsula, we caught a glimpse of our old camp, until the bluffs and the walls of Fort D removed it from our view. We had plenty of time to enjoy all the natural beauties, since we did not have guard duty as long as the boat was moving. Picturesque banks, where the bluffs in steep slopes drop down to the river, consist mostly of sandstone and alternate with the wide bottomland, which now—densely forested—is only a few feet above the low water level. The farther south we came, the more majestic the tree growth seemed to become.

At sunset we came to the mouth of the Ohio. A shot from the guard of one of the erected forts went off as we rounded the headland, and soon we were mooring alongside one of the boat docks of Cairo. Some goods were unloaded; passengers came and left the boat. One U.S. gunboat was anchored in the mouth of the Ohio, and eight to ten steamers were lying very close to each other at the landing, representing a small part of St. Louis. We stopped here until eight o'clock and, of course, had to guard our prisoners during this time, since it appeared that some of them were inclined to set foot on the free soil of Illinois.[6]

After we had departed, we rested for several hours until we reached Columbus around midnight. There we delivered four of our men to the officer of the guard, and after we unloaded a quantity of government goods, we steamed farther downstream.

Monday, April 20—At night we stopped once more to take on wood and then slept several hours until dawn. We had already passed Island No. 10 and docked right at New Madrid.[7] A large amount of corn in gunnysacks was taken on board, so one could be convinced the boat must sink under the freight stacked up everywhere. We then continued on our course. Around noon some forty cords of wood were loaded on the Missouri side of the river, about thirty miles north of the border with Arkansas. On the other, the east side of the river, we had [were passing] the state of Tennessee for some time. It was very warm, and real, genuine mosquitoes made their appearance.

We met four or five steamboats today, the same as yesterday. After dark we passed Fort Pillow, located on a high bluff, at a place where the Mississippi is narrow.[8] The river otherwise was quite wide today; frequently it looked like a lake—on both sides low banks resplendent with very lush tree growth. Extended plantations with lovely buildings alternated with the lonely hut of the woodcutter. Villages and small towns, so plentiful on the upper part of the river, were rarely seen here.

6. Cairo, Illinois, was a major Union base located on a peninsula at the confluence of the Ohio and Mississippi rivers. Coombe, *Thunder along the Mississippi*, 33–37.

7. In an effort to hold the Mississippi River, the Confederates had fortified Island No. 10, where the river made a large S-curve near the Kentucky-Tennessee border. After being cut off by Union troops and U.S. Navy gunboats, the garrison surrendered on April 8, 1862. New Madrid, Missouri, lies just downstream from Island No. 10 but north of the island as the crow flies. The campaign against Island No. 10 is discussed in Coombe, *Thunder along the Mississippi*, 81, 85–94.

8. The Confederates had evacuated Fort Pillow, on the Tennessee shore of the river, in late May 1862, after it was outflanked by Union forces moving into northern Mississippi. Coombe, *Thunder along the Mississippi*, 125.

Tuesday, April 21—Last night I had the last guard duty, but we did not dock anywhere until we stopped at the Memphis dock at three thirty in the morning.[9] We now closely guarded the deserters entrusted to us until it was complete daylight and then took them to the guardhouse in the city, where we delivered them to the commanding officer upon receiving a receipt. The military prison and guardhouse is housed in an elegant former store on one of the main streets of this lovely town. The public park, surrounded by a graceful iron fence, sits just in front of this lovely building.

These public squares are a real adornment to the city of Memphis. They are very well maintained; lovely, shady paths cross these little Gardens of Eden, and benches invite one to stay for a while. The gray squirrels here go about their business undisturbed, and they are so tame that they hop onto the visitor's shoulder to be fed by him. On the whole, Memphis is a lovely, friendly city, and for the well-to-do no more pleasant place can be found. Only the levee is ugly, despite the large traffic, and many boats are anchored there. However, Uncle Sam almost exclusively generates this activity. Huge [quantities of] supplies were lying piled up at the landing or were still in the boats of all kinds and sizes. Long rows of government wagons were continually taking the goods up into the city.

After we had finished our business and secured transportation for the trip back, I visited the city a little bit. It was a sultry morning, and around noon it rained some. As already mentioned, the city makes an extremely good impression, in fact, the prettiest city of all those I have seen so far. All houses, except the ones on the main business streets, are set back from the street, surrounded by shade trees and carefully tended gardens. Trees of all kinds, now in their most beautiful foliage, surround the houses, providing welcome shade against the heat, which is already very stifling. Furthermore, rows of trees are planted on the outside of the sidewalk on all the streets, trees that in part are already well grown and pro-

9. Union forces had occupied Memphis on June 6, 1862, following a naval battle in which the Confederate River Defense Fleet was destroyed. Coombe, *Thunder along the Mississippi*, 130–33.

vide welcome shade to the pedestrians. Everything indicated aristocratic elegance and refinement.[10] One almost never saw whites working, unless they were soldiers, and even Uncle Sam generally employs only Negroes.

Life is expensive in Memphis. Everything is almost triple the price for which it can be bought in St. Louis. A comrade and I had a noon meal in a restaurant, and each had to pay fifty cents for a meager meal, which only filled us halfway. There are many troops stationed in and around Memphis. The Twenty-fifth Indiana Regiment is provost guard; the provost guard is very strict here—beer may not be sold at all to soldiers. And only with great effort and secretly could we get a glass of bad lager beer for ten cents.

Today there was a battle eight miles from the city, and eighty prisoners were brought in from the battlefield.[11] In the afternoon we went back to the landing, where we found the *Champion*, a nice, large boat, ready to leave for St. Louis at four o'clock. Since the government had chartered it, our transportation pass permitted us space on it. Because there was almost no freight on board, we soon found roomy lodging on the lower deck. At the levee was a U.S. gunboat, an ordinary stern-wheel steamer. It has been enclosed and covered with iron plates. It has six small cannon on each side and in addition has firing ports for muskets. Four mortar boats, each outfitted for one of these monsters to which they are assigned, were also nearby. I counted over fifty iron cannons of large caliber on the levee, almost all spiked. They came from

10. Thomas E. Keen had also been impressed by Memphis when the First Nebraska was there in the spring and early summer of 1862. Potter, "I Thought It My Duty," 145. The city also drew favorable comment from army contract surgeon John Vance Lauderdale, aboard a navy hospital boat that stopped in Memphis on July 16, 1862. Josyph, *Wounded River*, 97. The public squares and shade trees seemed to attract most observers' attention.

11. Between April 18 and 24, Union troops from Memphis mounted an expedition to the Coldwater River and skirmished with Confederate forces. It was hoped the foray would divert the Confederates' attention away from Col. Benjamin Grierson's simultaneous cavalry raid through central Mississippi. All these efforts were related to Gen. Ulysses S. Grant's campaign against Vicksburg. Reports of the Coldwater expedition and its relationship to Grierson's raid are in *OR*, ser. 1, vol. 24, part 1, pp. 519–21, 554–59.

Island No. 10. Some men were busy drilling out the flash vents, and with success as it appeared.[12]

Many hundred bales of cotton were lying on the levee also, several of them half-burned. A drowned Negro had been washed up on the bank between the boats. No one took the body away. Cavalrymen who watered their horses at the place rode over the body. No preparations were made to remove and bury him. A Negress with two children came, obviously the family of the victim. All three were crying and sobbing wretchedly. Yet the body was still lying there as we left in the evening. A dead Negro is, of course, no more than a dead dog!

But the saddest sight I have ever seen, I saw today. The *City of Memphis*, a hospital boat, came up from Vicksburg with sick and wounded.[13] It moored next to us to replenish its cargo for the North from the hospitals of the city of Memphis. One full ambulance after another arrived, and the poor sick men and cripples of all kinds were then brought on board—those completely helpless on stretchers, those able to walk a bit supported by two attendants or limping by on crutches or two canes. [Some were] Missing legs and arms, some with both legs amputated. Many men were so weakened by sickness that they could not walk; their bodies were nothing more than skin and bones. The eyes were deep in their sockets, the cheekbones and chin stuck out, truly walking skeletons! The sight of these men, so thin, weak, and helpless like children, was almost more touching for me than to see all the pale, mutilated figures. It was enough to make one cry! Oh, war is a terrible thing.

12. Before the Confederates surrendered Island No. 10, they disabled the cannon by driving iron rods or spikes into the vents, where the primers would be inserted for firing. The spikes were then clinched inside the barrels with a rammer, preventing easy removal. Spiking prevented an enemy from immediately turning captured guns on their former owners. Nonetheless, as Scherneckau indicates, the spikes could be removed and the cannon restored to service. Switlik, *Complete Cannoneer*, 59–60.

13. John Vance Lauderdale provides a firsthand description of the role of navy hospital boats on the Mississippi River and the conditions thereon. Josyph, *Wounded River.* The navy's first hospital boat was the *Red Rover*, whose story is told in Kenney, "From the Log of the *Red Rover*."

A number of crippled and sick soldiers, most of them discharged, who were hurrying home, came on board our boat. Also a few who had received leave went with us. While I am writing this (in my pocket notebook), such an emaciated, hardly still humanlike form is lying not far from me, a young man, over six feet tall but just bones, covered with a wrinkled, yellow skin. The long, skinny hands appear transparent. The arms and legs are almost no heavier than those of a child. Only with great effort does he get up and drag himself away with the help and support of two canes. It is the first time I have seen so much human suffering; all in all it touches me deeply. I believe that the battlefield can hardly be worse than to take a cold-blooded look inside the hospitals, since the excitement in which a soldier finds himself in battle [distracts from the horror].

At about five o'clock our boat left the landing of the city of Memphis, and it seems to promise a quick journey, since it goes upstream faster than the boat, the *Nebraska,* brought us downstream.

Wednesday, April 22—Today we went upstream, nearly without stopping, sometimes in a race with a small steamer, *Glendale of Cincinnati,* which after all passed us by. We passed New Madrid, and around four o'clock in the afternoon we reached the now famous Island No. 10. It is only a flat island, partly under cultivation. Little could be seen of fortifications; I saw only a few mounted guns. A large number of blacks, of both sexes, came to the shore as we passed. I noticed a black sentry guard as well. A U.S. gunboat was lying at the landing of the island and inspected every passing steamboat; however, we did not have to stop. At sunset we came to Hickman's Bluff [Kentucky], a small town with fortifications above. During the night we passed Columbus and later Cairo. We did not leave the last place until dawn.

Thursday, April 23—In Columbus a number of military prisoners came on board, escorted by a detachment from a Wisconsin regiment and destined for St. Louis. We stopped several times to take on wood and also to load freight on board; also in Cape Girardeau, which we reached at eight o'clock in the morning, where we had to load four new ten-pounder cannons from the Allegheny arsenal.[14]

During this time we went on shore and greeted our comrades from the regiment stationed here. There was quite a bit of excitement; "general march" was struck this morning. The nine weak companies of our regiment, one company from the First Wisconsin Cavalry, and one from the Second Missouri Artillery Regiment made up the entire garrison. General Marmaduke is supposed to threaten this place; General Price, on the other hand, Ironton.[15] Forty men of the Second Missouri Cavalry Regiment were cut off by the rebels yesterday and taken captive not very far from the town, where Lieutenant Colonel Baumer is in command.

After this short stop we again moved on. We soon took on a considerable quantity of firewood, and at sunset we reached Chester, located on a high, steep bluff on the Illinois side of the river. Here, for the first time since my trip from New York, I set foot again on the free soil of the state of Illinois. To celebrate the event we drank a glass of miserable beer. Here the boat took on board a number of barrels of flour and then went upstream.

Friday, April 24—At sunrise we were awakened by the call "St. Louis!" We packed up our things, shouldered our rifles, and made our way to our old barracks. Here we found confirmed what we had heard in Cape Girardeau, namely, that our company would be

14. Because Scherneckau describes them as "ten-pounder cannons," the guns were probably three-inch Parrotts, commonly called "ten-pounder Parrotts." They were rifled, muzzle-loading field guns made at Robert P. Parrott's West Point Foundry. Hazlett, Olmstead, and Parks, *Field Artillery Weapons,* chapter 8. The Allegheny arsenal was at Pittsburgh, Pennsylvania.

15. Confederate general John S. Marmaduke, commander of the cavalry division, District of Arkansas, launched a raid into southeastern Missouri from his base in northeastern Arkansas. Although he threatened Union garrisons at Patterson, Bloomfield, and Cape Girardeau, and his troops fought several engagements with Union forces, the raid was a failure. Bailey, "Texans Invade Missouri." Confederate general Sterling Price, who led the Missouri State Guard at the outbreak of war, played a prominent part in battles and campaigns west of the Mississippi River, including Wilson's Creek, Lexington, Pea Ridge, Helena, and his 1864 Missouri raid. At this time Price commanded a division in the District of Arkansas. Sifakis, *Who Was Who in the Confederacy,* 231.

provost guard in St. Louis. Hence, they had left their old quarters and moved to the quarters of the provost guard on Washington Street, between Fifth and Sixth streets. There we found our comrades and our breakfast. On the entire trip we had nothing but bread and cold ham as well as sweet tea, for we tapped hot water from the steam boiler of the boat on some tea and sweetened it very strongly. Ten days' rations had barely lasted for six days.

Not only did we find the members of our company (H) here but also men from almost all companies of our regiment. They had gradually transported prisoners up here from Cape Girardeau and then were attached to our company. We take this as an indication that our entire regiment is destined to come here.

Our quarters as provost guard are in a very nice building in the middle of the city. The first floor, a one-time store whose windows consist of four huge glass panes, each as tall as a man and almost as wide, serves us as dining hall. The upper four floors serve as quarters, where we are housed by twos, fours, and so on, according to the size of the room. A comfortable stairway with mahogany railings leads to all floors and reminds me vividly of the spiral staircase in my parents' home. In short, the building is brilliantly set up but already badly damaged since it is used as a barracks. Captain Ivory has returned to his company and has the direct command.

I wrote in my diary and to Hedde and Egge. In the evening I was sent to the levee with five more men and a sergeant to inform all the boats there not to go downstream until further orders. A few captains, however, had special permission certificates from headquarters, and therefore we had to let them leave. Having taken this walk, we returned to our quarters. All nonessential troops have left St. Louis, even the greater part of the Thirty-seventh Iowa Regiment, the Graybeards. The old boys gasped under the large haversacks [when they marched] toward the Iron Mountain Railway station, as we arrived this morning.

Saturday, April 25—Three regiments came through here last night on the way from Rolla to Pilot Knob. Three regiments of Missouri militia have been put in service here in the city and three regiments each to guard the Iron Mountain Railway and three more to guard the railway leading to Rolla. The Graybeards have been moved to the Jefferson Barracks.[16] Here in the city everybody is in a state of greatest excitement.

I was not on duty today, and therefore I took some walks through the city. The evening was wonderful, and I enjoyed the lovely evening air until late at night. I wrote to Martin. St. Louis now looks ready for war. The militia, which has been called out, is gathering here; infantry and cavalry patrols pass through the streets. The guards were doubled around McDowell College and cannons brought up in the streets leading to it.[17] An uprising of the rebellious population was expected, since the leaders of the secessionists circulated rumors about the advance of the rebel generals Price and Marmaduke and attempted thereby to provoke disorder.

At sunset we had retreat as usual and, soon afterward, drill and parade through the streets, probably just to show what a well-trained provost guard was now maintaining order in the city! By the way, most of us desire that the secessionist gentlemen would let themselves go somewhat and give us an opportunity to step in. Our patrols had strict orders to arrest anyone who should make some disloyal remarks. The guards in the theaters had strict orders as well.

Sunday, April 26—It rained a little until about noon. As always there was the routine Sunday inspection by the captain. I had to go on guard duty. Three men and a corporal were sent to the office of the provost marshal general to take up honor guard. This place was on Fifth Street, just a block from our quarters here where I am writing this. For the first time, therefore, I stood honor guard on one of the busiest streets of the big city. I now had to salute, since many officers to whom the befitting honor had to be given hurried here and there.

Telegraphic reports that Cape Girardeau had been attacked arrived late in the evening, but the enemy had been beaten. Reinforcements under the command of our Colonel Livingston left

16. Jefferson Barracks, the largest military base west of the Mississippi, lay eight miles south of St. Louis. Gerteis, *Civil War St. Louis*, 1, 85.

17. As noted earlier, this former medical college at Eighth and Gratiot streets was being used as a Union military prison.

Gratiot Street Prison, Eighth and Gratiot streets, St. Louis (formerly McDowell's Medical College). Photograph by Emil Boehl, ca. 1868. VM90-000341, Neg. # PB111-14. Missouri Historical Society, St. Louis.

here for that place. Unfortunately we have to stay here and cannot participate in the fight in which our regiment has been involved. Most of those here would gladly have taken part in it, but who would have thought that such a sizable force would have attacked us there. We had a good night; slept in a corridor of the building.

Monday, April 27—More news arrived in the morning with the morning papers. It is said that our troops had beaten back an attack on Cape Girardeau with great loss to the enemy. This can hardly be otherwise, because I know the area. Our fortifications completely controlled the access roads and surrounding region. Twenty of our men are presumed wounded or killed. Naturally we are curious to find out more.[18]

This morning at eight o'clock I was relieved. I sent today's morning paper to Hedde. Paid Mr. Olshausen a visit in his office and found him very busy. Then I wrote in my diary and to Egge. Took various walks through the city; thunderstorm in the evening and rain during the night

Tuesday, April 28—The comrades previously attached to our company from other companies of our regiment went back to the regiment this morning, reducing our numbers significantly. Nothing to do. I again took walks through the city, mostly along the very busy levee. According to today's papers, three from our regiment were killed and three were wounded. I am acquainted with some of them.

In the evening I had patrol duty with some of the others. We had to visit the St. Louis Theater to arrest soldiers who are found there without a pass. There we got into an argument with the owner, who did not want to allow us to enter the hall with our rifles. Naturally we did not want to leave our weapons behind and sent a man back to get a ruling concerning a further course of action, since such a development had not been anticipated in our instructions. Since neither our captain nor the provost marshal could be found, it took a long time until we received instructions, and the play was over when they finally came. They were as follows:

18. The overall campaign is discussed in Bailey, "Texans Invade Missouri." The reports of the Union and Confederate officers are in *OR*, ser. 1, vol. 22, part 1. Lieutenant Colonel Baumer commanded the First Nebraska troops that were engaged, and his report appears in the same volume, pp. 267–69. He reported three killed and seven wounded. Dudley, *Roster of Nebraska Volunteers*, 18–19, 108–9, lists only two men killed in action at Cape Girardeau, Henry F. Smith of Company A, and Martin Agon of Company I.

we were to force entrance if we were refused and arrest everyone who resisted us and take them away to our jail. Tomorrow evening we will proceed accordingly.

The gentleman who denied us entry is supposed to be a good secessionist. I hope we shall meet him again, since I have obtained permission to be part of the action. It would do me some good to show the rude fellow the power of the bayonet. Not only did our captain send us this peremptory command but also a sergeant with four more men for reinforcement. He himself was on the way to the "war scene" when we met him and reported that the performance was over.

Wednesday, April 29—Today a comrade and I went for a walk out to the famous Benton Barracks, a creation of Fremont's, to whom Missouri owes so much. Similar fortifications set up around Cape Girardeau have just recently proven to be effective during Marmaduke's attack as the main support for our small garrison there. Twenty-five hundred against eight thousand of the enemy; where would we have been had we not been at that well-fortified post? That too was one of the so very costly and unnecessary expenses of the Fremont administration.[19] This barracks-camp, long rows of wooden houses inside a board fence on the former fairgrounds, is designed for eight to ten thousand men, and stables are at hand for two thousand horses. Furthermore, there are large open parade grounds, also splendid hospital buildings and still more.[20]

19. Marmaduke had only some four thousand men under arms during his Missouri raid, no infantry, and little chance of taking well-fortified Cape Girardeau. Bailey, "Texans Invade Missouri," 172. Scherneckau is being sarcastic by his reference to "Fremont's unnecessary expenses," although, in fact, Fremont had been implicated in fraudulent contracts for the construction of fortifications around St. Louis in 1861, contributing to his dismissal as commander of the Western Department. Shannon, *Organization and Administration,* 1:62–63.

Nevertheless, Fremont's attempt to effect immediate emancipation in Missouri had made him popular with many Germans, who were outraged when he was relieved from command. Bärner, "A Forty-Eighter Who Returned," 97–98.

20. Benton Barracks, located at the northern edge of St. Louis near the fairgrounds, was established by General Fremont and named in honor of his father-in-law, the former Missouri senator Thomas Hart Benton. The complex included five rows of barracks, plus warehouses, hospitals, and stables. Nearby was one of

At the time there were not many men there, only about twenty-five hundred war prisoners under guard, who were waiting to be exchanged in order to take up arms again.[21] The place is nicely laid out to some extent, with beautiful shade trees. Carefully tended lawns and parks surround the hospitals, offices, and residences of the officials. The barracks for the men consist of long rows of one-story wooden buildings, constructed in the same style as the Schofield Barracks I have previously described. It is fully three miles from the center of the city to this place. A horse-drawn tram goes to the main entrance, and for ten cents we secured our return trip to our quarters. Lovely houses with gardens built in the varied tastes and all kinds of styles beautify and to a degree disfigure these outer ends of the metropolis.

It was noon when we returned. In the afternoon, along with a detail, I had to straighten up the interior courtyard of the building where we live and clean it a bit. The floor was then dusted generously with chloride of lime to absorb a little of the stench raked up and to improve the air in the building.

In the evening the expedition, with the appropriate orders and a troop determined to carry them out, went to the theater. The scene from yesterday evening recurred; however, it ended differently this time. As the fine gentleman tried to hinder our access, he was taken by the collar, and without making a fuss, we transported him to our guardhouse. Then we returned and carried out our orders without further hindrance; however, we found only one

---

the several forts Fremont had ordered erected in a semicircle around St. Louis. Winter, *The Civil War in St. Louis*, 73–75.

21. Under an 1862 agreement between the U.S. and Confederate governments, captured soldiers could be "paroled" back to their own armies under the promise not to take up arms again until "exchanged" for an equivalent number of parolees from the other side. The exchange system broke down when the Confederates refused to include captured black Union soldiers under its provisions. Nevertheless, exchanges still took place until Union army commander Gen. Ulysses S. Grant suspended them in the fall of 1864. McPherson, *Ordeal by Fire*, 450–56. The men Scherneckau mentions were Union soldiers paroled by the Confederates. In 1862 Benton Barracks was named one of three Union parole camps where paroled soldiers were housed until they were formally exchanged. The men were probably under guard to prevent desertion. Winter, *The Civil War in St. Louis*, 73.

soldier without a pass. At that point we continued our patrol until after midnight, visiting all kinds of public houses without further results. Everyone who had no pass knew how to disappear one way or another as we approached.

Thursday, April 30—On guard duty today; had the same post again at the provost marshal's office. Today our Lieutenant Moore came up from Cape Girardeau and brought us interesting news. Our colonel is back as well. At three thirty in the afternoon, our post was recalled to be reviewed with the rest of the company. After we had first drilled a bit, Colonel Livingston and our Major Blacker, came and Colonel L. proceeded with the roll call.[22] After the review was over, we had to return to our post. Slept quite well there. We had a nice day, and the night was the same.

Recently our patrols have arrested many soldiers, often up to twenty in one night. The strict orders read to bring in any soldier found without a pass, furthermore, disloyal and drunken men. The U.S. Secret Police, who are much more familiar with the situation, help us in many ways and sometimes must also rely on our support.[23]

One of these detectives was constantly with the regiment last winter and made the tour down to Arkansas with us. Most considered him to be a loafer, or rather a professional gambler, who toiled with us in order to relieve the men of their money after payday at a convenient time. More informed men mentioned then that he was with the secret police and was pursuing an entirely different matter. After we had arrived in St. Genevieve on the Mississippi, he left us. And I only saw him here again since we are acting as provost guard and thus have come into contact with the police.

Many funny but also unpleasant scenes now take place as we carry out our daily patrols. Often it is necessary to use the rifle butt or bayonet to deal with rough characters. Through these nightly

22. Allen Blacker enlisted in 1861 as captain of Company D. He was promoted to major on October 4, 1862. He resigned March 1, 1865. Dudley, *Roster of Nebraska Volunteers*, 4–5.

23. Probably the U.S. Secret Service, organized by Allan Pinkerton to conduct intelligence operations. Faust, *Encyclopedia of the Civil War*, 586.

patrols I have become familiar with the darker side of a large city. Dives of all kinds, dark passageways and cellars, secret dance halls in back premises are the scenes of our nightly venture. We find our men in these places. Rarely do we meet resistance; sometimes we have problems only with drunken individuals. The female occupants of these houses were usually the only ones who protested vehemently when we led one of their visitors away. The soldier we get hold of without a pass knows we cannot do differently but take him with us, and therefore he is silent and surrenders to his fate. But still many escape, since these "dens" have so many exits that it is difficult for the guard to cut off the culprits' retreat.

Friday, May 1—Glorious weather, like yesterday. Was relieved this morning, wrote in my diary, polished the weapons, and slept the rest of the time. Toward evening we had steady rain, also during the night.

We now are hearing more and more details about the last battle at Cape Girardeau, and these are, of course, of great interest to us. All reports agree that our comrades have demonstrated great courage and that it is not just newspaper humbug. In the western army, without offending other regiments who are certainly just as competent if not better, our brigade consisting of the Eighth Missouri, Eleventh Indiana, and the First Nebraska has an especially good reputation when it comes to bravery and military training. Lieutenant Colonel Baumer was in command, and all reports agree that he was as cool-headed as if he were on the drill ground with us. In fact, the battle scene had been our old drill ground for regimental drill, and we had run over the same place in skirmish exercises, which was now undertaken by our skirmishers in deadly seriousness.

Only five companies of our regiment actually got into the battle. Two on the extreme left and two companies on the right flank had no opportunity to fire even one shot. The troops actually engaged, however, advanced so close to each other that they shouted out insults, at the same time looking for an opportunity to shoot at one another. Welfley's battery from the First Missouri Artillery Regiment did its best to control the entire area, stationed advantageously as it was. This is one of the batteries that made the march with us last winter. The admiration of the men for Colonel Baumer

Lt. Col. William Baumer. RG2411-7265, Nebraska State Historical Society, Lincoln. Digitally enhanced.

has most likely increased to a higher level than it already was. But why sum up still more details; the newspapers already will have provided more detailed reports before this gets into your hands.[24]

In the evening I was with a patrol to the Varieties Theater, where we arrested some twenty men who had managed to obtain admission without passes. Our jail was overflowing, but the larger part of the prisoners was released by the provost marshal's office during the night. All commissioned officers discovered without a pass must also give their name, rank, and regiment and must report the next morning at eight o'clock at the office of the provost marshal. Lieutenant Moore of our company is in charge of this part of our every-evening program.

The presentation, farces, ballets, fireworks, Negro songs, and dances were just bad, not what one would expect in a city like St. Louis. The theater was smaller than the one in Kiel and also not as elegantly decorated. Not only were the scenery and costumes bad; the numbers themselves were raw in word and action, common, and poorly played. It should not be permitted to produce such miserable things. Of course, ladies were not present in the audience, although most of the presenters were ladies. But the serving in those places was done entirely by girls, who brought the drinks to wherever something was ordered.[25] It was midnight before we were back in our quarters.

Saturday, May 2—I had guard duty this morning. Here in our quarters ten men and two corporals are stationed regularly to provide the necessary patrols and to guard possible prisoners or to escort them to wherever they are being transferred from here. Therefore, each of us had to be on our post for some two and a half hours of the twenty-four and had to patrol about three hours. In the evening I was with a patrol under the command of our lieutenant, off to the

24. He means that Nebraska newspapers with reports, and perhaps some soldiers' letters, describing the Battle of Cape Girardeau would already have reached his friends and relatives in the Grand Island settlement before he sent this installment of his diary.

25. This theater was probably the Varieties Music Hall, which featured "burlesque, can-can dancing, and sexy jokes." Van Ravenswaay, *St. Louis*, 537.

various theaters. However, we took no prisoners; it was the same way during the day, when we brought in only a few men.

Sunday, May 3—This morning, inspection as usual. I read and slept almost the whole day. How I shall get used to work again after such lazy life will be difficult. To lie around, sleep, or go for a walk is now the order of the day just to kill time. My hands are soft and delicate now, totally weaned from hard work.

In the evening several comrades and I visited a Methodist church not far from here. It was the most elegant church interior I have seen so far; yet there was generally no decoration on the walls, altar, or pulpit. Sixty gas flames in four large chandeliers gave a brilliant light. The floor was covered with a beautiful carpet, the seats and pews elegantly executed, lacquered, and covered with pillows of red damask. A small organ accompanied the choir of men and women. The sermon was pretty much unintelligible to me.[26]

After this was over and I had returned to our quarters, I felt so little inclination to sleep that I went out with a comrade. This time we took one of the Seventh Street cars in order to drive to the arsenal on the lower southern end of the city. It was about nine thirty and a beautiful night.[27]

Right next to the arsenal there is an amusement park, called Arsenal Park, coupled with a dance hall that is managed by Germans in the German manner. There was dancing, and, of course, the "gentlemen" soldiers were numerous. In the spacious pavilion was noisy dance music, _____ dances; in the adjoining rooms beer was being drunk. In short, it had great resemblance to the

26. This was the Methodist Church South. Thomas E. Keen, who evidently was one of the comrades who accompanied Scherneckau to the church, described the pastor's effort as "a kind of milk and water Copperhead sermon." Potter, "I Thought It My Duty," 157.

27. The U.S. arsenal at St. Louis was a major depot during the Mexican War and for later military campaigns in the West. Protection of the arsenal, and the munitions stored there, from Missouri secessionists was a major concern of U.S. authorities in early 1861. The arsenal was the assembly point from which regular and volunteer troops under Capt. Nathaniel Lyon marched on May 10, 1861, to surround and capture Missouri militia in what became known as the "Camp Jackson Affair." Winter, *The Civil War in St. Louis*, 34–54, esp. 38–40.

establishments in St. Pauli and at other places in Hamburg. Here as there, the same class of ladies made up the female dancers exclusively. Drunken soldiers without passes were here in great numbers. It is three miles to our quarters, and none of our patrols had ever disrupted the pleasures here. Our enthusiasm for duty did not go so far as to walk back that distance. Since we had stayed here too long, we found out that the tram was no longer running and now we had no choice but to march home on foot. Genuinely tired, we got back to our quarters after one o'clock, where I slept quite well the rest of the night.

Monday, May 4—Today on guard duty; had to patrol and stand on post for several hours. Wrote to Egge. The day passed as usual. Got to bed late, since we had to make an extended excursion through the most notorious neighborhoods of the city, whereby we got hold of various drunks.

Tuesday, May 5—Slept, read, and walked around a little. Today it was unusually cold for the season and so far south—true Nebraska March weather.

Wednesday, May 6—Today, still just as cold as yesterday. A coat is comfortable during the whole day. On guard duty, had the post in front of the office of the provost marshal. Had to salute a lot. Officers of all ranks from the last lieutenant to major general come and go.

It should be mentioned that all garden vegetables are already available here, despite the weather still being so cold. Lettuce, asparagus, spinach, onions, radishes, watercress, and others were available three weeks ago when we arrived here. I have seen the finest cauliflower, large firm heads, the first I recall having seen here, that is, in America. Excellent bundles of asparagus, displayed at the vegetable markets, make my mouth water every time I pass by there.

Our meals here are not very good. It is more the quality of the rations that we have received here in recent times than the preparation, although this also leaves something to be desired. Two of our own men take care of the cooking, but it is not as good as we had with the same rations, for example, in Schofield Barracks. Here we have been supplied with corn processed in still another way than the grits, of which I believe I have already written you. This is called hominy. This corn is only hulled and is just like the groats of wheat or barley. We received it instead of beans cooked with the meat. I think cooked with milk it must be quite tasty.[28]

The day passed as usual. In the evening we had a bit more excitement as often happens naturally in such a large city and under these situations. At about eight o'clock nearly all were already in their quarters, partly in bed. I was on the fourth floor, chatting with some friends, when suddenly a cry resounded that set our teeth on edge. "Murder, murder," "help, help," and at the same time a turmoil emerged on the street. Below in the guardroom the command sounded, "Guard, fall in." Everyone hurried down the stairs, rifle in hand, putting on cartridge pouches and bayonet. While I, with another man, was coming out first, the crowd of people just turned the nearest corner on Sixth Street. Since we assumed that one of our men was screaming for help and was perhaps being mistreated, we ran, without waiting for the others, and made our way through the crowd of people by using our bayonets, which had been fixed in the meantime.

We soon saw the cause for the mob. Two men were carrying off a Negro by force. A carriage was standing at the corner of the block, apparently to pick up him and his persecutors, but it drove off at high speed when they saw that we had stopped the kidnappers. It was clear and simple kidnapping, as is, unfortunately, still carried out here too often. The poor blacks know that the Union soldiers are mostly friends and almost always helpers when they are in trouble. Therefore, the poor fellow was delighted and shouted, when he saw our bayonets flashing about him—since by now at least a dozen of our men were on the spot—"Massa, now I am alright. I got my papers. These men have no right to take me."

The man who had arrested him now identified himself as a deputy constable of some county in the interior of Missouri. He

28. He had forgotten that he had previously eaten hominy on December 17, 1862, during the expedition in southeastern Missouri.

had warrants to arrest and return five or six Negroes who had run away from their owners. However, he had no right to detain free Negroes here who did not match the description in the arrest warrant [that he was claiming] had given him the authority to drag this black away from his family. Mr. Constable acted very surprised when the Negro, in our presence, now pulled out his pocket book and produced a completely valid pass and free paper issued by General Curtis, since he had been the property of a rebel in this state.[29] Enraged, he asked the black why he had not presented them earlier. He replied that they had not given him the opportunity to produce them. Besides, he had been afraid that they would have taken them away from him and destroyed them, whereby he would have then become completely defenseless. We took the Negro with the constable to the provost marshal, where the Negro could prove his identity sufficiently and was set free. What happened to the constable, I don't know.

I was really happy to have come to the aid of the poor devil at the right time, for if the white kidnappers had reached the carriage with him, he most likely would have been finished, and his free paper would have been of no use. Most of our men were on the side of the Negro, although they were unhappy to have run head over heels for a d——d nigger. Besides, they certainly would not have been quick as a flash had they known that it just concerned the weal and woe of a Negro family. That's the way Americans are. Their hatred for the Negro is, for the most part, hardly less than the hatred they bear for our enemies, the Southern

29. The Lincoln administration grappled with how to deal with slavery in Missouri. Because it did not want to alienate loyal slave owners or conditional unionists, Missouri was to be allowed to adopt a policy of gradual, compensated emancipation. The problem for Union authorities in Missouri lay in determining the status of blacks entering their lines. Slaves employed by the Confederates and captured by Union forces were considered contraband of war. Slaves who had escaped from their owners in one of the rebel states were, after January 1, 1863, freed by the Emancipation Proclamation. Slaves owned by disloyal persons in Missouri were freed under the Second Confiscation Act. Slaves owned by loyal persons in Missouri were to be treated with a "hands-off" policy for the time being. Former slaves of disloyal Missourians or escapees from rebel owners could be issued "free papers." A thorough discussion of this issue appears in Gerteis, *Civil War St. Louis*, chapter 9, esp. 277–78.

brethren. "I never was so glad in my life," the Negro said to us after he had obtained his freedom, "as when I saw the guard coming around me," and indeed he could congratulate himself; a horrible fate awaited him if the soul-merchants had succeeded in getting him out of St. Louis.

Last night [May 5] under the direct orders of the captain of our company, a strong detail of us made a round through the fashionable gambling halls. These night patrols are now armed with a navy revolver in addition to their rifles. However, we encountered no resistance anywhere; five to six fine gentlemen gamblers were arrested, and a quantity of cards, dice, etc., confiscated.

Thursday, May 7—Today before breakfast two of us were sent with three prisoners to Schofield Barracks. From there all of our prisoners are transferred on to their different assigned places. The day was spent with sleeping, reading, taking walks; boredom is taking the upper hand.

Friday, May 8—Glorious weather; loafing as usual. Some forty of our regiment came up from Cape Girardeau escorting secesh prisoners. From them we now hear more details about the participation of our men in the last battle. Our regiment pursued the rebels to the border of Arkansas, where they were engaged in a battle near Chalk Bluff. Two from our side were wounded, while the rebels, according to the statements of the prisoners, buried eighteen dead there.[30]

Saturday, May 9—Today I had no guard duty. A company from the Twenty-third Missouri Regiment is now stationed here and, together with us, carries out the provost guard duty. The captain of the above commands the whole so that the headquarter is in their barracks, corner of Fifth and Pine streets, a nice roomy residence

30. Dudley, *Roster of Nebraska Volunteers*, 72–73, 84–85, reports that Edwin Brown of Company F and Lewis Cunningham of Company G were wounded at Chalk Bluff. There was no major battle but some skirmishing as Union troops pressed the Confederate retreat across the St. Francis River into Arkansas. Bailey, "Texans Invade Missouri," 182–86.

with a yard, garden, and outbuildings, the confiscated property of a rebel. Therefore, we had to march to that place, and there we were assigned to our respective posts. We were lounging around there all day without doing any duty. Not until nine o'clock in the evening were we sent out on patrol, where we walked the streets until twelve o'clock and then went to our quarters and to bed.

The comrades from our regiment who are present here are reciting an accident that took place there [in Cape Girardeau] this week. A fellow member of Company C killed a comrade of the same company with a revolver, which he had handled carelessly in the tent.[31]

Sunday, May 10—Warm weather and very dusty, since today the streets were not sprinkled like on other days, which then dampens the dust and brings some cooling relief at the same time. The day passed in the same way as nearly all Sundays; in the evening the obligatory inspection and after that some drill.

At nightfall I went to the evening service, this time to the Union Methodist Episcopal Church, corner of Eleventh and Locust streets, the one I had heard favorable remarks about. This church is considerably larger and furnished more luxuriously inside than the one I visited last Sunday. Soldiers were treated especially warmly and, upon entering, were taken at once to the best front seats. Our ranks were, therefore, well represented, and even quite a few officers were in attendance, including Major General Herron, if I am not mistaken.[32]

The evening speaker was introduced to the congregation by the pastor, after he had delivered a really moving prayer. It was Senator Harlan of Iowa.[33] He is a very skilled speaker, and the sermon

31. The dead soldier was Corp. Israel Prince of Company C, who enlisted from Mt. Vernon, Nebraska Territory. Dudley, *Roster of Nebraska Volunteers*, 32–33.

32. Francis Jay Herron of Iowa commanded the Third Division, Army of the Frontier, Department of the Missouri, from October 12, 1862, to February 1863. Promoted to major general of volunteers, he commanded the Army of the Frontier from March 30, 1863, to June 5, 1863. Sifakis, *Who Was Who in the Union*, 194.

33. Republican James Harlan, who resigned from the Senate May 15, 1865, to become secretary of the interior. Sifakis, *Who Was Who in the Union*, 177.

was more a political speech than a sermon. He talked about the sins of the nation, which had brought on the current war as punishment. Among the principal sins of which we are guilty as a nation, he appropriately emphasized slavery, of course, and urged the inhabitants of this state to end it and not to let the great opportunity for emancipation pass by. Furthermore, he then made a sarcastic remark to the officers present about blasphemous talk and cursing, which is heard from the lowest lieutenant to the general, and that regulations emphatically forbid this! Such shocking behavior surely could not bring a blessing upon our arms, etc.

I believe this is the first sermon in my young life that I have followed with such an interest. To listen to such speeches and at the same time be seated leisurely on a soft seat is indeed worth the trouble of going to church. As I have already mentioned, this church is furnished with the utmost luxury, all for the comfort of the congregation. A large, full- and well-sounding organ accompanied the singing by a good choir of gentlemen and ladies. The pulpit for the preacher reminded me in some ways of the seats set up for the members of the Schleswig-Holstein government in the castle church in Kiel in order to attend the proceedings of the provisional assembly. Here too, velvet armchairs stood in a semicircle, while the background was draped with the Union flag over red damask. This political humbug in the church has its effect and draws a full house every time, as this evening, when it was packed.

I should also mention that we had some kind of service in our dining hall in the afternoon, where three individuals appeared and announced their intention to deliver a sermon. As a result some twelve to fifteen of us showed up and listened to a dull and incoherent presentation, as well as the singing of some hymns, whereupon the improvised reverends took their leave.

Monday, May 11—Today the anniversary of the capture of Camp Jackson was celebrated.[34] You probably will have already seen in

34. Camp Jackson at St. Louis had been named for Claiborne F. Jackson, secessionist governor of Missouri. He refused Lincoln's call for troops and began training state militia at Camp Jackson. U.S. regulars, along with Union volunteers and home guards (mostly St. Louis Germans), surrounded the camp and made

the papers a detailed account of the large festival parade long before this reaches your hands. The parade passed us here at our quarters. I was on guard duty in these quarters, where we maintain a post in front of the building. Besides, almost all the men were on duty, since the company of the Twenty-third Missouri Regiment, otherwise assigned to us, was involved in the festivities.

Tuesday, May 12—After I had stood my four hours during the night, I was relieved this morning. In the morning I slept and read; in the afternoon I wrote to Egge and in the diary. The weather by now is quite warm, so that even the nights cool off only little. The morning papers are now virtually devoured because of the events taking place in the East, without giving some explanation about the battles fought on the Rappahannock. The rumor spread here on Saturday and Sunday about the capture of Richmond, however, proved to be a newspaper hoax. The spirit of the Know-Nothings is rising again. The opportunity for that came when the Eleventh Army Corps, at the first attack, had been accused of panic and the Germans, for the most part, were blamed.[35]

Unfortunately we also have one or two "alien-haters" in our company, as I discovered yesterday.[36] But the majority is quite decent and on my side, since many of them are descendants from

---

prisoners of the Missouri militia on May 10, 1861, leading to violence between Union troops and St. Louis civilians in the aftermath. The Camp Jackson affair is discussed in Gerteis, *Civil War St. Louis,* chapter 4, and Winter, *The Civil War in St. Louis,* 34–54. The celebration Scherneckau mentions was the Camp Jackson Rally marking the second anniversary of the Union seizure of the camp. Theodor Olshausen helped organize the rally, and many German Americans participated. Bärner, "A Forty-Eighter Who Returned," 98.

35. The Know-Nothings were a nativist, anti-immigration party. Naturally Scherneckau was sensitive to criticism of the many Union soldiers who were Germans. He refers here to the Eleventh Corps of the Army of the Potomac, commanded by Gen. Oliver O. Howard, which included a large number of Germans. At the Battle of Chancellorsville on May 2, 1863, Howard's corps was on the right of the Union army and was routed by a flank attack by Stonewall Jackson's Confederates, leading to charges that the German soldiers were cowardly or incompetent. Sifakis, *Who Was Who in the Union,* 203.

36. Scherneckau probably overheard some disparaging remarks about Germans, prompted by their role in the 1861 seizure of Camp Jackson and their heavy participation in the Camp Jackson Rally anniversary observance.

Germans and other immigrants, and even if they only speak English, they often have parents or brothers and sisters who still speak our or another language besides English. Though it makes me very depressed to hear such narrow-minded and often-hostile attitudes expressed against my fellow countrymen, it was not really directed against me personally. The *St. Louis Republican* is clearly a medium of these people and carries infamous articles against the Germans.[37]

37. Despite its name, the *Missouri Republican* (St. Louis) was a Democratic newspaper. Scherneckau had probably seen articles in that paper critical of the St. Louis Germans and the city's German newspapers, which favored emancipation, the enlistment of black soldiers, and other "radical" war measures.

CHAPTER 8

Banishing the Secessionists, May 13–20, 1863

Wednesday, May 13—On guard duty again today. Suddenly, around noon, an order came for twenty-five men to get ready for immediate departure and an absence of at least twenty days. At one o'clock we lined up in front of the provost marshal's office, thirty-two men altogether, under the command of our captain. At this time we were informed about our assignment. We were supposed to take disloyal persons, who had been arrested one by one, in part by us, down the river and outside of our lines.[1] Several smaller details were sent out to bring the gentlemen, previously set free on parole, on board the steamer.

I marched with the larger detail to the McDowell College, so well known to us, where we took custody of eight gentlemen secessionists. From there we went to the Myrtle Street prison, where we received six more with whom we marched through town to the boat.[2] As we left Myrtle Street, our drummer struck up, and the shrill fifes joined in. However, they were interrupted in their play-

1. Thomas E. Keen of Scherneckau's company was also part of this detachment, and his account of escorting the civilians from St. Louis appears in his May 23, 1863, letter in Potter, "I Thought It My Duty," 155–57. Federal banishment policy in St. Louis is discussed in Gerteis, *Civil War St. Louis,* 178–86. Correspondence relating to banishment is in *OR,* ser. 2, vol. 5, pp. 319–21, 515, 537–39, 599–600, 954–55.

2. The *Missouri Democrat* (St. Louis) and *Missouri Republican* (St. Louis), both May 14, 1863, listed thirteen men: Charles Clark, James S. Daugherty, Daniel H. Donovan, George W. Dutro, Henry N. Hart, Mortimer Kennett, Owen Mency, Dr. S. Gratz Moses, Isaac J. Pollard, Christian Pullis, Samuel Robbins, Linton Sappington, and Christian Shaffer. Cited in Winter, *The Civil War in St. Louis,* 165n102.

ing, since Major McKenny, who had the command over the entire expedition, forbade it.[3] He did not want to attract unnecessary attention, since it already caused quite a stir when we led a number of civilians under such strong military escort through the main streets of the city. Many of them were well-known persons and among the wealthiest people of the city. Indeed, the excitement and tumult became so great that before we reached the levee the captain had to give orders to fix bayonets in order to make way and keep the pushing crowd at a distance. On the whole it was more curiosity and the desire to make fun of the prisoners that caused the mob to press around us, rather than any serious intention to set them free. On the contrary, it was a mob consisting mostly of the riff-raff of the city, which would rather have attacked them. One officer of our army with the insignia of an infantry major became so violent and insulting that, upon our captain's command, we arrested him and took him with us on board of our boat. This was ready for departure, and the large military detachment that was already on board met us and thus made it possible for us to reach it, since they cleared the way through the dense crowd.

In the cabin of the boat we set our gentlemen prisoners free, where they found several of their soul mates, among them a number of ladies who are so strongly spellbound by the South that the government decided to have them transported there. These ladies were brought on board by the U.S. police officers. Five obstinate Southern ladies, who had not accepted the parole that had been offered, had been left behind in the Chestnut Street female prison, and now were also brought on board by two of our men in an omnibus.[4]

3. Thomas I. McKenny had been a second lieutenant in the Second Iowa Infantry and was appointed an aide-de-camp to Gen. Samuel Curtis in 1862. He later rose to the rank of brigadier general of volunteers. Heitman, *Historical Register*, 1:672.

4. Thomas E. Keen was one of the two soldiers. For his account of the encounter with the women, see Potter, "I Thought It My Duty," 156. The Chestnut Street "female prison" was really the home of Mrs. Margaret McLure, one of the women being banished. Ten other women completed the group: Mrs. Charles Clark, Mrs. Addie M. Haynes, Mrs. R. Lowden, Miss Harriet Snodgrass, Mrs. Lily Frost, Mrs. Joseph Chaytor, Mrs. Montrose Pallen, Mrs. David Sappington, Mrs. William Smizer, and Miss Lucie Nicholson. Some were the wives of Confederate officers. Winter, *The Civil War in St. Louis*, 85–86.

At about five thirty in the evening the *Belle of Memphis* left St. Louis with us. Since it is a U.S. mail boat, we docked at nearly every landing. Of course, we had to set guards every time to prevent the gentlemen from going ashore. Furthermore, we had a post by our weapons and baggage and one in the salon of the steamer to maintain peace and order there. This is a medium-sized boat with side wheels, furnished inside most brilliantly. The gentlemen secesh enjoyed this, since they are all rich men. Naturally there was a lot of handshaking and farewells before we departed, and two or three times the order was given to drive away with the bayonet all citizens who did not belong on board. This helped a little and reduced the crowd around the guards. A German, a wholesale liquor dealer, is among these "friends of the South" and nearly the most hostile of all.

We also found our Negro robber in this group. I believe I have already told the story how, a few days ago, we rescued a poor devil of a Negro from the hands of an alleged constable. We then brought the man to the provost marshal, who deemed it proper to send him to Dixie, where nigger kidnapping is perhaps more popular. By the way, our aristocratic prisoners praised us greatly for the protection that we and our captain had provided against the insults of the people on the way to the boat.

Thursday, May 14—We were moving on all night, stopping frequently. This morning at eight o'clock we arrived at Cape Girardeau, where we greeted our comrades. We stopped there for about half an hour, since a great deal of freight was to be loaded and unloaded. I took the opportunity and went into town. There in the office of the provost marshal I met the now famous General McNeil.[5] At present our comrades stationed here are going up and down the river, sinking or otherwise destroying all [small] boats and flatboats to prevent ferrying across and smuggling from

5. Brig. Gen. John McNeil. Sifakis, *Who Was Who in the Union*, 259–60. His "fame" probably derived from his having ordered the execution of ten men at Palmyra, Missouri, on October 18, 1862, in retaliation for the presumed murder of a Union man. The episode became known as the Palmyra Massacre. Winter, *The Civil War in St. Louis*, 114.

the Illinois bank. Several times they have captured supplies from the rebels and taken away horses from them too.

Our trip promises to be very interesting, the weather is nice, and nature is at its finest. A little past noon we came to Cairo. There was a lot of activity; locomotives and steamboats competed with one another in blowing their whistles. Six to eight steam gunboats lay at anchor at the mouth of the Ohio. They were of all sizes, from small tugboats with only makeshift armor of iron plates on the boiler to the new monitor *Osage,* just recently here from St. Louis.[6]

After we had finished our business, we again went back downstream the Mississippi. Shortly before sunset we reached Columbus. Above the city are the fortifications set up by General Beauregard, now occupied by our troops. From a cliff, which falls off steeply into the river just below the batteries, the famous chain was stretched across the river.[7] In Columbus we unloaded a quantity of cargo and took on board two hundred sacks of corn and two hundred bales of hay for the army. Huge quantities of Quartermaster Department supplies are here in stock for the army in Tennessee. It was long after dark when we left the place. The night was cold, yet I slept quite well. Around midnight we passed Island No. 10, where we anchored at the gunboat stationed there to report about our boat, cargo, etc., as ordered.

Friday, May 15—When I woke up this morning, we were anchored at the Tennessee bank, taking on a considerable amount of wood. The day is gorgeous; the heat is agreeable due to our brisk speed on the river. The nights are quite cold. A little before noon we reached Fort Pillow, where we stopped and cargo was unloaded. Meanwhile, I wrote in my diary and to Hedde in order to mail it

6. The *Osage* was the first of the shallow draft monitors built by James B. Eads at St. Louis. It was launched in January 1863, but it grounded and was damaged in April. It was then sent to Cairo for repairs. Faust, *Encyclopedia of the Civil War,* 549; Gibbons, *Warships and Naval Battles,* 56–57.

7. Confederate general Pierre G. T. Bureaugard. Sifakis, *Who Was Who in the Confederacy,* 20–21. To prevent navigation, the Confederates in 1861 had stretched a chain across the Mississippi River at Columbus, supported by flatboats. Between the boats, "torpedoes" (mines) had been attached. *OR,* ser. 1, vol. 7, p. 534.

from Memphis. Here we unloaded the hay and corn for the government, which had been taken on board yesterday in Columbus.

Around four o'clock we arrived in Memphis. We now had to watch our prisoners, since they could move about freely on the entire upper part of the boat. As in St. Louis, there was a large crowd of residents here to see the gentlemen. Endless greetings and handshaking. The ladies were most arrogant in this, since they counted on exaggerated politeness by the "Northern mud sills."[8] One of them mentioned she could have escaped from us long ago if she had wanted to. And even now she could do so, for she could easily knock down such a little lad as I. I was on my post at the door of the salon at that moment. I acknowledged that it was a difficult assignment to guard ladies, but I would do my best to bring her safely to Dixie.

Most of the ones who shook hands with our prisoners were, of course, not better than those. However, I noticed one case where a friend who greeted one of the gentlemen from St. Louis did not agree with him, at least for public appearances. After they had shaken hands he said, "I am sorry to see you here." "Sorry," replied the prisoner, "you ought to rejoice!" The friend, who obviously could not think how to reply to this, turned around abruptly and left the salon. Furthermore, the gentlemen here seemed to have an extended circle of friends. Upon the news of our arrival, the crowd surged back and forth, until we finally had to seal off the entire boat to strangers. The people here had already heard the news that the government had confiscated all of the exiles' property. The name of the German secessionist among our prisoners is Shaffer. We spent the night on board.

Saturday, May 16—This morning the ladies were picked up from the boat by three ambulances and were taken under our escort to the station of the Charleston and Memphis Railroad, together with the gentlemen, who had to walk. The train was crowded; hence, all of us could not find room in the cars, and a large num-

8. Originally, the lowest timber or foundation in a structure, but here meaning the lowest stratum of humanity. In 1858 Senator James Hammond of South Carolina had given a speech in the Senate labeling the northern working class as "mudsills." McPherson, *For Cause and Comrades*, 154.

ber of the escort had to sit on the roof. This place was in many ways better than being crammed together into the crowded, hot cars. Besides, I had a great opportunity to see something of the area.

We left Memphis around seven o'clock in the morning. Memphis has delightful surroundings; pretty country seats in shady groves follow one after the other. Besides, I found here in Tennessee, as I had already discovered in Memphis, that every house was hidden as much as possible by bushes and trees. Therefore, throughout the entire region every farmhouse was located in the middle of a little forest, so that often one could not see the house in the shade of the majestic trees or the formal parks.

Here for the first time I saw extended plantations, though none were being cultivated as in peacetime; only a negligible small amount is now cultivated. The extensive clearings lie waste, the buildings often in ruins and abandoned. The extensive fields between the groves are similar to the large areas of arable land around the estates of the nobility in Holstein.

The area itself is slightly hilly, and the soil, a yellow loam, is annoyingly dusty. The plantations resemble small villages or are like our really large noble estates, due to the many outbuildings and Negro dwellings. On almost every plantation there is a cotton press out in the open. Running water seems to be rare; on the entire stretch to La Grange, we passed not a single brook but several swamps with yellow, standing water. In them I saw the slender cypresses, the tree of the South, of which I heard so much. Except for the vegetation and the fences and hedges of Holstein, this stretch I came through today is, from all I have seen in America, most similar to the fatherland.

Negroes were the sole workers on the land. They plowed between corn and cotton, while the women were busy with the hoe. The corn was already tall as a hand is high; the cherries on the tree were just now turning red; peaches were full-size, only the color was lacking. The cotton was already growing and was being worked over like corn but only in one direction, since it is planted in rows about two and one-half feet apart, and the stand is quite close together in the rows. Wheat and rye were headed out.

Troops were stationed along the entire railroad line. Near Memphis there was a considerable number from different branches of the army. Every stop, as well as all other important installations along the railroad, were protected. All kinds of blockhouses, fortifications, palisades in different sizes, shapes, and forms were to be seen. Even the smallest post had some kind of palisade to be protected until reinforcements could get through. Ramparts and even whole fortifications were erected at opportune locations; however, at the moment no troops at all were stationed there. In short, everything appears to have been done to make a disruption of traffic by the enemy impossible. It is an almost unbroken guard line from one of these small posts to the next. Naturally this requires a large number of troops.

The train stopped at almost all of the many camps to deliver the mail. Some of the weary soldiers at these stations had put up signs on which one could read in large letters the plea "throw off papers." Indeed, they have a boring job here along the railroad. A little before noon we arrived at our destination, La Grange, fifty miles from Memphis and only three miles from the border of the state of Mississippi. The southbound train stops here, since the line leads to Holly Springs, across terrain still disputed by both armies. However, the train still goes farther east to Corinth. Many troops are stationed here, and supplies of all kinds are stored here. The houses still standing in this little town show the signs of war.

Here our prisoners were delivered to the commander of the place, and under the escort of a cavalry company of the Sixth Illinois Regiment, they went farther on toward our advance posts. Seven ambulances took the prisoners, ladies and gentlemen, and two six-mule wagons brought the baggage. We left La Grange at the same time, three o'clock in the afternoon, to return to Memphis. Major McKenny went with the exiles to deliver them to their soul mates outside our lines. Captain Ivory stayed with us and was now in command.

Coming from Corinth, Adjutant General Thomas was on the train with us. At the first larger station to which we came, Lafayette, the troops were lined up, the Ninetieth Illinois Regiment of infantry and, with them, two cannons from some battery, manned by Germans. We stopped; the brigadier stepped out and addressed the men lined up. He is not an especially good speaker; however, I heartily endorse the content of his speech. I now have hopes that our government is on the right track when a man like General Thomas, who in the past was considered to be half a traitor and always a strong opponent of the drastic politics of the government (one need only recall the Fremont affair), expressed such words and that officially.[9]

The content of his speech, which we heard again and again, since he repeated it at every stop where troops were stationed, was in essence as follows. First, in the name of the president and the country he expressed his thanks for services rendered by the volunteers to the government and the public welfare. He then explained that he had come from Washington as inspector of the army but at the same time was authorized to get the troops in the field acquainted with the adopted policy of the government concerning a large class of the people. He meant the intended liberation and arming of the blacks! He knew what prejudices prevailed, how very many people, even soldiers, hated to see the Negroes armed. He himself had such prejudices, since he was born a Southern man and raised in the South. However, he had been converted. He had seen Negro regiments drilling and had to give them all the praise. Half of the men serving the heavy guns on our gunboats were blacks, and he had heard only praise from all their officers in regard to their courage and precision in battle. In Florida Negro regiments had distinguished themselves, etc. We only needed to look at other nations, at how England and France use them. Yes, even our enemies, the rebels, had regiments in service made up of Negroes. One of our generals, with whom he had spoken in Helena, had been guarded by Negro soldiers during his captivity by the rebels. The objection that Negroes would not make [good] soldiers was therefore untenable; his own eyes and all the reports of their officers had convinced him, etc.

9. Adj. Gen. Lorenzo Thomas in 1861 had investigated Gen. John C. Fremont's administration of the Western Department at President Lincoln's order. Thomas's report, in part, led to Fremont's dismissal and earned Thomas the enmity of radical Republicans. Nor did Thomas and Secretary of War Edwin Stanton get along. On March 13, 1863, Stanton sent Thomas to the Trans-Missisippi theater to recruit black troops. Sifakis, *Who Was Who in the Union*, 411.

Finally, after he had explained the objectives and wishes of the government in this regard, he asked the men to give their consensus and sincere support to this with three "hurrahs." Three cheers for the president were given, but there were too many Copperheads in the regiment to endorse the policy of the government.[10] Thereupon the general announced that he had the power to discharge dishonorably every officer and soldier who would oppose the policy in word or deed. He reminded them to consider what they were doing and gave them eight days to think about it. Then we went on farther. At two or three places this scene was repeated; however, there the soldiers were loyal and gave a strong hurrah for the president and his policies.

These speeches delayed us considerably, of course, and it was just before dusk that we reached Memphis again. This railroad is now operated exclusively by the government. The freight cars are marked "U.S.," and the passenger cars, "U.S. Military R.R." For the night we were quartered in a large building close to the depot. The entire Thirty-second Wisconsin Infantry Regiment was also quartered here. Furthermore, in the back of the building were large fenced-in areas for horses and mules. Fodder was stored here as well. The troops stationed along the railroad on which we traveled today were for the most part Illinois regiments, among others the 126th, 106th, and 41st infantry regiments, as well as various cavalry regiments. Tired from the heat of the day, I slept very well on the bales of hay, wrapped in a blanket.

Sunday, May 17—I wrote in my diary. We are waiting for transportation. Since it was Sunday, the necessary papers could not be

10. "Copperhead" was a term applied to "peace" Democrats, who opposed many Republican policies and urged restoration of the Union through negotiation and compromise. The Copperheads' opponents likened them to the poisonous copperhead snake. McPherson, *Ordeal by Fire,* 273. Other sources attribute the name to copper pennies worn as badges of identification. Faust, *Encyclopedia of the Civil War,* 564–65. The Copperheads generally opposed emancipation, which explains Scherneckau's reference. Fellow Company H soldier Thomas E. Keen said the Ninetieth Illinois was "composed entirely of Irishmen," whom he characterized not only as Copperheads but also as being intellectually and morally inferior. Potter, "I Thought It My Duty," 157.

issued, and we had to wait here all day. Even in war, where minutes can often be critical, Sunday is strictly respected by the Americans!

It was quite warm and unbearably dusty, since water was sprinkled only on the main streets. I took various walks through the city, among others to the camp area that our regiment had occupied last year, now taken over by the Twenty-seventh Ohio Regiment and a battery from Michigan.[11] I also visited a large, well-laid-out cemetery, lots of plants; also many graves were decorated with marble monuments.

Memphis, being one of the main cotton shipping locations has, of course, splendid facilities to receive this commodity. The warehouses and yards, all built of brick, mostly near the railroad, are now either partially in ruins or are being used by the government, like the building in which we are being quartered. The cotton shipping site seems to be chiefly on the Mississippi. A large number of bales are lying at the landing.

Monday, May 18—Last night I slept quite well. At noon we marched on board the steamer *Continental*, which was scheduled to leave for St. Louis at four o'clock. It had almost no freight but quite a lot of passengers, mostly military personnel. We took our place on the lower deck, which was completely empty.

We drew rations for three days, although we still had much more than we could use in that time, except perhaps coffee, which is usually made too strong to last long. Our rations received here consist of soft bread, a barrel of small, round crackers, which [dipped] in coffee soften just like zwieback and are therefore a kind of delicacy, at least for soldiers, a keg of potatoes, as well as cooked and raw ham. Only the best cuts of the last are eaten, all fat on it is thrown away. Furthermore, we drew coffee, sugar, soap, and candles.

A little after five o'clock, our boat finally left the wharf and went upstream quite rapidly. The *Continental* is a medium-sized boat

11. The First Nebraska Infantry had been in Memphis from late June to late July 1862. Because Scherneckau did not enlist until the fall of that year, he evidently learned these details from his comrades.

with side wheels and, as it seems to me, especially arranged for transportation of horses and cattle on the lower deck. The boat came from Vicksburg and had on board a large amount of cut up fence rails for fuel.

Tuesday, May 19—Moving quickly upstream we passed Fort Pillow at midnight. Getting up this morning, there were six boats visible on the river at the same time. I wrote in my diary. At approximately two o'clock we reached the fortifications near New Madrid, Missouri. A cannon ball fired across the bow of our steamer from the fort there across the river forced us to land in order to take on board a number of prisoners of war with an escort from the Thirty-eighth Iowa Infantry Regiment. Several Negro families also came on board to go to St. Louis. In the course of the afternoon we passed Island No. 10. Ten miles below Hickman we saw the few remains of the new steamship *Majestic*, burned there several weeks ago.[12] At sunset we passed Hickman and at midnight, Columbus.

Wednesday, May 20—We left Cairo before daybreak, where we had stopped for quite a long time. On this trip we met numerous steamships; among them also several boats of the Marine Brigade, light gunboats, each armed with eight to ten field cannons (six- and twelve-pounders). The artillerymen belonging to them, as well as infantry and cavalry, were on board, probably for landing purposes, since sailors in uniform were also visible, just like on our warships at sea.[13]

At eight thirty we arrived in Cape Girardeau, where we stayed several hours. We saw our comrades and received our mail, which sometimes is sent down by mistake with the letters for the regiment. I received a letter from Caroline. Two hundred men of the Missouri State Militia came on board here, all with horses, partly very good animals, but almost without weapons and everyone with-

12. *Way's Packet Directory*, 304, says the boat was burned May 6, 1863.

13. These soldiers were probably part of the Mississippi Marine Brigade, a special army unit composed of infantry, cavalry, and artillery carried on transports to counter Confederates and guerrillas who menaced Union outposts and shipping along the rivers. Bailey, "Mississippi Marine Brigade," 34.

out uniforms. They are going to Sulphur Springs, Missouri. More than half of the men are Germans and all from this area around Cape Girardeau. A cannon and several limber boxes were taken on board as well. General McNeil, who had been wounded by the accidental discharge of a pistol in the hands of one of the gentlemen in his vicinity, also went to St. Louis with this boat. Even though the weather is warm, it is pleasantly cool on board. We stopped several times to take on wood and reached Sulphur Springs at midnight, where the militia debarked.

CHAPTER 9

St. Louis Again, May 21–June 9, 1863

Thursday, May 21—We arrived at St. Louis around seven o'clock this morning and soon marched to our old quarters on Washington Avenue. Here we found our comrades, whom we had left behind, in good health; the sick ones had recovered for the most part.

Friday, May 22—This morning we drilled from eight to nine o'clock. Next, on my request, I received a pass from the captain and walked to Benton Barracks. A friend in the regiment had given me a message for his brother-in-law, who was supposed to be in the hospital there. It was very warm and dusty. I could not deliver the message, since the man had died yesterday!

Returning, I took another road and looked at one of the forts that Fremont had erected for the protection of the city. They are well set up, and the task was carried out with more care than Americans usually apply in building fortifications. They are the best-constructed bulwarks I have yet had an opportunity to see. A blockhouse in the interior with a bombproof roof is large enough to take in two companies. A drawbridge leads over the moat into the interior. Four or six guns of the heaviest caliber appear over the walls on each of these bulwarks.[1]

From there I went to the large water reservoir, visible in the far distance, which provides the city with drinking water. The water is pumped up by steam power from the Mississippi. The reservoir is

1. By the fall of 1861, under orders of Gen. John C. Fremont, ten forts and several detached batteries had been constructed ringing St. Louis to the west. Winter, *The Civil War in St. Louis,* 75–76.

Fortifications at St. Louis, Missouri. *Frank Leslie's Illustrated Newspaper,* August 16, 1862, p. 333, wood engraving by M. Henry Lovie. Neg. # Wars 160. Missouri Historical Society, St. Louis.

located on a natural high point, and in order to increase the pressure, it is raised considerably on an artificially elevated mound. It is a long rectangle built of bricks, except the upper six feet, which are boulders. The water was some twenty-five feet deep, yet it could hold forty feet of water. The outside wall is now being reinforced, since if the basin is full of water, the pressure is too great, and thereby a part of the wall, as well as the earth on the exterior of the hill, can burst and break apart. From the top level of this large pond, one has a marvelous view over the sea of houses, stretching far along the river but mostly darkened by thick smoke clouds from the countless smokestacks of the factories. Returning by another way, I saw a part of the city that was new to me. The night was warm; however, after the exhausting hikes of the day, I slept excellently.

Saturday, May 23—Today I was assigned to guard duty but had nothing to do. Patrols were sent out just after dark. Since I was in the last relief, my services were not needed anymore. Nevertheless, expecting to be awakened, I lay down on the bed fully clothed and slept until broad daylight. Today we had to take one of our comrades afflicted with smallpox to the hospital. There was great excitement when the case became known. However, I don't believe that it really was smallpox.[2]

Sunday, May 24—Wrote and sent off a letter to my parents. Yesterday we had to arrest one of our own men because the manager of an ice cream saloon not far from here accused him and someone else from Company G of our regiment of stealing two silver spoons. The latter is here on leave. A large number of men from our regiment are now coming through here going home on leave. The thief belonging to our company had returned just recently because he had deserted.

2. The Company H morning report, May 24, 1863, noted that Pvt. Andrew Miller had been sent to the hospital. He recovered, reenlisted, and deserted October 13, 1865, at Fort Sedgwick, Colorado Territory. NSHS RG18, roll 3; Dudley, *Roster of Nebraska Volunteers*, 98–99.

This small incident shows what kind of elements our corps consists of! It is the first theft that has been reported in which a comrade from my company was involved, but unfortunately it is not the first that was carried out by the soldiers and members of my company and the regiment. I read, wrote, and slept. In the afternoon at retreat (at sunset), the usual inspection went on, after which we drilled some.

The only pleasant time to take a walk now is in the evening right after sunset. I usually take advantage of this, since, being accustomed to physical activity, I feel the need for it. That was never the case in the past, and I never went willingly just to be walking. As in all American cities, it is deathly quiet here on Sundays; the city appears to have died out at least in many parts.

At nightfall I went to the Union Methodist Church, which I had visited two weeks ago. The pastor of the church preached this evening. He is a very proficient speaker and handles his theme with much warmth and expression. In the churches in America, however, attempts are made to achieve an effect much more through theatrical bearing and gesture than we are used to seeing on the pulpit. After the end of the sermon, the minister said that, in view of the latest news, he would take the liberty to change the program and, in place of a hymn, proposed that we sing a national song with organ accompaniment. He took the liberty, even though gathered in the church for other purposes, to announce the news just received at headquarters about the surrender of Vicksburg with the garrison under General Pemberton. An electric shock seemed to sweep through the audience, and a spontaneous thunder of applause broke out. It demonstrated that the congregation was composed predominantly of friends and supporters of the Union. In St. Louis this is not always the case at such a large public gathering![3]

Monday, May 25—Today on guard duty, that is, patrolling. Usually no patrols are sent out during the day. At nightfall we, the first

3. Gen. John C. Pemberton was the Confederate commander of Vicksburg, but the rumor about the surrender was false.

relief, went out and returned after eleven o'clock with four or five prisoners after we had roamed through a large part of the city. The second and third relief went out after us until about one or two o'clock. We were able to sleep the whole night. Divided up in this way, guard duty is not at all difficult. The evenings now are pleasant, and we go wherever we want to. The guard has completely free admission to all amusement places. Soldiers are very much attracted to beer gardens with music, and many are arrested there. Today we signed the payroll. Wrote to F. Schiffman in Africa.

Tuesday, May 26—Were paid off today. The privates received two ten-dollar notes and six one-dollar bills, making twenty-six dollars—two months' wages. It is nice to have this little bit of money. I wrote to Schuster Court in Omaha and sent him the rest of the amount due. As always after payday and also today, there were drunks already. Father's letter to me was forwarded by Hedde; I wrote on Schiffman's letter.

Wednesday, May 27—Did not feel well, had some diarrhea, took pills, wrote to Father and my siblings.[4] An order came for sixteen men to go as an escort to Helena, Arkansas; however, the order was cancelled. Our regiment has left Cape Girardeau to march to Pilot Knob. I wrote on the letter to my parents.

Thursday, May 28—Felt well again today and by afternoon was on guard duty. A lot of drunkards in the company; it really is a sad sight in what ways and how quickly many of these men get rid of their money. I finished my letters.

In the evening I went to the theater—Varieties Theater, the one I talked about before. The performance was miserable. Crude silly comedy, dances, songs, and Negro productions with bawdy jokes are the main subjects. The service introduced at many places here

4. One sibling was Marie Scherneckau, who came to the United States in 1908 and cared for her brother until his death. Pension file. In his diary entry for July 15, 1863, Scherneckau mentions writing a letter to "sister Sophie." On September 7, 1865, he noted receiving a letter from "Sophie and Ludwig."

is the Polka Salon type.[5] For twenty-five cents the performance lasts from about eight o'clock in the evening until after midnight, interrupted only briefly by intermissions.

Friday, May 29—Last night and this morning it rained quite severely. I wrote to Faber, finished the other letters, and mailed them off. It is rumored that we soon will be ordered away from here and back to the regiment! In the evening a friend and I made a rather complete tour of the saloons of the city. Ice cream, strawberries, and milk are now on the daily agenda. We drew clothing today. I took a pair of pants, socks, and a haversack.

Saturday, May 30—Had a severe rainstorm this morning. Since yesterday I am required to act as the servant, what they call in the army "dog robber," for my captain who is sick.[6] His previous orderly is also on the sick list. The captain had asked me to take his place until he is well again. I did not want to refuse. I do not know why he wanted to have me, except that the others, with very few exceptions, are not found here in the barracks very often because, since payday, most of them are staggering from one drunken stupor to another. I only hope that it does not last very long; I do not especially care for this position. It rained almost constantly today.

Sunday, May 31—A glorious day. Captain Ivory was up again today. He is often sick and has a very unhealthy facial color. The dark hair and beard have gained him the name "Black Bill" among us. It seems to me he is a Creole.[7]

As I hear, various members of our company have applied for commissions in the Negro regiments to be newly established. Even the captain is among the applicants. Colonel Livingston, as well as General McNeil, who regards our regiment highly since the last affair at Cape Girardeau, has recommended the applicants strongly. Also

5. His meaning is unclear. The Varieties Music Hall featured burlesque, cancan dancing, and other risqué entertainment.

6. A term applied to enlisted men who acted as personal servants for officers.

7. Ivory was a Pennsylvania native, but his ancestry is unknown. Dale, "Otoe County Pioneers," 5:1335–36.

General Curtis himself says he does not know the men, but the regiment has such a good reputation he is not reluctant to recommend them. So much for our "democratic abolitionists."[8]

Now about a more indecent side of the character of our men. About eight days ago a drunken soldier, who had fallen asleep in one of our beds, had his watch stolen while he slept. The victim did not belong to our company. A comrade, a member of our company, the day before yesterday had his whole cash reserve stolen, about eighteen to twenty dollars, while he slept in his bed, most likely drunk. The thief had cut open the outside pocket of the sleeping soldier's blouse and had removed the pocketbook with the money. Such thefts by our own comrades leave a very embarrassing impression. We have some repulsive characters in the company.

The day passes as usual. I do not need to do guard or any other duty. In the evening, the customary review. Mailed newspapers to Hedde. The bill for clothing drawn during the past year must be paid at the end of next month. Therefore, I calculated it out this evening. Following I present a list of the stuff drawn by me during the year, to which hardly anything else will be added before the first of July.

List of clothing drawn by me:

One overcoat	$9.50
Two pair pants	7.50
One pair pants	3.75
One hat, complete	2.02
Two pair of drawers	1.90
Two blouses	4.80
Two flan. shirts	2.92
One blanket	3.60

8. Scherneckau's comment about "democratic abolitionists" may refer to Captain Ivory's apparent interest in appointment to one of the black regiments. Ivory was a Democrat who had been appointed to offices in the Nebraska territorial bureaucracy before the war. Dale, "Otoe County Pioneers," 5:1335–36. Scherneckau's comrade Thomas E. Keen called Ivory "a rank Copperhead and a *traitor*" who had been run out of Iowa for his "secesh" principles. Potter, "I Thought It My Duty," 159.

Seven pairs of socks	2.24
Two pair of shoes, sewn	4.10
One haversack	0.48[9]

Prices of some articles that are usually used by soldiers:

Uniform hat, complete	$2.02
Forage cap and cover	0.74
Uniform coat	7.21
Pair of trousers	3.75
Blouse, unlined	2.40
ditto, lined	3.14
Flannel shirt	1.46
ditto, knit	1.30
Stockings	0.32
Flannel drawers	0.95
Ditto, knit	1.00
Bootees, sewed	2.05
ditto, pegged	1.48
Overcoat (cavalry)	11.50
Overcoat (infty)	9.50
Blanket (woolen)	3.60

So for the usual needs of a soldier. I am adding the prices of the three tents generally being used now to show how high it comes to equip and maintain such an army. The men of our regiment use this last kind of tent, while the officers have wall tents. Sometimes we were fifteen to sixteen men in each tent.

Wall tent (officer)	$53.56
Common tent (five men)	22.45
Sibley ditto (ten to twelve men)	63.71

9. Totaling this list reveals that Scherneckau had exceeded his forty-two-dollar annual clothing allowance by eighty-one cents. The price of soldiers' clothing and equipment varied somewhat during the war. Shannon, *Organization and Administration*, 1:98–99.

Monday, June 1—Cloudy sky and some rain. In the afternoon the marching orders came for early tomorrow morning. I wrote to Egge. Late in the evening I had to go to Hickory Street to claim a wagon from a government stockyard there, necessary for our baggage.

Tuesday, June 2—This morning at four o'clock, the drum and fife woke us up. Everything was packed up, a fast breakfast, and at five thirty the comrades marched off to the Iron Mountain Railroad station. I had to stay behind with Captain Ivory, since his former orderly is not yet well. The captain himself is also ailing and will most likely receive a furlough to restore his health. An abundance of clothing was left behind, much of it given away by the comrades who were leaving. I gathered a lot of it together to sell but couldn't get rid of it. As always I had nothing to do except an errand or to buy this or that for the captain from time to time. Boredom will torment me; I wish I could have marched away with my comrades! Since I have not kept any food here for myself, I eat with the captain, usually fetching the meals from the Planters' House, probably the best of the few restaurants still open in wartime.[10]

Most of my comrades call this the life, and many of them may envy me because I could remain here and not have duty, etc. I gladly would have traded with a comrade had not Ivory insisted so much on keeping me specifically. He is sick, and therefore I stayed with him. In the large Lindell Hotel, diagonally across from our apartment, some sort of festival was celebrated this evening by the ladies here; the proceeds are designated for the care of the wounded. It appeared to be well attended.[11] It rained frequently during the day.

Wednesday, June 3—Slept long, got our breakfast at nine thirty, read, and wrote. Boredom, as yesterday. Our regiment was

10. The Planters' House, one of St. Louis's grandest hotels, was located on Fourth Street between Pine and Chestnut, near the quarters occupied by the provost guards. Winter, *The Civil War in St. Louis,* 67.

11. This was a "Sylvan Fete" to raise funds for the Western Sanitary Commission. Women decorated rooms in the Lindell Hotel and presented tableaux and dances with seasonal themes. Gerteis, *Civil War St. Louis,* 210.

ordered to go to Vicksburg. Our colonel, Colonel Livingston, went with a special train to Pilot Knob. But Captain Ivory told me this evening that a counter order had been given and that the regiment would *not* go. The weather was nice; lately it has not been quite as warm as it was at the beginning of May. We have the fireplace burning the whole day!

Thursday, June 4—Like yesterday. From the *Republican* I see that "Old Abe," on the recommendation of Governor [Hamilton] Gamble of Missouri, wants to appoint our brave Colonel Baumer, whom I have often mentioned previously, to brigadier. I would be very happy if it happens. He is the darling of the regiment and a competent officer; was at first captain of Company B, which was formed entirely of Germans. His promotion happens due to his good conduct in the last battle at Cape Girardeau!

So I thought, and wrote this down. As I look at the newspaper again, however, I see that it is all a mistake. A Colonel Boomer from a Missouri regiment was intended who, as I recall, had distinguished himself at Vicksburg.[12] But it is excusable, since other people were misled and had pointed out to me the article in the *Republican.* Baumer, the Dutchman, likely will have to wait a while before he earns the star on his shoulder! No Gamble will intercede on his behalf. The day passed as yesterday.

Friday, June 5—Nice weather. After I had brought breakfast to Captain Ivory, I visited the men from our company in Hickory [Street] Hospital: two of our sergeants, one corporal, and a private. At present the company has little strength, especially the officers. Captain Ivory received leave; First Lieutenant Clarke is in the Schofield Barracks here in St. Louis as commandant; the second lieutenant [Stephen W. Moore] is also on leave; the second sergeant also has a post in the Schofield Barracks. The third and fifth

12. Col. George B. Boomer, Twenty-sixth Missouri, commanded a brigade in the Union Army of the Tennessee and fought at Island No. 10 and Corinth. He was a brigade commander under Gen. James B. McPherson at the siege of Vicksburg and was killed May 22, 1863. Sifakis, *Who Was Who in the Union*, 38.

sergeants are sick here in the hospital. The company is now led by the first sergeant [James I. Shaw].

The men in the hospitals here are well taken care of, and these comrades are all on the road to recovery. The hospitals here are very clean and especially airy—the ones I have visited. Iron bedsteads are used everywhere. The bed linens are very clean as well. At the moment a large number of officers from our regiment are here in town. Colonel Livingston is here again.

Saturday, June 6—Same as yesterday. Took care of various errands for the captain. He was almost always absent, and therefore I was pretty much tied up. Wrote to Martin.

Sunday, June 7—Steady rain today. Captain Ivory left for Pittsburg, Pennsylvania, today.[13] I helped him to pack his things and to look after them. For the rest of the day I had plenty of errands to run for him.

Monday, June 8—Yesterday evening I went to the Schofield Barracks to inquire about transportation to the regiment. There I learned that there will be no connection until Wednesday. On my return, I reached the German theater on Fifth Street between Franklin Avenue and Morgan Street. It really is more of a beer garden, combined with a small summer as well as a winter theater.[14] The latter is no larger or hardly as large as the Davenport German theater.

The performers, under the circumstances, played very well in the winter area because of the damp and cold weather. It was all in German and not such a humbug and as much shouting as in the English variety theaters here. There was no one but Germans, but not a soul that I knew. I felt strange and deserted among my countrymen! It was well attended, yet the military was poorly represented. I saw only two or three uniforms besides my own.

It was eleven thirty before the play was over. It got almost too cold even in the hall, since all doors were open. The playbill

13. Ivory had been given a twenty-day sick leave. Company H Morning Report, June 1863, NSHS RG18, roll 3.

14. Evidently he means there were indoor and outdoor theaters.

announced the play performed last night for today, that is, Monday. A clever arrangement to bypass Sunday. The large number of people gathered there must have known this; I had arrived by accident. Yet for once I was glad to have visited the German City Theater in St. Louis.

Slept last night in the room previously occupied by Captain Ivory. Took care of his orders in various parts of the city. A cousin of his lives in the southeastern part of St. Louis; nothing but aristocratic looking buildings and an entirely new area for me.

Around noon I had completed the various assignments, and I went to the hospital on Hickory Street to say good-bye to the comrades there from my company. For one of them I secured signatures from Colonel Livingston, the captain, and a lieutenant of our company to an application for an officer's commission in one of the Negro regiments.[15] They were given readily and with recommendations. In the evening I reported to the Schofield Barracks with my baggage to secure transportation to my regiment. Lieutenant Clarke of our company, who until now was in command here, has today been ordered to Rolla, Missouri. I am hoping to be sent on tomorrow.

Tuesday, June 9—Still no release from here. The barracks are overcrowded, at least four to five hundred men. Consequently, it is very loud and tumultuous in these small rooms. As always when so many are here, it is very interesting to see and to hear the men who come from all areas of the West. Right now there are about 150 paroled prisoners just up from Vicksburg, who are waiting for transportation to go to Camp Chase, Ohio. There are several slightly wounded among them, wounded and captured in the bloody battles previous to Vicksburg's siege.[16]

15. Sgt. Thomas H. Price, who later was commissioned in the Fourth U.S. Colored Troops. Dudley, *Roster of Nebraska Volunteers*, 90–91. Price had been in the Hickory Street hospital since May 12. Company H Morning Report, May 1863, NSHS RG18, roll 3.

16. These included the Battles of Raymond, Champion's Hill, and Big Black River, leading up to the siege of Vicksburg, which began when Grant's army surrounded the city on May 18, 1863. Coombe, *Thunder along the Mississippi*, 219–20.

One of them from the Twenty-fourth Indiana Regiment showed me the ball that shattered his shoulder blade, flattened out like a half-dollar on the hard bone. His arm was on the way to recovery. He described our loss of men as very heavy, like the newspaper reports, yet the fort [Vicksburg] is firmly surrounded and its capture only a matter of time. The brave Eleventh Indiana Regiment also has some of its members among the prisoners. All these were paroled by the rebels before they retreated to Vicksburg.

When the rooms are overcrowded, a frightful tumult emerges every time, a life-threatening mob at the three daily "feedings," and one is lucky if he can get only one of the different cooked items. If coffee, one has no bread, and if one first elbows for bread, the coffee will be gone in the meantime. Yet the cooks do their best, and usually there is enough available, only it cannot be distributed so quickly to the hungry souls!

CHAPTER 10

Building Fort Davidson at Pilot Knob, June 10–August 29, 1863

Wednesday, June 10—Since our transportation was issued yesterday evening, we left St. Louis on the Pilot Knob train at seven o'clock in the morning. It rained severely in the morning, but it became slightly better toward noon. We arrived in Pilot Knob around twelve thirty. Quite a number of comrades from the regiment were gathered at the depot. We camped close to town. It is very muddy here and in the surrounding area as a result of the constant rain. Because the mountains, which consist of nearly pure iron ore, are supposed to attract thunderstorms, it now looks like more rain.

Apart from our regiment, a battalion of the Third Colorado Infantry Regiment, the Third Missouri Cavalry Regiment, a battalion of the Thirteenth Illinois Cavalry, and the Third Iowa Cavalry Regiment are here. The rest of the troops gathered here earlier have gone off to Vicksburg. What our destination is, only the future knows.

I greeted the different friends that I have in the regiment and heard about the little events that happened since I have been gone. My friend Foster is still here, although he has received the official notice of his nomination from the adjutant of the Negro regiment. His discharge from our regiment has not yet been delivered.[1]

Germans have sometimes annoyed me when they so distorted our language with bits of English, but now I am almost doing the same thing. Yesterday I visited Company B of our regiment, which

1. Richard Foster's discharge to accept a commission in the black regiment would come on December 9, 1863. Dudley, *Roster of Nebraska Volunteers*, 118–19.

is made up entirely of Germans. Many are from North Germany; hence, they spoke Low German. As I tried to speak it, I got stuck, since I mixed in English words. Sergeant Burmester, who enlisted in Omaha, was born in Hamburg.[2] He had news from Omaha that P. [Peter] Steuben and Paulsen, previously of Grand Island, have done a good business there with their dairy.[3]

Thursday, June 11—Dry, but sultry and looking like rain. We received rations for ten days. I did some laundry in the brook that runs past the camp. In the afternoon we had some company drill. It is an especially nice campground that we are occupying; the ground dries quickly. Yesterday I received a letter from Court; wrote to Egge today. The pontoon train that accompanied us last winter is here with us again. Five to six thousand men of our cavalry are supposed to be in Patterson, but I do not know to which regiments they belong. This evening, a dress parade.

Our regiment's flags, which were entirely shot to pieces in the last battles at Cape Girardeau, are barely holding together. A shell went through the Stars and Stripes, ripping a huge hole in it. The flag of the territory (Nebraska) is tattered by many rifle shots. In the battles of Fort Donelson and Shiloh they had not been damaged as much as in these last actions.

Friday, June 12—We had several thunderstorms today, with them intense heat. I was cooks police for the day. In the evening, dress parade. Today our First Lieutenant Clarke arrived here from Rolla. New rifles for our regiment arrived from St. Louis as well.

During my absence from the regiment, it received new tents, that is, repaired old ones. No matter what, these are better than the ones we last had, which no longer protected against the rain.

2. Adolph Burmester of Company B. Dudley, *Roster of Nebraska Volunteers*, 22–23.

3. The *Tri-Weekly Nebraska Republican* (Omaha), January 4, 1864, and surrounding issues, has an advertisement by J. T. Paulsen, who offers milk for sale. According to Andreas, *History of Nebraska*, 800, John Steuben, a native of Holstein, operated a dairy on the Military Road near Omaha beginning about 1870, but his relationship to P. Stueben, if any, is unknown.

They are Sibley tents, as we had before, three for each company. Some of these tents were captured from the Confederates, made in Nashville, Tennessee, and marked "C.S.A." I am now lodging in the tent of our captain with the first sergeant and several other comrades, since none of the commissioned officers of the company is here. First Lieutenant Clarke has not yet reported back to the company.

Saturday, June 13—Had to take up guard duty in the camp tonight. It was very hot, with signs of a thunderstorm. At night it is icy cold, and there is heavy dew. I slept out in the open, and I was warm enough, but when on guard in my overcoat, I could not keep sufficiently warm in the freezing morning air.

Sunday, June 14—Just after we were relieved from duty, we had a regimental inspection; however, I did not have to show up for it. I climbed Shepherd's Mountain during that time; our camp is situated at the foot. From the top one has a nice view over all the camps with the town of Pilot Knob in the background, wedged between the mountain of the same name and two others, nearly as high but not quite so steep. Almost all of it was once thick forest, but the part easily accessible has been cut down and used.

One or two regiments of the cavalry left their camp next to us yesterday and marched southward. The one regiment had two small howitzers, each with two horses and an ammunition cart alongside, each cannon pulled by only one horse. The gun crew was mounted as well. It really seemed to be the flying artillery.[4]

General Davidson with his staff came from St. Louis, and after he had inspected the troops who were just leaving, he returned to St. Louis. It was again unbearably hot. A former barber, now belonging to our company, opened a barbershop, that is, a kind of bower where he has placed his "chair," which is nearly always occupied.

This evening after the dress parade our regimental chaplain, Reverend Tipton, preached in an open area in the middle of the

4. "Flying artillery" was a term applied to a battery in which all the cannoneers were mounted, which would have been the case with artillery attached to a cavalry regiment.

tents. Since the sun was low on the horizon, it was pleasantly cool following the heat of the day. After the presentation was opened with some spiritual songs, the men sat down, sitting on the ground in a circle with uncovered heads, listening to the speech. As always the sermon was frank and well selected with regard to the audience. The Reverend Tipton is an unpretentious man and therefore is loved by all, even by these rough fellows who pay little attention to the laws of God or man!

While we were listening to the sermon, the neighboring Colorado regiment had their evening parade, and the field music for this sounded across to us. Officers and cavalrymen galloped past, displaying a living picture of a war camp. In the middle of this edification, we are reminded of the purpose for which thousands so motley are gathered together.

Monday, June 15—Very warm, like yesterday. Due to the absence of all our commanding officers Lieutenant Donovan of Company K took over the command of our company.[5] In the morning we had some drill for a very short time. As always at six o'clock in the evening, dress parade.

It appears that there is the intention to send out a large expedition from here. More troops arrive daily from St. Louis and Rolla; some are immediately going farther on; some are making camp here. Yesterday, Merrill's Horse, a fine regiment, came through here. The First and Eighth Missouri and First Iowa cavalry regiments came through here today.[6] Nearly eight to ten thousand men must be stationed between here and Van Buren, mostly cavalry and light artillery. Hundreds of wagons with six-mule teams are being outfitted here. I just wish we could join the expedition. I

5. Edward K. Donovan, who later became captain of Company F and was mustered out July 1, 1866. Dudley, *Roster of Nebraska Volunteers*, 66–67, 116–17.

6. Merrill's Horse was the Second Missouri Cavalry, organized by Lewis Merrill under the authority of Gen. John C. Fremont in the fall of 1861. At the time of Scherneckau's writing, the unit was serving in the District of Southeastern Missouri, Department of the Missouri. Dyer, *Compendium*, 1303. The Second Missouri Cavalry and the other regiments mentioned were part of the district's cavalry division. *OR*, ser. 1, vol. 22, part 2, p. 345.

did not become a soldier to be so inactive. Received Egge's letter of the seventh of this month.

Tuesday, June 16—Very warm. We had drill as usual in the morning and afternoon, today under our new commander, who seems to be more concerned about us than any one of our own officers. Even though the exercise is not very strenuous, it is sufficient to bring out the sweat. Our campground is without shade, and the sun burns on our tents without mercy; therefore, it is unbearably hot inside. To remedy this misfortune, we have built various huts of leafy branches in which we pass the hot daytime hours. They are somewhat more airy and shady. Wrote to Egge. Dress parade as always.

Wednesday, June 17—Finished and sent off the letter to Egge. While our company was stationed in St. Louis, we had one case of smallpox; the patient is still in the hospital there. Another sick man, of the same kind, was taken from us to the smallpox hospital last Saturday. Since then the sanitation and ventilation of the tent, as well as of the entire camp, has been carried out more strictly. No smallpox cases have been found in other companies. I am convinced these men have picked up the contagious matter in the immoral houses they visited. A number of men who never had been vaccinated have now, wisely, been vaccinated.

It was intensely warm, yet we had drill two times, and in the cool of the evening, dress parade as usual. Afterward I took a long walk over the surrounding hills to view the grandiose arrangements that are being made to prepare an expedition from here.[7] Hundreds of wagons covered with white canvas, driven together in large trains, and thousands of mules as teams for them, penned up in numerous large corrals, are visible from the surrounding heights. There is lively activity everywhere; long wagon trains are busy from morning to night delivering the necessary forage from

7. The cavalry force under Gen. John Davidson was preparing to join Gen. Frederick Steele's campaign to take Little Rock, which Union forces accomplished on September 10. DeBlack, "1863," 90–94.

the railway station to the various places for the thousands of artillery and cavalry horses. Everything is coming from St. Louis. The other supplies for the men, the quartermaster and commissary stores, are held in the sheds right by the railroad station. Most likely, however, the shipping of these last mentioned supplies will start when the wagon trains are ready to load them and to follow the departing troops. Most of the wagons and mules are arriving here from Rolla.

Thursday, June 18—After we had endured our morning drill a bit, a severe thunderstorm with rain erupted and cooled down the air somewhat. We raised our tent slightly, that is, above the ground, to let the air on the ground freely circulate and so secure a somewhat cooler camp. This happens as follows. The pole set in the tripod in the middle of the tent is replaced with a longer one, and instead of the customarily used tent pegs, others are made of the desired length, so that the underside of the tent, otherwise touching the ground, is now eight inches, one, or even two feet from the ground, depending on the new length of the center pole.

At six o'clock in the evening, instead of the usual dress parade, we had to march to the railroad station, where we, in company front, had to receive General Davidson, who was coming with a special train. It was night, however, before he arrived. We welcomed him with drum rolls and present arms. He walked the front, his head bare, and expressed several words of thanks and joy to see *us* again and [said] that he had not expected such a formal reception and therefore did not show up in uniform. He noted further that our colonel would also be here on Monday or Tuesday. General Davidson is the commander of the district and at the same time the commander of the expedition departing from here.[8]

Friday, June 19—Right after reveille we drilled in the cool morning until breakfast time. I had guard duty today, which will be relieved at eight thirty. Today I was on guard duty in town, that is, post

8. At this time Davidson commanded the District of Southeastern Missouri in the Department of the Missouri, as well as being in direct command of the district's cavalry division. *OR*, ser. 1, vol. 22, part 2, p. 345.

guard, which has to protect the military prison and the public property, as well as to supply the miscellaneous honor posts. The men for these guard posts are provided by the Third Colorado Infantry and our regiment. The cavalry furnishes the pickets. Two large sheds make up the prison rooms, containing mostly prisoners of our own men, as well as several residents of this area suspected of spying, these last ones in chains. Six posts are placed at the prison, and four more in town. At night it rained a little, and it was cold and unpleasant.

Saturday, June 20—Was relieved. Did not feel well and slept almost the whole day. Today Colonel Livingston arrived from St. Louis. In the evening he attended the dress parade. The night was very cold, and the weather was also quite cool during the day.

Sunday, June 21—Right after the usual Sunday inspection, I made a trip to Shepherd's Mountain, where a rich lead vein had been mined in the past. A railroad at least three miles long, going down the mountain, brought the ore directly to the furnaces at the foot of Pilot Knob. The cars ran down by their own weight and then at least partly half a mile up the hill again, crossing the open area where the troops are now camped. Going up empty, they probably were pulled by horses or mules, since there were not two tracks as at Pilot Knob, where the full car that comes down pulls up the empty one. All these works are now halfway in ruins. Traces of former structures on the top of the ridge show that before the war there were inhabitants even at this elevation. Wherever the rocks, which are visible so frequently, permit it, this mountain is densely forested like all those around, hindering a broad view. Today it was pleasantly cool, and therefore I could take this walk without perspiring too much.

Another smallpox patient from our company was taken to the hospital today.[9] Most likely the disease had been transmitted to him from previously afflicted men. This evening we received different

9. Probably Corp. Egbert Shaw. Company H Morning Report, June 1863, NSHS RG18, roll 3. If Shaw was the soldier stricken with smallpox, he survived to be mustered out on November 10, 1864. Dudley, *Roster of Nebraska Volunteers*, 92–93.

guns, old muskets that had been repaired and then polished a bit. Our men who already had muskets kept theirs. Hence I kept my old rifle.[10] We also received bandoleers for our cartridge pouches that until now we had carried on the belt going around the body. These wide straps crossing over the left shoulder are not at all popular with our men, but one certainly will have to use them. There is a round shield on this strap, affixed so that it appears on the middle of the chest. This brass emblem has the American eagle on it with the caption "E pluribus unum."

Monday, June 22—At eight o'clock this morning, a big inspection; I was on cooks police for the day. The inspection was postponed until five o'clock in the afternoon, and right after it ended, dress parade was held. Colonel Livingston himself inspected the troops. We had to put on the new shoulder straps; every disregard was reprimanded. Colonel Livingston also conducted the dress parade himself. He is indeed a man who knows how to give orders; as soon as he gives the word of a specific command, everything happens at once. Actually he is not that popular—not like Baumer—but his abilities are recognized. Miscellaneous orders were read: first announcing that Colonel Livingston had taken command of this post, then various regulations aiming at stricter discipline. For that goal a provost guard, some forty men strong from our and the Colorado regiment, is stationed in town.

Our Company H also had to change its position in the regimental front. Instead of standing on the right hand of the flags, as previously, we are now to the left of them, and instead of marching ahead of the flags as before, when converting to marching order, we are now positioned behind them. The positions the companies have to take when marching up in regimental front depend on the length of service, as company commander, of the officer leading the company. Due to a mostly cloudy sky it was a cool day. Received a letter from Hedde.

10. The smoothbore muskets that many of the men had were being replaced with rifle-muskets, designed to shoot the conical minié bullet. Some men, including Scherneckau, already had the rifled arms, which they kept. Ordnance reports, MS129, Livingston Papers.

Tuesday, June 23—Overcast sky, rain toward evening. I was on guard duty. The prisoners were taken to Fort Curtis, located in Ironton, where they have to do earth work, since a trench is to be put around the fort.[11] The dirt dug up is to be thrown against the logs of the breastworks. Company C of our regiment is stationed here.

From the fort one has a wonderful view of the whole area, first of Ironton and Arcadia, our old campground of last spring. Now it is taken up by the camp of the First Iowa Cavalry Regiment, which, like the rest of the area, was covered with rows of white tents. All these tents were the so-called shelter tents—small, miserable rags of canvas stretched over a horizontal bar resting on two forks and then secured to the ground on both sides with pegs. The open gable-ends can be closed with fitting triangles of canvas. Such a small tent is designed for three men, and each of the three carry the parts of such a tent, so that wagons are not necessary for the transportation of the canvas houses.

Eight cavalry regiments were camped directly around the fort. Four cannons from a Missouri battery and two from the Second Illinois Battery, all six-pounders, were set up directly below the breastwork. Another battery of six cannon was camped on this hill as well. All of these troops passed in a large inspection before General Schofield, who was here from St. Louis. The latter and General Davidson also came riding into the fort, completely without any attendants, where we were at work with our prisoners.

Fort Curtis is armed with three thirty-two-pounder pivot cannons, three eighteen-pounder howitzers for field service, and two six-inch mortars.[12] At five thirty we again escorted our prisoners, about forty, back into the prison at Pilot Knob, at which point we could go home. One had escaped during the day. It rained steadily all night. One of our smallpox patients died yesterday in the hospital.[13]

11. Fort Curtis was located between Ironton and Arcadia.

12. The howitzers were more likely twenty-four-pounders. The mortars he saw were probably twenty-four-pounder Coehorns, which had a bore diameter of nearly six inches. Ripley, *Artillery and Ammunition*, 368.

13. Pvt. John Kellerman, Company H, who had enlisted from Madison County, Missouri. Dudley, *Roster of Nebraska Volunteers*, 98–99.

Wednesday, June 24—No roll call, either last evening or this morning, due to the heavy rain. Toward noon it became dry, yet humid, cloudy air. Both our lieutenants are back again. The Colorado troops have moved a little farther away from us, since their old campground had to be cleared to make room for a fortification to be built there.

After the meal, I climbed Pilot Knob. Only one of the two tracks that were laid to bring the ore from the heights to the furnace is now in use, since the ore at the foot of the mountain is shipped farther on directly by the railroad. In the past the loaded car pulled the empty cars up the mountain. Some ten to twelve workers were busy blasting the ore loose and getting it down. I waited for a blasting. The pieces were thrown far and wide; ten to twelve tons of ore were broken loose.

From the heights of the mountain, I had a beautiful view. Close by are the three towns, the white camps round nearby, and the wagon trains driven up in a charming symmetry. Farther away were mountains barely less high, all wooded, rarely showing a clearing with a small house. I forgot to mention that the iron ore from here is now taken to Iron Mountain and is smelted there. The smelter furnaces here have not been used since the outbreak of the war, half destroyed by fire and in ruins. By the rocks near the top of the mountain, I found blackberry vines with almost ripe berries, also raspberry vines but no berries yet.

Thursday, June 25—Overcast sky like yesterday, heavy rain in the afternoon. Wrote to Hedde, Giese, and Egge.[14]

Friday, June 26—Sultry and rain showers. I was cooks police. Today the work began on the new fortification. Five hundred men from various cavalry regiments showed up, and our regiment provided a fatigue party of 150 men as well. Had visits from General Davidson and Colonel Merrill. The fortification is a star-shaped bulwark, built of earth walls. The breastworks are supposed to be covered

14. Henry Giese was another of the German settlers at Grand Island and a native of Schleswig-Holstein. Andreas, *History of Nebraska,* 939.

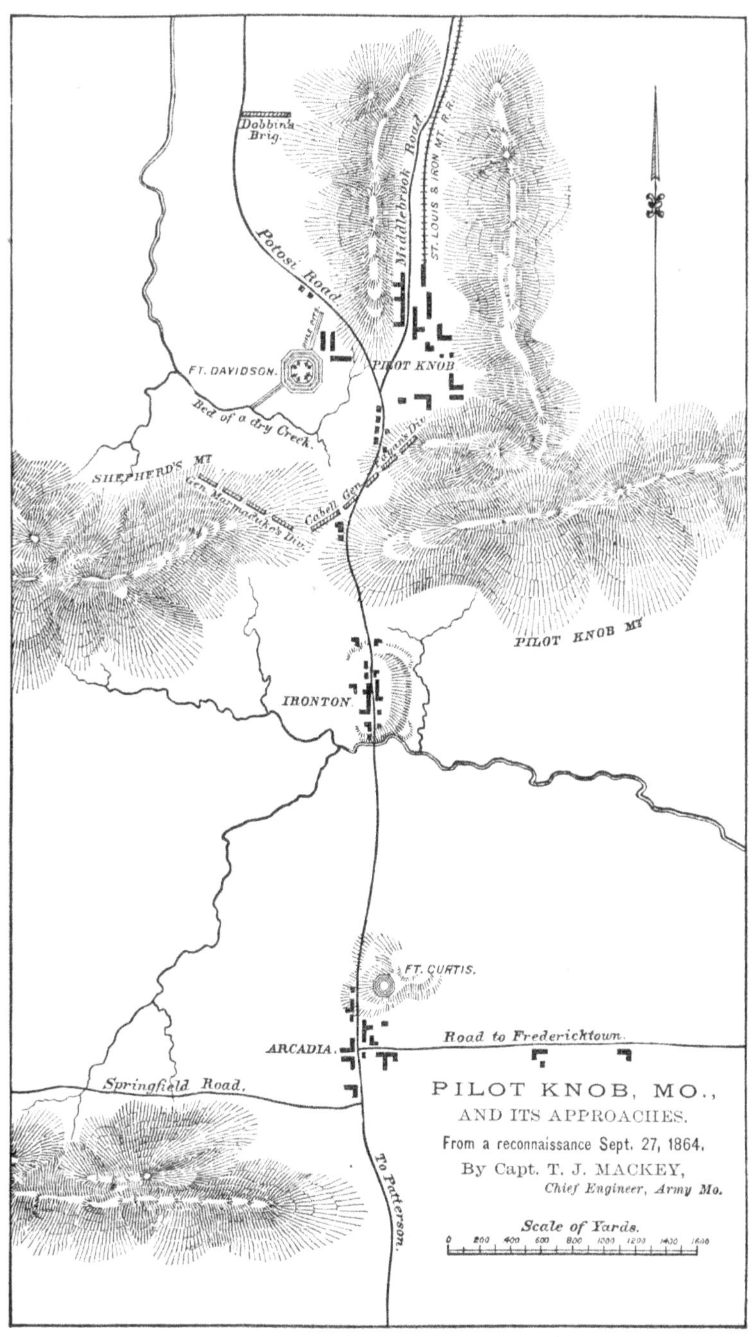

Wartime map of Pilot Knob showing Fort Davidson, which the First Nebraska helped build in the summer of 1863. *The War of the Rebellion*, ser. 1, vol. 41, part 1, p. 708. Digitally enhanced.

on the inside with logs. A German engineer is in charge of the work.[15] It rained in the evening and during the night.

Saturday, June 27—Rain showers and muggy. All men who were not on guard or other duties worked on the fortification. Work was done in two shifts; every half hour the rested men went to work again. Of course, no one overworked himself. As a soldier one is not particularly inclined to do hard work; one is not used to it. Even though I did not exert myself, several blisters appeared on my hands from the shovel handle. In the afternoon a strong detachment of cavalry came and lent a hand. The abundance of hands at work advanced the project quickly; the ramparts were raised noticeably. In the evening each worker received a schnapps. I bathed in the creek near our camp. This can be done here, since there are no mosquitoes in this area.

Sunday, June 28—Today on camp guard. All men not on duty worked several hours on the fort. The air was muggy, stifling. Detachments of the Colorado regiment were constantly busy felling the trees around the bulwark, partly to use the wood for building the fort and, at the same time, to clear space as a field of fire for the fort's cannons. It is said that the First Brigade of the First Division of the Army of Southeastern Missouri is to leave here today, southward.[16] General Davidson looks over the progress of the bulwark daily.

Horses and mules are stolen here every night, by soldiers, of course, who sell every animal as long as it does not yet have the

15. According to Special Orders No. 50, HQ, District of Southeastern Missouri, October 1, 1863, the officer in charge of the fort's construction, at least at that time, was 2nd Lt. Fred Smith of Company F, First Nebraska, who was then being reassigned to the regiment. Orders, NSHS RG18, roll 3. Smith's Compiled Service Record, roll 21, indicates that in July and August 1863 he served as assistant engineer. He was dismissed from the service by court-martial January 16, 1864. Dudley, *Roster of Nebraska Volunteers*, 66–67. The completed fortification would be named Fort Davidson.

16. The brigade, commanded by Col. Lewis Merrill, comprised the First, Second, Seventh, and Eighth regiments of Missouri volunteer cavalry. *OR*, ser. 1, vol. 22, part 2, p. 345.

U.S. brand. Our regiment is notably distinguished by the large number of such thieves. In this way farmers and other private persons lose some valuable horses or mules. Last night our regimental physician lost his riding horse in this manner.[17] There must be a large number of well-skilled horse thieves in our regiment.

I am suffering from a stubborn constipation, probably as a result of the diet. I also have small boils over my whole body. The water with its very heavy iron content, I believe, causes the latter evil, since so many suffer from the same. Toward evening we had thunderstorms and very heavy rain during the first part of the night.

Monday, June 29—Before we were relieved this morning, we had a strong thunderstorm again and steady rain. More troops arrived from St. Louis yesterday to join the expedition. Among them were the Third Missouri Cavalry Regiment and a part of an Illinois battery, as well as the Twenty-fifth Ohio Battery. By noon the weather cleared up, and then we had a nice day. But the steady rain has made it very muddy.

Furthermore, there is the stench of the many dead horses and mules. This makes our present campground extremely unpleasant, if not really unhealthy. The dead animals are usually left lying on the surface only a short distance from the camp, or if buried, they are covered only very superficially with soil. The cadavers are around us in such large numbers that the stench is really pestilential. A large number of these poor animals died here in the corrals after we had returned from our expedition to Arkansas.

A small detachment worked today on the fort. This evening we had dress parade. Various orders were read. Since Colonel Livingston has departed for St. Louis, the regiment is under the command of Captain Curran.

Tuesday, June 30—Although the evening was wonderful and the sky clear, during the night we had a very severe thunderstorm with

17. Dr. William McClelland, who had enlisted as assistant surgeon, and was appointed regimental surgeon on September 7, 1862. He served with the regiment until it was mustered out on July 1, 1866. Dudley, *Roster of Nebraska Volunteers*, 4–5.

heavy rain. Lightning and thunder, storm and rain, raged terribly, and various tents were blown over, yet we were spared and remained dry. The little brook has swollen up to a raging stream. At nine o'clock there is inspection for two months' pay.

Before we could march up from the regiment's front in companies for this inspection, we had to fall in in a quarre [square], front toward the inside. Colonel Livingston gave a speech and decorated a piper from Company A with a medal for bravery displayed in the last battle of Cape Girardeau.[18] Five more of our men are to be rewarded the same way for bravery displayed there. The entire regimental band had thrown away their drums and fifes and had taken up rifles and had fought in the ranks.[19]

After the inspection all men not on duty were ordered to work on the fortifications. Every Negro was seized and put to work at the fort. In the afternoon a number of the white inhabitants of the area, who had been summoned to work on building the fort, came also. The day was nice and not so warm. The teams dragged logs out of the woods up here into the fort.

Wednesday, July 1—It was a nice day, not too warm. We all had to work on the fort. Also a small detachment from the cavalry came, as well as a few locals and Negroes, but in general little was accom-

18. This may be Pvt. James Boyce, a bugler in Company A. His service record includes a letter from Col. Robert Livingston that mentions Boyce as "a noble brave soldier who won a medal for gallantry at Girardeau." No description of his deed was provided. Compiled Service Records, roll 3. Boyce was mustered out at the expiration of his service on August 27, 1864. Dudley, *Roster of Nebraska Volunteers,* 14–15. Either Scherneckau was mistaken when he wrote the day before that Livingston had gone to St. Louis or the colonel had returned after only a brief trip.

19. The First Nebraska band, initially composed mostly of Germans from Company B, was mustered out, along with other regimental bands, by Special Orders No. 206, HQ, Army of the Southwest, August 18, 1862. Dudley, *Roster of Nebraska Volunteers,* 6–7. Nevertheless, the regiment later had a band, if an unofficial one. According to an article reprinting a letter by bandleader Henry Vogt in the June 30, 1865, *Nebraska Republican* (Omaha), the band had been organized in July 1863. The men provided their own instruments. Some of the bandsmen were buglers and drummers in their official capacities. Vogt had enlisted from St. Louis in May 1863 as a bugler in Company B and was appointed chief bugler of the regiment on August 11, 1864. Dudley, *Roster of Nebraska Volunteers,* 6–7. Here, however, Scherneckau evidently means the drummers, fifers, and buglers when he refers to "the band."

plished. Soldiers don't like to work. There was plenty of beer, at least much more than I wanted to drink. We signed the payroll. It tried to rain a few times but did not amount to much.

Thursday, July 2—A wagon from the Christian Aid Society brought a load of religious tracts and leaflets. I took a German edition of the New Testament.[20] A few days ago we again drew rations, and this time we got dried apples and syrup for variety. This worked better on my digestive system than all the pills and salts from the doctor, and I feel much better now than in the last two weeks. Early in the morning the bugle called us to work.

Today a detachment from the Colorado regiment came to help us. The teams dragged logs out of the woods. Negroes and locals also helped, so the breastworks grew considerably. The fort is not very extensive, but the walls are unnecessarily thick and the trenches, therefore, deep and wide. On the south side a covered path leads under the wall into a long trench with breastworks on both sides so that it can be used as a rifle pit for musket fire, which would cover the front of the fort. This trench coming from the fort toward the small creek in an obtuse angle will lead into it and should serve as a way to the water at the same time.

After the men were paid off, the greater portion of the cavalry left us, as I hear. A detachment of the Third Missouri Cavalry Regiment, which is still here, also helped in building the fort. In general the building of this fort is not very popular, either among the men or the officers, in part because we do not think that it is necessary to build more fortifications here but even more because the location of the fort is regarded as unsuitable. Several of the surrounding heights completely overlook the fort. Although a layman in these things, this last reason appears to me to be quite serious. I do not believe that the fort could be held, should the enemy be able to bring cannons onto the above-mentioned heights.[21]

20. He may mean the Christian Commission, organized in November 1861 by Protestant ministers and YMCA officials to provide nursing care, books and pamphlets, and other comforts to the troops. McPherson, *Ordeal by Fire*, 386.

21. Scherneckau was remarkably prescient. On September 27, 1864, Gen. Sterling Price's Confederate Army of Missouri attacked Fort Davidson. Although the Confederates emplaced field artillery on Shepherd's Mountain overlooking

Part of the regiment was paid off this evening. The weather was warm, and several times it tried to rain.

Friday, July 3—The last four companies of our regiment were paid off this morning. I wrote to Egge. Very warm. In the afternoon we had to dig. Of course, as soon as money was available, there were drunks. Sent twenty dollars to Egge. In the evening and during the night it rained quite a bit.

Saturday, July 4—At sunrise a salute by the thirty-two-pounders of Fort Curtis was fired, and at the same time, the reveille of the field band and bugles woke us up.[22] At eight o'clock I had to take up guard duty, which was staffed unusually heavily, probably to suppress fights that might break out. I was on guard duty in town; my post was in front of headquarters. During the course of the day, almost all of the officers got pretty drunk. Every company in the camp received half a keg of beer. Of course, there were a great many drunks.

At nine o'clock in the morning, the preacher gave a speech inside the unfinished fort. My duty prevented me from hearing it to the end. The beginning was quite good. At noon two six-pounder howitzers fired another salvo. They were set up close to the camp, and from there they fired shells in different directions to test the range to various heights where the enemy might try to settle down. They were the first shells I had seen being shot and exploding. Some were thrown completely over Shepherd's Mountain. Their whistling in the air does not exactly sound pleasant, but

---

the fort and opened a brief bombardment, they then tried to carry the fort in a series of infantry assaults, which the badly outnumbered Union garrison repulsed, causing significant Confederate casualties. Had the Confederates had more, or heavier, guns, they likely could have bombarded the fort into submission. On the night of September 27, however, the Union forces withdrew from Fort Davidson, fearing they could not resist renewed attacks from their numerically superior foe. The First Nebraska did not take part in the battle, having returned to Nebraska by that time. Brownlee, "The Battle of Pilot Knob."

22. Fort Curtis, between Ironton and Arcadia, was abandoned in favor of Fort Davidson because the former was too far from the railroad and supply depot at Pilot Knob. *Guide to Civil War Activities.*

it is pretty to see them explode: at first the small smoke cloud in the air, then the report of the explosion.

The result of all that beer was excessive drunkenness and then fights! I saw really brutal fights; the men struck each other with their fists until the blood was flowing freely. Large crowds gathered around these fighters and encouraged them all the more. The officer of the day, whose duty it is to suppress all such disturbances of the peace, did not appear at all. The officers who are not on duty are usually the first among the public watching the fight and trying to regulate and coordinate the battles systematically. Our first lieutenant [William T. Clarke], who today was officer of the day, is himself a big rowdy and therefore did not bother. Very warm day.

Sunday, July 5—Six prisoners, secesh spies and letter carriers for the rebels, whom we were guarding here, escaped last night. All were in chains, and even though the guards discovered it immediately, so far they have dodged any pursuit. One of them was condemned to be shot. The men on guard, one of them from our company, were arrested this morning and put in irons.[23] Also the officer of the guard and the field officer of the day, a captain of our regiment, are under arrest. Colonel Livingston is determined to punish the guilty men with extreme severity! I was lucky that this time I was not on duty at the guardhouse. Very warm in the morning; storms and heavy rains in the afternoon. In the evening, a sermon by our chaplain (while I am writing this down). A lot of money is gambled away, as always after payday. Professional gamblers take the money from the greenhorns.

Monday, July 6—Very hot in the morning, then in the afternoon thunderstorms and heavy rain. Work was done on the fort. Since

23. Pvt. John C. Douglas of Company H and Pvt. Thomas Mason of Company D were subsequently court-martialed and punished for letting the prisoners escape. General Orders No. 81, HQ, Department of the Missouri, St. Louis, August 17, 1863, copy in possession of James E. Potter. Douglas reenlisted November 10, 1863, and deserted August 16, 1865, when the regiment was serving in Nebraska. Dudley, *Roster of Nebraska Volunteers*, 96–97.

the cavalry left here we hear all kinds of rumors of their battles with the rebels not very far from here. This evening we heard the boom of cannons from the direction of Fredericktown. Whether it was only a salute or whether a battle took place there, one cannot say, of course.

Tuesday, July 7—Today I was on guard duty; as always, all kinds of rain showers. The work on the fort is progressing very slowly, since the rain so often interrupts the work, and if work is being done, it does not amount to much. Never did the thought occur to me, as I left Germany and my father's home, that on this day, the seventh of July, I would be handling a musket for Uncle Sam![24]

Wednesday, July 8—Very warm weather today. After I was relieved I was lying on my bed in the tent while the remaining men worked on the fort. When relieved from guard duty we have no more work to do that day. Suddenly a bugler in the fort blew assembly. All the men were soon gathered there. After silence was established, the assembly came to order, and our Colonel Livingston stepped up. At first he informed us of all kinds of good news: Vicksburg had surrendered; our troops had driven back an attack on Helena and were also victorious in Pennsylvania. As a result of all this good news, he gave us a holiday, then closed the meeting amid a thousand shouts, Hurrah![25]

Just as on the Fourth of July, each company received half a barrel of beer. Drunks and fights were the result. Unfortunately, our company distinguished itself in this especially; due to drunkenness there were bloody heads among the best of friends. It is really brutal how these men beat up each other! Also the officers were soon drunk, many of them beastly, dead drunk. Even the officer du jour could barely stand on his legs!

24. This was his father's birthday, as he noted in his diary after he returned to Nebraska in 1864.

25. The surrender of Vicksburg on July 4 followed the Army of the Potomac's victory over Robert E. Lee's Army of Northern Virginia at Gettysburg the day before. *American Heritage Civil War Chronology.*

At sunset a salute was fired by the two cannons of the Second Illinois Battery. Like on the Fourth they threw shells on and over Shepherd's Mountain. Setting the fuse mostly on 2½ to 3½ [seconds], the shots usually exploded half a mile distant, just before they touched the ground. In the evening fireballs and rockets were shot from headquarters.

Thursday, July 9—Very warm, like yesterday. A full workday, yet the soldiers have not accomplished much. This way it will still take a long time until the fort is finished. Wrote to Hedde. One can find many wild berries in this area, and some of them are brought into camp for sale; among them are the following: blackberries, dewberries in English, also on the hills a small variety of raspberries, sometimes called blackberry; blueberries are also found here in abundance, huckleberry.

Friday, July 10—Not as warm as yesterday. We worked on the fort. Heavy oak logs are now being used to build the foundations for the gun emplacements, of which six are to be set up, one in each corner. The trench is fifteen feet wide at the top, with a depth of twelve feet.[26] At the ground the wall has a thickness of eighteen feet, sloping off at the top so that the breastworks show a thickness of only about nine feet. The breastwork, five feet high, is covered with planks on the inside.

Saturday, July 11—I was on post guard, which we now take up together with the Colorado regiment. Foggy weather. I had to guard the prisoners going to the fort to work. Therefore, I was relieved of the night duty. Slept under the open sky; quite cold, but it did not rain, although it threatened. Our men who are sitting in chains in prison since the escape of the prisoners are now undergoing an investigation. One of the secesh who had escaped at the time has been captured again and now is making very compromising statements about one of the guards. He states that he

26. The trench or ditch was outside the walls of the fort, as an obstacle to an infantry assault.

had bribed the soldier guarding the door. Two graybacks, as we call the gray-clad soldiers of the regular army of the South, were brought in yesterday, presumably deserters. They belong to Marmaduke's troops, who are supposed to be in our area.[27] One of them wears the proper uniform: gray trousers, gray coat with blue lapel and collar, and a black hat.

Sunday, July 12—Was relieved this morning. No work on the fort; cold weather, overcast sky.

Monday, July 13—Cold and gray sky, as yesterday. Had to work on the fort. I mentioned some time ago that a member of our company has set up a barbershop out in the open. On an average he makes two to three dollars daily. Some days it goes up to eight to ten dollars. But if he must be on guard duty, of course, he cannot pursue his business.

Tuesday, July 14—Warmer weather again today. I went on guard duty here in camp. With the warmer weather the flies are unbearable, especially during mealtime. Other pests don't bother us as much, except now and again the annoying lice. It is very difficult to keep them away when one has to camp for so long at the same place. Every third or fourth day, one is on guard duty and has to be stationed at the guardhouse, where lice are crawling in abundance. I wish we would march on again! The nights here are almost always cold, cool enough to sleep comfortably only under two woolen blankets. On guard my overcoat proved very useful against the sharp morning air. Sent off a letter to Egge.

Wednesday, July 15—Was relieved and had the day off to rest. The weather was pleasant. Lieutenant Colonel Baumer returned to the regiment today and was received as the darling wherever he appeared. The work on the fort is progressing slowly. Whiskey is distributed to the working detachments. The beer that we received

27. Gen. John S. Marmaduke, who had led the April 1863 raid on Cape Girardeau.

during the first days of work was, as I now learn, paid for by the neighboring brewery as a fine because it had sold some to the soldiers without permission; a good idea! Today I had a dish that I had not eaten since I came to America. I bought whortleberries and a pint of milk for six cents, which with a bit of sugar made a good hors d'oeuvre to the beans and bacon. I wrote to sister Sophie.

Thursday, July 16—Was cooks police today. It is said that our advance post was attacked yesterday. It is not known which troops did this and how strong they were. However, one can assume that there are no forces of any significance in the area, so to speak, at the rear of the strong army that left here recently. The Third Missouri Cavalry Regiment provides the advance post duty here. Pleasant weather, not too warm.

Friday, July 17—On guard duty in town. There we have to guard the prisoners and government property. Besides, there are several posts now in the new fort, which has been named "Davidson." Two thirty-two-pounders, pivot guns, have been set up there. They were taken from the fort [Fort Curtis] in Arcadia. It appears that it will be abandoned.

Two sergeants from our company received orders yesterday to report in Cincinnati. They will take an examination before they receive their commissions as officers in a Negro regiment, for which they had applied. Friend Foster still does not have his release from our regiment in his hands, apparently due to chicanery, and therefore will most likely lose his position.

From the St. Louis newspapers I take it that the Sioux are restless in the area of Hall County and that the party of the government surveyors in that region has asked for military protection so that they can continue their work. Rumors about disturbances and skirmishes with bands of Indians are being spread here in the Nebraska regiment. But private letters to us have not yet verified these rumors. However, I look forward very much to receiving letters from you.[28]

28. Scherneckau and his comrades may have heard about a June 22, 1863, skirmish between soldiers of Company D, Second Nebraska Volunteer Cavalry,

The farmers of the area now come here daily to the camp with vegetables, butter, eggs, etc., like we used to peddle at Fort Kearny. Butter is about twenty cents a pound, and eggs fifteen to twenty cents a dozen. There are only few vegetables available. Milk is brought to the camp by farmers living nearby or other owners of cows and sold at five cents a pint. The poor peddling farmers, unfortunately, are too often robbed and cheated by the scoundrels, of whom the regiment has plenty. Yesterday, a farmer driving around here in camp almost had his horse stolen from his wagon, and he did not get back his rope and bridle. A pail of butter was stolen from another wagon while selling from it was underway. But this time the people got their butter back, and the soldiers suspected of the theft were put into the guardhouse. Another pail with fourteen pounds of butter, however, disappeared without the thieves being detected. So much for the honesty of the Noble Nebraska Volunteers!

Horse thieves, gamblers, swindlers, etc., are almost in the majority. I find only a few among the comrades who, after a longer acquaintance, can claim my respect. The braggarts, flatterers, and sycophants, who succeed the best, are without merit or principles. This creates an emptiness and loneliness in me, and I often feel depressed and homesick! I just wish we would soon have some activity again. The night was unusually mild. My post was in front of headquarters, a row of tents on a lovely place in town at the foot of Pilot Knob.

Saturday, July 18—Overcast, foggy weather. Was relieved and had the day to relax. As usual all the men not doing duty elsewhere had to work on the fort. Today another bit of talented thievery by the Braves. A large number of the belts with the square buckles or, better, plates, to hook the belt together in front, which were recently delivered to the ordnance officer stationed here, were stolen little by little. The infantry of our regiment, especially, took these

---

and Sioux Indians near the Pawnee Agency in Nebraska. One soldier was killed, and one was wounded. The agency was some fifty miles northeast of the Hall County German settlement. R. T. Beall to Robert Knox, adjutant general of Nebraska, November 21, 1865, correspondence of the First Nebraska Volunteer Infantry/Cavalry, NSHS RG18, box 2.

instead of the oval plates with "U.S." on them and used these so-called eagle plates on their body belts, just because they probably look a little better and are easier to keep shiny. This morning at inspection for guard duty, all the men who were wearing these cavalry plates were arrested, and all tents were then searched for more, but not many were found, since most men had gotten wind of it and got rid of the offending plates.

Sunday, July 19—Cool weather. This morning I had guard duty again, since so many men are required to fill all the posts. To my great joy the mail brought a letter from my parents, sent straight to this regiment. Since I was super numerae, I slept very well all night in the guardhouse. There are now about seventy prisoners under guard there, mostly deserters from the various regiments in the district. Besides these, a number of other soldiers are there for various offences—neglect of duty, insubordination, drunkenness, etc.—also several of the local residents, who are under suspicion of having had business with the enemy. Spies and deserters from the rebel army are likewise being held as prisoners there. A court-martial is in session here at present to pass sentence upon them.

Monday, July 20—Relieved this morning after we had taken the prisoners to work at the fort. Wrote to Father and Sophie. The day was very warm.

Tuesday, July 21—Today I had to work on the fort; it will be finished soon. Besides four thirty-two-pounder pivot guns, there are now three twenty-four-pounder howitzers, field cannon, in place, as well as two six-inch mortars.[29] In the center of the fort a bombproof powder magazine and supply house is now being built.

Wednesday, July 22—Today I had to take up post guard. Had one of the posts at the railway station, where quartermaster and commissary stores are to be guarded. Besides the posts set out by the camp

29. The seven large guns were in place during the September 27, 1864, Battle of Pilot Knob, supplemented by six three-inch ordnance rifles brought up just before the Confederate attack. *Pilot Knob,* 9, 13.

guard, fourteen sentries are now set out by us and the Colorado regiment. Five of them are around the guardhouse, number six is guarding the ordnance supplies, seven and eight are at the railway station, nine is at headquarters, ten at the tent of the court-martial. The rest are guarding cannons and ammunition in the fort. The night was warm; at the same time there was heavy dew. Finished my letter to Father and sent it off.

Thursday, July 23—Was relieved and had the day to rest. As always, work on the fort. The weather was quite warm. With the last rations we received new potatoes, which make for a pleasant change. I wrote to Hedde. As expected, the brave General Davidson advanced in his old-fashioned, easygoing way. Instead of advancing with his troops as quickly as possible—his force was almost exclusively mounted and light—and attacking in Arkansas, thereby threatening General Price's army in the rear and on the flanks and perhaps cutting him off entirely from Little Rock, he is now lying between Cape Girardeau and Bloomfield with his force, as it is said, building fortifications. After all the lengthy preparations here, stockpiling all kinds of material and supplies, he goes only to Cape Girardeau. There, if he had thought of it or intended it before, he could have equipped his expedition at less cost and in less time without being forced, as it is now, to have his supplies hauled through swamps and over steep hills between here and Bloomfield! There is only one word for this kind of warfare. General D. might be fit for the Army of the Potomac, but here in the West his strategy is unsatisfactory. He is one of the "smart West-Pointers."[30]

Friday, July 24—This morning I again took up guard duty as a substitute for the comrade who had been taken to prison, arrested for stealing. He had stolen the watch, the revolver, and money from a comrade of Company E while he was drunk, fast asleep. The accusation is, of course, true without a doubt, but it is questionable if it can be proven.[31] Since I have come into such close contact with so

30. Davidson graduated from West Point on July 1, 1845, twenty-seventh in a class of forty. Davidson, *Black Jack Davidson*, 23.

31. This may be Pvt. Edward P. Goulding, who was confined in the guardhouse on July 25 and released the next day. Company H Morning Report, July 1863,

many men, my judgment for or against a man, as I have frequently noted, depends very much on my impression of his looks, especially his facial expressions. It has been this way with this comrade: all along his appearance, especially his face, was the most repulsive of all those in my company. I do not believe that I have spoken more than a hundred words with him since I joined the company, though I did not know anything bad about him. I only learned of it yesterday after his arrest became known, though the theft had been committed when we were still stationed in St. Louis. Several of the men whom I expected to be of better character due to their physiognomy unfortunately did not turn out to be as such upon close acquaintance, although my judgment almost always proved to be true with the ones who showed evil in their faces. Unfortunately, we just have too many evil and rough fellows among us. Only a very few satisfy the requirements that I demand from an educated person. Among them, above all, I value—as I have frequently mentioned—Foster from Company K of our regiment.

I again had the post in front of headquarters. General Fisk has now taken over the command of the District of Southeastern Missouri, replacing General Davidson.[32] It is to be hoped that the latter will now advance. The general has his tent next to the headquarters, set up next to that of our Colonel Livingston. A third sergeant [Thomas H. Price] of our company left us today to pass his examination in Cincinnati before he can obtain his commission in a Negro regiment. Our orderly sergeant is now the only noncommissioned officer in our camp. At night we had a severe thunderstorm and rain.

Saturday, July 25—Relieved this morning and rested all day. No work on the fort. Yesterday our men felled trees to build the powder magazine in the new fort. Since a large review is to be held tomorrow, there was general cleaning and polishing of weapons and other equipment in camp. I did not feel entirely well.

NSHS RG18, roll 3. Scherneckau reports the unnamed soldier's release in his July 27 entry. Goulding reenlisted in November 1863 and deserted September 7, 1865, at Plum Creek, Nebraska Territory. Dudley, *Roster of Nebraska Volunteers*, 98–99.

32. Brig. Gen. Clinton B. Fisk. Faust, *Encyclopedia of the Civil War*, 261; Sifakis, *Who Was Who in the Union*, 137.

Sunday, July 26—Had to report in sick today, a kind of colic with severe stomach pains that made it impossible for me to take up guard duty, as I would have had to do if I had been well enough. A heavy dose of pills gave me relief during the day. At nine o'clock our regiment marched out for review, which was held in the vicinity of Ironton. Every man not on guard duty or sick had to go along, even the cooks and all other men who were listed in the morning report as on daily duty had to march along with their respective companies, knapsack on the back with the overcoat tied on top. It was very warm, and naturally, the men were sweating very much in the heavy uniform coat (dress coats) with the packs. Since our Captain Ivory has not yet returned, First Lieutenant Clarke is now commanding the company. He is more popular than Ivory was. But Clarke loves whiskey, and we often see him under the influence, again this afternoon, when he was beastly drunk. A nice example this commissioned officer is giving his men, yet he is not the worst in the regiment by far. Had dress parade again for the first time this evening.

Monday, July 27—I felt better, although still weak and exhausted from the strong dose of medicine that I had taken yesterday. We are not working at the fort anymore except for a few soldiers from our and the Colorado regiment ordered there as carpenters. The prisoners will have to finish the earthwork that still has to be done. In the coolness of the evening, we had battalion drill for one and a half hours, and at sunset, dress parade again. An order regulating the daily drill times was read, as well as the judgment regarding the scoundrel I had talked about several days ago who had been arrested because of theft from a comrade. They only sentenced him to repay the money, which will be taken out of his next pay, and he is already free. Although the court-martial has been in session a long time, only a few verdicts have been reached so far, and the prison is still filled with prisoners under many different charges. Since I felt better, I took part in the drill. The night was icy cold.

Tuesday, July 28—This morning, right after breakfast, drill from six to eight o'clock. Since I was feeling better, I did not visit the doctor anymore. The day was tolerably warm. Although it is much farther south, I do not find it much warmer here than in Nebraska at this time of year. However, the nights are definitely colder here, even icy. None of Nebraska's warm nights with mosquitoes, in which it is almost impossible to get any sleep. Two thick woolen blankets are hardly warm enough for cover. At five thirty regimental drill, and dress parade at seven o'clock. In the afternoon, along with a detachment, I had to get a load of kitchen wood for our cooks.

Wednesday, July 29—Camp guard duty today; had a post in the fort, which is occupied by our camp guard. It was not very warm, drilling, dress parade as usual at sunset. The fort is close to completion; the carpenters assigned to it are diligently at work. The Negroes and prisoners still have to work on the unfinished earthwork. The powder magazine is being built underground with the heaviest oak blocks. The hole dug out for it is at least eighteen to twenty feet deep. Considering the small area of the fort, it seems to me that too much work and expense are being wasted on the interior equipment for this merely unimportant location.[33] The night was again very cold; wrapped in my overcoat and walking back and forth, I was still freezing.

Thursday, July 30—Relieved; drill in the evening and dress parade as usual. It was stifling hot. A small fatigue party from our regiment had to work on the fort.

Friday, July 31—Company drill right after breakfast; again a detail for the work on the fort. Warm and very stifling during the day. As I indicated earlier, drills are only in the morning and evening so that we can rest during the heat. But at noon the tents are very hot. In the evening, first battalion drill and then dress parade.

33. The Fort Davidson earthworks survive, now the focal point of a Missouri Historic Site at Pilot Knob, including a visitor center that interprets the September 26–27, 1864, battle. Upon evacuating the fort, the Union forces blew up the powder magazine, leaving a large depression within the earthworks that remains today.

Saturday, August 1—Was on guard duty in town today; the heat was oppressive, yet it was somewhat tolerable through a good breeze. By sending [prisoners] to St. Louis, by passing judgment and discharging some, the guardhouse has been emptied quite a bit. Its cleanliness has improved considerably, as also by whitewashing the whole building. The night was pleasant. [The diary from August 2 to August 29 was lost.]

CHAPTER 11

Guarding the Navy Yard at Carondelet, August 30–October 24, 1863

[Sunday] August 30—I have to update my diary for more than just a day. Unfortunately, I lost my knapsack on the trip here [to St. Louis] from Pilot Knob, or more correctly, it likely was stolen. On Thursday, the twenty-seventh of July [August], we received marching orders to go to Kansas City.[1] Early on in the morning of the twenty-eighth, preparations were made for departure, yet the signal to strike the tents was not given until noon. Soon this was done, the wagons loaded, and the regiment in rank and file. I followed on the wagon of our company, since I still felt very weak.[2] A long train of railway cars was waiting for us. Our wagons with their loads were pushed from the platform directly onto the flatcars, two [wagons] onto one [flatcar]. Freight cars were furnished with seats for the men.

After our animals also were all on board the train, we finally left Pilot Knob a little after six o'clock. The night was not very cold, yet the arrangement for sleeping on the small benches without backs was not up to much. Around midnight we arrived at the depot of the

1. Rumors must have spread that additional Union troops were to be sent to western Missouri in the wake of guerrilla William C. Quantrill's August 20 raid on Lawrence, Kansas. Kansas U.S. senator James Lane advocated a retaliatory strike into western Missouri. After discussion, Department of the Missouri commander John M. Schofield prohibited Lane's foray. On August 25 Thomas Ewing, Jr., the Union commander in western Missouri, issued the infamous Order No. 11 that evicted the entire population of several counties. President Lincoln suspended the order in November. Etcheson, *Bleeding Kansas*, 239–42.

2. Perhaps he was still suffering from the sickness he had reported on July 26 or had suffered a relapse.

Iron Mountain Railway, not having had much sleep. We stayed in the car the rest of the night, that is, all men who did not go out for another drink. Unfortunately, there were not just a few, as many drunken men could confirm at daybreak. I still had several hours of sleep, until at daybreak the regiment marched off to Camp Gamble.

At the beginning of the war this [camp] became famous as Camp Jackson. It is located to the west of the city. I stayed with the wagons of the regiment, which around noon were finally unloaded, and they then followed the regiment out on Olive Street, where the camp is located.[3] On arrival there we found that our Company H had been ordered to Carondelet, a suburb of St. Louis on the Mississippi south of the city, to guard the navy yard there. Companies B, D, and I were ordered to Schofield Barracks, Company E to the Gratiot Street prison, Companies F and G to the Myrtle Street prison. The rest of the regiment remains in camp, a nice place covered with shade trees.

After we, that is, Company H, had eaten a noon meal in a rush, we marched off to Carondelet. I rode the greater part of the way, since I am still very weak, and besides I had a severe headache. Colonel Livingston is now the local commandant of St. Louis, and the Tenth Kansas Regiment has been transferred to Kansas instead of us.

Carondelet, about six miles from the center of the city of St. Louis, is quite a sizable place built along the river. A well-maintained street leads there from St. Louis; extensive fruit orchards are on both sides of the road. The peach trees are quite heavy with the red-glistening fruit, a truly splendid sight. We set up our tents right behind the Union Iron Works, where the river gunboats are built, on a hill covered with shade trees, a schoolhouse in the middle, which is now our kitchen.[4] We have a beautiful view from here, over the city, the river, and into Illinois, the state lying across

3. Camp Jackson/Camp Gamble was bounded by Grand Avenue, Laclede Avenue, Lindell Street, and Olive Street. A map is in Winter, *The Civil War in St. Louis,* 46.

4. This shipyard was operated by James B. Eads, who built several ironclad gunboats for the U.S. Army and Navy. Winter, *The Civil War in St. Louis,* 77–78; Gerteis, *Civil War St. Louis,* 237–53.

from us. As the baggage was unloaded, I discovered to my dismay that my knapsack had disappeared, had been stolen. I do not lose much in the way of clothing, but I am pained the most by the loss of my writing case with all the letters that I have received so far. Besides, I also lost some of the diary.

The night was very cold. Although I slept with a comrade under two heavy woolen blankets, I still woke up several times due to the cold. Our duty here consists in guarding the navy yard only at night; we have no duty during the day. This morning I drove with our team to St. Louis to see if I could find some trace of my knapsack. Since a number of men from our company are stationed there as provost guard, I had some hope, but it was useless. Our wagon went back to Camp Gamble, since we do not need a team here.

Today rations were sent out to us. I went back to the arsenal and rode with an omnibus from there for ten cents all the way to our campground. In the afternoon I wrote in my diary, so long neglected. Second Lieutenant Moore now commands our company, since the captain is still on leave. The first lieutenant in Pilot Knob [William T. Clarke] stayed on as a member of General Fisk's staff. As I had mentioned, the night of our arrival in St. Louis we had a large number of our men drunk, and on the day of our arrival they were spread across the city, still very much under the influence of the whiskey.

This afternoon, one of the eleven-inch Columbiads was transported here from St. Louis. A two-wheel wagon provided with very high wheels, like the ones used to transport steam boilers, was hitched to eight horses, and they pulled this giant hanging between the wheels with ease. A gunboat is anchored here, almost completed. It will receive two towers [turrets] and, inside each, two of these eleven-inch "destruction deliverers."[5]

Monday, August 31—Again a cold night, and during the day, not very warm either. I am feeling better, but I suffer from constipa-

5. The gunboats were armed with smoothbore Dahlgren guns, not Columbiads. For details on these two types of cannon, see Ripley, *Artillery and Ammunition*, chapters 4 and 5. The large cart used to transport the cannon was called a sling cart. Ripley, *Artillery and Ammunition*, 239–40.

The former Eads boatyards in Carondelet. A postwar photograph by David C. Humphries, ca. 1882–85. Neg. # Outside StL. 117. Missouri Historical Society, St. Louis.

tion. We were mustered today for two months' pay. Lieutenant Colonel Baumer mustered our company here. I wrote to Egge. Sergeant Price received his commission as first lieutenant in the Fourth Regiment Colored Troops of the regular army. Sergeant Adamson went with the recruiting detachment to Nebraska.[6] In the evening I received a letter from Egge.

Tuesday, September 1—We had some warmer weather than the last days. In the afternoon we had an hour of drill, but I am still on the sick list and so was not involved. We are camped here at a very busy place. Right at our feet the Iron Mountain trains go by day and night. A little farther away the imposing steamboats glide up and down the Mississippi. Besides, all day long the navy yard, with its three hundred workers, makes a racket, constant hammering is sounding up from there. So far I like it here, but, of course, it is not why I joined the army. I always wished for activity in the field. It seems to be my fate to be kept away at all times from all major action in the field. Otherwise we have it as pleasant here as soldiers could wish for. We receive our flour, and for that a baker delivers good fresh bread every day. Other provisions, which we have in surplus, we can trade for things we want. A few days ago we thus traded a dish of fish for several bars of soap, etc. The camp here is called "Mary Belle" after a sign on a shed that served as quarters for the troops stationed here last winter; now, however, it is in need of major repairs to make it livable again.

Wednesday, September 2—I wrote to Pilot Knob. The weather is somewhat warmer again. Fine apples and peaches are cheap here. At some places one can get them free for the gathering under the trees. We signed the payroll.

Thursday, September 3—We received orders to get ready for inspection, but the officers did not appear. The weather is still not very warm.

6. Aaron M. Adamson was discharged December 31, 1863, to accept a commission in the First Missouri Colored Troops. Dudley, *Roster of Nebraska Volunteers*, 90–91.

Friday, September 4—Since I have been plagued with toothache for some time, I obtained a pass yesterday and went to St. Louis and then to Camp Gamble, where Companies C, A, and K, as well as the regimental staff, are located. The bad molar was pulled, and I feel very much relieved.[7] In the evening I returned with the train of the Iron Mountain Railway, which runs every two hours between Carondelet and St. Louis, for fifteen cents. The camp was in high spirits, since the newly appointed lieutenant had ordered several barrels of beer, and, as usual, not just a few of our men enjoyed too much of the good thing.[8]

In St. Louis last night the provost guard had been ordered to be ready on the shortest notice at all times, since it was expected that a strong number of sympathizers with the South would cause unrest in the city. The government cotton lying on the landing in such large quantities was to be burned and if possible the prisoners in McDowell College to be set free. Jeff. Thompson is there in custody.[9] During the night strong detachments of infantry and cavalry patrolled the streets of the city, but the peace was not disturbed.

Saturday, September 5—A nice day. Yesterday I found an old knapsack, turned it in today, and received a new one for it. Uncle Sam is surely the best man in the world; he hands out new things for old worn-out ones! Unfortunately, I do not have much to fill it with! I received only the most necessary pieces of clothing as replacements for the ones I had lost with the knapsack. As a common soldier it is better

7. He first reported suffering a toothache on November 14, 1862, and frequently thereafter.

8. He means the former Sergeant Price, who had been commissioned a lieutenant in the Fourth U.S. Colored Troops.

9. M. Jeff. Thompson was the Virginia-born mayor of St. Joseph, Missouri, before the war and organized secessionist militia in the region. He also cut down the U.S. flag flying over the St. Joseph post office. Filbert, *The Half Not Told*, chapter 2. Thompson later entered service with the Confederate Missouri State Guard and raided in southeastern Missouri during the early months of the war. In the summer of 1863, Thompson led men, known as "Swamp Rats," in northeastern Arkansas and southeastern Missouri until his capture on August 22. He was sent to federal military prisons and paroled in August 1864. He commanded a brigade in Shelby's Division, Army of Missouri, during Price's 1864 raid into Missouri. Sifakis, *Who Was Who in the Confederacy*, 280.

that one does not carry too much ballast around, especially since we can get whatever we wish in the way of clothing almost any time.

Some time ago I reported as ready for duty, but so far I have not been ordered to do any guard duty. In the afternoon a carriage brought the paymaster, and we received our pay for two months. We are the last company of our regiment to be paid off. Yesterday, when I was in St. Louis, I found several men from our regiment who had not one cent of their pay still in their possession; either it had been stolen or they had already squandered it within twenty-four hours. The men are made drunk and then "sounded," as the technical expression goes, all by their alleged friends! One could almost become a prohibitionist when one sees the effects of brandy in the army!

This time we were paid off in old notes, notes that had already been in circulation. This is the first time we have been paid off in [old] greenbacks; previously we always received them fresh from the presses.

Sunday, September 6—A general "leave for an outing"; only a few remain in camp. Most of them go to St. Louis to have a good time. In the evening I was on guard duty for the first time in a long while. There are only three posts to fill. Each man is on his post for three hours, so that there are only three reliefs from dusk until daybreak. The night was mild and nice.

We have here a truly troubled neighborhood. Several times the residents of the surrounding huts (shanties) called for the guard. These were mostly Irish men and women, drunk, fighting with one another. Of course, we don't pay any attention to these small family quarrels, since, according to the orders we have received, we should not get involved in the affairs of these neighbors.

Around ten o'clock, a little farther away, we heard loud screams and thereupon a rattle as if someone was seriously wounded. Since many of our comrades had been in the city tonight and were drunk, for the most part, it was feared that it was one of ours who had gotten into a fight and was being ill treated. The sergeant and I hurried over to the place and found an old man lying on the ground near a small tavern. Two very tipsy Irishmen were busy with him. The old man, a German, was unable to speak; a bloody wound on his head had caused him to collapse. The Irishmen stated they did not know how the man had received his wounds, which obviously had been inflicted with a sharp instrument, like a hatchet, for example. At first they did not even want to take the wounded man into the house, but upon our insistence they finally agreed. As he was being carried in, he regained consciousness, probably through the pain this caused. He complained mainly about his back. Since he spoke only German, only I could understand him. As much as I could make out he had been attacked by two Irishmen and knocked down; however, he did not accuse any of those present. We took down the names of everyone present. After his wounds were cleansed and dressed, we went back to our post. I then stood my time on the post, from eleven thirty until two thirty, slept the rest of the night. Wrote to Hedde.

Monday, September 7—The old man is still living. The sergeant reported the incident this morning. Our lieutenant likely will turn it over to the appropriate authorities. Since we arrived here the weather has become a little warmer. Even here on this elevation during warm quiet nights mosquitoes get into the tent once in a while. But, of course, the dear little animals don't bother an old acquaintance like me. I now treat myself daily with lovely fruits, apples and pears as well as peaches. The first ones are peeled, and the skin is removed from the peaches. Then I cook them into a sauce in my large quart tin cup, put in a good handful of sugar, and have a delightful dish for dessert. Besides it is very beneficial to one's health. One of our doctors visits us occasionally in order to give the sick the necessary medicine or to put them in the hospital. However, we have almost no cases of sickness at all.

Tuesday, September 8—A warm day. After the meal I went to the docks next to the navy yard where steamboats are built and repaired. A boat, the *New Iowa,* was pulled completely out of the water by steam power.[10] The screw-conveyor was applied here. Eight screws with the corresponding wheels can be set in motion by the machine. Only

10. This may have been the *Iowa,* no. 2766 in *Way's Packet Directory,* 225.

five of them were applied with this boat. The boat, resting on the skids that had already been pushed underneath it when in the water, is moved little by little so that someone sleeping on board would not be aware of it and be highly surprised to find himself on dry land upon awakening.[11] Four boats are now lying there to be repaired, while another, quite large, is being newly built.

Wednesday, September 9—It was cooler again and threatened to rain. Storms and heavy rain the better half of the day. In the evening I had guard duty. The night was pleasant.

Thursday, September 10—Together with a comrade I obtained a pass today. At nine o'clock we went to St. Louis with a train leaving from here. Had myself photographed; for two dollars I received six pictures.[12] Subscribed to Olshausen's paper for another six months. The location of the printing shop as well as the office has now been moved to Chestnut Street and has been greatly enlarged and improved. Mr. Olshausen was very busy in his private office upstairs, and therefore I did not bother him. Because I had heard nothing from Hedde for so long, I had nothing new to report from there, since Olshausen is always anxious for information. At noon I ate in an eating house, made various purchases. St. Louis now is hot and too fast-paced; our camp here suits me much better. Since we missed the train leaving at four o'clock, we had to be patient until the six o'clock train brought us home.

Since two so-called provisional regiments are being formed in the city, naturally only militia for thirty days, it is said we will have to get

11. The Carondelet works were originally known as the Carondelet Marine Railway Company due to an innovative system of rails and conveyors used to move boats from the river to construction or repair facilities on shore and vice versa. Coombe, *Thunder along the Mississippi*, 19. It is probably this mechanism that Scherneckau describes. In August 1862 surgeon John Vance Lauderdale's hospital boat was drawn out of the river at Carondelet by this machinery. Josyph, *Wounded River*, 137.

12. At one time the Hall County Historical Society in Grand Island, Nebraska, had a photograph of Scherneckau as a soldier. The society's collections were transferred to the Stuhr Museum of the Prairie Pioneer in the 1960s, and the photograph cannot be found.

out of here soon, but I do not believe it.[13] If we are sent to the Missouri border to fight the angry men from the free state of Kansas, General Schofield and the copperhead governor will find that they have chosen the wrong men for this, since we surely will make common cause with the Kansas boys.[14] We would help to eradicate the border tramps, alias bushwhackers, with fire and sword.

That is the state of mind in our corps, as it is in the majority of the old regiments. They are without exception staunch radicals. Pacifists, Copperheads, are thoroughly hated, more than the enemy facing us. We respect the latter because he has enough courage to take up arms and openly oppose us, whereas we despise these Northern traitors. Woe to them if they give us an opportunity to move against them; only sharp bullets will be fired there! Surely, no one is more tired of the war than the old soldiers, and they would rather see peace concluded today than tomorrow, but not at any price. Having carried the burden of the war for so long, they are willing to carry it through to the end rather than grant any of the demands of the secesh.

Friday, September 11—In St. Louis yesterday I saw our former colonel, now General Thayer, who is here on leave.[15] I wrote to my parents and sent them an issue of Frank Leslie's newspaper and a picture of St. Louis. In the afternoon we had a short time to drill. In the evening, guard duty. The night was warm at first, but it became cold and windy toward morning.

13. Provisional enrolled Missouri militia regiments were organized in 1863 by the state government of Missouri, the men to be drawn from the enrolled Missouri militia, but as full-time troops. The policy produced debate over whether such a "state army" was legal, and most of the regiments were disbanded in November 1863. Missouri newspaper comment on the issue appears in *OR*, ser. 1, vol. 22, part 2, pp. 555–65.

14. It is clear that Scherneckau was in favor of a retaliatory strike by Kansans in response to Quantrill's sack of Lawrence. Union commander Gen. John M. Schofield and Missouri governor Hamilton Gamble both supported the gradual emancipation of slaves in Missouri, which made them Copperheads in the eyes of those who favored immediate emancipation. Gerteis, *Civil War St. Louis*, 270–71. The German-language newspapers of Missouri had harsh words for Schofield and Gamble and their "Copperhead" policies. *OR*, ser. 1, vol. 22, part 2, pp. 547–55.

15. John M. Thayer, who led the First Nebraska during the early months of its service before being promoted to brigadier general.

Saturday, September 12 [*Sunday, September 13*]—The weather was colder. I wrote to Egge and sent him a calendar. Inspection in the morning. The day was nice. At sunset we saw a big fire beginning on the levee of St. Louis. Soon it was evident that steamboats were burning. Two of them, burning, came downstream; however, they ran ashore long before they could reach us.[16] I was on guard duty; the night was nice. We have received a new recruit, a loafer from the village here.[17]

Monday, September 14—Four steamers burned down last evening: *Imperial, Hiawatha, Post Boy,* and *Jesse K. Bell.*[18] The private from our company under arrest since the Fourth of July because of the five escaped prisoners at Pilot Knob came back to duty again today. After he had been in detention pending trial for almost six weeks, he was given another two months in prison, which he survived in our guardhouse. The main guilty person is now serving six months at hard labor in the penitentiary in Alton and will receive a dishonorable discharge after serving the sentence.[19]

In St. Louis the military is creating quite a tumult, since they beat each other and stab and shoot each other while drunk. A member of Company E from our regiment has to spend two months penalty in Alton and will receive a dishonorable discharge

16. By all accounts (and as Scherneckau says in his September 14 entry), the steamboats were burned on Sunday, September 13. He evidently misdated this entry, perhaps when transcribing the diary.

17. Probably Neal Murphy, who enlisted September 10, 1863. He turned out to be a faithful soldier, serving until the First Nebraska was mustered out in July 1866. Dudley, *Roster of Nebraska Volunteers,* 98–99.

18. The loss of the steamboats was attributed to arson by Confederate agents. Additional boats were burned in early October. Winter, *The Civil War in St. Louis,* 88. On October 8, 1863, General-in-Chief Henry Halleck wrote to Brig. Gen. Robert Allen in St. Louis, remarking that "the burning of steamers on the Mississippi River is really a very serious matter." If the incendiaries were caught, said Halleck, "they should be tried by a military commission and, if found guilty, immediately hung." *OR,* ser. 1, vol. 22, part 2, p. 618.

19. Scherneckau is referring to Pvts. John Douglas of Company H and Thomas Mason of Company D, about whom he had written in July from Pilot Knob. A federal military prison was at Alton, Illinois, across the river from St. Louis. It also housed Confederate prisoners of war. Winter, *The Civil War in St. Louis,* 152–54. Mason of Company D was apparently "the main guilty person," though Dudley, *Roster of Nebraska Volunteers,* 50–51, records him merely as being mustered out on August 24, 1864.

after completing his prison term. He shot at an officer and wounded him on the head.[20]

In the evening I got acquainted with a German who came to shoot a dog. There are enormous numbers of dogs here. He believed our regiment was composed only of Germans. Since he was not able to speak English, luckily he met me right away. I was ready to do him the courtesy; went with him to his house, where he introduced me to his family, a wife and two daughters. The people are Tyroleans and speak a very poor German, since all the time they heard and spoke only Italian.

The man is a ship's carpenter and is now working here on the gunboats; earns two and a half dollars a day. Mechanics and engineers receive from three to five dollars a day. Every piece of iron that is used in the building of the boats must be weighed, also every nail and bolt. The iron plates cost six cents a pound. The smaller ones weigh two hundred pounds or more, the larger ones four hundred pounds or more, and how many of them are used to make the armor of the ships. Each of the eleven-inch cannons, with the gun carriage and all that goes with it, costs six thousand dollars.

Tuesday, September 15—The day was very warm; we had to drill in the afternoon. My new acquaintance sends milk for my coffee; the little girls are becoming quite devoted. Had guard duty. The night warm and still, the mosquitoes very annoying.

Wednesday, September 16—We have a new recruit! How long will they recruit? And how long do they think they can keep these men?[21] I hope we will all be dismissed together when the term of enlistment of this regiment has run out.

Fruit is cheap; large nice apples cost forty cents a bushel, the same for delicious peaches. I wish I could get some to you in

20. The Descriptive Book for Company E lists three men who served time in Alton for unspecified crimes: John Foster, Thomas Kennedy, and William O'Byrne. NSHS RG18, roll 3.

21. This recruit was Joseph Robertson, who enlisted September 14, 1863. He deserted September 8, 1865, when the regiment was serving in Nebraska. Dudley, *Roster of Nebraska Volunteers*, 100–101.

Nebraska, so fresh from the tree! Some rain in the afternoon. Since we always had the freedom to visit the city that, so to speak, surrounds us, this [privilege] was abused by many of the men. They got drunk and then were lying around in the saloons, did not return to camp, and their duty was neglected. As a result the increased guard and other duties were placed onto the shoulders of those more sober comrades who stayed behind. Lieutenant Moore, therefore, sent out patrols and had all men arrested who were found in the city without permission. These then received extra duties during the day. No one may leave camp anymore without permission.

The story of the Tyrolean from the Italian border, whom I had visited again in the evening on his insistent invitation, was very interesting. The man had served in the Austrian army for eight years under Field Marshal Radetsky, had participated in the entire revolution in Lombardy.[22] As a veteran he has been very partial to soldiers, and in the family I am always received very warmly. As I said, I enjoy them very much, despite the deficiency in German. It seems to me that previously they clearly had been used to lighter wine; unfortunately, here they took to the much stronger and destructive whiskey, which was sampled very frequently, not only by Mr. Kuhn himself, but his wife also took sips. Not that I would say that they got drunk, just taking sips in excess and nearly want to force it on their guest. They own a lot with two small houses on it, as well as a garden and yard in which they keep several cows and calves.

Today, when it was already dark, Company A from our regiment arrived here as reinforcements; really just twenty men strong, since so many of the company are absent on other duty. Toward morning we had rain.

Thursday, September 17—Rainy weather, cool air. In the evening I had guard duty; it was a cold, stormy night. Since we now have

22. Josef Radetsky was an Austrian field marshal. In the war of 1848–49 against Sardinia, he won victories at Custozza and Novara. He was governor of Upper Italy from 1849 to 1857. Johann Strauss (the elder) composed the "Radetzky March" in his honor. *Columbia Encyclopedia,* s.v. "Radetsky, Joseph."

more manpower, two more sentries were posted around the wide area that we have to guard, so that the perimeter can now be guarded fairly well. It was really cold, lying on the hard ground under only one wool blanket.

Friday, September 18—A cold, sharp wind raged all day, and it felt very much like fall, amazingly early this year for this latitude. In the afternoon I inspected the shipyards and gunboats. Civilians are not allowed at all, unless taken inside by a known and responsible person. We soldiers are, of course, regarded as good, loyal Union men and can enter without problems. Naturally I cannot give a[n adequate] description. There is too much to express here in words; one must see it.

These armor-plated monsters are all iron. The deck resting on strong iron beams first has an iron plate, about half an inch thick, then a layer of gutta percha, on top a layer of four-inch-thick pine planks and over this a layer of one-inch-thick iron plates, all joined together with countless rivets and iron screw bolts. The two towers, standing on the deck, consist of eight iron plates, each one inch thick, one riveted to the others, thus forming a compact wall eight inches thick. The roof is formed of several layers of railway rails on top of one another, then covered with iron plates. These towers are rotated by steam, quickly or slowly as needed. The two cannons in the towers are also maneuvered by the steam-driven machinery. Although the boat rises only about three feet above water, the space below deck is still about ten feet high in the middle. But there are, of course, no windows or hatches on the sides. The light can come only from above, from the deck, through the few entrances. Besides, there are a number of holes in the deck, each about six inches in diameter, covered with thick glass. The space, naturally, is very limited. The machinery, the two towers, and the coal require too much space. The area intended for the crew and officers is covered on the inside with lovely pinewood, while everything else is iron and therefore fireproof. The machinery drives two screws, which are protected with strong armor at the stern, also the rudder. The boats all have flat bottoms. The sides above water are covered with two-and-a-half-inch iron armor plates, while about an eighteen-inch thickness of wood is placed behind

USS *Milwaukee*, one of four Eads ironclads Scherneckau saw being built at Carondelet in the fall of 1863. U.S. Military Academy Library, West Point, New York.

the armor, again covered on the inside by a half-inch iron plate. So far, only a very superficial description of the gunboats.[23]

To describe the work done there and how it is done is much more difficult, especially for someone who knows as little about it as I do. One just has to see how the building material is handled here, which consists mostly of iron of all sizes and strengths. Planes, drills, and saws are busy on the heavy iron blocks; the chips fly here in such a way as if a carpenter would be working a pine board. Steam power sets all these tools into motion. A man only has to set up the material and guide the machine. Powerful drills make the countless holes in the plates; planes smooth out the sides of the plates so that they connect tightly to one another. Drills and chisels combined make up the saws, which cut all kind of shapes out of the iron plates. In short, the iron must give in to the mighty tools driven by steam power, tools that man has at his disposal. Pulleys, rolls, and levers are used to lift these iron piles and to move them to their place of destination. More than twenty eleven-inch cannon barrels are already lying here finished, waiting for the completion of the boats. All parts of the boats above the water level are painted in "hideous gray"; the part underwater, however, is painted red.

In the evening I visited my Italian again, who can tell very interesting stories from his military life. Unfortunately, he uses too much liquor. We had some drill.

[Scherneckau does not explain the gap from September 19 through October 7.]

Thursday, October 8—In the morning it is quite cold now. Reveille is sounded, but since no roll call is usually taken, everyone stays in bed, for the orderly sergeant does not appear. Windy. Life here is very monotonous, no letter and nothing to write. Some drill.

23. These were the new, double-turreted monitors *Winnebago, Milwaukee, Chickasaw,* and *Kickapoo,* as Scherneckau notes in his entry for October 21. For specifications, see Gibbons, *Warships and Naval Battles,* 12. Gerteis, *Civil War St. Louis,* 250–52, discusses Eads's innovations, in particular his revolving turret, which differed in construction and operation from the turret on John Ericsson's original *Monitor.* Each of the four monitors of the *Winnebago* class had one Eads turret and one Ericsson turret.

Friday, October 9—In the morning we heard that our regiment had gone to Jefferson City, except for the detachment forming the provost guard, and we should get ready to follow at any minute. I do not know what the reason can be to order our regiment away so suddenly. It left St. Louis at midnight.[24] Received a letter from Hedde and answered it. Some drill. On guard duty in the evening. The night was cold and the wind calm.

Saturday, October 10—Life as always. The greater part of the provost guard also left St. Louis in order to march against the rebels threatening the railway near Syracuse.

Sunday, October 11—The usual inspection of the company. Cold. In the evening it began to rain; I had to take up guard duty. Heavy rain and thunderstorm at night, an extremely unpleasant post on the shore of the Mississippi. Blinding lightning made the darkness all the more noticeable!

Monday, October 12—Cloudy, cold weather, some rain in the evening. In the afternoon I went to St. Louis with several comrades to hear Jim Lane speak.[25] We used the train. The passes from our company commander had to be countersigned by the provost marshal in St. Louis, since the regulations are now very strict in this regard. Only about thirty men of our regiment still remain in St. Louis as provost guard, supported by militia, the Invalid Corps, and three companies of blacks. The latter are stationed in the Schofield Barracks and make good soldiers. The Seventh, Ninth, and Tenth Minnesota regiments of infantry arrived here yesterday and today.

In the Turner Hall "J" Lane gave a splendid speech in front of a large, enthusiastic audience. We were almost the first of the audience in the hall and got good seats. Hundreds had to be turned

24. In October 1863 Confederate cavalry commander Joseph Shelby led a raid into Missouri. Among the troops dispatched in response were some men of the First Nebraska. *OR*, ser. 1, vol. 22, part 1, pp. 664–68.

25. U.S. senator James Lane of Kansas had been active in the free-soil movement during the "Bleeding Kansas" days of the 1850s. Despite being a sitting senator, Lane had secured a Union brigadier general's commission in 1861. See Etcheson, *Bleeding Kansas*, and Castel, *Civil War Kansas*, for Lane's story.

away without having seen or heard Lane. The general [Lane] scarcely found room on the podium for himself; the place was packed, the crowd so eager to hear the famous speaker. Mr. Praetorius introduced the general with several words, yet it took some time before he could get attention.[26] About ten o'clock, the meeting was over.

Our pass was valid until eleven thirty tonight. At a little after eleven o'clock we left St. Louis with the last train for Carondelet. Near the Iron Mountain railroad station, a major fire had broken out. A large building packed with government supplies was in flames. It had been filled with corn, hay, bacon, lard, and flour. The powerful steam hoses could only confine the flames to the building, in which they surged between the massive walls and bubbled like in a cauldron, despite the four or five fire hoses that were hurling the water four stories high. Fire is so common that even this significant event attracted only a few people, no crowd, no blocking of the streets, no military; hardly a single policeman was visible near the site of the fire. We were back at camp again about twelve o'clock.

Tuesday, October 13—Cold weather. In the afternoon I made a longer visit to the iron works, where one can always see something new! The towers of the gunboats are completely finished in the workshop. The holes for the bolts are drilled by steam-driven machines. Eight plates, one inch thick, form the walls of the towers. Twenty plates in each position make 160 pieces for each tower, which are strongly bolted and riveted together. The weight of these towers when they are brought on board, finished, is given at forty tons.

In the evening I took up guard duty. Fear seems to prevail now that an attempt will be made to set this place on fire. We do not have sufficient manpower to surround this very extensive installation adequately with posts. But we will apply the utmost vigilance

26. The lecture was held in the meeting hall of the Turnverein, a German social and gymnastics society. On November 30, 1864, Emil Praetorious became part owner and editor-in-chief of the *Westliche Post.* Gerteis, *Civil War St. Louis,* 327; Winter, *The Civil War in St. Louis,* 108–9.

to prevent these valuable buildings from also becoming prey of the flames. Woe to the men who try to sneak through in the darkness of night.

Wednesday, October 14—Dreary weather. We had to undergo an investigation, since a businessman of the city was swindled with a fifty-dollar note altered from a two-dollar bill. The businessman had given ten dollars in merchandise and the rest in cash. Of course nothing was found. The swindler most likely had used our uniform to divert suspicion from himself to the soldiers. In the evening, a little drill.

Thursday, October 15—Warm weather today. Even though it really is not my favorite work, I could not avoid having a washday. Here where there is the possibility I usually have it washed. But the weather was so tempting that I got at it myself. In the afternoon I went with several comrades for a walk in the neighborhood, through the extensive fruit orchards. Of course we brought our haversacks back to camp, stuffed.[27] The owners are now busily occupied picking fruit. They pay seven cents a barrel for picking. Three of our men tried it yesterday but gave it up, since at this low price they could not earn an adequate day's wage. Because the trees are mostly low and full of fruit, apple picking could be done quickly. It was quite warm.

Friday, October 16—Nice weather; on guard duty in the evening. The night was unusually mild.

Saturday, October 17—Rainy weather; our tents are poorly suited to keep us dry. Yesterday two boats, loaded with troops, went down-

27. Although some soldiers apparently regarded the apples as theirs for the taking, the orchard owners considered it theft. On December 9, 1863, Mrs. L. C. Duvall of Clayton Road, "near St. Louis," complained in a letter to Col. Robert R. Livingston and asked him to assess his soldiers for the apples they took from her orchard. What's more, they had destroyed piles of apples lying on the ground, waiting to be pressed for cider. She wanted payment for fifty-three barrels of apples. The result of her plea is unknown. RG129, Livingston Papers.

stream. I imagine they were the Minnesota regiment that had arrived recently. The hunters among us now and then go over to Illinois to hunt. The game consists mostly of tree squirrels, which are abundant. Today we had a good meal from them. They are shot with our Springfield muskets, a sign that they are good rifles and we are just as good marksmen. The head is usually the target, and when the minié bullet hits it, it is removed completely. Apples, hazel-, wal-, hickory, and pecan nuts are here in abundance. We also have grapes, pawpaws, chestnuts, medlar, and quince here.[28] Indeed, I have eaten more different fruits since we have been here than ever before.

Sunday, October 18—Today it is a year since I enlisted; it flew by quickly. I have learned and seen many things. All in all, I do not regret that I became a soldier! Where will I be next year at this time? Very windy last night and today; the usual inspection, guard duty in the evening. The night was calm but cold. In the afternoon I went over to Illinois to gather nuts and pawpaws. Some go out to get apples, others nuts; others bring home squirrels, etc., from their excursions, so that we are always well provided with the delicacies of the season.

Monday, October 19—A typically Nebraska storm still rages today. In the afternoon I was out and gathered hickory nuts, as big as the average walnut. I saw a new fruit today that grows wild here, "dattelpflaume" in German according to the dictionary, "persimmon" in English. However, the frost has not yet been hard enough to make the fruit tasty.

The *Winnebago*, the gunboat that had been launched quite some time ago, tried out her machinery again. Powered by steam, the towers turned around fast or slowly, as required. Admirable.

Tuesday, October 20—Overcast sky, very cold at night.

28. Medlar is a small tree of the rose family, producing a small, brown, applelike fruit.

Wednesday, October 21—It was very cold this morning; a crust of ice covered the water. Some drill; on guard duty in the evening; the night was cold. Today the gunboat *Winnebago* went upstream a short distance for the first time, quite slowly and clumsily; these ships are no fast-sailers. The *Milwaukee, Chickasaw,* and *Kickapoo* are the names of the three boats still on the dock.

Thursday, October 22—It snowed heavily today. Four inches are already on the ground. It is uncomfortably cold in our tents, where we have no stoves like last winter.

Friday, October 23—Cold, yet it thawed quite bit during the day. In the evening we received orders to keep ourselves ready for immediate departure; however, our release did not come, and I still had guard duty this evening. The night was very cold.

Saturday, October 24—We waited impatiently for relief. At around three o'clock in the afternoon a company of the Tenth Minnesota Infantry Regiment arrived. At five o'clock we marched off—the road was very muddy from the melting snow—until we reached the sidewalks of St. Louis. At seven o'clock we were at Camp Gamble, where our old regiment was camped. Since no space had been left for our tents, we set up our tents on the left wing. The supper once again tasted outstanding after we had marched the ten miles and the conditions were pretty much as we had been used to last winter in the field. Camp Gamble is on Olive Street, about two and a half miles from the center of the city, on a nice place with trees.

CHAPTER 12

Mounting the First Nebraska, October 25–December 9, 1863

Sunday, October 25—This morning Colonel Baumer was making the regimental inspection. It is like last time, the old familiar faces around us and lots of stories to tell about the last expedition to Tuscumbia, which must have been very interesting.[1] I went with a few comrades to a church on Chestnut and Twelfth streets, which I had visited previously. In the evening, dress parade with full regimental music.

Lieutenant Colonel Baumer is now commanding the regiment. At present it is more complete than I have ever seen it since I joined it, partly because there are new recruits and partly because men who were in the hospital before or had served detached from the regiment now make it appear full-strength. It is cold, and the melting snow makes it muddy, yet it is tolerably dry in camp. Since we received straw on Saturday evening, we had quite good beds in our tents.

Monday, October 26—At nine o'clock we once more had drill for the whole regiment, under Baumer's command. The day was cold, and we made a fire in the tent. Since we had no stoves like last winter, the bottom of one of our kettles was knocked out and hung up under the tripod that supports the tent pole. The fire lighted under it burns merrily and carries the smoke away quite well.

1. Tuscumbia is a small town southwest of Jefferson City, in the region where Union forces were sent to counter Shelby's raid. Some men of the First Nebraska arrived there on October 14, 1863, and remained for several days. Company I Morning Report, October 1863, NSHS RG18, roll 3.

It is a magnificent area; gardens surround beautiful villas that are hidden among the woods. We are camped on the site of the former rebel Camp Jackson, which luckily was taken in a surprise attack by the troops under Lyon and General Siegel three [two] and a half years ago before the secesh gathered there could carry out their plans for St. Louis. Fort No. 6 is close to the camp and now controls the whole place, as well as Olive Road.[2] Four thirty-two-pounders are set up, manned with Negro troops. We had dress parade, as always now, with full music. I wrote to Governor Saunders.[3]

Tuesday, October 27—Today somewhat warmer weather. In the morning, company drill. Companies D and C marched into the city today for duty there. The teamster of Company D was shot and killed in a fight with a civilian in a house of ill repute in St. Louis.[4] In the evening it began to rain seriously; our poor tents hardly kept us dry.

Wednesday, October 28—The weather was somewhat better. In the afternoon Clark, the teamster, was buried not far from our camp in the Wesleyan Cemetery with full honors. This cemetery is filled with graves of soldiers that, numbered in long rows, give a somber impression and are well suited to raise serious thoughts in oneself. Every grave bears a number and the first letters of the name on a wooden board. It is, by the way, a nice place, with fine monuments

2. A map of the St. Louis fortifications is in Winter, *The Civil War in St. Louis*, 75.

3. Only a few of Nebraska governor Alvin Saunders's papers are found at the Nebraska State Historical Society, and they do not include any correspondence for 1863, so the subject of this letter remains unknown.

4. Pvt. John A. Clark was killed at a brothel/saloon on Almond Street operated by John and Aleck Vanderwerker. While Clark and several comrades were passing the place, one of them said, "Here's a nigger who_e house, let's clean it out!" After entering the establishment and quarreling with the proprietors, the soldiers left the building. Witnesses reported that Aleck Vanderwerker followed them out and fired his revolver, the bullet striking Clark in the back of the head. Clark was a native of Platte County, Missouri, about twenty years old, who had enlisted at Nebraska City in 1861. His parents still lived in Nebraska City at the time of his death. "A Young Man of the 1st Nebraska Shot," *Nebraska City Daily Press*, October 31, 1863, reprinting undated article from *Missouri Democrat*; Dudley, *Roster of Nebraska Volunteers*, 48–49; Compiled Service Records, roll 5.

and trees. As usual the men of the company fired the customary salute over the grave. The chaplain spoke a few appropriate words in which he also touched upon how sad it is that a young man must lose his life in this manner, through his own fault, and at a place where he had no business to be, while the country that way lost the services due to it. Rain again during the night.

Thursday, October 29—The weather got better during the day. I had to go into the city, together with the men who had enlisted with me, to be mustered in once more, since, as they say, the papers issued at that time have been lost. It was very muddy. In the evening we had dress parade. At that time an order was read whereupon we are to be changed into a cavalry regiment without delay.[5] Recruits are to be enlisted, enough to bring the regiment up to its full recommended strength. But how this will be done is a puzzle. We certainly will not get the necessary numbers of men from Nebraska, and here in Missouri we are not allowed to recruit.[6]

Friday, October 30—It turned colder, and instead of rain we had snow. It snowed during the entire night and during the day until it stopped toward evening. We, the recruits entitled to bounty, went to the city again and received twenty-seven dollars paid by the U.S. official. Captain Ivory returned with us from the city in order to take over command of the company. There are several inches of snow, lots of mud in camp.

Saturday, October 31—Last night we had a hard frost, and it was unpleasantly cold this morning when standing at attention in rank and file at reveille, yet we had to do it. I had to step in as company cook, since no volunteers were to be found as before, and it was my

5. Following Department of the Missouri commander Gen. John Schofield's recommendation, Gen. Henry Halleck authorized mounting the First Nebraska as cavalry on October 10, 1863. *OR*, ser. 1, vol. 22, part 2, p. 627.

6. By Special Orders No. 213, November 20, 1863, Missouri Adjutant General's Office, the First Nebraska was authorized to recruit in Missouri, provided the regiment furnished certified copies of all muster rolls of Missouri residents, so they could be credited to Missouri's quota under the presidential call for troops. Copy in Robert R. Livingston file, Compiled Service Records, roll 14.

turn to do fatigue duty. There are two of us, and one Negro. Water is brought to us, as well as firewood. In the afternoon, muster in again by companies for two months' wages. Lieutenant Colonel Baumer was the mustering officer. The weather got better, but the snow, which disappeared as quickly as it had come, made it very muddy in the camp.

Sunday, November 1—A nice, warm day; the ground is drying rapidly. Cooking is quite an easy job. Mornings and evenings there is coffee, sometimes tea; furthermore, bacon is fried, and the bread that the baker brings every day is cut and handed out by the cooks, who must see to it that all receive an equal portion. For the noon meal we cook beans with bacon or fresh meat; instead of beans, rice or hominy, that is, rough-ground corn. We also must oversee the distribution of rations of soap, candles, vinegar, molasses, etc. Two members of our company now have their families here. They each have a tent for themselves and get rations for their own use. Yesterday we received rations for ten days for forty-eight men, the present strength of the company, the men who are qualified to receive rations.

Monday, November 2—We struck our tents and packed up to set them up again in another camp nearby. The tents had hardly been rolled up when it started to rain, that is, quite seriously. We received new, that is, repaired, Sibley tents for our old tents. After we had to wait in the rain for a time as usual, we started and took our respective spots on the new, staked-off campground. The rows of the company's tents are now far enough apart from one another to place several rows of horses between every two companies. It rained hard during the whole day, and the "moven" was, therefore, not a pleasant assignment. Naturally, we now take up a rather large stretch, which goes along Olive Street toward the city.

The place is a high, dry ridge, sparsely covered with trees. The Pacific Railway leaves the city southward, not far from here.[7]

7. The Pacific Railroad connected St. Louis and Sedalia. The Atlantic and Pacific Railroad branched off to Rolla. See map in Fellman, *Inside War*, 9.

Three forts control this entire region with their heavy cannon and thereby the main roads that come from the west, yet their pivot guns can just as well be turned toward the city, if necessary. These small forts are all independent enterprises with drawbridges on the sides extending toward the city. Bombproof log houses are in all the larger ones. It cleared up toward evening. For us cooks it was an unpleasant day—wet, dirty, and cold.

Tuesday, November 3—A nice, warm day; our campground is already dry again. Today we cooked goose soup. A member of our company killed four of them with a single shot, out of a flock that walked around on the campground, tame ones naturally. Here, of course, foraging in this way is not allowed, but that is not all. Even pigs, just killed, sometimes find their way into our kitchen. Saddles and fences were brought to camp today; also ropes were stretched out to tie up the horses. Today was election day in the state of Missouri, and all men who were from Missouri and who had entered our regiment voted.

Wednesday, November 4—The enlisting in the veteran regiment begins.[8] The weather was nice but very windy for cooking.

Thursday, November 5—Mailed off a letter to Egge. The weather is nice. I was released from kitchen duty, since a volunteer for my replacement had been found.

Friday, November 6—Today the first cavalry equipment was handed out. The boys appear in the jackets with the yellow stripes. We also received the crossed sabers of the dragoons instead of the bugle, which the infantry wears on its hats. I did not receive a jacket, since

8. The original three-year enlistments of the majority of Union soldiers would expire in the summer of 1864, and they would be free to leave the army. In order to prevent this potential loss of manpower at a critical stage in the war, the government, under General Orders No. 191, offered inducements for reenlisting. They included a thirty-day furlough, a $402 bounty, a special uniform chevron, and the right to be known as veteran volunteers. *OR*, ser. 3, vol. 3, pp. 487, 795–96, 1084. Something over half of the veteran soldiers in the Union army reenlisted, including many in the First Nebraska. McPherson, *Ordeal by Fire*, 409–10.

I still have a brand new infantry uniform coat. In addition to this a poncho, the waterproof rubber blankets that the cavalry receives. They have a hole in the center to put one's head through. With this cover the whole body is protected against rain. We also received boots, but I could not find any that would fit me.

In the afternoon I went to St. Louis. There I visited a small museum on Fourth Street, where a few live animals are shown, as well as curiosities from the animal kingdom, among them a black wolf, a California lioness, and various badgers, a wildcat caught in Missouri, raccoons, a nice specimen of an eagle, and finally, a number of monkeys. The admission for the above show was expensive enough at fifteen cents for so much humbug as was presented in the "museum." The weather was pleasant.[9]

Saturday, November 7—All of us men who were not then on duty had to march to the city with rifles and in the infantry uniform. There we had to form the honor guard for a major killed at Vicksburg to give the customary salute over his casket at the graveside. The rest of the regiment appeared in cavalry uniform with side arms, that is, bayonets. With our band ahead we marched down Olive Street, then over to Market Street, up to Seventh, on it to Gratiot Street, where we stacked our rifles for a pause. There we met with a detachment of the Tenth Minnesota Regiment, so that our detachment to fire the salute was now some 150 men strong. The major of the Minnesota regiment then took over the command of our troops. Next we marched to the police station on Chestnut Street, where, after some delay, we took delivery of the hearse with the coffin. With arms reversed and funeral march, we then went to Locust Street, close to Eleventh Street, where the funeral service was held in a church. Meanwhile, we stacked our rifles in the street.

9. This museum has not been identified. It sounds more like an exhibit akin to a circus sideshow. The major museum in town, the St. Louis Museum, was on Market Street opposite the courthouse and featured extensive exhibits of natural history specimens, mummies, geological collections, paintings, and other curiosities, which hardly sounds like the museum Scherneckau visited. Information about the St. Louis Museum is courtesy of Dennis Northcott, reference archivist, Missouri Historical Society, St. Louis.

Not until one o'clock did we start marching again, along Eleventh Street, all the way out of the city, until we finally reached the Bellefontaine Cemetery, a magnificent park with really fine gravestones and monuments.[10] After a few brief words by the minister at the open grave, the coffin was lowered, and we fired three volleys over the grave. Very tired and hungry, we finally arrived at camp after dark. All in all, we had marched at least twenty miles. The weather was nice, yet the roads were partly dusty.

Sunday, November 8—This morning at ten o'clock the signal to fall in sounded, this time without arms. Only the bayonet as side arms, with our cavalry uniform, made a ridiculous impression. I had borrowed a jacket from a comrade. I am having my uniform coat made over into a regulation jacket. From the discarded coattails, I will get a vest.

Today Captain Welker, who fell in the Battle of Champion's Hill, was to be buried.[11] Like yesterday we marched with our regimental music, first to Gratiot Street and from there to the Chestnut Street police station, from where we moved on with the body at one o'clock. Since the deceased had previously belonged to the St. Louis police, they now showed him the last honors. Therefore, a company of the police corps was armed with muskets to fire the salute over the grave. We, together with detachments of the Minnesota regiments and detachments of the artillery, were under the command of Captain Majors of our regiment.[12] We marched

10. The history of this cemetery, along with some of the notable individuals interred there, is found in Winter, *The Civil War in St. Louis,* 110–33.

11. Capt. John Welker, Company B, Twenty-sixth Missouri Volunteer Infantry. The Battle of Champion's Hill occurred on May 16, 1863, as Gen. Ulysses S. Grant's army maneuvered to lay siege to Vicksburg. An officer of the St. Louis Police Department had recovered Welker's body from the battlefield grave. Welker was a Mexican War veteran who had served three years as a police officer before joining the army in 1861. Accounts of his death, and his funeral at the Holy Trinity Church, appear in the *Missouri Republican,* November 6, 7, 8, and 9, 1863, courtesy of Dennis Northcott, Missouri Historical Society.

12. Thomas J. Majors commanded Company C. He was commissioned as major on May 1, 1864, and was mustered out July 1, 1866. Dudley, *Roster of Nebraska Volunteers,* 4–5, 30–31.

along Fourth Street to Washington Street, where we walked up to Ninth Street, and then on Ninth we marched almost out of the city to a Catholic church on Eleventh Street, where the coffin was carried into the church after we had formed lanes with the police corps. As soon as this was over, we disbanded, leaving it at the end to the police to accompany the body to the grave. Then I went home, that is, to Camp Gamble on Olive Street, through the northwestern part of St. Louis, the most direct way possible. The marching today was more annoying than yesterday, since we had more dust.

Monday, November 9—Quite a cold night; also a cold wind is blowing today. Had to go on guard duty today. The duty is easy, and since we don't have drill, we have little to do. The evenings are quite pleasant, even though cold. We rest around the lively burning fire in the tent; song and stories shorten the time until tattoo calls us to line up; afterward, one usually goes to bed.

Tuesday, November 10—The day was nice; was released from guard duty. The men enlisting in the veteran corps from our company, twelve men, were mustered in today, and each was paid sixty-two dollars as bounty.[13] Of course, there were several drunks.

Wednesday, November 11—Went to the city with our teams, where we had to load hay, corn, and oats for the mules and horses belonging to the regiment. In the afternoon we also got straw from there, which was allotted to us for our beds. These buildings on Main Street containing quartermaster and commissary stores are all guarded by Negro soldiers—young, strong men. The uniform looks better on many of them than on some of the white soldiers in our regiment. Weather windy, yet not very cold.

Yesterday [Nebraska] Governor Saunders was here. We had dress parade; after we had formed a quarre, he spoke several

13. The men were Sgt. James I. Shaw, Corp. John Adams, and Pvts. James Bowen, John Boyles, John Douglas, William Erwin, Paul Fitzpatrick, Edward Godsell, Edward Goulding, Ira Howe, Jacob Kinsey, Francis Lohnes, Isaac Sager, and Samuel Vogan. Dudley, *Roster of Nebraska Volunteers*, 90–103.

words to us; however, he is a poor speaker. Colonel Livingston also spoke several words regarding reenlistment in the veterans' corps.

Thursday, November 12—Finished a letter to my parents, received a letter from Egge in the evening; very windy.

Friday, November 13—Unpleasantly windy. In the afternoon I went with a comrade into the city to visit Ed. Keen from our company, who is in the Hickory Street hospital.[14] The hospitals of our army are really worth a visit. The nice furnishings, cleanliness, and comfort for the patients have certainly gone as far as can be wished and expected. In this regard the government has done much. But quite a bit also happens through private charity. Ladies, members of societies formed for this purpose, come every day distributing presents to all the sick, comforting the suffering, and inquiring about their wishes, which they carry out whenever possible, or see to it that they are fulfilled. After retreat I took another extended walk in St. Louis by gaslight.[15]

Saturday, November 14—An unusually strong guard was made up from the regiment this morning and a camp guard organized with some twenty posts, enclosing the entire camp and preventing anyone from leaving without a pass. This is the result of many thefts, fights, etc., recently perpetrated by some of the men, for which we all must suffer now. Weather more pleasant.

Sunday, November 15—Had to go on guard duty today, the most unpleasant of all guard duties, camp guard, to guard our own comrades. During the daytime, when all eyes are focused on the cordon of guards, no one can pass, of course. But as soon as it is dark, naturally, everyone who wants slips through. The result today is that more men than usual were picked up by the provost guard and delivered here in spite of the cordon of guards. Our

14. Keen's letters to his family from the hospital appear in Potter, "I Thought It My Duty," 163–65.

15. For St. Louis hospitals and women's nursing and charitable work, see Gerteis, *Civil War St. Louis*, chapter 7.

first sergeant, or "feldwebel" [James I. Shaw], was among them. He is still under arrest. The day was cold, looking like snow.

Monday, November 16—The night was quiet and more agreeable than I had anticipated. We received an order to put out all fires on our post, just as if we were standing before the enemy. Yet no one obeyed the order, and the fires were started again, despite it having been stated that if a man were encountered with a fire on his post he would be arrested immediately and sent to the Myrtle Street prison. We risked it and had fire until morning. Yesterday evening a detachment of sixty men was sent into the city to double the usual guard on the levee. They came back this morning.

Today distribution of the sabers began; each company also received a small flag like the ones the cavalry regiments have, stars and stripes, but cut out on the very end like the Danish marine flags. In a blue field, surrounded by the stars, is the letter of the respective company.[16]

Tuesday, November 17—Since the unusually strong guard is still needed, I had to do guard duty again today. The weather is nice and warm; the night was bearable.

Wednesday, November 18—The weather is still pleasant. I sent a letter to Egge. Today we stretched our rope in front of our row of tents in order to hitch the company's horses there. Drumming and fifing is now a thing of the past. All signals, as well as reveille and tattoo, are now given only by the bugle, and instead of the infantry signals, the signals for the cavalry, not yet well known to us, are given.

Thursday, November 19—Strong wind; rain in the afternoon. We received our saddles today, all very new. They are the so-called McClellan type, a wooden sawbuck covered with leather; also saddlebags, straps to tie up the blankets, a leather halter, a rein to hook on to the halter when riding through water. Besides these, a regular bridle and a strap for fastening blankets.

16. A cavalry guidon.

Friday, November 20—During the night the rain turned into a snowstorm; it was still snowing in the morning, but [the snow] was gone by noon. Yesterday the strong guard around the camp was removed. We are free again, no longer restricted to the roads of our tent city. This guard duty and confinement within the borders of our camp was a punishment for the thefts, etc., that had been committed, for which the entire regiment was made responsible.

This morning we marched, each of us with his halter and bridle, to Benton Barracks, about three miles northwest of here. It was very muddy! There we received 250 horses from the extensive government stables, and we returned to camp mounted. The horses were distributed to the companies according to their color. The officers drew lots for this purpose, so Company K received the white and gray-white ones, Company G the black ones, Company E the chestnut bays, Company B the red-white ones, Company I, F, and H the dark brown ones, A and G the light brown ones, and Company D the rest of the horses. Our company did not receive horses today. Companies K, G, I, F, and a part of E received their horses.

Saturday, November 21—This morning, with halter and bridle, we lined up again in order to get three hundred more horses from Benton Barracks. We had started in that direction when a counter order arrived. Headquarters in the city had requested 150 men, "armed and equipped." Fetching horses, therefore, was cancelled, and at around eleven o'clock, playing infantry again, we started out for the city. We were in two sections; the last, some 100 men, was ordered back. I was in the first group, about 50 men strong.

We marched to the Gratiot Street prison (McDowell College before the war), where we reinforced the guard from the Ninth and Tenth Minnesota regiments. Some men of the prison guard had been ordered last night to the state of Illinois. It was rumored that Copperheads there tried to stir up trouble. At the distribution of the guard duties, I was super numerae and as such did not have much to do. However, in the evening three more posts were set up inside the vast building. All in all, it requires twenty-three sentries to surround the prison. Seven of them are in the courtyards and passages inside the strange building, which reminds me vividly of the old manors at the large estates of the nobility in Schleswig-Holstein. An octagonal tower in the middle of the front rises two stories above the building. It is built of stone, with pointed Gothic windows, all heavily barred; the connecting wings of the building are half stone, half brick masonry, three stories high. On Gratiot Street the wings are one story higher, since on the back the first story is the basement.

I was posted in this basement, containing the kitchens in the back. A partition, provided with doors and windows, separated me from a large room, where a section was used as a dining hall. Two-thirds of the room, divided by a wooden wall, was furnished with beds for some two hundred men. My instructions were to permit no one into the kitchen and, of course, have my gun loaded. A corporal constantly makes the rounds to control the posts. It is, therefore, no small undertaking to break out of here. Instead of doors the sleeping quarters of the prisoners have strong iron bars, and since lamps are burning, the post can pretty well see what goes on in there. I believe there is room there for fifteen hundred prisoners; however, at present it is occupied by about six to seven hundred.[17]

The row of houses across from the prison is used as barracks and as a hospital for the sick secesh. The office of the guard is there, as well as offices and residences for some of the officers. At the moment three or four companies of the Invalid Corps, which is in the process of formation, are located there. Men from the whole army are represented in this corps. I found a German among them who earlier had belonged to the Twelfth Missouri Regiment. Ernst Arp, as he told me, was a lieutenant in Company F of that regiment, only Germans. He had taken money from comrades, which they had asked him to send home. He had spent it and then vanished. But, as he told me, [Arp] was recently seen here in St. Louis. This swindle, of course, has brought him the scorn of his former comrades.

Sunday, November 22—At nine o'clock in the morning, we marched off again and met a strong detail of our regiment, which was in

17. The St. Louis military prisons and conditions therein are described in Gerteis, *Civil War St. Louis*, chapter 6, esp. 170, 186–95.

part to take our place and in part to guard the levee against arson to boats and wares stored there. Tired, stiff, and sore from the little bit of riding the day before yesterday, I came home again; slept the largest part of the day. It dried up quickly.

Monday, November 23—This morning, eighteen men from our company were detached for guard duty in the city. Once more our detail went to the Gratiot Street prison and another to the levee. The night was cold and some rain fell.

Tuesday, November 24—Was relieved this morning; a cold, windy day. Most of our horses had been brought into camp yesterday and were now handed over to the companies without regard to color. We turned in our haversacks today. Drew a saddlecloth, currycomb, and brush, as well as a linen sack for feeding the horses (nose bag). I had barely made it home when I had to go with a detail to Benton Barracks to get the rest of the horses, about one hundred of them. We have a lot of fun; falling off is the order of the day, since the horses have had much rest, and some of them are still young. Our company received a total of sixty-one horses. They are fed and watered mornings and evenings. Each horse receives three quarts of oats or corn daily, besides fourteen pounds of hay for the day.

Wednesday, November 25—A lovely day. Today the company was divided into three squads, one for each of the three tents. Graded according to height, I was ordered to the third tent, among only small men! I lost my bunkee this way, whom I had had for a long time. All tent comradery was broken up, a general moving about took place. Today we also received our revolver, Remington pattern, similar to the "Colts" dragoons six-shooters.

Around noon we had the regular inspection; some lieutenant from General Schofield's headquarters eyed us, and then the farce was over. We are, of course, still quite clumsy in the use of the new weapon as well as with the horses. I have received a dark chestnut bay, young and good on its feet and at the same time a good trotter. We had considerable freedom to choose the horse that we wanted. I chose this one since he seemed to be best at trotting.

The horses are quickly being shod; the blacksmiths are working day and night. Wrote to Hedde and to the private secretary of the governor, Mr. [E. P.] Brewster.

Thursday, November 26—At four o'clock reveille sounded, since Companies I, F, K, and C had orders to be ready to march at seven o'clock; they had to go by train to Rolla, Missouri. The horses are being shod in great haste, here in camp and in the city. In the afternoon I had to go to the city on fatigue duty, that is, to load corn and hay on the wagons. At the Hickory Street hospital I said good-bye to our comrade Keen. In the evening I received a letter from my parents with their photograph. Great joy.

Friday, November 27—Our unit had some drill today to learn how to put on the saddle and to mount, to hold the reins, etc. The sergeant who was in charge in the tent drilled us. In the afternoon we had to ride to the city, to the government's smith on Hickory Street. Only a few of the ten horses we had brought were shod, since so many had been ahead of us, despite that in the spacious workshop eight to ten horses were being worked on at once. It rained all afternoon, and the waterproof covers to hang over us [ponchos] were put to good use.

Saturday, November 28—A very cold, stormy morning. The rain had stopped at night, and a hard frost set in; the wet tent was frozen stiff and glittered like a glass mountain. I had to go on camp guard duty to keep watch over quartermaster stores. The regiment was paid off. Since I had not yet signed the roll, I did not yet receive my pay. My horse was shod today.

Sunday, November 29—Last night it was very cold, even standing guard by the fire. The teamster of Company D, a brother of our first sergeant, was killed by his team of mules, which had run away with him.[18] This was the second teamster of the company who had lost his life here in St. Louis, since he was half drunk, like the first,

18. Pvt. William H. Shaw, who enlisted from Nebraska City in 1861. Dudley, *Roster of Nebraska Volunteers*, 50–51; Compiled Service Records, roll 21.

who had been shot to death. The weather was still very cold but not as windy.

Monday, November 30—Early this morning the bugle woke us up. It had been a very cold, moonlit night. But we still had to get up and feed the horses. Then we began packing up and tying on to the saddles. This way of packing all our belongings was still completely new to us. Therefore, we did not know what to do with our things. Many articles of clothing and the like had to be left behind, since the bundles at the back and front of the saddle became too large. Besides, our old muskets with bayonet and bullet pouch had to be tied to the horse. Oh, how we cursed these old, heavy things! Yet they must come along.

At eight o'clock in the morning, the tents were finally down and loaded up, and we set out for the depot on Fourteenth Street, the Pacific Railroad. The horses were loaded onto the rail cars, and at noon they went off with the larger group of the men. I stayed behind to go along with the saddles and baggage and with the company wagons. We followed at about four o'clock in the afternoon. Around sundown we arrived at Franklin, where a track branches off to Sedalia, leading in a northern direction, while the main line leads southward to Rolla. Here we stayed overnight. I slept in the baggage car, where our saddles and baggage were stowed.

Tuesday, December 1—I had my breakfast in the restaurant. Around ten o'clock we left Franklin. The area resembles the one through which the Iron Mountain Railroad travels. Some different tunnels have been blasted through the rocks, and deep cuts have been made through the ridges of hills. Toward Rolla the area became flatter, sparsely wooded, even flat, prairie-like expanses. At three o'clock in the afternoon we were in Rolla, a sad-looking little place in a hilly area sparsely covered with shrubs. Nearly all of the buildings are now being used by the government, and were built as barracks and warehouses, probably by the government. We saddled up quickly and rode to the area where our four companies, which had arrived first, were camped three miles from the depot. Having arrived there we unsaddled, tied the horses to the bushes, and made our beds between them just as we found space. Our wagons reached us late in the evening, yet we all were lying down, already asleep.

Wednesday, December 2—"Erhebt Euch von der Erde, ihr Schlaefer aus der Ruh" [Sleepers awake, arise from the earth, etc.] were my thoughts this morning as the bugle sounded.[19] The horses neighed around us. Everyone sprang into action. I had slept very cold; we had enough over us, but the ground beneath us was too cold. The day became very nice and warm, just as if we had been transferred into another climate.

We saddled up again, since we had to move about a thousand paces farther on to make camp. This time we set up camp differently from all previous ones we had made. Six companies were all in a line, then two companies on each flank, stretching at right angles about as the following drawing shows. From this you can see that the horses are inside the tent line, three tents to each company. The officers' tents are twenty paces back, across from the horses of their respective companies. We brought our tents over, and soon we were set up. Our wagon was brought over with the team of another company, since our mules were still all behind. My bunkmate and I made up a bed-base. Young hazel brush and, on top of that, a layer of dry leaves that we scratched together made a really good bed and kept us away from the dampness of the ground. It is amazing how fast soldiers get things set up. As soon as the tents are raised, arrangements are made for cooking, wood is brought in, ropes stretched out for the horses, saddles hung up, beds made, the weapons—and what a mass of those we have now—brought into the tent, a fire started in the middle, and we are ready.

This evening a number of men who had stayed behind in St. Louis arrived, as well as the mules. The men detailed to recruit also came, since they were ordered to return to their companies, because no more recruits are to be enlisted, since we are going to Batesville to fill up the regiment with Union men there. Colonel

19. According to Edith Robbins, this is the first line of a poem by Max von Schenkendorf (1783–1817), whose work appeared in a popular book of patriotic songs and writings published in 1848.

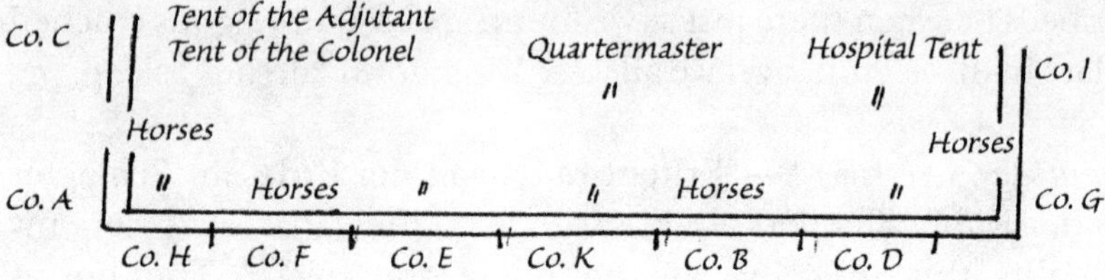

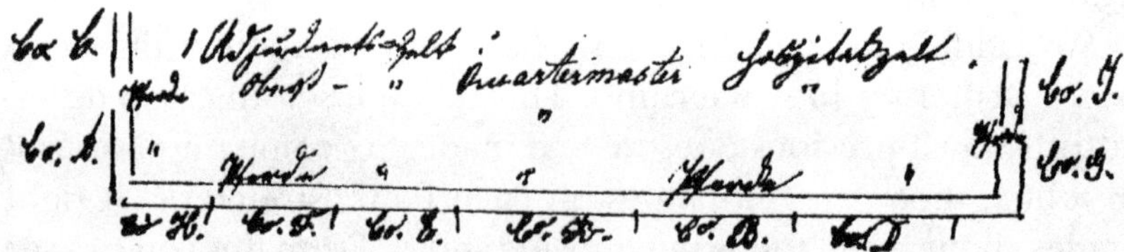

Scherneckau included this drawing of the First Nebraska Cavalry camp in his diary entry of December 2, 1863. August Scherneckau Diaries. MSS2698, Oregon Historical Society Research Library, Portland.

Livingston is commander of a district in Arkansas with headquarters in Batesville.[20]

Thursday, December 3—Cold in the morning but nice weather during the day. We have enough oats and corn but no hay since we left St. Louis. I wrote to Hedde and to my parents. We had some drill on horses before noon, on foot in the afternoon, instruction in fencing [with the saber]. In the evening we draw hay.

Friday, December 4—A really warm, sunny day. I rode to town with five or six soldiers from our company to have the rest of the horses

20. Livingston had been assigned to command the District of Northeastern Arkansas by Special Orders No. 327, Department of the Missouri, November 30, 1863. Included in his command were a battalion of the Eleventh Missouri Cavalry and one section of Battery D, Second Missouri Artillery. He was charged by General Schofield "to destroy, drive out, or capture the guerrilla bands which now infest the district" and "organize as many troops as can be obtained for the general service." *OR*, ser. 1, vol. 22, part 2, pp. 725–26.

shod. For this reason we were up soon after three o'clock and feeding. Before daybreak we were at the government smith. The government here has large workshops of all sorts and warehouses for the needs of the army, as well as large stables and yards for horses and mules. The town is very scattered and built irregularly on several bare hills. It is nearly as large as Nebraska City, but all wooden buildings, many of them log houses. I noticed that the courthouse, located on one side of the town, is the only one that is built of bricks. It was quite busy in the small streets, though almost all military and government wagons, only now and then a farmer with an ox team. Colonel Livingston is here in town. By noon I was at home again; in the afternoon, some drill with the saber.

Saturday, December 5—This morning I was detailed for fatigue duty with some forty men. We marched to town and reported there at headquarters. However, we were sent back again, almost up to our camp, where there is a government corral holding several hundred wild mules. We had to catch sixty of them—not an easy job. Most of them had already been broken, that is, were halfway tamed. But now, fully rested and hence vigorous, we had to run quite a bit before we had a rope on them. Those government men assigned to the yard caught them with a lasso (I wouldn't dare to claim that this is spelled correctly), which some of them understood quite well how to throw skillfully. Always tied together in fours, we brought them [mules] to the smiths in town, where they were shod. Also, no small task for the workmen. Having been shod we then led the mules back.

These draft animals are all intended for one of the trains, which have to go to Arkansas with us; they are now being equipped here in all haste. Some of the wagons standing here are already loaded. It is almost as in Pilot Knob last spring before General Davidson began the march with his corps, only not as grandiose. The day was delightful and warm. One section of the Eleventh Missouri Cavalry Regiment is changing its camp today and is going with us on the march to Batesville.

Sunday, December 6—A nice day. Before noon we passed in review. At that time one of our men had the bad luck to be thrown from his horse. However, he escaped without serious injury. The horses and the men who rode them made it through the maneuver better than one probably had anticipated. In the afternoon I wrote to Egge, sent him ninety dollars. In the evening I was ordered to guard the horses. For this reason six men are now designated from each company, always for twenty-four hours. This has been ordered after several horses were stolen or ran away.

Monday, December 7—Today it became colder. We had regimental inspection, which was conducted by Colonel Livingston. Since I was on guard duty, I was exempt. After the mounted inspection was over, the men then were inspected with their infantry equipment, that is, their muskets and the appropriate equipment. It is really too much to ask from us that we belong to both branches at the same time, to carry the weapons and keep them in good order.

Tuesday, December 8—Was in town from early morning until sunset. Had to catch mules, which had been shipped here by train. A desperate piece of work to capture these two hundred mules and then have them shod. Many, especially the young animals, apparently had never been shod; they had never been touched by men. You can imagine how much work we had before we got them back from the smiths and delivered them to the government yard. The day was quite pleasant.

Wednesday, December 9—My first task was to bring in water for the cooks. Warm weather. All preparations were made for the departure tomorrow. One wagon after another of the various trains came from town loaded and set up camp in our vicinity. These wagons are loaded in part with provisions for us, in part with uniforms, weapons, and ammunition for companies being formed in Arkansas. Also forage for several days is being taken for our horses; afterward, we will have to forage!

Lately several men from our regiment have been seriously injured as the horses threw them. One from our company was kicked by a mule this morning and quite severely wounded. He was doing the work I had to do yesterday! We drew a complete supply of ammunition, forty cartridges for the musket and forty-eight for the revolver, per man. Each company had to haul five boxes of each on their wagon, that is, five thousand of each kind.

A few days ago Captain Ivory returned to the company. It had been under the command of our first lieutenant, although the captain was with us, but always unwell, at least so he appears. The Third Colorado Regiment, previously stationed here, went by train to St. Louis yesterday. Four companies of the Ninth Minnesota Infantry Regiment took up their position here. Besides these, a mounted Missouri militia is stationed here. Refugees from Arkansas and southwestern Missouri are living here in large numbers, mostly women and children. The government supports them to some extent and gives the men employment as teamsters and as other workers.

CHAPTER 13

The March to Batesville, December 10–30, 1863

Thursday, December 10—Late in the evening [December 9] the order to be ready to march at five o'clock in the morning was recalled, and the time was set for twelve o'clock noon. By that time everything was ready, the wagons packed, and a little after twelve o'clock we rode into regimental line. Our Colonel Livingston once more rode down the front, then we wheeled off and moved on in a southeastern direction. The musicians played cheerful tunes, the company flags were flapping in the wind, and happily we rode off into the country, a dry, stony area overgrown with oaks.

We made another twelve miles, where we camped at a creek. A few deserted houses and devastated fields still showed signs of earlier camps. Our entire company had to go on advance post. Without even dismounting we rode into the darkness. Always three men on a post, who relieved one another. The third stood watch alongside the saddled horses while two slept. Besides, no fire! However, the night was mild, even though very dark. This was our first picket duty as cavalry.

Late in the evening the five companies of the Eleventh Missouri Cavalry Regiment arrived as well as two six-pounders, a section of a battery of the Second Missouri Artillery Regiment. Of course, our company, like several others, had not set up tents. At reveille the posts were drawn in. We had breakfast and got ready to march off, on

Friday, December 11—With music sounding we went off again. The wagon trains are still behind, guarded by a detail of the Eleventh Missouri Regiment. We marched some eight to ten miles and camped at midday at a small creek, the second we encountered since we left Rolla. Here we were to expect the trains.

The area is settled only sparsely; rarely is a good farm and house to be seen. The weather is exceptionally mild. In general we ride pace and dismount every eight to ten miles to go on foot for a mile or more, a relief for us as well as for the horses, since the load with our "odds and ends" is already quite a weight without the rider. The old muskets, cartridge pouches, and bayonet are the main trouble.

We set up our tents, and it turned out well, since it rained some during the night. I had to go on duty and guard the horses. The additional horses of each company are loaded with the fodder for the trip. Each company drew oats, rations for their horses for two days. The weather is warm, so we did not make fire in the tent.

Saturday, December 12—This morning it rained quite severely, yet the tents had to be taken down and the horses saddled. All troops left us; only the four companies H, B, I, and D of our regiment stayed behind to serve as rear guard for the train. But it took a long time before it reached us. We unsaddled again and went into the vicinity to forage; oat sheaves and hay soon were plenty at camp. In the afternoon we practiced shooting with our revolvers.

Finally the wagons caught up with us, but it took a long time until they were past; it went on forever. They moved forward only very slowly, often getting stuck; the mules were overworked, tired. The drivers, men of all sorts, also many sailors among them, did not know how to handle the poor animals. But it is no surprise, considering how wild and little trained they still were when we took them to the smiths to get the first horseshoes they ever saw. Wagon shafts were broken off, and other problems were created by animals and men. The road too was very bad, run down by endless wagon trains. We then saddled up and followed slowly for several miles where the train stopped, and we also put up our tents. The other companies stayed behind. During the night it rained quite heavily.

Sunday, December 13—Overcast day with some rain. We had a fast breakfast, while our Company I overtook us. Some of the wagons left camp as well before we were ready. We soon overtook them and went ahead, until we came to a small place a little after noon, where headquarters and the rest of the regiment were. We camped next to the town of twenty houses, of which only half were occupied. The rest of the day we took things as easy as possible. The weather was unpleasant; the fine rain turned into snow, and a hard frost appeared during the night.

Monday, December 14—Everything had arrived with the train, and as the advance guard we moved forward rapidly and made some twenty miles this day. (Here ends the first part of this diary.)

(Continuation of this diary, in part reported in letters to friends in Grand Island, Hall County, Nebraska.)

Camp near Batesville, Arkansas,
[Wednesday] December 30, 1863
Dear Egge,

You will have discovered that recently you have not been overwhelmed with letters from me as in the previous months. The reason, I had neither the time nor the opportunity! For the first time since I became a soldier, I could not continue my diary, and there is no possibility of sending off letters every day, even if they had been written. It is now said that mail might leave from here on the first of next month, and I will hurry to have a letter ready to go. What will happen to the diary, I do not know yet. I have neglected it very much by now, and I do not know if I will find time to continue it in the future. Duty is tough, and there is much to do as a cavalryman.

We had a very interesting time on the march to here. As a cavalryman one has a lot to do, but also a lot of fun. We were attacked several times when we went out in small detachments to forage, killed various guerrillas, took several prisoners, and made short work of them. Upon marching into West Plains, where we had been last winter, we surprised three notorious bushwhackers. One of them escaped at night. The other two were to be shot according to martial law. As we marched them out to the place of execution, they tried to escape, but both were shot down before they went very far.[1] West Plains exists only in name—the town has been burned to the ground, not a single house is standing, only a chimney now and then indicates where stately houses stood last winter. On our march we again approached Salem in Arkansas, which has disappeared as well.

From there we arrived in an area new to us. The closer to the White River, the more developed was the otherwise very hilly, mountainous landscape. Large farms, plantations worked by Negroes, became more numerous and were, at least partly, under cultivation. Here the rocks are mostly sandstone, while in Missouri limestone is predominant.

The last ten miles were over exceptionally rough terrain. Tall, often vertical, rocks were on both sides, while the road followed the brook or a branch of the White River, "bayou" as they call them here.[2] We had to ride through this bayou no less than sixteen times, the last time crossing over on a good bridge, the only one I have seen in Arkansas so far. Riding through this branch, the horses nearly had to swim at times. At one place the road followed the course of the river, while on the other side the rocks rose vertically to a height of three to four hundred feet, leaving just enough room for a wagon track or two riders riding side by side.

It was here a year ago that the wagons of General Curtis were attacked by the guerrillas as he was on his expedition from Pilot Knob. [They had been] hurling large rocks down on the wagons from these stone walls adjacent to the road and thereby smashed them to pieces. [The guerrillas] first had to be driven from the heights in a fight in order that the troops could proceed.[3] We

1. Scout William Monks also reported the capture and execution of these men at West Plains. Monks, *History of Southern Missouri*, 77–78. When Livingston's command arrived at Batesville, he reported they had killed fifteen guerrillas and captured seventeen during the march. *OR*, ser. 1, vol. 22, part 2, p. 750.

2. This stream was likely Poke Bayou, which flows into the White River at Batesville.

3. Scherneckau is mistaken about the details. Gen. Samuel Curtis led his Army of the Southwest along Missouri's southern border after his victory at Pea Ridge, Arkansas, on March 7–8, 1862, and turned south at West Plains, Missouri, to Batesville, where his command arrived on May 3, 1862. He had a skirmish out-

passed the bottleneck safely, since we had cover on both sides of the road from detachments dispatched earlier. However, close to town, shots were fired on our advance guard, but no one was wounded, while we killed two of the bandits, and one was taken prisoner.

The very lovely situated town [Batesville] looked deserted. None of the many stores was open, since for months all trade had been at a standstill and all businesses had been closed. There were very striking houses occupied by wealthy people, who, even with all their money cannot buy even the most necessary things, since they are not available. Not to mention sugar and coffee, even salt is not available, since it comes from Memphis or Arkadelphia in the south of the state and is priced here at $1 a pound. A pair of pants of common cloth costs $100 to $125. All this is calculated in Confederate money; $4 to $5 of this money is now necessary to buy one dollar in greenbacks. The houses of the city are, in general, surrounded by gardens and hidden under trees, many of them cedars, which grow here like the pine trees on the rocks and hills.

The place is about the size of Omaha, yet it is built more compactly. It is located half a mile from the White River, between this [river] and the frequently mentioned bayou that empties into the river below the city, therefore, on a type of peninsula. The city is old in comparison with cities of the Northwest.[4] An impressive church, a courthouse, and various other important buildings are here. A large stone building, occupied by stores below and a large hall above, belonging to the Freemasons, is now being used as a warehouse for our commissary department. A large hotel is closed, as are the rest of the stores, which have large signs with announcements of everything to be had inside, while the doors

side the town but did not mention being bombarded with stones. *OR*, ser. 1, vol. 13, p. 64. Although Curtis threatened the capital at Little Rock, he could not subsist his army so far from his base of supplies and finally marched to occupy Helena on July 12. Shea, "1862," 41–44.

4. Batesville, the county seat of Independence County, was named for Judge James Woodson Bates, first delegate to Congress from Arkansas Territory. He established a law practice in the town in 1823, which had been platted in 1821. *Historic Batesville.* An overview of the Civil War in and around Batesville appears in James, "Civil War Years." A recent study is Mobley, *Making Sense of the Civil War.*

and windows are shut and empty shelves and chests and crates belie the pompous advertisements.

Besides, nearly all the inhabitants are strong secesh, although most admit their cause is desperate. After all, they have not had news, papers, etc., for months and know little of what is going on in the world. We are, of course, in the same situation until a mail connection is established and secured. Jacksonport, thirty miles below on the White River, is a military post from which we will need to get our supplies; boats cannot come here because of the present water levels.

We are the first U.S. troops here since General Curtis's expedition came through here almost two years ago. Currently we are reduced to three-quarters rations; pigs and feathered fowls have had to bear the consequences. Just now my company with several other companies is out on a reconnaissance mission. They went away yesterday while I was out serving as escort for a train to bring in corn. These forage trains have been attacked by the guerrillas several times already. Usually the desperados escape, since they are good riders, riding over sticks and stones with their horses where we cannot follow them. I have somehow missed participating in these exciting events. So it was yesterday, when I was with the advance guard, while the small detachment that formed the rear guard had to endure a real stampede by the teamsters, who thought they had seen a few bushwhackers. The civilian and Negro drivers unhitched their saddled mules from the team to get themselves to safety and left the rest of the team standing. All were detained [by the rear guard] except one Negro. He came to camp and caused great commotion, since for a time it was generally believed that they were either killed or taken prisoner.

The weather is extremely mild. During the marches we had, in fact, several cold days, but it is now as warm and nice as a Nebraska summer. Only once in a while do we have rain. It is so today, as you will see from my letter. The possibility of writing is not up to much; the materials are wet and poor.

We marched into town on the twenty-fifth of this month with full music, bringing our prisoners with us. Our company had to guard them on the last days of the march, as well as here in camp. I expect we shall have to shoot some of them. It seems that Livingston, the commander of the district and of the whole expedition, wants to deal seriously with this mob.[5]

Even though stiff from much riding, I have never been sore. Our saddles are comfortable, and my horse trots easily. The marching was not hard; we rarely made twenty miles a day, but getting the forage, after we were in camp in the afternoon, was exhausting for horses and men, since sometimes we had to go eight to ten miles. But my time is up; I must go on guard duty. It is not unusual to have guard duty four out of five nights. Write again soon; greet Hedde; I hope to be able to write to them soon. [The letter continues on January 1, 1864.]

5. On December 25, 1863, Livingston issued a proclamation "To the Citizens of Northern Arkansas." He extended protection to those who had always been loyal, those who had renounced allegiance to the Confederacy, and those who would subsequently lay down their arms. "Return to your firesides and the bosoms of your families, and as far as in my power lies, I will protect you and yours from harm." He also warned that his troops would mete out death to guerrillas, bushwhackers, and jayhawkers wherever they were found. The proclamation appears in the *Batesville (Ark.) Bazzoo,* February 6, 1864, a newspaper published by soldiers of the First Nebraska. Dennis Northcott of the Missouri Historical Society, St. Louis, provided a copy of this issue, which is in the society's collections.

Subsequently, Livingston issued a less conciliatory general order, dated January 11, 1864, which outlined regulations, based on the laws of war, that would apply to the inhabitants of the District of Northeastern Arkansas. The order defined martial law, spies, brigands, and guerrillas and specified the penalties to be imposed upon those found in violation of the regulations. In some cases, the penalty was death on the spot. *OR,* ser. 1, vol. 34, part 2, pp. 65–67.

CHAPTER 14

Scouting and Skirmishing in Northeastern Arkansas, January 1–March 31, 1864

[A continuation of the letter to Heinrich Egge, begun on December 30, 1863.]

[Friday] January 1, 1864—A Happy New Year to all of you!

The mail is not leaving until tomorrow, under guard to Little Rock, one hundred miles from here, so, therefore, I will add a few words. The weather has changed; it rained terribly as I had to go on picket duty. Furthermore, it got cold during the night, and the rain changed to snow. Soaked and cold, everything froze solidly—coats, saddle and harness, the boots on your feet. The poor horses, saddled and bridled, naturally suffer greatly, just as the men do. This duty is extremely hard; the cold weather comes so suddenly and then it is so penetrating that one has no idea how to keep warm. In order not to go on duty right away today, I had put myself on the sick list, since I really felt exhausted and worn out. Therefore, I can still add a few more words. You must excuse my sloppiness. I have neither the time nor the desire to copy it again. As I went on picket duty the day before yesterday, I put the sheet of paper, already written, in my writing case, which I always have with me in my saddlebag. As you can see, the rain and snow found their way into it. I hope you can decipher it.

My company returned from the expedition and brought back twenty-six bales of confiscated cotton. The snow and rain is causing the White River to rise and I hope will make it possible for a boat to reach us with provisions, as well as mail, letters from you and from Germany. The quartermaster of this brigade is going to Little Rock with the guard escorting the mail in order to arrange, I hope, that we will receive our food the same way as the other army units in the Southwest. Please write from time to time so that once the mail gets through I will be sure to receive a letter. Now I must feed [my horse], and therefore I will close.

It is quite cold now; several inches of snow cover the ground. I hope you had a pleasant Christmas, and also entered this new year hale and hearty. The holidays passed rather depressingly for me. Christmas Eve I was on duty guarding the captured guerrillas, and yesterday evening I went to bed early in the cold tent.

[Monday] January 11, 1864 (Letter to Hedde, written in Little Rock)

Since you have not heard from me for so long, you will not be very surprised to find my letter dated from here. I had no time or opportunity to write before. Also mail was sent out only once, by which I had written to Egge from Batesville. The combination of hardship, duty, and, for these latitudes, the astonishingly cold winter prevented writing and the continuation of the diary.

You will have seen from my last letters from Rolla that our destination was Batesville in this state. On the twenty-fifth of December, we marched into the latter place with a large number of prisoners, after we had shot about a dozen in occasional skirmishes on the march. Each one of these bandits captured with a weapon in his hand is shot, mostly on the spot, or if brought in, they are judged as quickly as possible and the sentence carried out at once. Our Colonel Livingston is on the right track in this respect, which makes him popular, both among the troops as well as a not inconsiderable Union element of the population.[1] These unionists are, to some extent, real martyrs to the cause and have suffered constantly under the reign of the rebels. They are now enlisting by the hundreds to take revenge on their enemies. However, our regiment did not benefit from any increase, since a regiment of mounted infantry, as the expression is, is being formed in

1. Both the official Union policy toward guerrillas and the interaction between Union troops and guerrillas in the field is detailed in Fellman, *Inside War*, chapters 3 and 4.

Batesville, the Fourth Arkansas.[2] When we left the city, four or five hundred had already joined.

That I came here happened as follows: an escort of ten men from the Second Battalion of our regiment went with the quartermaster, Lieutenant Thompson, and our mail on the second of this month from Batesville to here.[3] After they had been gone for several days, rumors circulated that they had been attacked but had fought their way out. Colonel Livingston was concerned about the safety of the mail, and dispatches that were anticipated in return, and sent us, some sixty men from the four companies of the Second Battalion of our regiment, to proceed in their direction, to Little Rock if necessary. Theoretically, we received three-fourth rations for three days, nine crackers and a pinch of coffee and some sugar for each man.

Meanwhile the White River was frozen over in places, and the small flatboat was also frozen tight. Nobody thought the ice would be strong enough to support even one man. By putting planks on top, we managed the crossing, to the amazement of the locals, and rode off. The [Little] Red River was frozen over, and we, in fact, glided over the smooth ice, barely three inches thick, also over the several bayous, our horses with only worn-out horseshoes. For miles we rode through swamps overrunning with water, then ice, and it is a miracle that we, along with the horses, did not break our necks and legs. Only one man was slightly hurt in a fall with his horse.

We saw no enemies, but our mail escort had surprised five guerrillas in a house, shot one, and brought one prisoner along to Little Rock. We left the banks of the White River near Batesville at two o'clock in the afternoon on the seventh of this month. On the ninth at sunset we came to our advance post on the north bank of the Arkansas River, across from Little Rock. [We] made 110 miles in three half [two and a half] days. Our men from the mail escort are still here and the heroes of the day! But I must close, I am writing

2. On December 31, 1863, Livingston wrote, "Col. E. Baxter, of this place, has authority from Major-General Steele to raise a regiment of mounted infantry for twelve months, or during the war, and has now 131 men." *OR*, ser. 1, vol. 22, part 2, p. 756.

3. Lt. Charles A. Thompson. Dudley, *Roster of Nebraska Volunteers*, 4–5.

this in the blacksmith shop, where we are getting our horses shod correctly. Tomorrow, most likely, we will return. I hope to hear from you soon.

[Wednesday] January 20, 1864 (Letter to Egge, written in Batesville)

I am still without news from you! The mail seems to have not yet found its way to us. I only hope I will not be left empty-handed when, one of these days, it does come through! I hope Hedde received the newspaper that I sent him from Little Rock. We were there, some sixty men from our battalion. As I mentioned in the last letter, our mail left for Little Rock right after New Year's with an escort of about ten men, along with our quartermaster, to take the necessary steps regarding our arrangements for supply. After they had been gone several days, rumors of a disturbing nature reached Batesville, which persuaded Colonel Livingston to send us after the mail escort. Of course, we expected to meet them on their return from Little Rock. Later we learned that they had never intended to return this way overland but wanted to try to go by steamer, down the Arkansas River, and then on the White River back to Batesville.[4]

We crossed the White River, which was frozen over in places, at the sawmill in town by placing long planks on the ice and then leading our horses across on these, one after the other, a truly "Yankee" idea. Since the ice was barely three inches thick and strong enough to support even a single man only in a few places, long boards were first laid crosswise about every ten to twelve feet, planks resting on these, over which we then safely walked with the horses. However the ice bent so much in the middle of the river that the water came rushing over it. We managed the crossing without breaking through, and by two o'clock in the afternoon luckily we were all on the south bank and took up our march over the snow-covered road.

It was really difficult for our horses to go on. The previous days it had thawed a little, the current cold weather had formed a crust on the snow, and with each step they were breaking through. For

4. But as will become clear, all the soldiers returned overland to Batesville.

the same reason it was impossible for us to walk, although it was very cold sitting on the horse. Just before sunset we fed [the horses] and then rode throughout the night until two hours before daybreak. We once more stopped at a farm, fed, and ate something in a hurry and were in the saddle again before the sun was up.

It was still early in the morning when we crossed the Little Red River on the ice; the ferry had become ice bound. Searcy was the next town, two miles on the other side of the river, once a really impressive town with several large brick buildings, churches, and so on, but now totally deserted. All stores were closed, and hardly a person could be seen on the street. Barely one in ten houses was still occupied, as we find to be the case in all these little towns. The South feels the effect of the war severely, while business prospers in the North.

At dark we arrived in Austin, a small town consisting of a few houses, at the moment almost all of them occupied by the Eighth Missouri Cavalry Regiment. They received us warmly and gave us feed for our horses as well as provisions for ourselves, since the nine crackers and the pinch of coffee that we had been issued were all gone. We stayed here all night and unsaddled our horses for the first time since we had left Batesville, after having ridden some seventy-five miles.

The next day we passed a more swampy area, swamps traversed with bayous, which we crossed sometimes on bridges, sometimes on the ice. We passed Bayou Meto with the destroyed bridge in the last-mentioned manner. It was here that Marmaduke had challenged the crossing by General Davidson. The extended campgrounds stretched for miles along the road we had come. The battlefield was located between the camps of both armies. The trees still bore the marks of the battle that had taken place here. Trees a foot in diameter had been cut down by cannonballs; others were riddled with small balls, etc.[5]

5. For the Union campaign against Little Rock, and the city's surrender on September 10, 1863, see DeBlack, "1863," 90–94. Two of the principal combatants were Union general John W. Davidson and Confederate general John S. Marmaduke.

Here we were still fifteen miles away from Little Rock. Farther along the way we occasionally found fortifications used to fight for the road; trees and brush were chopped down to secure an open field for the cannons. Several miles below Little Rock we came to the Arkansas River, to the long trenches put up by the rebels, built up with gun emplacements, breastworks, etc., stretching for miles along the river and the road. Our troops had bypassed these fortifications by crossing the river below them with pontoons, which they had brought along, and the enemy, threatened on the flank, had to retreat in great haste.

By sunset, we reached our advance guard and camped on the bank across from the city. The pontoon bridge, which at other times connects the banks, can be used only halfway across the river; the rest has to be crossed on the ice. In addition, a steam ferry was operating somewhat below, where the river was open, to deliver supplies of all kinds to the city from the cars of the railroad, which ends here. This railroad comes from DeVall's Bluff on the White River, where the larger steamboats deliver the goods and load them on the railroad.[6] While we were camped here, three steamboats came up the river, packed with government supplies, the first ones in a long time.

Little Rock is a pleasant city, even though from the river it doesn't appear very attractive. The streets are straight and broad, and an active military life prevails. Civilians are seen only rarely. Aside from the sutlers and some speculating Jews, almost none of the businesses are open. The government, of course, uses many of the buildings for storage, stables, and so on. At least ten to fifteen thousand troops are stationed here and in the area. Most of them are housed in barracks, which they have built themselves, log houses with fireplaces where one can live quite comfortably. During the three days we spent in Little Rock, we too were assigned to such lodging and with *full rations* besides!

6. This was the Memphis and Little Rock Railroad. Although the terminus was at Memphis, Tennessee, the rails originated on the west bank of the Mississippi and extended to Madison, Arkansas. There was a gap in the line between Madison and DeVall's Bluff, where the rails resumed and continued to Little Rock. Freeman K. Mobley, Batesville, Arkansas, to James E. Potter, February 13, 2005.

Iowa, Illinois, Missouri, Indiana, and Ohio regiments were here; also several of the new regiments now forming, consisting of Arkansas men and called "mountain feds," "feds" for federals, as we call them, to distinguish them from the enemy, the Confederated Southern States. They probably are called mountain federals because many of these new soldiers were hiding in the mountains or conducted a kind of guerrilla warfare while the rebels had the upper hand here. When our troops marched in, they found their way into our camp with horses, old rifles and muskets, just as it is happening in Batesville, where the Fourth Arkansas Regiment is quickly filling up. Our regiment, however, has received only a few recruits so far. These "feds" ride mostly small ponies or mules, which are especially well suited for this area. In general, they receive infantry uniforms and, as weapons, muskets or flintlocks, besides a revolver.[7]

I also saw Negro troops here, who, it seems, were assigned mainly to fatigue duty. General Steele, in command here, is having the city fortified.[8] It is said a Southern army, eight to ten thousand men strong under General Price, is camped some seventy miles southwest of here, apparently in winter quarters!

Here we found our thirteen men from the mail escort who first left Batesville. They had not considered returning the same way they had come. They wanted to go by train from here to DeVall's Bluff and, from there, try to get up the White River by taking one of the steamers to Batesville.[9] On their trip they had taken five rebels by surprise, killed one of them, taken two captive, and two escaped. They had paroled one of the prisoners and brought the other to Little Rock. They were now going back with us the same way we all had come. However, we needed three and a half days to make the trip this time.

7. The story of one such family of "mountain feds," the Williams family, is told in Barnes, "The Williams Clan."

8. Gen. Frederick Steele commanded the Arkansas Expedition, Army of the Tennessee, and later the Department of Arkansas. Sifakis, *Who Was Who in the Union*, 388–89.

9. He means the steamboats that were to deliver supplies. At this time, however, boats could not run up the White River to Batesville, on account of low water, and were forced to stop at Jacksonport. *OR*, ser. 1, vol. 34, part 1, p. 62.

On the return trip we routed out four guerrillas at a house, but they quickly evaded all pursuit with their fresh horses, which are accustomed to this rough mountain area, while our animals are stiff and tired. My horse has become really skinny, although still safe on his feet, yet he is too heavy for such a rough area. On this march we crossed the Boston Mountains, a chain of hills between the White and Red rivers. I got a few half frozen toes on the first night ride that we made on this trip, and they are still swollen and sore.

The duty is exhausting. Picket duty and foraging as well as patrolling the surrounding area keep you always busy. Some evenings, just relieved from guard duty and tired out, you think you can lie down, when an order comes to saddle up. You could then ride ten or fifteen miles, search through half a dozen houses, and return to camp in the morning dead tired and exhausted. At present a battalion is on an expedition where they are supposed to have ambushed and captured a band of one hundred men in camp; thirty of these were brought in today. This way it is rather difficult for the bandits to maintain themselves.[10]

Currently several detachments have been sent down on both sides of the river toward a steamboat that is supposed to be icebound forty miles from here with one hundred thousand rations for us, along with clothing and weapons. An army corps, reported as anywhere from two to eight hundred men strong, in fact properly enlisted men of the Southern army, is presumably at the river seventy miles above Batesville. Since an attack from them was suspected, and since only a weak garrison had been left behind here, we had our horses saddled for several nights and slept on our weapons. But enough of this, my time is up. Since I am now the cook of one of the sections, I must take care of supper.

[Sunday] January 31 [Letter to Heinrich Egge, written in Batesville]

Quite a long time has passed since I had an opportunity to write. On the twenty-second of this month, our battalion was

10. The report of this foray, under command of Capt. Thomas J. Majors of the First Nebraska, including a detachment of the Eleventh Missouri, is in *OR*, ser. 1, vol. 34, part 2, pp. 140–43. An account also appears in the February 6, 1864, issue of the *Batesville (Ark.) Bazzoo.*

ordered to get ready to march. On the twenty-third at nine o'clock in the morning, we fell in to march off, provided with two days' bread ration and rations for five to six days of coffee, sugar, and salt. Any man who could be spared at all had to go. Besides the four companies H, I, D, and B that belong to the battalion, all men of the First Battalion fit for service were also ordered out. The First Battalion was still in Jacksonport, thirty miles below on the White River, where the steamer was being unloaded, since the river had been too shallow to allow it to come farther up.

Our company was 37 men strong, the remaining companies had about the same, so our regiment provided about 120 to 130 men. Ninety men from the Sixth Missouri Cavalry Regiment had arrived here from Springfield several days ago as escort with dispatches and now went out with us. Therefore, we probably were 250 to 300 men strong, under command of Lieutenant Colonel Baumer.[11] Of course, we did not have baggage, except for one or two packhorses, which carried cooking pots and a couple of frying pans. We had guides and scouts with us, who were, as we soon found out, of great importance to us.

We left from here in a northeastern direction. But it is impossible for me to write down the daily events and incidents, as I did before in the infantry, keeping a diary and recording daily happenings. It was all quite interesting, and I just wish I had been able to make daily notes. We never stopped more than four to five hours and always had half of our horses saddled. It is not an exaggeration to say that we spent fully two-thirds of the time in the saddle. We kept east of the road on which we had come when we marched to Batesville. On the first night we ambushed and surrounded a small place called Evening Shade. However, we found that the "customers" we had expected to find there had left.

The next day we came within fifteen miles of Salem, where we crossed the country road that earlier had taken us to Batesville, and turned southwest, where, as our scouts and spies had learned,

11. Baumer's report of this expedition is in *OR*, ser. 1, vol. 34, part 1, pp. 63–67. He gives the troop total as 202 officers and men of the First Nebraska and 95 men of the Sixth Missouri State Militia, plus 5 guides. A brief account also appears in the February 6, 1864, issue of the *Batesville (Ark.) Bazzoo.*

there was to be a band under Freeman.[12] On that day our advance guard wounded and captured one of Freeman's men. We took another with us, a farmer, since he had made the mistake of thinking we were Confederate troops and offered to lead us to Batesville to seize it from the federals. Before evening, however, he discovered that he had made a small error.

We usually found plenty of corn, oats, or cornhusks on the large plantations that we encountered now and again. Their smokehouses had to yield the meat to us, which was then distributed by the quartermaster. But on occasion one also helped oneself. Almost every evening we had honey. Mush had to take the place of bread, since we had neither time nor opportunity to make anything else out of the cornmeal. Of course there were soon lame and tired horses due to the fierce riding. However, we soon found replacements on the way. Wherever a good horse or mule was found, it was pressed into service. The old horse, if totally worn out, was left behind or, if rapid improvement was expected, taken along. Yet, my horse made the whole trip without getting lame, although it was still very haggard from the ride to Little Rock when we left camp again.

The next morning, our entire force was divided into two groups, which rode toward the White River on two different roads. In a mill we found a lot of corn, as well as wheat flour, obviously ground for our enemies. We took with us as much as we could carry. Close to the mill several of Freeman's men were captured, who apparently had been left behind to guard the supplies.

In Mount Olive we again joined up with the other section. This is a small place on the White River. Our section arrived first at the town. Our advance guard shot a man on the street who had run

12. Col. Thomas R. Freeman, who led troops in southern Missouri and northern Arkansas at this time. At least some of his soldiers were regularly enlisted in the Confederate army, and correspondence in the *OR* addressed to Freeman by Gen. Joseph O. Shelby, the Confederate cavalry commander, indicates Freeman was a recognized Confederate officer. *OR*, ser. 1, vol. 34, part 4, pp. 632, 637, 677. Col. Robert R. Livingston also exchanged correspondence with Freeman on an officer-to-officer basis. *OR*, ser. 1, vol. 34, part 2, pp. 232–34, 310. From Scherneckau's account, however, it seems the Nebraska soldiers considered Freeman's men little better than guerrillas.

away as he was hailed. This is the first man I have seen killed in this war! As his wife, who lived in the town, told us, he was on leave from the Southern army. Most of these men, now in arms here against us, are either deserters or soldiers on leave from the Confederate army. They do not want to surrender so they will have to go back to the army.[13]

We were now closest to our enemies, the notorious Freeman gang, whom we had been chasing for so long. Sylamore, a little place eight miles from here, is supposed to be the headquarters of the gang. We crossed the rather broad and raging river here at a very good ford. The road always passed close to the river, down the White River. The news about the enemy was now more accurate, and we prepared for a tough battle. On one side was the river, on the other the cliff rising up steeply three to four hundred feet, leaving just enough room for the road so that two riders had exactly enough space to ride side by side. This was the approach to the nest and headquarters of the gang, and therefore easy to defend, even against a superior force.

We had followed this road for about half a mile when our head [of the column] reached the town, where they were fired at from the houses and the thicket. At once the bugles sounded "gallop" to come to the aid of our advance troops; however, we did not get to see the enemy. A sergeant of our advance guard was wounded in the leg.[14] The balls and buckshot whistled over our heads as we rode through the Sylamore Brook that empties here [into the river] and reached the town with the same name.

Right behind the few houses, a mountain rose high, overgrown with cedar shrubs. The smoke of the shots fired at us was still rising

13. Confederate soldiers who were captured by Union troops knew that they might be returned to the Confederate army's jurisdiction under the parole and exchange agreement between the Union and Confederate governments (see chapter 7, note 21). If these men had deserted from their units or were absent without leave, they risked being punished, or even shot, once they had been turned over to the Confederate authorities, which explains their reluctance to surrender.

14. Sgt. William Millen of Company G. *OR*, ser. 1, vol. 34, part 1, p. 65. Millen survived his wounding but was discharged for disability on March 13, 1865. Dudley, *Roster of Nebraska Volunteers*, 78–79.

halfway up, but everything was quiet now as we wheeled by the left into line at the very foot of the mountain. "Dismount" was the next command; every fourth man had to hold three horses, while the rest formed lines as infantry. I was one of the horse-holders, however, but immediately found a man who traded with me, whereupon I took my place in the ranks. We had our rifles and revolvers; however, we left the saber with the horses.

Company B from our regiment went to the right of us, while the unit from the Sixth Missouri detachment formed the line to our left. We were under the command of our Lieutenant Moore and, as skirmishers, proceeded in an extended line, covering the entire front side of the mountain. As fast as possible we climbed over rocks and fallen trees toward the peak. Where it often seemed impossible for us to get through on foot, we found paths recently made by the hooves of the ponies and mules of our enemies. Not a shot fell; not a man was to be seen.

Gasping and tired we finally reached the peak, at least half a mile from where we had started. A deep ravine and another mountain ridge appeared and on the latter, a few of the last riders were still galloping away. Several shots were fired. Then again we pursued them in a long line, searching the area as on a battue [hunt]. We climbed this way for another three or four miles, where we encountered the road on which the enemy had withdrawn and whose rear guard had fired on us.

As we stopped here for a moment to catch our breath, a troop of butternuts appeared some three hundred paces from us, on small horses and mules. Since we were quiet they apparently did not know whether we were enemies or some of their own men. Because some of them were wearing blue coats, we were just as uncertain. Since our scouts were also wearing these coats, we were afraid to shoot at our own men. One of these riders came still closer and called to us. We answered "friends." Another called, "Come over and see," at which point the bushwhacker turned his horse around, and as soon as we saw the movement we fired, yet the troops were riding away at full speed, untouched. We pursued them but without result; a gray felt hat was all we found.

Now three or four miles away from the main force, we turned around, since it was evening and we were without provisions and on foot. But the main force had followed slowly and soon met us. Our horses had been brought along, and after we mounted, we followed in the direction the enemy had taken. After dark our skirmishers, covering the flanks, saw a long row of fires. Again we dismounted and spread out toward the suspicious fires in greatest silence. However, we found that it was a clearing where dead trees and brush had been set on fire. We rode several miles and stopped about eight miles from the little town, which we had passed, in order to feed. At three o'clock in the morning we mounted again and went back the same way to Sylamore.

And like yesterday, from here we went over the mountains again in skirmishing order, while the mounted ones waited on the road, until we had reached the riverbank so as to cut off the retreat of any of the enemy who had pressed this far. But nobody was seen, a truly miserable result after all our efforts. Only three riders, about to board a flatboat, were on the other side of the White River, but they quickly turned around when we appeared at the bank. A volley from our muskets got one of them down from his horse, but the others helped him to escape, leaving one horse behind.

Then the bugle blew the signal to assemble. Soon we were together amidst the houses, just starting to feed the horses and taking care of ourselves, when once again shots were fired on us from one of the hills surrounding us on all sides, though not injuring anyone. The line of skirmishers was immediately set up again, and double-quick we ran to the hill. We had to wade the creek, reaching up to the knees—I was in shoes—and then clamber up the steep stone walls, crawling from bush to bush through gaps in the rock. Yet in the excitement of the moment one can endure and make astonishing jumps.

But as usual the scoundrels were too quick for us. They did not even take time to fire at us and sought their safety in flight. We could see some men only a great distance away, whose hasty retreat we accelerated with several shots. Like the mountain we had searched yesterday, this one was also full of horse tracks from the guerrillas, real trails, almost all of them leading in the direction of the town, which appeared to be their headquarters.

Tired, we turned around and ate a meal such as rarely had tasted better, although it was only freshly salted pork, with mush and hot coffee, also cornbread baked on hot stones at the fire. The freshly ground corn meal and the ham were from the supplies we had seized here. Also a large supply of fodder for the horses served us in good stead. Company D went up the creek for several miles, where they burned down a mill, which had delivered flour to the rebels.

During the time we were lying down, enjoying the short break and the warm sun, some men blessed with good eyes discovered at that point several men on their horses on top of the stone walls that we had searched that morning, watching us in the valley. It was too far and too high to be able to shoot at them successfully. Since we now knew the terrain a little better, some of us thought it might be possible to cut off their retreat. Our lieutenant did not want to give us permission to undertake the expedition. Thereupon we went to Baumer, who told us to try our luck and spoil the spying for the fellows.

Five of us, therefore, took our revolvers, muskets, and our horses, without saddles, in order to ride through the brook. One comrade went with us and took back the horses. At the same time four men from the Sixth Missouri Regiment rode through the brook farther down, leaving their horses behind, and climbed the rocks there, while we were on the left, and so got the enemy between us. They, of course, had seen our movements and considered their retreat, using the peak of the mountain, which extended farther back on a ridge.

Since we found quite accessible trails, sometimes around steep rocks, rising straight up, we could move forward on them really quickly. Large boulders, cedar brush, etc., concealed our enemies, and only the breaking of a dry twig or a stone crumbling away revealed that we were near them, although perhaps one hundred feet below. One of the Sixth Missouri boys first discovered a lad who was just about to take aim at him with his long squirrel rifle. The cocking of the gun betrayed him; a carbine shot cracked, hit; he jumped; a second shot from our side brought him down; he fell at least fifty feet into a crevice in the rock, where he disappeared.

From the flank of our position where we were posted, we climbed as quickly as possible toward the trail, obviously leading along the mountain ridge, to cut off the retreat for the rest of the bandits we were attacking, while the right wing of our position [force] drove them into our arms. We reached the top in time to see two men on our left hurrying down toward the valley. [We saw] two more with their horses on the same plateau as we were, their backs turned toward us, since they apparently had heard our comrades and expected to be attacked by them, not anticipating that in the meantime they had been enveloped and we had come upon them from the rear. There was the danger that both men, running away, would be soon hidden by cedar brush. We fired on them and forced at least one of them into several involuntary jumps, grabbing his head with both hands. The bushes, however, concealed him from our sight, and we saw none of them again. This was the first human being at whom I had shot, very calmly and quite deliberately, and who, apparently, also had been hit.

Since we had to climb down a steep rock wall at least two hundred feet, we gave up trying to find out what success we had and turned toward the camp, for we were already past the allotted time and still had to go about three miles. But we heard our comrades, who made up this climbing party with us, shooting various times. In the meantime they had encountered the other two and had killed both. Soon they arrived at camp, shortly after us, having carried off two horses, weapons, and the like. The entire commando then rode about another fifteen miles, where we camped at a farm.

This night we lay down on the ground in battle formation, holding our horses by the reins, for we were in the vicinity of the enemy. Our scouts had brought exaggerated reports about their strength, so Colonel Baumer feared an attack, but without justification. The rebels ahead of us were only concerned with their retreat.

The next morning we came upon the rear guard patrol that had been left behind. Since we surprised them, we were able to take seven of the ten men prisoners, two were shot, while one escaped. Riding farther on the shortest trails through the wilderness, several more stragglers from Captain Freeman's corps were killed. We arrived at the campground, where the band had stayed last night. There again we surprised five of the pickets and took them prisoner. The campfires were still burning where some two to three hundred men had camped last night.

We now took up the chase with vigor. At the next houses we learned that the wagons, with an escort of some thirty riders, had recently passed by. The advance guard, strengthened by our company, now received the order to go after them right away. At full gallop we thundered along the rocky road as fast as the horses could run. For four or five miles we stayed pretty much in rank and file, the slower horses holding back the others. But then the ones in front saw the last of the wagons, and with wild shouts they stormed forward, the best horses riding past the others.

I was soon among the first of the riders, and immediately the wagon train was taken; the escort, scattered in all directions, was riding away, since they were better mounted, while our animals had very little breath left, due to the demanding chase up to now. Three men were shot and five captured, three teamsters and two cooks.[15] There were only three wagons, two with four horses hitched and one with six horses, loaded only with cooking utensils, horseshoes, etc.

The first wagon had some officers' baggage on it, which was plundered. At the moment I still have a shirt of Captain Freeman's here, which I took, also a number of letters from a mail pouch to be taken through to Missouri, which came from the Army of the South. I am enclosing some of them. I also took a large map of the state that way. Since we probably had little chance to catch up with the band scattered through the mountains, we now returned to Batesville, our headquarters. We brought about forty prisoners back to camp, as well as a number of horses and mules. But I must close; I have taken too much time for this letter already.

Only now that I am cooking do I find a chance to write these days; otherwise I would not have time or opportunity for it. The men who are not on guard duty or other duty in camp are constantly on raids, during which guerrillas are shot or brought in as prisoners, along with many horses. Four days ago, I was ready to end this letter, when suddenly "boots and saddles" sounded, and everyone was in the saddle within a few minutes. It was said our advance post would be attacked by a detachment of two hundred men.

15. One of the rebels killed was a "Captain Franks." *OR,* ser. 1, vol. 34, part 1, p. 66.

So we chased out for all it was worth, but it seemed to have been a false alarm. At least we found no one, although we went out six to seven miles, where we found our forage train with about twenty men as escort, to which another thirty men from our detachment were added for reinforcement. I was among those who had to make this expedition, so unexpectedly and not at all prepared, from which I returned only the day before yesterday. I was absent for three nights, without blankets or food literally, since we left camp in the greatest hurry.

This is action, indeed, even though at times hard and tiring, but still exciting and interesting. Cavalry is the weapon for me! My horse has now become quite skinny but still makes it just as well as any of the others. To ride twenty or thirty miles does not make me any more tired than two to three miles I did before. But one cannot go without sleep, and sometimes one is overcome with fatigue; therefore, I have slept in the saddle for miles.

But enough of that. Yesterday [February 9] a steamer arrived here with supplies, and I expect that tomorrow, or at least soon, our letters will leave with it.[16] There is still no mail here for us! A detachment from our regiment, some fifty men strong, just returned from a reconnaissance. Forty-five miles northeast from here they met with united bands of various guerrilla captains, five to six hundred men strong, and had to withdraw from this superior force. We took six prisoners but lost some thirty men as prisoners; however, only one from our regiment. The others were from the Eleventh Missouri and Fourth Arkansas regiments, called mountain feds.[17] I assume that now we will leave soon to attack these united bands, and therefore I hurry to end these lines.

You or Hedde write occasionally anyway, so that if our mail arrives I will be certain to receive at least some letters. You will not believe how much I long to hear anything from Grand Island again. It is now two months since we had mail, and everyone is as impatient as I am! I am placing these sheets in several envelopes and hope they will reach your hands safely. Let Hedde read this too; I really have no time to write.

16. This was the *Dove*. *OR*, ser. 1, vol. 34, part 1, p. 132.
17. The reports of this skirmish are in *OR*, ser. 1, vol. 34, part 1, pp. 131–35.

You won't believe how much we are constantly in action; there is no hour at night or day in which we must not be ready to mount and maybe ride forty or fifty miles in one stretch. Since recently, here in camp, we have been living only on mush and fresh beef, one learns to get along well on this! A few days ago I had breakfast at a wealthy planter's, and I had a quite decent breakfast. I was served by blacks, who were half dead with fear, since their masters had told them that the Yanks would massacre all the Negroes. They now did their best to please the rough soldiers.

Yet I am well and happy and hope you dear Grand Islanders can report the same about yourselves. Write occasionally and address it as always. I will send you a small newspaper published here as soon as I can get an issue. It is edited and printed by several comrades in the regiment.[18] Share it with Hedde as well as other documents I will enclose. Please also save these letters and diary entries for me. Send me a lot of news, since, of course, we do not receive any newspapers. How about your trip to Germany?

Whether I will receive my release in June has still not been decided.[19] However, cavalry in the field is my ticket, as it is said in the soldier's language. Excuse the poor writing and style!

In great haste, your friend,

August

[*Wednesday*] *February 10, 1864*, Batesville, Arkansas, USA

[*Friday*] *February 26, 1864* (letter to Egge)

Prevented by constant duty, I hurry now to let you have at least a few words from me. This afternoon the escort will leave with the mail, and until now I have been able to write just one letter to Mad[am] Hedde. Several days ago we received the only mail since we left Rolla, Missouri. I received eight letters, among them two from you, dated November 28 and 30 last year, so very old. I hope you have received my letters, mailed from here (Batesville). I also received a letter from Pundt, obviously too late. However, I did not withdraw the money, since at the end of this month I can expect six months' pay. Yet I will not draw any pay before we get to a place

18. This was the *Batesville (Ark.) Bazzoo.* Only the February 6, 1864, issue, vol. 1, no. 2, seems to have survived, cited from the collections of the Missouri Historical Society.

19. He discusses his prospects for a furlough in his March 2 letter.

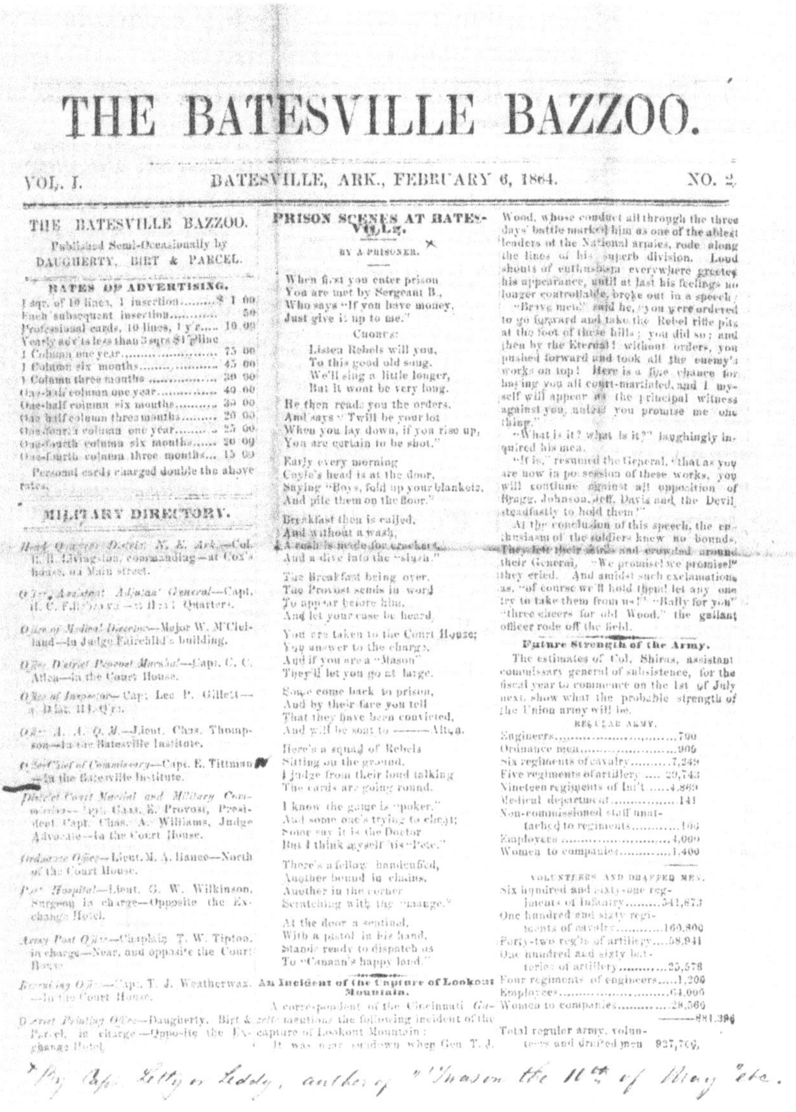

THE BATESVILLE BAZZOO.

VOL. I. BATESVILLE, ARK., FEBRUARY 6, 1864. NO. 2.

THE BATESVILLE BAZZOO.

Published Semi-Occasionally by
DAUGHERTY, BIRT & PARCEL.

RATES OF ADVERTISING.

1 sqr. of 10 lines, 1 insertion	$ 1 00
Each subsequent insertion	50
Professional cards, 10 lines, 1 y'r	10 00
Yearly adv'ts less than 3 sqrs $1 ᵖ line	
1 Column one year	75 00
1 Column six months	45 00
1 Column three months	30 00
One-half column one year	40 00
One-half column six months	30 00
One half column three months	20 00
One-fourth column one year	25 00
One-fourth column six months	20 00
One-fourth column three months	15 00

Personal cards charged double the above rates.

MILITARY DIRECTORY.

Head Quarters District N. E. Ark.—Col. R. R. Livingston, commanding—at Cox's house, on Main street.

Office Assistant Adjutant General—Capt. H. C. F. [illegible]—at Head Quarters.

Office of Medical Director—Major W. M'Clelland—in Judge Fairchild's building.

Office District Provost Marshal—Capt. C. C. Allen—in the Court House.

Office of Inspector—Capt. Lee P. Gillett—at Dist. H'd Q'rs.

Office A. A. Q. M.—Lieut. Chas. Thompson—in the Batesville Institute.

Office Chief of Commissary—Capt. E. Tittman—in the Batesville Institute.

District Court Martial and Military Commission—[illegible] Chas. E. Provost, President. Capt. Chas. A. Williams, Judge Advocate—in the Court House.

Ordnance Office—Lieut. M. A. Hance—North of the Court House.

Post Hospital—Lieut. G. W. Wilkinson, Surgeon in charge—Opposite the Exchange Hotel.

Army Post Office—Chaplain T. W. Tipton, in charge—Near, and opposite the Court House.

Recruiting Office—Capt. T. J. Weatherwax.—In the Court House.

District Printing Office—Daugherty, Birt & Parcel, in charge—Opposite the Exchange Hotel.

PRISON SCENES AT BATESVILLE.

BY A PRISONER.*

When first you enter prison
You are met by Sergeant B.,
Who says "If you have money,
Just give it up to me."

CHORUS:

Listen Rebels will you,
To this good old song.
We'll sing a little longer,
But it wont be very long.

He then reads you the orders,
And says "'Twill be your lot
When you lay down, if you rise up,
You are certain to be shot."

Early every morning
Coyle's head is at the door,
Saying "Boys, fold up your blankets,
And pile them on the floor."

Breakfast then is called,
And without a wash,
A rush is made for crackers,
And a dive into the "slush."

The Breakfast being over,
The Provost sends in word
To appear before him,
And let your case be heard.

You are taken to the Court House;
You answer to the charge,
And if you are a "Mason"
They'll let you go at large.

Some come back to prison,
And by their face you tell
That they have been convicted,
And will be sent to ——— Alton.

Here's a squad of Rebels
Sitting on the ground,
I judge from their loud talking
The cards are going round.

I know the game is "poker,"
And some one's trying to cheat;
Some say it is the Doctor
But I think myself 'tis "Pete."

There's a fellow handcuffed,
Another bound in chains,
Another in the corner
Scratching with the "mange."

At the door a sentinel,
With a pistol in his hand,
Stands ready to dispatch us
To "Canaan's happy land."

An Incident of the Capture of Lookout Mountain.

A correspondent of the Cincinnati *Gazette* mentions the following incident of the capture of Lookout Mountain:

It was near sundown when Gen T. J. Wood, whose conduct all through the three days' battle marked him as one of the ablest leaders of the National armies, rode along the lines of his superb division. Loud shouts of enthusiasm everywhere greeted his appearance, until at last his feelings no longer controllable, broke out in a speech:

"Brave men," said he, "you were ordered to go forward and take the Rebel rifle pits at the foot of these hills; you did so; and then by the Eternal! without orders, you pushed forward and took all the enemy's works on top! Here is a fine chance for having you all court-martialed, and I myself will appear as the principal witness against you, unless you promise me one thing."

"What is it? what is it?" laughingly inquired his men.

"It is," resumed the General, "that as you are now in possession of these works, you will continue against all opposition of Bragg, Johnson, Jeff. Davis and the Devil steadfastly to hold them!"

At the conclusion of this speech, the enthusiasm of the soldiers knew no bounds. They left their arms and crowded around their General, "We promise! we promise!" they cried. And amidst such exclamations as, "of course we'll hold them! let any one try to take them from us!" "Bully for you" "three cheers for old Wood," the gallant officer rode off the field.

Future Strength of the Army.

The estimates of Col. Shiras, assistant commissary general of subsistence, for the fiscal year to commence on the 1st of July next, show what the probable strength of the Union army will be.

REGULAR ARMY.

Engineers	700
Ordnance men	906
Six regiments of cavalry	7,249
Five regiments of artillery	20,743
Nineteen regiments of Inf't	4,869
Medical department	141
Non-commissioned staff unattached to regiments	166
Employees	4,000
Women to companies	1,400

VOLUNTEERS AND DRAFTED MEN.

Six hundred and sixty-one regiments of Infantry	541,673
One hundred and sixty regiments of cavalry	160,800
Forty-two reg'ts of artillery	58,941
One hundred and sixty batteries of artillery	25,578
Four regiments of engineers	1,200
Employees	64,006
Women to companies	28,366
	881,394
Total regular army, volunteers and drafted men	927,769

*By Capt. Lilly or Leddy, author of "Invasion the 11th of May" etc.

The Batesville (Ark.) Bazzoo, published by soldiers of the First Nebraska. Archives: Civil War Collection. Missouri Historical Society, St. Louis.

where we have an opportunity to send it off safely. From yours and Hedde's letters, I understand that you have had an unusually cold winter. Here too the weather was quite cold for this latitude. But it was warm and nice the last few weeks.

As mentioned above, we have exhausting duty here. The enemy here is nothing more than unorganized gangs made up from inhabitants of the area and deserters of the Army of the South. The cowardice of the men from the Eleventh Missouri Regiment made it possible for these bushwhackers to take a train of some thirty wagons a while ago.[20] They seem to be afraid of our regiment. Wherever we had encountered them we were victorious, almost without loss on our side, whether we faced many or few. It is often quite an exhausting life but also a lot of fun as a cavalryman in the field. We have ridden many hundreds of miles around the area, sometimes lived well, sometimes endured hunger.

It is now said that various gangs are congregating around us, and several days ago they even demanded that Colonel Livingston hand over the place. We will give the lads a warm welcome should they actually have the courage to attack us here. Previously they never resisted when we were the attackers. A quick, reliable horse and a good shot are the best things for a rider in this kind of warfare. I have quite a good horse, as I found out in a number of chases that we have had. I was never far behind the best horses of our company. Shooting, however, is another matter, and to be honest, I don't believe that any ammunition shot by me has harmed anyone. Yet the comrades who were with me in the small fight we had some time ago near Sylamore maintain that at a distance of three hundred yards my old musket caused one of the butternuts to make several mighty leaps, whether hit or not.

But before I close, just a few words about my affairs there. As soon as I find the time, I will write more. I thank you for all the trouble and inconveniences you have had on my account. Dispose of that money that you do not need for yourself as if it were your own; that means lend it to people in the settlement who are good

20. The escort included men of the Eleventh Missouri Cavalry and the Fourth Arkansas Mounted Infantry, commanded by Capt. William Castle. Captain Castle was killed, and thirty-five wagons and twenty-nine soldiers and some teamsters were captured. *OR*, ser. 1, vol. 34, part 1, p. 132.

for it. Hedde is too worried [to lend money], even when he does not benefit from it, so he would keep the money in his hands. To deposit the money in the bank does not seem as good to me as loaning it out to people in Grand Island.[21] I am happy to hear of the progress in our settlement, and my thoughts are always there, where I would like to own a piece of land for sure. Sell all my things, only not books and clothing. If the latter is ruined, however, or causes too much trouble for you to keep, dispose of them too. Let me hear from you soon.

Yours

A. Scherneckau

Greet all the settlers sincerely from me. Alas, how often I think of the delightful hours we bachelors have experienced together.

Batesville, Arkansas

[Wednesday] March 2, 1864

Dear Egge:

Although I do not yet know how this letter will reach you, I am writing it anyway. Since I have a moment's time, I will make use of it and then send off the letter as soon as a chance presents itself. Maybe we will leave this area soon in order—just imagine!—to go to Omaha in Nebraska? But in any case I think this letter will reach Nebraska before us.

We have to thank the veterans' movement for this Nebraska trip if it happens. The order regarding the admission to this new organization just established states clearly—in order to make the entry into it more attractive—that as soon as three-fourths of the required recruits assigned to a certain company have reenlisted, and who must all belong to one and the same company of the present regiment, the whole company or, in some cases, the regiment shall be sent back to the state or territory, where they will be given leave for thirty or sixty days! This is now the case with Company H and several others of the regiment. All these veterans will soon be going from here to Cape Girardeau, and all recruits with them. The old soldiers who could have reenlisted but did not do so, however, have to remain behind here, at least for the present. I will also be entitled to

21. Probably some of his pay that Scherneckau had been sending home from time to time.

a leave, and should we get to Omaha, I will use it to visit my Grand Island friends. I am only afraid that it will still be rather cold at your place, since we have endured a cold winter here. This leave will not cost me anything, and I am considering staking out a claim again and holding it until I have served out my time.

At the moment things are quiet. Due to our raids we have greatly disrupted the gangs gathering around us and have partly driven them away, partly scattered them. Therefore, our pickets are no longer alarmed as often, and we sleep several nights in a row without being awakened to saddle horses and to stand in battle lines. However, fodder for our animals is in extremely short supply. The immediate surroundings are completely drained; therefore, our wagons must go out three to four days' march in order to get corn. The roads are horrible, and therefore the forage parties cannot always return at a specific time, so the horses must go hungry. My horse is nothing but skin and bones, and I don't even want to be seen by him, since he neighs every time he sees me, for he hopes to be fed.[22] We also are not amply provided with food, yet we are awaiting a boat with provisions soon, since the last rain has caused the river to rise.

Yours
August

Batesville, [Sunday] April 17, 1864[23]

Dear Friend Faber:[24]

For a long time I have neglected to write to you. The circumstances here made it impossible and you must forgive me. I

22. The Company H morning reports for March and April 1864 record the dearth of forage almost daily. NSHS RG18, roll 3. Because so many troops from both sides had been scouring the countryside, and Union supply lines could not always be kept open due to enemy activity or low water in the rivers, forage was scarce. On April 16, 1864, Colonel Livingston reported, "my stock is dying daily for want of food." *OR*, ser. 1, vol. 34, part 3, p. 181.

23. As Scherneckau mentions in the next chapter, some of his diary pages and letters were lost after he was wounded on March 31. Although he began writing this letter to Faber while he was lying in the Batesville hospital, it has been included in this chapter because it covers events that occurred before he became a casualty.

24. Faber was in Germany. Scherneckau received a letter from him on March 30, 1863, and wrote to Faber on April 5 and May 29, 1863.

received the last letter from you just before we left St. Louis, Missouri. Whether I answered it then, I no longer know. If I did, I hope the letter reached you long ago. You will surely not do as I have and make me wait so long for an answer. Any news from home [Germany] and also from here [the United States] that we receive in camp is valued highly. You cannot imagine what excitement the arrival of the mail causes in camp. It is then twice as hard to have to leave empty-handed, when one had so confidently counted on news from home.

But now a bit as excuse and explanation for my long silence. If you have heard anything at all about me through my parents, you will have learned that our regiment, while stationed in St. Louis, was changed into a cavalry regiment. Initially we kept our infantry weapons but received a revolver and a saber, and at the same time we were also stuck into the yellow-striped jackets of the cavalry. We hardly had received our horses when we were ordered here, without having learned to use the saber and even much less how to ride correctly. We barely learned how to get on and off the saddle.

Our colonel is commander of the District of Northeastern Arkansas and received the order to set up his headquarters here in Batesville on the White River. We went by train from St. Louis to Rolla, 110 English miles. From there we marched here, escorting a long wagon train loaded with supplies, as well as arms and uniforms. The latter were intended for a new regiment to be organized in the vicinity of Batesville. It is now at full strength and stationed here as the Fourth Arkansas Volunteer Infantry Regiment.

On December 25 last year we arrived here. Without having had any significant skirmishes on the way, we still brought forty to fifty prisoners with us. On the march here, we had a martial law execution, two jayhawkers. I suppose you already have seen that wording in the newspapers; it means no more and no less than the highwayman in England or the thief in Italy or Spain. Here they are dressed as Union soldiers or they pretend to be members of the Confederate Army, just as it fits their plans. But in fact they belong to neither but live on thievery, whether taken from the Union's faithful people or from those associated with the Southern states, just as it works out. As mentioned above, we took two of these bandits as prisoners. Since they were known and notorious in the area, our commander, Colonel Livingston, decided to set an example. At sunset they were to be shot by a detachment from our regiment. As we marched out to the place with them, where their graves were already dug, they both made an attempt to escape at the same time. However, they were immediately shot down. Since then there are no such formalities. If such notorious criminals fall into our hands, they are simply taken aside by a few men ordered for that purpose, and one does not see them again.

A major offense was the wearing of our uniform. Entire detachments of the enemy, often only robbers and desperados, performed their robberies and acts of violence in the name of the federals, as the U.S. troops are called here. Therefore, it was announced publicly, and the enemy informed through intermediaries, that no prisoners would be taken who were found in our uniform. Several times I looked on when such were shot, although they had thrown away their weapons and were ready to surrender! But it was absolutely necessary since, frequently deceived by the uniform, we did not fire promptly and the enemy then escaped, or when they misled us and we regarded them as our own men, they took us by surprise. As soon as the order became known to the enemy, we found, when following on the heels of fleeing bands, coats and other parts of our uniforms thrown along the road on which they were retreating, getting rid of them as they rode.

We soon found out that we had our hands full. The mountainous area was especially well suited for guerrilla warfare. Supplying our horses with feed was one of our main activities. Strong detachments always had to go with our forage trains; besides, the fodder in the vicinity soon became scarce, and we often had to get corn thirty to forty miles away, over appalling roads. Food for us also became scarce, since steamers couldn't come up to the city because of the low water level.

We have had an exceptionally hard winter in all states of the Union. Here too it was unusually cold and more snow than the inhabitants were used to seeing. Just at the coldest time, in the middle of January, a detail of sixty men from our regiment was sent to Little Rock, 110 miles from here, to the commander of the department, General Steele, with dispatches and mail. I also made the trip; it was hard for men and horses, fast riding, with the crossing of frozen streams and brooks. The horses, having only worn-out horseshoes, skidded and slid, and it was a miracle that not more fell and got hurt. We had to cross over the Boston Mountains and in general had a very rough and barely cleared road on the whole stretch. Yet we had no fights to face, although the enemy was reported to be in considerable strength between here and Little Rock.

We rested several days on the banks of the Arkansas, on which Little Rock is located. I visited the city, which has really nice buildings: churches, the state capitol, U.S. arsenal, university, penitentiary, etc. It was lively there, as every place where the uniform of the United States is seen in large numbers. At the time, there were supposed to have been not less than thirty thousand men in winter quarters in and around Little Rock. How warm and nice those barracks seemed to us in comparison to our smoky tents, where we rarely could sleep undisturbed one night during a week. We returned on the same road, although somewhat more at leisure than when we had come. The bands of guerrillas now appear to be gathering around Batesville.

Besides our regiment, some five hundred horses strong, there are just about as many of the Eleventh Missouri Regiment and two cannons. The Missouri cavalry regiment, so far, has not been very trustworthy. A train of thirty wagons was seized by the enemy from a detachment of that regiment that was to be its escort. The one hundred Missouri men left the train to its fate and fled in confusion; the wagons were burned, and the mules driven off. Since then we have recaptured many of the mules from them [the enemy]. On one expedition recently undertaken we tracked down a band, supposed to be two hundred men strong, which had its camp in a remote area. Men familiar with the region led us over mountains and steep cliffs to their campground, but we found the band had deserted the place, maybe an hour earlier, their campfires still burning.

On their retreat they had divided into two columns, one of them taking the train with them. First of all, our task was to pursue this one and, if possible, capture the wagons and destroy them. The advance guard, made up of our company, therefore received the order to pursue, while the main force followed more slowly.

We then went on at a gallop, and it became a long race. Only after five to seven miles of breakneck riding did we see the escort of the wagons. With a loud hurrah, spurring on the horses to their utmost, we drew our revolvers and began to shoot into the troops. An officer tried in vain to rally them into a formation to oppose us, but he was shot off his horse, and the rest scattered in all directions. The three wagons were soon in our hands. Two of them had nothing more than cooking utensils and some food. The third wagon contained the baggage of officers and some rebel mail, letters from the soldiers of one of the Southern armies to their families who live in Missouri. Everything was plundered, and whatever we could take with us, we dragged along. I took a number of letters, some writing paper, and a clean shirt from Colonel Freeman, which came in handy at that time. Then we cut up the wagons with the axes found there, and set them on fire. On the same expedition we had several small skirmishes with parts of the same band. [The letter ends abruptly.]

CHAPTER 15

A Casualty of War and a Furlough to Nebraska, April 1–July 5, 1864

(Here an additional part of my letters and diary pages was lost. Besides, I was forced for some time to stop writing down my experiences, for I was wounded.[1] So I am starting again in the hospital in Batesville, Arkansas.)

Tuesday, April 26—The wounds are nearly healed; however, I still spent the day in bed. The steamboat *Lloyd* came up the White River loaded with forage for the garrison.[2] The water level of the river and also in the bayou Poke, which empties here into the river, is so high that the steamboat could come up the bayou to the bridge in the middle of town.

The garrison here consists now of the Fourth Arkansas Regiment and a company of the Eleventh Missouri Cavalry under the

1. On March 31, 1864, a fellow soldier accidentally shot Scherneckau as he was approaching a picket post to relieve the guard. On March 12 his company had boarded the steamboat *Miller* to go up the White River to load forage. The boat ran aground March 16 and remained stuck until April 4. During this period, the soldiers established picket posts near the river to protect the helpless steamboat against guerrillas. Company H Morning Report, March–April 1864, NSHS RG18, roll 3. It was at one of these posts where Scherneckau was wounded. His company commander, Capt. William W. Ivory described the incident in an April 1, 1864, letter: "Augustus Scherneckau (one of my best men) was badly shot in the left leg by one of my own men. . . . Scherneckau was on his way to relieve him and got outside of the man." Evidently Scherneckau had become disoriented and approached the post from beyond the lines, rather than from within them. Ivory commented that he had often warned his noncommissioned officers against letting soldiers relieve picket posts without the noncoms' oversight. Scherneckau file, Compiled Service Records, roll 20.

2. The official name of the boat was *Q. Lloyd*. *OR*, ser. 1, vol. 34, part 3, p. 257.

command of Lieutenant Colonel Stephens from the last regiment.[3] The cavalry is quartered in the courthouse; the mountain feds have their tents by the bridge at the bayou. The hospital is a two-story brick building; our room on the upper floor was previously used as a print shop. The lower front part of the building was a store. These buildings, however, were all empty when we arrived here, with pompous signs and announcements of the businesses, but nothing in back of them. But things have changed since then; refugees occupy all the houses and have had to build new huts to find shelter. The government also uses a number of buildings for various purposes.

Since the feds arrived here, the town has changed, very much to its advantage. Yankee speculation brought in all kinds of merchandise and found a ready market, because such things were not to be had here for years. Not only greenbacks but also gold and silver filled the merchants' pockets. Hundreds of the residents nearby came in daily to see and buy the splendors being offered. The churches were opened again, and our regimental chaplain held Sunday services. Even the town clock at the courthouse tower was again set in motion by hands skilled in these things and now tells the time with loud strokes, while announcing that the Yankees have their hand in the game here and that the old sad times of anarchy and mob rule are over.

The weather is very warm; the trees, for the most part, are green, but from my bed I can't see much of nature. Today, we had one of the Memphis newspapers from the sixteenth of this month, which had, indeed, more recent news than we were used to getting for a long time. The newspapers tended to be a month old before they reached us and were then sold for twenty-five cents each. Fred Elwood, my comrade here in this sad hospital life, bought four

3. Lt. Col. John W. Stephens, who was left in command at Batesville when the majority of the Union forces there moved to Jacksonport in mid-April. Colonel Livingston ordered the move because "shipments of supplies and forage to this point [Batesville] have been dangerously dilatory in reaching here." He also noted that navigation to Batesville was problematic during much of the year. Furthermore, Livingston believed the enemy threat was increasing east of the White River, and Jacksonport was a better base from which to operate. *OR*, ser. 1, vol. 34, part 3, pp. 181–82.

dozen eggs for one dollar today. Besides, we have to pay fifty cents a pound for butter, soft, white, and watery.

Wednesday, April 27—I finished a letter and sent it to Egge. The boat left today, loaded mostly with cotton. My leg was hurting me more than usual; a change in the weather is imminent, and I am afraid that with my wound I will have a dependable barometer for some time at least. The treatment of my wound is fully in accordance with the coldwater method. Nothing but coldwater compresses have been applied from the time of my injury until now, changed frequently at first but now only at longer intervals. The same treatment is applied to all cases. The healing is achieved only through coldwater treatments, even where a limb has been amputated. Severe thunderstorms with heavy rain in the evening. This weather causes quite a bit of pain in my wounds.

Thursday, April 28—Overcast sky; I was not well today, most likely due to the change in the weather. An attempt to walk on crutches turned out badly. I cannot yet take it to let the leg hang down. As long as I have it in a horizontal position, all is well. I can sit up if I have the leg on one chair and sit on another. We received onions and eggs from friends in the area.

Friday, April 29—It was a long, sad night for me; the storm continued and my leg was too fidgety! Besides, my digestion is also out of order, most likely caused by lying still for so long. Unfortunately, the medical supplies left behind here are so few that scarcely any laxative in sufficient quantity is available. I believe this happened on the assumption that we would soon follow the regiment to Jacksonport. Up to now, however, no boat has come up the river for this purpose. The weather is still rainy.

Wednesday, May 4—Today I feel remarkably better in every respect than in the last few days. The weather is nice, and we are looking forward to the arrival of a boat. I mailed off a letter to Egge. My friend Elwood is all but fully recovered; his wound is healed, even though the ball still sticks somewhere to the bone. The rifle ball [that struck him] was not as large as the pointed balls that our revolvers shoot. He must have been wounded by a so-called squirrel rifle.[4] Actually, Elwood should be in the convalescents' ward, but he remains here to keep me company and to assist me. He is, however, mostly absent during the day. The days are very long for me; to have to lie all the time on the same spot is not easy.

Thursday, May 5—Beautiful weather, but being in bed it does me little good. The wounds are beginning to heal now. Began a letter to my parents.

Friday, May 6—As yesterday, wrote and read.

Saturday, May 7—Finished a letter to my parents; wrote to Mr. Olshausen. Today we had fresh fish from the river, which some officers caught yesterday. Furthermore, we had only cornbread, since the wheat flour, as well as all other supplies, are nearly used up. The arrival of a boat is anxiously anticipated.

Sunday, May 8—Beautiful weather; unfortunately, I can only enjoy it from my bed. My wounds are healing well; my appetite is returning, now that there is not much food available. Cornbread, desiccated potatoes, some ham, molasses, and very little coffee are about all that is still served. The days are already quite long; at four thirty in the morning it is daylight, and darkness does not fall before seven thirty in the evening.

Monday, May 9—Yesterday evening our regimental surgeon, Dr. McClelland, came up from Jacksonport. The assistant surgeon, who had stayed here with the hospital, is sick and asked for Dr. McClelland to come up here.[5] The doctor describes Jacksonport

4. Corp. Frederick M. Elwood had been wounded in the hip during a skirmish with guerrillas on April 2, while Company H was guarding the stranded steamboat on the White River. He rose to the rank of sergeant before being mustered out on July 1, 1866. Dudley, *Roster of Nebraska Volunteers,* 92–93; Company H Morning Report, April 1864, NSHS RG18, roll 3. Many of the irregular troops the Nebraska soldiers were fighting were probably armed with a motley collection of civilian weapons, including small-caliber hunting rifles.

5. George W. Wilkinson was the assistant surgeon. He was mustered out in July 1866. Dudley, *Roster of Nebraska Volunteers,* 4–5.

as a low-lying, unhealthy place, exposed to floods from the White and Black rivers.

Another unfortunate incident took place there the night before last. One of our pickets shot the corporal of the guard. The corporal happened to be outside the sentry line and came toward the sentry from the outside. After three warnings he did not stop; at that point the guard fired and killed him on the spot.[6] Our whole regiment is still there, except a detachment that has gone to DeVall's Bluff, since General Steele had drawn together any troops that could be spared to maintain his connections with the Mississippi.[7]

Incidentally troops are now on the way to relieve our regiment here, which will then go north to enjoy the furlough. The flies are already annoying here and bother me while I am writing this. Wrote to H. Thomson [in Grand Island]. Since the smoked ham, as well as meat in general, is all gone, roaming pigs were killed for us today, and therefore we have fresh meat.

Tuesday, May 10—Heavy rain fell last night, and today it is still cold and rainy. Because rotten flesh grew out of the healing wound, it was cauterized today. We are looking forward impatiently to the arrival of a steamboat. We are even in danger of running out of coffee. The food we still have on hand, however, is well prepared. We have a German from Company B as a cook, who also bakes our bread. Fortunately several barrels of flour were confiscated from one of the merchants. This way we at least get rid of the cornbread for a while.

Wednesday, May 11—Today a detachment of our troops came up from Jacksonport. Three steamboats with all kinds of supplies were there. One of them is supposed to come here tomorrow to bring provisions to this place. We, patients of the hospital, will be

6. Corp. James Hutton of Company E. Dudley, *Roster of Nebraska Volunteers*, 56–57. It is clear that Captain Ivory's admonition, following Scherneckau's accidental wounding by a fellow soldier under similar circumstances barely a month before, had gone unheeded.

7. Steele's Union army had just limped back to Little Rock after its disastrous foray south of the Arkansas River as the northern prong of the equally disastrous Red River campaign. See Sutherland, "1864." The Arkansas and White rivers, along with the Memphis and Little Rock Railroad, provided Steele's principal supply line to the Mississippi.

Corp. James Hutton, Company E, First Nebraska, was shot and killed accidentally on May 7, 1864, while on picket near Jacksonport, Arkansas, RG2057-40, Nebraska State Historical Society, Lincoln. Digitally enhanced and restored.

sent to Jacksonport by boat, where a hospital is already set up. How long we will have to remain there is difficult to say. General Steele's operations seem to take all disposable troops. We from the Nebraska regiment, therefore, should not count on seeing the North as soon as we previously had hoped.

Thursday, May 12—Constantly the nicest weather; no boat showed up. Since coffee and tea are now completely used up, a substitute is cooked from the roots of the sassafras tree, which grows wild here. I have a strong aversion to this beverage. The smell alone reminds me of a medicine that I must have taken once before.

Friday, May 13—Last night a man died in our room. He had been brought here just recently from another ward. For a long time he had suffered from an inherited scrofulous illness. He belonged to Company G of our regiment and had been recruited here.[8] Another man, a resident from the neighborhood whose foot had been amputated, left us yesterday, since his leg had healed. So only three are left here in this room. They are a person from the Eleventh Missouri Regiment, F. Elwood, and me. Elwood, however, has recovered and will leave the hospital as soon as we are in Jacksonport.

Great excitement today; the entire garrison in this town must evacuate this place grown dear to us in order to join up with the main force.[9] It is said the enemy has gathered around us in sizable numbers. I wish I were now able to serve again. Around noon two steamboats came up from Jacksonport, and loading of both vessels began immediately. Not only is the military leaving this place, but also all the merchants and all the families who have taken refuge here, whose men are serving mainly in the Fourth Arkansas Regiment, have to flee. The boats, therefore, were loaded with women and children and all kinds of goods. The larger of the two boats, *Pocahontas*, a side-wheel steamboat, took us on board this very evening. We had a good place on the deck immediately behind the main salon. However, the food was not adequate—nothing more than dry bread and water for the evening meal.

Saturday, May 14—Bread and water for breakfast. F. Elwood brought me something from the breakfast at the table in the cabin, which

8. Dudley, *Roster of Nebraska Volunteers*, does not list any member of this company who died at Batesville on May 12. As a recruit from the area, he may not yet have been formally mustered in, and no record survived to reach the Nebraska adjutant general's office.

9. Livingston's order to evacuate Batesville is in *OR*, ser. 1, vol. 34, part 3, pp. 562–63.

did me much good. We left around nine o'clock in the morning. Only a few miles below Batesville, rifle shots were fired on the boat and returned from the boat without result, just a great deal of screaming and excitement in the cabin among women and children. Even though our boat was quite heavily loaded and therefore running deep, not once did we run aground, which, considering the rather low water level, surprised me.

As we approached Jacksonport, the banks were lower, and swamps appeared, partly under water. We passed the mouth of the Black River, all lowland, and there was Jacksonport, right below where the mouth of the Black River joins the White River, mostly wooden buildings, only a few made out of brick. It is not much smaller than Batesville, but as much as I have seen of it, not nearly as beautifully situated. There, most of the residences were surrounded by gardens. The houses there, mostly painted white, were shaded by bushes and trees in all tints of green, from the dark cedar to the light green of the willows. I had made my observations while I was being driven in the ambulance from the hospital to the steamboat. Jacksonport, on the other hand, lies directly on the sandy riverbank and is prone to floods caused by both streams. During the dry season, such as now, it is quite a pleasant place, however.

The boat had hardly landed when comrades from my company came on board to greet me. These visits went on the whole evening. The kindness thus extended to me was very comforting. It was though we had been separated not for only three weeks but for a whole year! A little after four o'clock, I left the boat and was carried on a stretcher to a hospital not far from the landing. I was taken to the second story of the building, where by now there are eight men, most of them not yet able to leave their beds. The building, a large wooden building, was previously used as a store. It is quite cool and airy up here. One man from the Eleventh Missouri Regiment died just after we had been brought here.

My comrades soon brought me a really fine supper and buttermilk to drink because we had not eaten since morning. At eight o'clock in the evening, we received a cup of warm tea and with it dry bread. This cup of tea was the first warm food provided by the hospital since we had eaten lunch in Batesville the day before.

Sunday, May 15—The whole day I had plenty of visits by comrades from my company. Besides, I also received a dear, long letter from my parents yesterday evening. Today I wrote nearly all day and mailed off letters to my parents, Keen, C. Hedde, Thomson, Egge, and Mr. Olshausen. In the afternoon the man who died yesterday was buried, the regimental band playing a funeral march. In the evening, the troops arrived here from Batesville. They had marched overland and were also welcomed by our band.

Monday, May 16—Our food is still not very much! Since we arrived here we are receiving something new in beverages—ready-made coffee! That's coffee, sugar, and milk, all together in a can, ready to use, just to be poured into hot water. It is a fair drink, weak in coffee, of course, and tastes more like oil than milk.[10] The warm season of the year is already very much in evidence; it was a hot day. All the men who visit me here are sunburned, some of them brown like an Indian, while lying in the dark in bed, I am pale like the color of the bed sheet on which I am lying.

This morning we had cornbread for breakfast, since the bakery had not been ready to deliver the required wheat-flour bread. At lunch we had salted fish, mackerels I believe, desiccated potatoes, as well as a very good pea soup, the first decent food we have had since we have been here. They say we have a food supply for the entire garrison for three months, as well as large supplies of corn and oats.

The boys tell me that the duty here is very strenuous since the last battle that took place nearby.[11] Guard duty or fatigue every day. Much of the surrounding forest had to be cut down in order to secure better clearance for the gun emplacement. Minor fortifications are also constructed. The unloading of the steamboats is a lot of work too, and the usual cotton must be loaded on. It is amazing

10. Instant coffee was introduced during the Civil War. One version was prepared as a paste, including milk and sugar. Lord, *Collector's Encyclopedia*, 113.

11. The battle referred to occurred on April 20, when Confederate forces under Gen. Dandridge McRae were repulsed in an attack upon the Union camp at Jacksonport. The reports of Colonel Livingston and Lieutenant Colonel Baumer are in *OR*, ser. 1, vol. 34, part 1, pp. 893–97.

how many cotton bales now come to light, and the gentlemen owners become loyal. They render the oath of allegiance to the Union when Yankee steamboats arrive to take it to market, where the good people receive Uncle Sam's greenbacks for it. The *Pocahontas* left the day before yesterday; early this morning the other boat, the *Little Marte*, left the dock. The *Sunny South* came up this morning from DeVall's Bluff.

My leg swelled up again; flaxseed was placed on the almost fully healed bullet hole to open it up once more to provide an outlet for the pus. Dr. McClelland looked at the leg today and gave his opinion: the bone was damaged, and small splinters of the bone, which still had to come out, were causing the current inflammation. But the doctors who have been treating me until now disagree, and I also do not believe that the bone is injured.

The steamboat went back to DeVall's Bluff this very day. This evening the quartermaster sergeant of our company brought me some underwear, which I had asked him to draw for me, also several newspapers to read, old, of course, from March and April, but nevertheless still new for me. Quite warm again.

Tuesday, May 17—Because Dr. Wilkinson from our regiment is still ill, we have had, since we arrived here, a doctor from the Eleventh Missouri Regiment as hospital doctor. We had fresh meat for breakfast and lunch today, but it was very tough. Again, the day is very warm. Although there is enough fresh air here in our attic, we are nevertheless directly under the shingles of the roof, since no floor has been laid on the joists above us. When the sun burns straight down on the roof, it is very hot here in the afternoon. The framework of the building, if one can call it that, is constructed almost entirely of cypress wood; only the siding, weatherboards, is of pine. Even the floors are of cypress, which is very similar to pine, only there are very rarely knots in the wood of the cypresses, which grow everywhere here in the swamps.

A few more sick men were brought to our ward; one of them died during the night. My leg is really painful today; the flaxseed poultices were continued. My comrades still come to see me daily and chat for a while, so time here is not so boring, as sometimes in

Batesville. A man from Company D of our regiment drowned today in the White River.[12]

(Here again is a gap, I am missing the days from April [May] 17 [18] to 27 [25], which I spent in the hospital in Jacksonport, and when I was put on board a hospital boat on the twenty-fifth, which was to take us to DeVall's Bluff.)

[Thursday] April [May] 26—On board the steamboat. We discovered that besides our boat two other boats were leaving Jacksonport too.[13] Right below Jacksonport we had to stop, since two boats were lagging behind and completely out of sight. We waited there for at least an hour without seeing the boats, and at that point, our boat received the order to continue. We then steamed on again. Completely contrary to our expectations, we were not bothered. Either the guerrillas respected the hospital flag that we were flying, or there were none of these gentlemen in the area.[14] For breakfast and also in the evening we had crackers and some tea.

Friday, May 27—We went all through the night, and at daybreak we arrived here in DeVall's Bluff, where other boats were anchored. There seems to be a lot of activity. At noon we were taken from the boat and brought to one of the wooden shacks, of which this place is made up, built helter-skelter around the railroad station.[15] At the steamboat landing, also linked with the railroad, the government has constructed sheds, and large quantities of all kinds of supplies are stored.

12. Pvt. Jordan Orton, Company D. Dudley, *Roster of Nebraska Volunteers*, 50–51.

13. On May 22 the First Nebraska was ordered from Jacksonport to DeVall's Bluff. *OR*, ser. 1, vol. 34, part 3, pp. 718–19. The federals were abandoning Batesville and Jacksonport to Gen. Joseph Shelby's Confederates because of lack of horses, shortage of forage, and untenable supply lines. Sutherland, "1864," 126.

14. The hospital flag was a yellow banner with a green *H* in the center. Lord, *Collector's Encyclopedia*, 111. Earlier hospital flags were plain yellow, as described by surgeon John Vance Lauderdale on May 28, 1862, with respect to the flag on his hospital boat, the *D. A. January*. Josyph, *Wounded River*, 75. A red cross was not adopted to designate hospitals and other medical facilities until after the Civil War.

15. The Memphis and Little Rock Railroad.

Eighteen patients, most likely the weaker ones and those who cannot help themselves, are quartered in the lower part of the house, and I am among these. The upper story can be reached only from the outside with a ladder. Our hospital accommodations are really getting worse each time. The convalescents are put up in this attic, about twenty, thus making some forty sick and wounded men in all. In our room the flies are most hideous, more persistent than I have ever encountered before.

In the evening a train brought the Eighteenth Illinois Infantry Regiment on its way north to be discharged, since their enlistment has expired. In this important location, as well as along the railroad, there are, of course, quite a few troops stationed; one or two gunboats are also lying here. None of the six boats that left with us has arrived here yet.

Saturday, May 28—Today the small steamboat *Lloyd* from the fleet left behind came down. Several of the boats had run aground. One of the gunboats lying here and the *White Cloud* went up to their aid. Although I still don't have my crutches, I was up today, however, and hopped around without them, whereby I caught quite a cold. There was beer in half barrels. We knew how to roll one into our room, and, of course, we soon had lager by the bucketful. At least six to eight thousand troops are located here. The cavalry has some nice horses, which have not yet experienced starvation like our poor animals. The 8th Missouri Cavalry, 12th Illinois Cavalry, and 9th Iowa Cavalry are here, as well as the 126th Illinois Infantry, 7th Missouri Artillery Regiment, and Negro troops.

Sunday, May 29—Nine of the very sick men from this hospital were sent to Little Rock today. The Eleventh Missouri Cavalry Regiment arrived here today, coming down on this side of the White River. Our regiment crossed the river, arriving here at almost at the same time as the Missouri regiment. Also the rest of the fleet, which had departed with us, got here safely today.

I even had various visits from friends in my company—Elwood, as always, the first. Colonel Livingston, riding by with his staff, came in for a moment. However, he did not appear to be very happy with the place in which he found us. Livingston, especially, devotes very commendable attention to the hospital.[16] Therefore, as we were landing in Jacksonport, the colonel was almost the first one to come on board to see his sick and wounded men. An old member of our regiment, "Dobblin" of Company G, became ill on the march here, where they had to swim through various bayous.[17]

Monday, May 30—Elwood visited me again. Two men, members of our company, were brought in today, the one wounded, shot through the side shortly before we left Jacksonport, the other sick.[18] The weather here is warmer and, at the same time, dry. There are neither wells nor springs here; we have to rely entirely on river water. The area is low by the river, little knolls now and then, all eagerly sought after for building sites. Boats depart and arrive here almost daily; one from St. Louis is here on the banks of the White River; besides, two or three trains come and go daily.

Tuesday, May 31—Convalescents and some of the medical orderlies were released today, since this hospital is to be closed as such, and the patients will have to go back to their regiments. Nevertheless, more patients arrived here, even though it is no longer regarded as a hospital but only as a temporary refuge until the men can be discharged to their various regiments, sent to Little Rock, or released on leave. For the first time this afternoon, I went out of the house on crutches and quite far, almost too far to make it back safely. I was very tired. The Third Cavalry Regiment of the regular army is also here.

Wednesday, June 1—Doctors, regimental chaplains, and members of the U.S. Christian Commission visited us today. They found the arrangements here not exactly satisfactory, but as I said, this is no longer regarded as a hospital but only as a temporary refuge. We had some rain today, yet it was still very sultry.

16. Livingston had been a medical doctor in civilian life.

17. No person with a name resembling "Dobblin" is found on the roster of Company G in Dudley, *Roster of Nebraska Volunteers*. Perhaps Scherneckau was using a nickname.

18. The wounded man was probably Pvt. Ira Howe, wounded in action May 24. He was discharged for disability from the hospital at Fort Leavenworth on May 26, 1865. Dudley, *Roster of Nebraska Volunteers*, 98–99.

Thursday, June 2—It rained quite heavily today. I received a letter from friend Keen and answered him; mailed a letter to Hedde. In the evening Colonel Livingston came back from Little Rock. Just now large wagon trains are being outfitted here. One section of the troops has marching orders; it appears as if General Steele will take the field again.

Friday, June 3—After intermittent rain showers yesterday and the day before, it is raining constantly today. One of our patients died last night; he belonged to the Eleventh Missouri Regiment. Even though large warehouses and sheds are here to store the government goods, a great deal still lies outside, which can no longer be put into the buildings. Extensive piles of hardtack boxes, barrels, corn, and oats, etc., are lying along the railroad and on the riverbank. More sheds are being constructed.

The troops located here have ample work to do. The unloading of the boats and loading of the railroad cars is a constant job. Negro and white troops together have to do this work. It is gratifying that those men, recently so hostile toward the Negroes, must now admit that the blacks make good soldiers, learning the necessary drills, standing under fire as well as white regiments, and even more important, being able to tolerate the climate better than they.

Saturday, June 4—Today quite a number of our patients went to Little Rock. With them also went John Brandon, who has been my neighbor in the ward ever since I have been in the hospital. He has become a complete cripple, caused by one shot. Due to carelessness by his officers and the doctors, it was neglected to draw up his discharge. Hopefully it will not take too long until he receives his papers in good order.[19]

Although the red clay soil had become a vast amount of mud due to the wet weather of the last few days, it dried up rather quickly today in the heat.

19. No soldier by this name is recorded in the records of the First Nebraska. The man was probably from one of the other regiments.

Sunday, June 5—Again one from the Eleventh Missouri Cavalry died last night. This new regiment, it seems, is losing many men due to sickness and incompetent and careless doctors. Quite warm. The *Westmoreland,* a large boat, came upstream today. I counted ten steamboats at the landing, besides the two gunboats.

Monday, June 6—It was very warm. A strong detachment from our regiment unloaded the *Westmoreland.* It is said we are to go on it to St. Louis.[20] It has five thousand sacks of corn and oats on board and one hundred wagons, besides harnesses to hitch up teams. The hospital is packing up; all beds, bedding, etc., must be turned in. I limp about as best I can, but I don't get far, and I am sick of this place.

Tuesday, June 7—It looks like rain and is somewhat cooler. My leg also forecasts a storm. Two gentlemen and a lady, members or only agents of the U.S. Christian Commission and the Sanitary Commission, visited us today, distributed tracts, good words, and made some promises, which so far have not yet been fulfilled. The hospital does not look very inviting; all linens have been taken off the beds, also the pillows; only the bedsteads with mattresses have been left. The gentlemen visitors were very surprised to find us so uncomfortable; however, the circumstances were explained to them. There are now only seven or eight patients here. They all belong to our regiment, waiting for the departure of the boat to St. Louis. I limped on my crutches to the landing today, where my comrades are unloading the boat, only a few hundred steps, yet it was like a journey for me. Sent a letter to Egge.

Wednesday, June 8—After we had several good rain showers yesterday, more rain fell during the night and today. This cools the air

20. On June 1 orders were issued furloughing the reenlisted veterans of the First Nebraska, to depart on the first boat arriving at DeVall's Bluff. The men who had not reenlisted would remain behind. Orders, NSHS RG18, roll 3. The adventures of the nonveterans and recruits who remained in Arkansas are discussed in Potter, "First Nebraska's Orphan Detachment."

considerably. At night, however, it was so stifling hot again that, although we were in a very drafty, wooden shack where doors and windows are open, we could not fall asleep due to the heat. It got better only toward morning. The boat was unloaded, and those men from our regiment returning to Nebraska as veterans went on board. We hospital rats stayed for the night in our old quarters. There are eight of us here, six of them sick—all showing symptoms of dysentery—and two wounded.

Thursday, June 9—The night was cool and pleasant; today nice weather but bottomless mud. This mud makes it impossible for me to dare to go beyond the door on crutches. Toward evening we patients were taken on board the *Westmoreland*, that is, with the help of several comrades I "crutched" myself there. Staterooms were available for the weakest of the sick. I, however, was lying like the rest on the floor of the cabin. The boat has no freight except for the horses, which are the private property of the officers. The veterans turned in their horses and kept only saber and revolver. Furthermore, families of white and black refugees were housed on the lower deck.

General Steele arrived with the evening train from Little Rock and was received with military honors. The rest of the Third Michigan Regiment was with him on the same train. Our regiment's band played, a section of the local garrison paraded, and the artillery fired a salute! The steamboat is completely taken over by us, even the "Holy of Holies," the ladies' cabin, is not spared. Wild rackets were heard through the entire length of the hull, as if we were lying in bivouac on shore. General Steele came on board for only a moment. Our colonel himself was lighting his way. Nevertheless, they had trouble finding their way through the groups sitting and lying everywhere without stepping on men, since none of the men took the trouble to get out of the way for these illustrious persons. The unfamiliar noise and the hard bed kept me awake for a long time.

Friday, June 10—At daybreak, reveille woke me up once again, and right after that our steamboat departed too. The *Mayflower* met us just below DeVall's Bluff, loaded with government supplies. A gunboat went downstream ahead of us. We found another one a few miles farther, stationed in the middle of the river, the shiny brass cannons looking quite friendly from the gun ports. The river makes many unusual and short turns, but it is small. Our band played for the changing of the guard and also every time we passed a boat. We passed several villages that, like almost all in this state, are deserted and in ruins, often quite nice locations with large buildings. Turtle eggs were visible now and then on the barren sandbanks, also at other places where they had already been buried in a hurry by the creatures. The turtles are plentiful here and rather large.

We met two other government transport boats, escorted by the gunboat no. 30.[21] Shortly afterwards we overtook the gunboat, which had so far gone before us, and soon left it behind. These gunboats all are stern-wheelers, covered only with planks and thin iron plates. It seems that the crew was made up, for the most part, of blacks.

As we came farther downstream, the shore became flat and partly swampy. Numerous arms, bayous, branch off. The current is hardly noticeable; the water looks yellowish-green, while around Batesville it is a clear, rapidly flowing river. At sunset we reached the Father of Rivers, the truly majestic Mississippi. How much larger and mightier is this river here at its lower course, compared to the other rivers, which bring quite substantial amounts of water into the main stream. The Mississippi in this area looks more like a lake than the large river I had admired in St. Louis.

There is a marine station just below the mouth of the White River in the Mississippi; two gunboats were there. A few huts and warehouses on the shore of the swampy island made up the settlement. The inhabitants, all Negroes, were cutting wood for the steamboats. We also stopped here to take on wood. Napoleon is twenty miles below, lying in the Mississippi at the mouth of the Arkansas River. At high water the steamboats can go directly from the White River to the mouth of the Arkansas River over land, so to

21. Gunboat 30 was probably the USS *Fawn*. A photograph of *Fawn* in the Naval Historical Foundation collection, taken at DeVall's Bluff on December 31, 1863, shows the numeral 30 on the stern-wheel vessel's pilothouse.

USS *Fawn* (Gunboat 30), which operated on the White River near DeVall's Bluff, Arkansas, in 1863–64. NH54093, Naval Historical Center, Washington, D.C.

speak, which has been flooded to a certain depth by the overflowing rivers, and then into the Mississippi. The gunboat escorting us soon came from the mouth of the White River behind us and moored at the station.

As darkness set in we were moving again, now upstream. It rained hard. After we, that is Potts, Elwood, and I, had taken our places in the rear cabin and lay down to sleep, our regimental band gathered around us.[22] Since they played their blaring tunes for quite a while, they made our heads "swim," if one may use the expression.

Saturday, June 11—When we woke up the boat was at Island No. 66, another government wood station with a small garrison of blacks. During the night, we had advanced only a little. At one o'clock, daytime, we came to the town of Helena. Here, close to the river, the government had extensive farms, with nice fields of corn and cotton. Somewhat above the town two gunboats were at anchor; a third one sat on a sandbank, high and dry. Near the town firewood was taken on board again. Memphis, upstream, is eighty-five miles from here, and it is the same distance to the mouth of the White River. Several steamboats passed us here, and we did not move again until close to sunset. It rained quite severely, like yesterday.

Sunday, June 12—While having the changing of the guard with cheerful music it rained again, as it had earlier yesterday evening. The weather then improved and was nice when we reached Memphis slightly before noon. A dozen boats were lying at the landing where there was, however, little activity since it is Sunday.

One of the fully ironclad gunboats was lying here, as well as a couple of howitzer boats.[23] A large raft of sawed lumber was pushed downstream by a steamboat and passed us here. Despite the strict ban and the alert guard many men still succeeded mak-

22. Corp. Jonathan J. Potts of Gage County, Nebraska, had enlisted in 1861. Dudley, *Roster of Nebraska Volunteers*, 92–93.

23. Some of the smaller gunboats may have been armed exclusively with howitzers, which are cannon with large bores and sub-caliber powder chambers, designed to throw shot or shell at relatively short ranges.

ing it to the city. Just above the city we again took on wood, which delayed us there until midnight.

Today a battle had taken place with rebels not very far from the city. Reinforcements had been sent out from Memphis, since in the beginning, as it seems, our troops had gotten the worst of it.[24] After sundown our men, I mean the soldiers, persuaded by whiskey and by the influence and good example of the officers, helped bring in wood. Colonel Livingston himself worked hard.

Monday, June 13—Our steamboat is moving only very slowly ahead. The steamboat *Perry,* which we left behind at DeVall's Bluff, arrived in Memphis just after us but has already left the city long before us.[25] A dispatch boat of the fleet overtook us in the morning and was also soon out of sight; it was going so much faster! We passed Fort Pillow a little after noon. A small gunboat was lying there. We met several steamboats, heavily loaded. The weather is nice.

Tuesday, June 14—At reveille we passed New Madrid. A gunboat was lying at anchor across from the town. Ten miles farther up we came to Island No. 10, now completely abandoned, the fortifications without cannons, the barracks in ruins, not even one gunboat now stationed at such an important passageway. At about eleven o'clock we passed Hickman, where a small garrison is stationed. A gunboat was lying there in the middle of the river.

In the afternoon we reached Columbus, an important military post. Four of the one-hundred-day regiments were there, as well as Negro artillery.[26] Belmont, known for the battle that took place

24. Scherneckau had heard about the Battle of Brice's Crossroads, or Gun Town, Mississippi, on June 10. An expedition under Brig. Gen. Samuel Sturgis had been ordered from Memphis to northern Mississippi to destroy railroads and disperse or defeat Gen. Nathan Bedford Forrest's Confederates, but Forrest routed the Union forces. Following the defeat, Sturgis's column retreated to Memphis. The correspondence and reports are in *OR,* ser. 1, vol. 39, part 1.

25. This boat was probably the *Peri. Way's Packet Directory,* 367.

26. In the spring of 1864 the governors of Ohio, Indiana, Illinois, Iowa, and Wisconsin tendered a force of eighty-five thousand men to the federal government to be enlisted as U.S. volunteers for one hundred days' service. These troops would relieve veteran soldiers who had been guarding forts, arsenals, and

here, lies a little downstream, in Missouri, on the bank of the river.[27] Our food here on board is not very satisfactory. They say the arrangements for cooking are very poor. Coffee and crackers, mostly with raw bacon, are all that we can be lucky enough to have at present. Also the coffee is still very weak since we cannot boil it, and the water from the steam boiler does not extract it.

About three o'clock in the afternoon, we went from the muddy and yellow Mississippi into the mouth of the Ohio River and laid to at Cairo, where about a dozen steamboats and a gunboat were lying. Here we had an opportunity to draw clothing, since Colonel L. wanted to deliver his men back home in decent outfits, as is only proper.[28] We took on coal, which kept us here until ten o'clock in the evening. The town has really grown since I was here last, and new buildings are constantly being built. During the night we did not move for several hours in order to take on wood.

Wednesday, June 15—A sergeant of Company A from our regiment, who had been quite sick since we left DeVall's Bluff, died yesterday just before we reached Cairo. This morning we met various steamboats, among others a hospital boat, painted red.[29] The others were loaded with supplies, also with horses, mules, and slaughter cattle for the army. We caught up with the *Clara Bell*, which showed various bullet holes through her cabins, pilothouse, and stack.

---

other installations and release the experienced men for combat duty. It was hoped this plan would help the Union armies win the war more quickly. President Lincoln accepted the governors' proposal on April 24, 1864. The hundred days' men are discussed in *Report of the Adjutant General*, 35–39; and Reid, *Ohio in the War*, 208–220.

27. On November 7, 1861, Brig. Gen. Ulysses S. Grant led Union troops in an attack on a Confederate outpost at Belmont, Missouri, across the Mississippi River from Columbus, Kentucky, but the Union forces were forced to withdraw. *American Heritage Civil War Chronology*.

28. As the Nebraska veterans boarded the *Westmoreland* at DeVall's Bluff on June 9, Colonel Livingston issued an order that read, in part: "The regiment is going home where anxious hearts and eyes await them, and the col. comdg. looks to his officers that the men may be presented in such a manner as will gratify the highest hopes of those who love them." NSHS RG18, box 3.

29. This was likely *Red Rover*, the navy's first commissioned hospital ship. Kenney, "From the Log of the *Red Rover*" 47.

Below the Red River a battery of rebels had fired off several volleys at the boat, but she was not damaged enough to be captured.[30]

The area is improving, both on the Missouri as well as on the Illinois side; farms under cultivation and occupied houses are becoming more numerous. At ten o'clock in the morning, we laid to at Cape Girardeau, with lively music like at all the other places, which soon brought the whole population to the shore, where wild handshaking took place between citizens and soldiers. Then first Sergeant Kidder was buried.[31] All men present from the regiment followed in full dress in reverse order, the officer corps closing the procession with the colonel the last in file. After this was over, the citizens handed out beer and whiskey to the soldiers. At around twelve o'clock, when we wanted to go on, there were several very drunk men and quite a few very tipsy ones who required a long time to come on board. Several fell into the water, since they tried to come on board after we already had shoved off. Brawls could not be avoided due to the confined space on board. Still 150 miles from here to St. Louis.

Thursday, June 16—We passed St. Genevieve before sunrise, and we laid close by on the Illinois side to take on wood for the last time on this journey. The weather became unpleasant, and rain fell. Colonel L. had ordered assembly sounded, and inspected the men on the hurricane deck. Then with a few brief words he urged the men to behave well upon our arrival in St. Louis (very necessary warning). Soon we reached Carondelet. The three gunboats under construction there last fall had been launched and, two of them were still lying there in the water but, as it seems, almost finished.

Around twelve o'clock we arrived at the landing in St. Louis with full music, crowding into the rows of steamboats. The levee, as before, is still filled with boats along its entire length, among them

30. *Clara Bell* had been the headquarters boat during the Red River campaign and, as Scherneckau notes, received some damage from Confederate gunfire. Worse was to come, however, when the boat was destroyed by Confederate artillery on July 24, 1864, while operating on the White River in Arkansas. *OR*, ser. 1, vol. 41, part 1, pp. 87–88.

31. Daniel E. Kidder of Plattsmouth, Nebraska Territory. Dudley, *Roster of Nebraska Volunteers*, 8–9.

many new and large ones. Colonel Livingston went ashore immediately. As soon as he returned, the men had to fall in with their weapons. Along with the garrison's and our own band, we then paraded through the streets to Washington Hall, on Poplar Street between Third and Fourth streets, where they had set up a banquet. A red-silk printed ribbon, tied to the chest, indicated the veterans.[32]

In the meantime, however, I went on my own through the streets with another comrade, took a bath, etc., ate in the evening, and returned on board. The veterans were scattered all over town, since the red ribbons saved them from arrest. Although the men have little money, there still were a lot of drunks. After the tiring tour on crutches, I slept well in the cabin.

Friday, June 17—Today we spent the day in eager expectation, but we were deceived. Nothing was done to pay us off as we had hoped. Lots of activity went on at the landing; all kinds of goods were loaded and unloaded. We are at the landing of the Missouri River steamboats. Alongside us is the *Kate Kinney* for St. Joe and Omaha. She is unloading bacon, smoked sides, hams, and shoulders, and is taking on flour, as well as a lot of furniture for Omaha, besides ironware, stoves, etc., also a large quantity of pine boards. My friend Keen was here yesterday, also again today. Last fall he had been left behind here, sick in the hospital, but he is now well.[33]

Saturday, June 18—A humid hot day. We signed the payrolls, were then ordered to go to Schofield Barracks No. 2. These are not the

32. This ribbon or badge was provided by the reception committee and was not an official army insignia. Each veteran in several Iowa veteran regiments arriving in St. Louis in March 1864 received a badge and ribbon with the regiment's name and the words "veterans" and "St. Louis, Missouri" printed beneath the U.S. coat of arms. According to an undated *Missouri Democrat* (St. Louis) article, reprinted in the *Nebraska City Daily Press*, March 25, 1864, "the Reception Committee has tendered the same courtesy to all veterans arriving in St. Louis." An account of the reception for the First Nebraska veterans appeared in the *Missouri Democrat*, June 17, 1864, reprinted in the *Nebraska Republican* (Omaha), June 24, 1864. The account said there were 320 veterans. About 270 nonveterans remained behind in Arkansas, according to the *Nebraska Republican*, July 15, 1864.

33. Keen would be discharged on July 7, 1864, at the expiration of his enlistment. Compiled Service Records, roll 12.

transportation barracks, where I had been several times before but just one street beyond, located on Chouteau Avenue. They are larger, but built in the same style as no. 1 barracks. A man from Company C died just before we left the boat; dysentery was the cause of death.[34] The barracks are in a filthy state; the bugs threaten to eat us up; bedbugs, fleas, and lice are here in abundance. No sign of a paymaster. In the evening I took a walk, that is to say I used the streetcar for most of the way. At night I again slept well since the unusual activity of the day had tired me.

Sunday, June 19—Time passes slowly for us here; the air in the barracks is stifling hot, almost like at the hospital in DeVall's Bluff. Of course it is not possible for me to go very far. Stayed in the barracks all day, although no guards hinder us to exit or enter. The entire guard here consists of one sentry guarding the commissary supplies that we have on hand. Jews and dealers of all kinds pester us here, praising their goods to get us as customers when we have been paid off. Some of our boys have already changed and appear in civilian dress a la mode or also in the assigned uniform, but made of better cloth usually worn by the officers. The officers are setting a bad example in putting on the nonmilitary apparel. However, I will be happy with the uniform issued by Uncle Sam. The prices here are very high, especially for clothing.

Monday, June 20—The weather turned somewhat cooler, yet it did not lead to rain. In the afternoon, at two o'clock, our anticipation was finally fulfilled. The paymasters with their tin boxes full of greenbacks paid off the men at various locations at the same time. Jews, runners for all kinds of businesses, female peddlers, etc., swarmed immediately into the yard of the barracks, as if they had smelled that money had arrived.

Most of our men did not ponder very long but rushed to town in great haste to make their purchases at the stores previously selected. It was clothing above all, either military or civilian. Newly fashioned civilians were scattered all over town in a few hours, and

34. Pvt. Samuel Stanley, who enlisted from Mt. Vernon, Nebraska Territory. Dudley, *Roster of Nebraska Volunteers*, 40–41.

it often happened that I did not immediately recognize the men, my old comrades, in their new suits. Many look quite uncomfortable in the newly purchased garb, as if it did not belong to them. But others, who had lived in the city before they became soldiers, felt more at home with it.

With Keen, Elwood, and Potts, I boarded the streetcar and accompanied them to the store of Kahn and Schloss on Fourth Street, a couple of German Jews, and like almost all Jews, clothing merchants. Our regiment, especially, seems to patronize these people, and in a short time they sold at least five hundred dollars worth of goods. The suits were from twenty to fifty dollars and more. One also could buy hats, shoes, and suspenders. A bath and the barber came next, and often a spree closed this day. I bought a wool shirt, then limped to the office of the *Westliche Post*, again paid for a year, until June 20, 1865. Mr. Olshausen was not at home. From Fourth Street I then took the streetcar and rode back to our quarters.

Tuesday, June 21—A warm day. The furlough papers were issued for those men who wished to leave here. The members of our regimental band, as well as all commissioned officers, received the order to go to Omaha, along with the rest of the men not given leave here. In the afternoon I was about town with Keen and bought a traveling bag, etc. The weapons were also turned in today, yet there was chaos beyond description. Orderly calls sounded, yet there was no sergeant who bothered about this, since most of them already were on leave.

By this time many were leaving the city with trains from the Illinois side. The rest, perhaps eighty men, received orders to be at the North Missouri Railroad station at one o'clock at night. Five or six government wagons took our baggage there. This new station is now much farther beyond the old place on the St. Louis levee. Since we did not know this, we had left the streetcar too soon and had to go about three-quarters of a mile on foot until we finally reached the station. The branch line along the landing between the North Missouri Railroad and the Iron Mountain Railroad, laid down by General Fremont in those days, has been removed, and therefore the station of the former has been relocated all the way to New Bremen, in the north of the city.

Ed. Keen bid farewell; it was almost nine o'clock in the evening. My things, under the care of our Negro, Harrison, luckily had all arrived.[35] I ate a hasty supper and then lay down to sleep on one of the platforms with other comrades.

Wednesday, June 22—After a good night's sleep, I woke up again about five o'clock; it was time to board the train. We left St. Louis just as the sun came up over the Illinois hills on the other side of the river. It was a bright day but hot and dusty, since it had not rained for so long. The corn is unusually slow in its growth due to the continuing drought; in many places it still was not even a hand high. Soon we arrived at St. Charles on the Missouri River.

While the ferryboat *Omaha* carried across two passenger cars and the locomotive, we passengers were taken across by the steamboat *St. Charles*, and soon we were on the lovely prairie of northern Missouri. How good it is to see the green expanses on the horizon once again, always pastures bordered with woods, which are now visible to the traveler's eye. Northern Missouri is a beautiful area; delightful prairie farms in near view, meanwhile, the charming houses are often located in the shade of groves.

At two o'clock in the afternoon, we took our seats in the cars of the Hannibal and St. Joe line in Macon City; from there we still had more than two hundred miles to St. Joe. Although we stopped twice for meals, I still had only crackers and cheese today.

Thursday, June 23—At one thirty this morning, we finally came to a stop in St. Joe; missed the omnibus, and I had to go the entire way to the Saunders House on foot, at least three-fourths of a mile. Quite a number of our men had taken quarters here, officers and

35. Harrison Johnson, who enlisted at Batesville on February 15 or 25, 1864, and was carried on the rolls of Company H as "undercook." Dudley, *Roster of Nebraska Volunteers*, 102–3; Compiled Service Records, roll 12. Johnson stayed with the regiment until it was mustered out in July 1866 and remained in Nebraska. He worked as a janitor at the state capitol building and other government buildings in Lincoln until his death on May 22, 1900. Johnson is buried in the veterans' circle at Lincoln's Wyuka Cemetery. *Nebraska State Journal* (Lincoln), May 23, 1900.

privates. Four comrades from my company had one room with two beds and we all slept quite well, I believe, despite the _____ soft bed. This hotel is an impressive building, the lower floor built of cut sandstone, the rest of bricks.[36]

We woke up a little after six o'clock, despite having gone to bed quite late and exhausted. After we had completed our morning toilet, we went to the basement to eat our breakfast. It was good enough for a soldier returning from the field, even if it proceeded rather rigidly and formally. Most of the officers of our regiment are lodged here, as well as many of our men, so I am not short of company or conversation. All morning I was lying around in the barroom in true loafer style and outside the house, since I did not feel inclined to limp about town. Of course, I, as a soldier, could not avoid being treated several times by loyal guests. After the noon meal I took my siesta in my room until I was called for tea. Wrote and read in the meantime.

Friday, June 24—Warm and windy. I wrote to my parents in the morning, which [the letter] I sent off at once. Like yesterday, was lying around in the hotel, and yet took small outings into town. Boats come and go, up and downstream, but we must wait for Colonel Livingston before we can leave for Omaha.

We have discovered that we have selected one of the best houses, that is, hotels, in town, not the cheapest, but for the money the most respectable and of best value. The food is quite good, amply stocked with all kinds of tasty dishes; also delicacies of the season are not omitted. Had ice cream for dessert today.

Saturday, June 25—After I had made miscellaneous purchases in the morning, I wanted to pay my bill to the innkeeper after lunch, when to my amazement I discovered that Mr. Saunders refused entirely to accept any payment from me. Not so much the money but the apparent attitude of the people pleased me most. This very afternoon we went on board the steamboat *Colorado*, and the

36. The Saunders House, at the corner of Third and Faraon streets, was operated by Richard and John Saunders, Jr. *History of Buchanan County*, 296.

colonel and the rest of the officers arrived with the evening train. We left St. Joe a little after midnight.

Sunday, June 26—The Missouri is quite high but has not gone over its banks. The boat is making good time against the increased current. A number of goods and machines are on board, threshing machines for the Mormons, bound for Salt Lake City. Eleven hundred Mormons are staying with their wagons and cattle in Wyoming, just beyond Nebraska City on the Missouri.[37] In the evening we reached Brownville, where we laid to for a moment. A large crowd had gathered on the shore and greeted us with shouts of "hurrah." Arago, almost completely settled by Germans, we passed in the afternoon, like all these places, with cheers and full music.[38]

Monday, June 27—Reached Nebraska City in the morning, where a large amount of freight was unloaded. Nobody bothered about us! Toward evening we came to Plattsmouth, where Colonel Livingston lives, as well as most of Company A. Here we were greeted warmly and unloaded some freight. At sunset we passed the mouth of our old Platte River. At night we reached the Council Bluffs landing, and with daybreak we came to Omaha, where we laid to just across from the Herndon House.[39] It rained hard during the night, yet it cleared up at daybreak.

Tuesday, June 28—As soon as wagons came down, I rode with the baggage to the Douglas House. With cannon salutes, band music, under our old and new flags, the few men, maybe fifty, marched around in the city and to the capitol, where a splendid banquet was given. In the evening there was a ball. However, I was there neither for the meal nor in the evening. I went to the Douglas House and to bed at a proper time.

37. The small town of Wyoming had become the major outfitting point for Mormons migrating from the Missouri River to the Salt Lake Valley of Utah.

38. Arago, a small village in today's Richardson County, Nebraska, is no longer extant.

39. Omaha's premier hotel.

Wednesday, June 29—Made the acquaintance of Mr. Burmester; visited Steuben, Greve, and others. In the evening I drove with Burmester two miles out of Omaha, where we camped.[40]

Thursday, June 30—It had rained severely during the night; the road in the hills had become quite slippery. We overtook a company of the Second Nebraska Cavalry Regiment, on foot with its German Captain Kuhl, which was on the way to Genoa.[41] We camped again on this side of the Elkhorn Bridge.

Friday, July 1—The road to Fremont was very bad. We overtook Mr. Martin with both his wagons at Rawhide Creek, where he was delayed since the road was too bad for him. Stopped for the night several miles east of the North Bend.

Saturday, July 2—The road was somewhat better, and we made it to eight miles east of Columbus. However, we got bogged down at an especially bad place and had to unload.

Sunday, July 3—Right after the "escort" passing through on the way to California, we went over the Loup Fork, which was still very high and not easy to cross. In the evening we camped together with the escort at Prairie Creek.[42]

40. Perhaps Emil Burmester, an Omahan who served in Company B, and P. Steuben, whom Scherneckau had mentioned earlier.

41. This was Capt. Henry Kuhl and Company C of the First Battalion, Nebraska Veteran Volunteers (cavalry). Many of these men had formerly served in the Second Nebraska Volunteer Cavalry, which had been mustered out in the fall of 1863. The First Battalion, Nebraska Veteran Volunteers, was mustered in in the spring of 1864. Dudley, *Roster of Nebraska Volunteers*, 136–37, 144–45.

42. The Emigrant Escort service from the Missouri River to the West Coast was authorized by the secretary of war in 1861 and continued for several years. Capt. Medorem Crawford, who had first gone overland in 1842, led the escort west from Omaha. *OR*, ser. 1, vol. 50, part 2, p. 51. Crawford's journals of the Emigrant Escort survive and are listed in Mattes, *Platte River Road Narratives*, entries 1811, 1838, 1888, and 1939. The latter is Crawford's journal for 1864.

Monday, July 4—The road got somewhat better, and we came as far as the Warm Slough, where we camped alone; heavy rain in the evening.

Tuesday, July 5—Again it was difficult to drive. The mules were tired when we reached Viereggs. There we acquired an extra team and drove up to Stolley's. We received a friendly welcome; stayed there overnight.[43]

43. Henry and James Vieregg were early settlers in the vicinity. Once Scherneckau arrived in Grand Island, he continued his diary for less than a month. The entries from July 6 to July 31 have not been reproduced.

Epilogue

ONCE HE ARRIVED IN GRAND ISLAND IN JULY 1864, August Scherneckau continued keeping his diary for less than a month, recording only brief entries relating to farm work, visits to friends, and his impressions of the settlement. While he was at home recuperating from his wound, dramatic events were transpiring in Nebraska's Platte Valley. In August 1864 Lakotas and Cheyennes raided stagecoach stations and road ranches along the Platte from Julesburg to Fort Kearny and eastward to the Little Blue River, leaving many as smoking ruins and killing ranchmen, settlers, and overland travelers. The furloughed veterans of the First Nebraska were quickly recalled to Omaha and sent out to garrison larger posts, such as Fort Kearny and Post Cottonwood, as well as tiny, one-company enclaves adjacent to stagecoach and telegraph stations. With the Civil War still raging in the East, it fell to volunteer regiments, thinly dispersed west of the Missouri River, to counter the Indian threat to overland travel and communications.[1]

It was February 1865 before Scherneckau was well enough to rejoin his company. On February 23, 1865, he left Grand Island and resumed writing in his dairy. Five days later he was reunited with his Company H comrades at Midway Station, adjacent to William Peniston and Andrew J. Miller's ranch, some sixty-five miles west of Fort Kearny. "The buildings here are all built of cedar logs or are adobe houses," he wrote on March 1. "The large stable

1. A classic account of the role of one of the volunteer regiments involved is by Eugene F. Ware of Company F, Seventh Iowa Volunteer Cavalry in *The Indian War of 1864*.

has room for sixty horses; furthermore, there are several smaller facilities, blacksmith shops, etc. A large, two-story cedar log house is not yet finished. The stage company has a station here to change their teams."[2]

Escorting stagecoaches between the stations, usually located about ten miles apart, was one of the soldiers' main jobs. They accompanied the stages "ten miles out and ten miles back." Between times, the men were detailed to cut firewood, build or repair quarters, hunt, or travel to Fort Kearny or Post Cottonwood for supplies. It was demanding yet often monotonous duty, punctuated occasionally by a frantic and usually fruitless chase after Indians who had swooped down to steal a few horses or threaten a passing wagon train. The soldiers were mounted on barely serviceable horses and, as Scherneckau noted, "This duty is quite strenuous, especially for the horses, since the stage drives fast indeed, and we, of course, must remain with the coaches on the way up, as well as back."[3]

During this period, Scherneckau found less to inspire his powers of description, and his diary entries are often brief, matter-of-fact notes about the weather, his boredom, or military routine. He was already familiar with the Platte Valley landscape from his years in the Grand Island settlement, and the pace of his life had slowed from the exciting days of guerrilla hunting in Arkansas. From time to time, however, something noteworthy happened and he would record it in more detail.

After some sixteen months as a mounted regiment, beginning at St. Louis in the fall of 1863, the First Nebraska finally began receiving cavalry arms to replace their infantry rifles. On March 14 Scherneckau noted that his company still had the short Enfield rifles, "one of the best firearms in the army, but not on horseback. A part of our regiment has now received the Joslyn carbine, a rear loader with copper shells (without the copper cap). These are, of

2. The station belonged to Ben Holladay's Overland Stage Company, which carried the U.S. mail. Root and Connelley, *Overland Stage to California*, 47–48.

3. Scherneckau diary, Saturday, May 13, 1865. McDermott, *Circle of Fire*, 158–59, calls the lack of good horses the army's "Achilles Heel" during the Plains campaigns.

course, more appropriate for mounted men than the antiquated system of the front loaders with copper cap."[4] On June 30 his company finally received the carbines: "We turned in our rifles, and for the first time we are actually equipped as cavalrymen."

Exposure to the harsh Great Plains climate brought many miseries. The nearly constant traffic along the Platte by stagecoaches, freight wagons, emigrants, and soldiers churned the soil into powder. When the wind blew, conditions were barely tolerable, as on March 17:

> A terrible storm arose, which forced dust through all the cracks and splits of our old sod houses. Never before have I experienced so much dust, although indeed, I had previously seen quite a bit of it, especially here in Nebraska. But I was never before in such a dusty and sandy area. Everything was packed with fine sand and dust. A train of government wagons came through here at the same time, escorted by the company of Pawnee Indians [the Pawnee Scouts], now on good ponies, equipped and armed just as we are. It was a miserable day to have to ride in such dust. We were not even twenty paces from the large, very busy road, yet the dust clouds were so dense and thick that often we could not see the vehicles passing by.

Guarding stagecoaches, carrying dispatches, and escorting officers frequently sent the men from Midway Station to other Platte Valley outposts, including Post Cottonwood (later Fort McPherson), established by Eugene F. Ware's Seventh Iowa Volunteer Cavalry in 1863. Scherneckau paid his first visit to Post Cottonwood on April 9 during a blinding snowstorm and found a substantial complex:

4. The First Nebraska carried muzzle-loading Enfield and Springfield rifle-muskets in Arkansas and turned them in when the men were furloughed. When the regiment was ordered to the Platte Valley in late summer 1864, Enfields were requisitioned in Omaha. By summer 1864, however, some of the volunteer units on the plains began receiving breechloading carbines. Most of the First Nebraska was armed with Joslyn or Merrill breechloaders by fall 1865. Ordnance reports and other documents on the regiment's small arms are in the Livingston Papers and in NSHS RG18, box 2.

The Platte has fairly good timber here on the islands, mainly cottonwood but also cedars. The bluffs stretch out close to the river, and the canyons hold lots of cedar. All buildings here have been built of nice cedar logs. East of the fort there are two to three ranches, stores, the post office, etc. The government buildings, barracks, and stables, and so on, form a square, which on the outside is surrounded by a kind of crude palisade, not over five feet high and constructed of cedar posts and logs. The open square [parade ground] in the center has a flagpole just like in the square of Fort Kearny. Also a row of trees is planted around the square, but they do not seem to thrive especially well. . . . It seems to me that this place has many advantages over Fort Kearny as far as location is concerned. Also, as a fortified place, at least against Indians, it is also worthwhile.[5]

News from the East, or other reminders of the war, provided occasional diversion. On April 7 Scherneckau reported that the men of Company H hung out a large U.S. flag to celebrate the anniversary of the Battle of Shiloh. Three years earlier, before Scherneckau enlisted, the First Nebraska had participated in the second day's fighting of that bloody Union victory. On April 10, while Scherneckau was at Post Cottonwood, the officer of the day read a telegram signed by Secretary of War Edwin Stanton and President Abraham Lincoln reporting the surrender of Robert E. Lee and his army. "Our regimental band played several national melodies, and, despite the bad weather, general cheerfulness prevailed."

More somber news came five days later: "Yesterday evening [April 15], through a passenger on the stage, we received the first reports of the murder of the president. Many debates about the value of Lincoln. Several put him higher than Washington." On April 19 at noon, "we fired a salute of twenty-one shots each from our rifles for the funeral of our president. It was raw and windy."

Although Scherneckau reported occasionally about Indians raiding wagon trains or running off livestock, he had only one

5. The principal ranche at Cottonwood Springs was that of Charles McDonald. Ware describes it in *The Indian War of 1864*, 46, with additional notes at 440. The history of Post Cottonwood/Fort McPherson is in Holmes, *Fort McPherson*.

close brush with the elusive warriors. He and another soldier escorted two officers to the next station west of Midway on May 12:

> When we arrived at Smith's Ranch, the fight with the Indians had just ended, and they were across the river on the north side with forty head of cattle. A comrade from my company was wounded in the hip by an arrow, a sergeant from the Black Horse Cavalry fatally, and three others lightly. One of our horses had three arrows in his haunch. The Indians had several dead; one of them fell into our hands.

Several companies of cavalry from the nearby stations tried to cross the Platte River in pursuit but succeeded only in wetting their equipment and ammunition, while the Indians escaped. Only later did Scherneckau learn that the wounded "comrade from my company," Pvt. Francis W. Lohnes, had been awarded the Medal of Honor for his conduct in the May 12 skirmish at Smith's Ranch, the only soldier of the First Nebraska to be so recognized during the war.[6]

During his service on the Platte, Scherneckau rubbed shoulders with the "galvanized Yankees," Confederate prisoners of war released to serve in the West as U.S. volunteer infantry.[7] Ten infantrymen from the Third U.S. Volunteer Regiment were detailed to each Platte Valley stage station to supplement the mounted details from the First Nebraska. According to Scherneckau, "These former rebel soldiers make good comrades, and there are many decent men among them." On July 29, while returning to Midway with a load of supplies from Fort Kearny, he spent the night at a ranche garrisoned by U.S. volunteers:

> Some were former soldiers of the Southern army, then prisoners of war who, as galvanized Yanks, voluntarily entered into the service of Uncle Sam against the Indians. Almost every second

6. The story of the skirmish, and the career of Pvt. Francis Lohnes, is found in Potter, "Congressional Medal of Honor." Sgt. Hiram Creighton of the First Battalion, Nebraska Veteran Volunteers, was the soldier who was mortally wounded.

7. See Brown, *Galvanized Yankees.*

man seems to play the violin. Songs and dancing alternated and kept us all awake for a long time. On an average, the men of the Northern armies are much less talented when it comes to music than what I have seen so far of the enemy brethren of the South.

Alcohol was a perennial problem in the army, more so when bored soldiers were stationed at road ranches well stocked with this commodity. On May 26 Scherneckau reported that a Company E soldier had murdered a mixed-blood scout near Midway Station. "The Indian had been employed by the government as a guide and translator and was on his way to headquarters in Julesburg. The soldier was drunk and deserted after the deed."[8] On Independence Day 1865, "most of our men are on a spree, as they call it; they get insanely drunk, as drunk as only Americans can be. Very delightful company! Very boring day! I just drank a glass of bad ale, which only makes matters worse." On August 23, while at Post Cottonwood, Scherneckau encountered the First Nebraska's commanding officer, Col. William Baumer, "quite drunk." On September 3 he noted that the men of his company owed ranchmen Peniston and Miller more than three thousand dollars for whiskey, of which only about nine hundred dollars had been paid.

Many of Scherneckau's entries for 1865 mention the constant wagon traffic moving along the trail. Many of these wagons were

8. Pvt. Joseph Dougherty shot and killed Joe Jewett. Both men had gotten drunk at Mullaly's Ranche, according to Capt. William W. Ivory of Company H to Acting Asst. Adj. Gen. John Q. Lewis, May 27, 1865, in Dougherty's Compiled Service Record, Roll 7. Ware, *The Indian War of 1864*, 139, 245, and 342, identifies Jewett as an old hunter and stage driver who had been a guide for the army. Dougherty was arrested for the murder a few days later and confined in the Fort Kearny guardhouse. While there, he wrote to his mother, a domestic employed by H. D. Cooke of the financial firm of Jay Cooke and Company, which was in charge of selling bonds to finance the Union war effort. The soldier asked his mother to request that Cooke intercede on his behalf with government officials. Cooke wrote Gen. John Pope, commanding the Military Division of the Missouri, asking for clemency for Dougherty. In the meantime Dougherty escaped from the guardhouse. The clemency plea brought results with the issue of Special Orders No. 46, Headquarters of the Army, February 22, 1866, which ordered Dougherty restored to duty without trial. He rejoined his company and was mustered out on July 1, 1866. Compiled Service Records, roll 7; Dudley, *Roster of Nebraska Volunteers*, 60–61.

hauling supplies for Gen. Patrick E. Connor's pending expedition against Indians in the Powder River country of present Wyoming, which embarked from Fort Laramie on July 30.[9] Many other freighting outfits were transporting machinery and supplies to gold mining camps in Montana or to western military posts. Some wagons carried "saw-, quartz-, and grinding mills, mowing and threshing machines by the dozens." Scherneckau was astonished by the size of the wagons being used by a Nevada mining company: "These latter wagons are the largest and strongest that I have ever seen so far. They were hitched up to eight mules each and harnessed like the military wagons. Our army wagons are real buggies compared to these. The wide tires of the wheels were one inch thick, the back wheels of the wagons almost seven feet in diameter, everything else in proportion."[10]

Although he recorded fewer observations about the vagaries of human nature during this period than during his service in the South (his opportunities for personal interactions were now more limited), Scherneckau occasionally weighed in on such topics. One comment related to Harrison Johnson, a black "undercook" who enlisted in Company H at Batesville, came with the regiment to Nebraska, and faithfully served out his enlistment. As Scherneckau had revealed earlier, he saw qualities in African American soldiers that he found wanting in some of his white comrades. One such opinion surfaced when his company received new horses: "Many of the horses were difficult to tame; bridle-bit and spurs had to be put to use to the extreme. Our Negro cook broke one of them with only saddle and bridle. None of the [other] men felt brave enough to risk his life in taming this animal. So much for the despised black race."[11]

9. The Powder River Expedition is a focus of McDermott's *Circle of Fire.*

10. Scherneckau diary, August 8, 1865. On freighting in 1865 see Lass, *From the Missouri to the Great Salt Lake.*

11. Scherneckau diary, May 17, 1865. Scherneckau first mentioned Harrison Johnson in his diary entry of June 21, 1864. Johnson earned further respect on November 6, 1865, when Indians attacked a Company H detail near Lodgepole Creek in the Nebraska Panhandle. Company commander Capt. William Ivory reported that "Harrison Johnson, col'd cook . . . behaved very well, fired several shots." Manuscript History of Company H, First Nebraska Veteran Volunteers, NSHS RG18.

Several Omaha Indians of mixed-blood ancestry also served in the First Nebraska, and these men too earned Scherneckau's respect. After a clothing issue he wrote, "The three Indians in our company signed the list for clothing received all in their own handwriting, while ten to twelve of the civilized Americans, who often had an opportunity to get a good education, indicated their name with an *x* for want of something better. The poor *ignorant* Reds and Blacks in the Promised Land!"[12]

In September 1865, a month before he was to be discharged, Scherneckau's Company H was ordered away from Midway Station, where the men had spent the summer building substantial quarters, and sent to guard the isolated mail and telegraph route between Fort Sedgwick at Julesburg and Mud Springs Station in the Nebraska Panhandle.[13] Desertions increased dramatically, including Medal of Honor recipient Francis W. Lohnes. The desertions were indicative of the weariness and frustration of soldiers who felt they deserved to go home now that the war was over. Nevertheless, many of the men hung on grimly until the last of the First Nebraska Veteran Volunteers were finally mustered out on July 1, 1866.

Scherneckau, however, was eligible for discharge when his three-year enlistment expired. On October 15, 1865, he and two other soldiers left Company H's camp near Julesburg, en route to Fort Kearny. There, on October 22, "I then received Shannon's and my papers, that is, three muster out rolls and for each of us a discharge. With that, we were released from service without further formalities." The "Little Dutchman's" war was over.

Scherneckau continued writing in his diary for only two more weeks. The brief entries reflect his easing into the routine of civilian life. Once back in Grand Island, Scherneckau lived for a time with Heinrich Egge and leased Egge's farm for two years. In

12. Scherneckau diary, September 17, 1865.

13. The stage route and telegraph line went north from Julesburg to intersect the North Platte Valley near Chimney Rock. Mud Springs was a former Pony Express station, now a telegraph station, which had been attacked by Indians in February 1865. McDermott, "We Had a Terribly Hard Time."

December 1867 Scherneckau bought 160 acres of Hall County land, for which he received the patent on November 2, 1868.[14] Trouble had been brewing, however, ever since the Union Pacific Railroad began laying track through the Platte Valley in 1866. Contractors virtually denuded the riverbanks and islands of trees to provide ties and firewood for the construction gangs. Because the river woodlands adjacent to the settlers' land had not been surveyed and the settlers claimed them only by "squatters' rights," their protests about the tree cutting fell on deaf ears. Scherneckau, for one, felt he had been robbed, and the loss of the timber "eventually led me to emigrate to a country where there was a natural supply of fuel without shipment."[15]

In the meantime, however, Scherneckau returned to his native land and married Cecile Moeller of Kiel, whom he brought to Nebraska in June 1868. His bride had been born March 15, 1844, at Elmshorn, Holstein.[16] He kept his Hall County land until 1870, when he sold it to Egge. The spring of that year found the Scherneckaus in Cheyenne, Wyoming, but they soon moved to The Dalles on the Columbia River, and in 1874 to a locality named Cross Hollows in the grasslands of north-central Oregon.[17]

Cross Hollows, in Wasco County at the intersection of two ravines with natural springs, served travelers along a trail from the Columbia River to gold mining camps farther south. When the Scherneckaus arrived at Cross Hollows, they purchased Thomas Ward's inn and blacksmith shop. A few years later they built a store, saloon, and a new sixteen-room inn. August and Cecile Scherneckau were soon doing a booming business, enabling them to invest in land and sheep. In 1879 Scherneckau became the Cross Hollows postmaster, and later served another term. By the late 1880s the Scherneckaus

14. Heinrich Egge, diary; Sw 1/4, Sec. 1, Twp. 11N, Rg. 9W, Tract Book 105, RG509, Records of the U.S. General Land Office, NSHS.

15. Stolley, "History of the First Settlement," 75–76; Scherneckau, "Her Quota Furnished," 80.

16. *Astoria (Ore.) Daily Budget,* December 31, 1907.

17. Tax lists, real estate, 1868–71, RG260, Records of Hall County, Nebraska, NSHS; Pension File.

had prospered and decided to move to Astoria, Oregon, selling their Cross Hollows properties to one of their employees.[18]

The Scherneckau name would live on in the Cross Hollows region. When the Columbia Southern Railroad reached the area in 1900, a town named Shaniko (which was the local pronunciation of Scherneckau) sprang up to become an important shipping point for area woolgrowers. After a rival railroad was completed nearby in 1911 and Shaniko lost its monopoly, the town began to wither. By its centennial year in 2000, it counted only about thirty residents.[19]

Scherneckau's war wound had damaged the bone in his leg, leaving him with a partial disability. In 1875 he qualified for a veteran's pension of twelve dollars a month. At some point, he became an American citizen. After he moved to Astoria, he was active in the community's affairs, helping organize the Commercial Club and serving as its first president. He also joined Cushing Post 14, GAR, was elected to the city council, and served a term in the state legislature.[20] In 1897 the Scherneckaus traveled to Europe to sightsee and visit relatives. Back home in Oregon, Cecile Scherneckau died on December 31, 1907; the couple had no children. In 1908 August Scherneckau's unmarried sister, Marie, came to the United States to care for her brother.[21]

In February 1912 Scherneckau and his sister decided to visit their homeland again. On January 6, 1913, he was living in Luebeck, Germany, where he was stranded when World War I broke out, unable to collect his Civil War pension from 1916 until 1919. Once the war was over, August and Marie made their way back to the United States. In June 1920, en route to the West Coast, they stopped in Grand Island, where August Scherneckau reminisced about his life in Hall County during the 1850s and 1860s and renewed acquaintances with a few old friends. The feeble old man

18. Rees, *Shaniko,* 5.

19. Rees, *Shaniko,* 1; *Bend (Ore.) Bulletin,* July 11, 1999, May 9, 2000.

20. *Astoria (Ore.) Budget,* April 12, 1923.

21. Pension File; shelf list, MSS2698, August Scherneckau Diaries, Oregon Historical Society Research Library; *Astoria (Ore.) Daily Budget,* December 31, 1907; *Grand Island (Nebr.) Daily Independent,* January 7, 1908, and June 5, 1920.

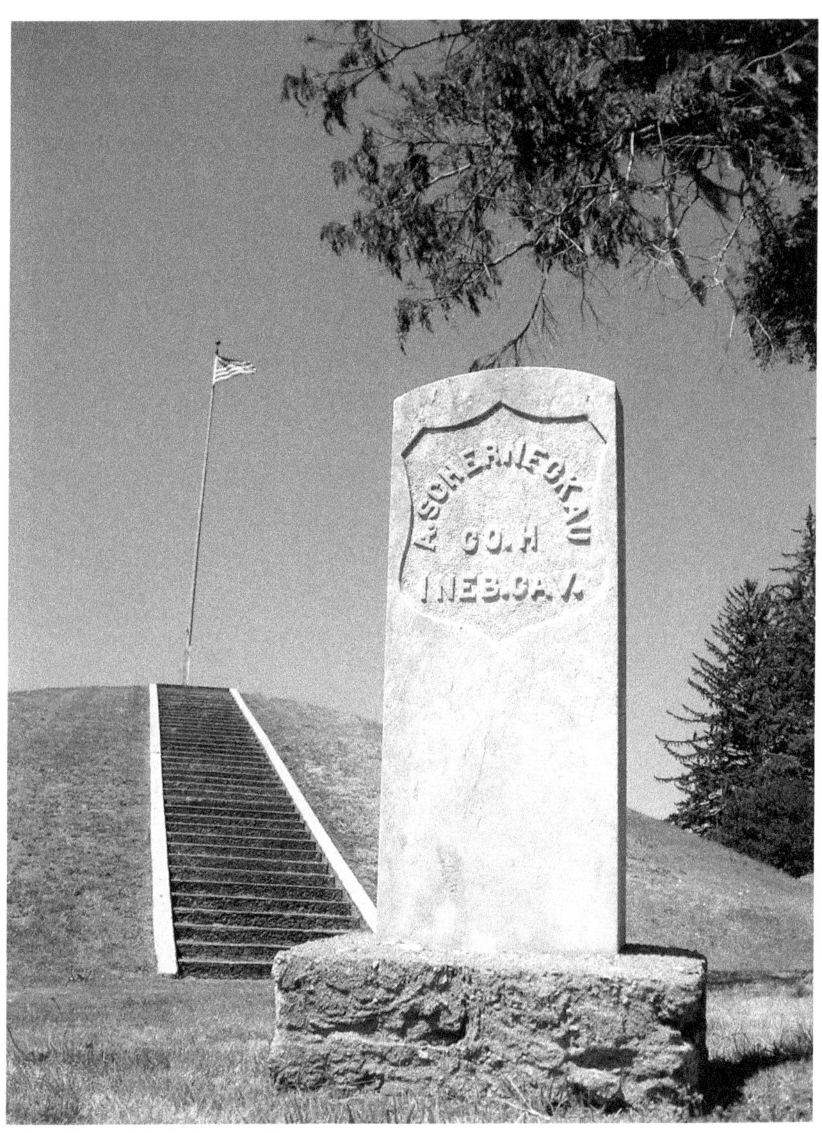

August Scherneckau's grave, Oceanview Cemetery, Warrenton, Oregon. Courtesy of Joshua Salber and Vincent Sproul, Warrenton, Oregon.

lived with his sister at 1518 Eleventh Street in Santa Monica, California, until he died on April 11, 1923, at the age of eighty-five. His ashes were buried at the Oceanview Cemetery near Astoria, Oregon, under a veteran's marker inscribed simply, "A. Scherneckau, Co. H, 1st Neb. Cav."[22]

22. Pension File; *Grand Island (Nebr.) Daily Independent,* June 5, 1920; Rees, *Shaniko,* 8; Sheri Salber, Warrenton, Oregon, to James E. Potter, August 6, 2005, enclosing photograph of Scherneckau's grave. Letter in author's possession.

Bibliography

Unpublished Sources

Compiled Service Records. First Nebraska Volunteer Infantry/Cavalry and Second Nebraska Volunteer Cavalry. National Archives Microfilm Publication M1787. RG94, Records of the Office of the Adjutant General, Washington, D.C.

Correspondence of the First Nebraska Volunteer Infantry/Cavalry. RG18, Records of the Nebraska Military Department. Nebraska State Historical Society, Lincoln.

Dale, Raymond E., comp. "Otoe County Pioneers: A Biographical Dictionary." 10 vols. Unpublished typescript, 1961–65. Nebraska State Historical Society, Lincoln.

Egge, Heinrich. Diary. In Esther Bienhoff, "The Original German Settlement at Grand Island, Nebraska, 1857–1866." Master's thesis. University of Nebraska, 1929. Nebraska State Historical Society, Lincoln.

Koenig, Henry. Letter. Pundt and Koenig Papers. RG0790. Nebraska State Historical Society, Lincoln.

Letters Sent, Fort Kearny, N.T. RG393, Records of U.S. Army Continental Commands. National Archives and Records Administration. Microfilm. Nebraska State Historical Society, Lincoln.

Livingston, Robert R. Papers. MS129. Nebraska State Historical Society, Lincoln.

Manuscript History of Company H, First Nebraska Volunteer Infantry/Cavalry. RG18, Records of the Nebraska Military Department. Nebraska State Historical Society, Lincoln.

Orders, Morning Reports, and Descriptive Books. First Nebraska Volunteer Infantry/Cavalry. RG 18, Records of the Nebraska Military Department. Microfilm. Nebraska State Historical Society, Lincoln.

Population Censuses of Hall County, Douglas County, Nebraska Territory, 1860. National Archives Microfilm Publication M653, roll 665. RG29, Records of the Bureau of the Census, Washington, D.C.

Scherneckau, August. Diaries. MSS2698. Oregon Historical Society Research Library, Portland.

———. Pension File SC139–742. Civil War and Later Pensions. RG18, Records of the Veterans' Administration. National Archives and Records Administration, Washington, D.C.

Tax Lists, Real Estate. RG260, Records of Hall County, Nebraska. Nebraska State Historical Society, Lincoln.

Tract Book 105. RG509, Records of the U.S. General Land Office. Nebraska State Historical Society, Lincoln.

Newspapers

Astoria (Ore.) Budget
Astoria (Ore.) Daily Budget
Batesville (Ark.) Bazzoo
Bend (Ore.) Bulletin
Daily Omaha Nebraskian
Grand Island (Nebr.) Daily Independent
Missouri Republican (St. Louis)
Nebraska Advertiser (Brownville)
Nebraska City Daily Press
Nebraska City News
Nebraska City People's Semi-Weekly Press
Nebraska Republican (Omaha)
Nebraska State Journal (Lincoln)
Omaha (Nebr.) Weekly Herald
Page County Herald (Clarinda, Iowa)
Tri-Weekly Nebraska Republican (Omaha)

Published Sources

American Heritage Civil War Chronology. New York: American Heritage, 1960.

Andreas, A. T., comp. *History of Nebraska*. Chicago: Western Historical, 1882.

Bailey, Anne J. "The Mississippi Marine Brigade: Fighting Rebel Guerrillas on Western Waters." *Military History of the Southwest* 22 (Spring 1992): 31–42.

———. "Texans Invade Missouri: The Cape Girardeau Raid, 1863." *Missouri Historical Review* 84 (January 1990): 166–87.

Bailey, Anne J., and Daniel E. Sutherland, eds. *Civil War Arkansas: Beyond Battles and Leaders*. Fayetteville: University of Arkansas Press, 2000.

Bärner, Ralf. "A Forty-Eighter Who Returned." In Brancaforte, *The German Forty-Eighters in the United States*, 93–102.

Barnes, Kenneth C. "The Williams Clan: Mountain Farmers and Union Fighters in North Central Arkansas." In Bailey and Sutherland, *Civil War Arkansas*, 155–75.

Becher, Ronald. *Massacre along the Medicine Road: A Social History of the Indian War of 1864 in Nebraska Territory*. Caldwell, Idaho: Caxton Press, 1999.

Berrey, Lester V., and Melvin Van Den Bark. *The American Thesaurus of Slang*. New York: Thomas Y. Crewell, 1947.

Bradbury, John F., Jr. "'Good Water and Wood but the Country Is a Miserable Botch': Flatland Soldiers Confront the Ozarks." *Missouri Historical Review* 90 (January 1996): 166–86.

———. "'This War Is Managed Mighty Strange': The Army of Southeastern Missouri, 1862–1863." *Missouri Historical Review* 89 (October 1994): 28–47.

Brancaforte, Charlotte L., ed. *The German Forty-Eighters in the United States.* New York: Peter Lang, 1989.

Brown, D. Alexander. *The Galvanized Yankees.* Urbana: University of Illinois Press, 1963.

Brownlee, Richard. "The Battle of Pilot Knob, Iron County, Missouri, September 27, 1864." *Missouri Historical Review* 59 (October 1964): 1–30.

Castel, Albert. *Civil War Kansas: Reaping the Whirlwind.* Lawrence: University Press of Kansas, 1997.

Christ, Mark K., ed. *Rugged and Sublime: The Civil War in Arkansas.* Fayetteville: University of Arkansas Press, 1994.

Columbia Encyclopedia. 6th ed. New York: Columbia University Press, 2001.

Cooling, Benjamin Franklin. "The First Nebraska Infantry Regiment and the Battle of Fort Donelson." *Nebraska History* 45 (June 1964): 131–46.

———. *Forts Henry and Donelson: The Key to the Confederate Heartland.* Knoxville: University of Tennessee Press, 1987.

Coombe, Jack D. *Thunder along the Mississippi: The River Battles That Split the Confederacy.* New York: Bantam Books, 1998.

The Daily News' History of Buchanan County and St. Joseph, Missouri. St. Joseph: St. Joseph Press, n.d.

Davidson, Homer K. *Black Jack Davidson: A Cavalry Commander on the Western Frontier.* Glendale, Calif.: Arthur H. Clark, 1974.

Davis, William C., ed. *The South Besieged.* Vol. 5 in *The Image of War, 1861–1865.* Gettysburg: The National Historical Society, 1983.

DeBlack, Thomas A. "1863: 'We Must Stand or Fall Alone.'" In Christ, *Rugged and Sublime,* 59–103.

———. *With Fire and Sword: Arkansas, 1861–1874.* Fayetteville: University of Arkansas Press, 2003.

Dudley, Edgar S., comp. *Roster of Nebraska Volunteers from 1861 to 1869.* Hastings, Nebr.: Wigton and Evans, 1888.

Dyer, Frederick H. *A Compendium of the War of the Rebellion.* Des Moines: Dyer, 1908.

Etcheson, Nicole. *Bleeding Kansas: Contested Liberty in the Civil War Era.* Lawrence: University Press of Kansas, 2004.

Faust, Patricia L., ed. *Historical Times Illustrated Encyclopedia of the Civil War.* New York: Harper Perennial, 1991.

Fellman, Michael. *Inside War: The Guerrilla Conflict in Missouri during the American Civil War.* New York: Oxford University Press, 1989.

Filbert, Preston. *The Half Not Told: The Civil War in a Frontier Town.* Mechanicsburg, Pa.: Stackpole Books, 2001.

Frank Leslie's Pictorial History of the American Civil War, edited by E. G. Squier. New York: Frank Leslie, 1862.

"The German Settlement of Grand Island." *Mississippi Blätter.* In Robert N. Manley, *Platte Valley Chronicles: Tales from Nebraska's Pioneer Trails.* Grand Island, Nebr.: Hall County Historical Society, 2001.

Gerteis, Louis S. *Civil War St. Louis.* Lawrence: University Press of Kansas, 2001.

Gibbons, Tony. *Warships and Naval Battles of the Civil War.* New York: Gallery Books, 1989.

Glaab, Charles N. *Kansas City and the Railroads: Community Policy in the Growth of a Regional Metropolis.* Lawrence: University Press of Kansas, 1993.

Guernsey, Alfred H., and Henry M. Alden. *Harper's Pictorial History of the Great Rebellion.* Chicago: McDonnell Brothers, 1866.

A Guide to Civil War Activities in the Southeast Missouri Region. Perryville: Southeast Missouri Regional Planning and Economic Development, July 2002.

Hart, Herbert M. *Old Forts of the Southwest.* Seattle: Superior, 1964.

Hazlett, James C., Edwin Olmstead, and M. Hume Parks. *Field Artillery Weapons of the Civil War.* Newark: University of Delaware Press, 1983.

Heitman, Francis B. *Historical Register and Dictionary of the United States Army.* 2 vols. Washington, D.C.: GPO, 1903.

Historic Batesville: A Walking and Driving Tour. Batesville, Ark.: Batesville Preservation Association, n.d.

Holmes, Louis A. *Fort McPherson, Nebraska, Fort Cottonwood, N.T.: Guardian of the Tracks and Trails.* Lincoln: Johnsen, 1963.

James, Nola A. "The Civil War Years in Independence County." *Arkansas Historical Quarterly* 28 (Autumn 1969): 234–74.

Josyph, Peter, ed. *The Wounded River: The Civil War Letters of John Vance Lauderdale, M.D.* East Lansing: Michigan State University Press, 1993.

Kaufmann, Wilhelm. *The Germans in the American Civil War.* Translated by Steven Rowan. 1911. Reprint, Carlisle, Pa.: Kalmann, 1999.

Kennedy, Joseph C. G. *Population of the United States in 1860.* Washington, D.C.: GPO, 1864.

Kenney, Edward C. "From the Log of the *Red Rover,* 1862–1865: A History of the First U.S. Navy Hospital Ship." *Missouri Historical Review* 60 (October 1965): 31–49.

Lance, Donald M. "Settlement Patterns, Missouri Germans, and Local Dialects." In *The German American Experience in Missouri: Essays in Commemoration of the Tricentennial of German Immigration to America, 1683–1983,* edited by Howard Wright Marshal and James W. Goodrich. Columbia: Missouri Cultural Heritage Center, 1986.

Lass, William E. *From the Missouri to the Great Salt Lake: An Account of Overland Freighting.* Lincoln: Nebraska State Historical Society, 1972.

Lewis, John G. W., ed. *Messages and Proclamations of the Governors of Nebraska.* 4 vols. Lincoln: Nebraska State Historical Society, 1941–42.

Lonn, Ella. *Foreigners in the Union Army and Navy.* Baton Rouge: Louisiana State University Press, 1951.

Lord, Francis A. *Civil War Collector's Encyclopedia: Arms, Uniforms, and Equipment of the Union and Confederacy.* Seacaucus, N.J.: Castle, 1987.

Manley, Robert N. *Platte Valley Chronicles: Tales from Nebraska's Pioneer Trails.* Grand Island, Nebr.: Hall County Historical Society, 2001.

Mantor, Lyle E. "Fort Kearny and the Westward Movement." *Nebraska History* 29 (September 1948): 175–207.

Mattes, Merrill J. *The Great Platte River Road: The Covered Wagon Mainline via Fort Kearny to Fort Laramie.* Lincoln: Nebraska State Historical Society, 1969.

———. *Platte River Road Narratives.* Urbana: University of Illinois Press, 1988.

McDermott, John D. *Circle of Fire: The Indian War of 1865.* Mechanicsburg, Pa.: Stackpole Books, 2003.

———. "Crime and Punishment in the United States Army." *Journal of the West* 7 (April 1968): 246–55.

———. "No Small Potatoes: Problems of Food and Health at Fort Laramie, 1849–1859." *Nebraska History* 79 (Winter 1998): 162–70.

———. "'We Had a Terribly Hard Time Letting Them Go': The Battles of Mud Springs and Rush Creek, February 1865." *Nebraska History* 77 (Summer 1996): 78–88.

———. "Were They Really Rogues?: Desertion in the Nineteenth-Century U.S. Army." *Nebraska History* 78 (Winter 1997): 165–74.

McPherson, James M. *Ordeal by Fire: The Civil War and Reconstruction.* New York: McGraw Hill, 1982.

———. *For Cause and Comrades: Why Men Fought in the Civil War.* New York: Oxford University Press, 1997.

Mobley, Freeman K. *Making Sense of the Civil War in Batesville-Jacksonport and Northeast Arkansas, 1861–1874.* Batesville, Ark.: Freeman K. Mobley, 2005.

Monks, William. *A History of Southern Missouri and Northern Arkansas. Being an Account of the Early Settlements, the Civil War, the Ku-Klux, and Times of Peace,* edited by John F. Bradbury, Jr., and Lou Wehmer. Fayetteville: University of Arkansas Press, 2003.

Morris, Larry E. *The Fate of the Corps: What Became of the Lewis and Clark Explorers after the Expedition.* New Haven: Yale University Press, 2004.

Morton, J. Sterling, succeeded by Albert Watkins. *Illustrated History of Nebraska,* vols. 1–2. Lincoln: Jacob North, 1905–1906.

Official Records of the Union and Confederate Navies in the War of the Rebellion. 31 vols. Washington, D.C.: GPO, 1892–1922.

Pilot Knob, Missouri, 125th Anniversary Commemoration. Missouri Civil War Reenactors Association, 1989.

Potter, James E. "A Congressional Medal of Honor for a Nebraska Soldier: The Case of Private Francis W. Lohnes." *Nebraska History* 65 (Summer 1984): 245–56.

———. "The First Nebraska's Orphan Detachment and the Skirmish at Grand Prairie, 1864." *Nebraska History* 81 (Spring 2000): 35–39.

———, ed. "'I Thought It My Duty to Go': The Civil War Letters of Thomas Edwin Keen, First Nebraska Volunteer Infantry." *Nebraska History* 81 (Winter 2000): 134–69.

Pritchard, Russ A., Jr. *Civil War Weapons and Equipment.* Guilford, Conn.: Lyons Press, 2003.

Puschendorf, L. Robert, and James E. Potter, eds. *Spans in Time: A History of Nebraska Bridges.* Lincoln: Nebraska State Historical Society and Nebraska Department of Roads, 1999.

Rees, Helen Guyton. *Shaniko: From Wool Capital to Ghost Town.* Portland, Ore.: Binford and Mort, 1982.

Reid, Whitelaw. *History of the State during the War.* Vol. 1 of *Ohio in the War: Her Statesmen, Her Generals, and Soldiers.* Cincinnati: Moore, Wilstach, and Baldwin, 1868.

Report of the Adjutant General of the State of Indiana, vols. 1–2. Indianapolis: State Printer, 1865–69.

Ripley, Warren. *Artillery and Ammunition of the Civil War.* 4th ed. Charleston: Battery Press, 1984.

Robbins, Charles G. *A Physicist Looks at the 1860 and 1870 Hall County Censuses.* Grand Island, Nebr.: Stuhr Museum of the Prairie Pioneer Press, 1983.

Robbins, Edith. "A Forty-Eighter on the Town-Building Frontier." In Brancaforte, *German Forty-Eighters,* 67–78.

Rogers, Fred B. *Soldiers of the Overland: Being Some Account of the Services of General Patrick Edward Connor and his Volunteers in the Old West.* San Francisco: The Grabhorne Press, 1938.

Root, Frank A., and William E. Connelley. *The Overland Stage to California.* Topeka, Kan.: n.p., 1901.

Scherneckau, August. "Her Quota Furnished." In *History of Hall County, Nebraska,* edited by A. F. Buechler, R. J. Barr, and Dale P. Stough, 77–80. Lincoln, Nebr.: Western Publishing and Engraving, 1920.

Shannon, Fred Albert. *The Organization and Administration of the Union Army.* 2 vols. Cleveland: Arthur H. Clark, 1928.

Shea, William L. "1862: 'A Continual Thunder.'" In Christ, *Rugged and Sublime,* 21–58.

Sheldon, Addison E. *Nebraska: The Land and the People.* 3 vols. Chicago: Lewis, 1931.

Sifakis, Stewart. *Who Was Who in the Confederacy.* New York: Facts on File, 1988.

———. *Who Was Who in the Union.* New York: Facts on File, 1988.

Stolley, William. "Defense of Grand Island." *Nebraska History* 16 (October–December 1935): 221–27.

———. "History of the First Settlement of Hall County, Nebraska." Translated by Harry Weingart. Special issue, *Nebraska History* (1946): xii, 1–90.

Stoy, Vera. *Kiel auf dem Weg zur Großstadt: Die städtebauliche Entwicklung bis zum Ende des 19. Jahrhunderts.* Kiel: Ludwig, 2003.

Sutherland, Daniel E. "1864: 'A Strange, Wild Time.'" In Christ, *Rugged and Sublime,* 105–44.

———. "Guerrillas: The Real War in Arkansas." In Bailey and Sutherland, *Civil War Arkansas,* 133–53.

Sweet, J. Hyde. "Old Fort Kearny." *Nebraska History* 27 (October–December 1946): 233–43.

Switlik, M. C. *The Complete Cannoneer.* Jackson, Mich.: Antique Ordnance Artificers, 1971.

Tucker, Phillip Thomas. Introduction to *Memoirs of the Rebellion on the Border, 1863,* by Wiley Britton, 5–13. Lincoln: University of Nebraska Press, 1993.

van Ravenswaay, Charles. *St. Louis: An Informal History of the City and Its People, 1764–1865.* St. Louis: Missouri Historical Society Press, 1991.

Varley, James F. *Brigham and the Brigadier: General Patrick Connor and His California Volunteers in Utah and along the Overland Trail.* Tucson: Westernlore Press, 1989.

Walton, George. *Sentinel of the Plains: Fort Leavenworth and the American West.* Englewood Cliffs, N.J.: Prentice-Hall, 1973.

The War of the Rebellion: A Compilation of the Official Records of the Union and Confederate Armies. 128 vols. Washington, D.C.: GPO, 1880–1901.

Ware, Eugene F. *The Indian War of 1864.* Edited by Clyde C. Walton. Lincoln: University of Nebraska Press, 1960.

Watkins, Albert. *History of Nebraska,* vol. 3. Lincoln: Western Publishing and Engraving, 1913.

Way, Frederick, Jr., comp. *Way's Packet Directory, 1848–1994: Passenger Steamboats of the Mississippi River System Since the Advent of Photography in Mid-Continent America.* Revised ed. Athens: Ohio University Press, 1994.

Winter, William C. *The Civil War in St. Louis: A Guided Tour.* St. Louis: Missouri Historical Society Press, 1994.

Index